WORLD TRADE ORGANIZATION

Dispute Settlement Reports

1999
Volume V

Pages 1797-2094

CAMBRIDGE
UNIVERSITY PRESS

PUBLISHED BY THE PRESS SYNDICATE OF THE UNIVERSITY OF CAMBRIDGE
The Pitt Building, Trumpington Street, Cambridge, United Kingdom

CAMBRIDGE UNIVERSITY PRESS
The Edinburgh Building, Cambridge CB2 2RU, UK
40 West 20th Street, New York, NY 10011–4211, USA
477 Williamstown Road, Port Melbourne, VIC 3207, Australia
Ruiz de Alarcón 13, 28014 Madrid, Spain
Dock House, The Waterfront, Cape Town 8001, South Africa

http://www.cambridge.org

Printed in the United Kingdom at the University Press, Cambridge

French edition and Spanish edition paperbacks of this title are both available directly from WTO Publications, World Trade Organization, Centre William Rappard, 154 rue de Lausanne, CH-1211 Geneva 21, Switzerland http://www.wto.org

ISBN 0 521 80324 1 hardback
ISBN 0 521 00568 X paperback

THE WTO DISPUTE SETTLEMENT REPORTS

The *Dispute Settlement Reports* of the World Trade Organization (the "WTO") include panel and Appellate Body reports, as well as arbitration awards, in disputes concerning the rights and obligations of WTO Members under the provisions of the *Marrakesh Agreement Establishing the World Trade Organization*. The *Dispute Settlement Reports* are available in English, French and Spanish. Starting with 1999, the first volume of each year contains a cumulative index of published disputes.

This volume may be cited as DSR 1999:V

TABLE OF CONTENTS

Page

INDIA - QUANTITATIVE RESTRICTIONS ON IMPORTS OF AGRICULTURAL, TEXTILE AND INDUSTRIAL PRODUCTS

Report of the Panel

WT/DS90/R

Adopted by the Dispute Settlement Body on 22 September 1999 as upheld by the Appellate Body Report

TABLE OF CONTENTS

I. INTRODUCTION

1.1 On 16 July 1997, the United States requested consultations with India, pursuant to Article 4 of the Understanding on Rules and Procedures Governing the Settlement of Disputes ("DSU"), Article XXII:1 of the GATT, Article 19 of the Agreement on Agriculture (to the extent it incorporates by reference Article XXII of the GATT), and Article 6 of the Agreement on Import Licensing Procedures (to the extent it incorporates by reference Article XXII of the GATT), concerning quantitative restrictions maintained by India on the importation of a number of agricultural, textile and industrial products (WT/DS90/1). The United States considered that the quantitative restrictions maintained by India, including, but not limited to, those tariff lines notified in Annex I, Part B of WT/BOP/N/24, appeared to be inconsistent with India's obligations under Article XI:1 and XVIII:11 of the GATT 1994, Article 4.2 of the Agreement on Agriculture and Article 3 of the Agreement on Import Licensing Procedures. At the same time, Australia, Canada, the European Communities, New Zealand and Switzerland requested consultations with India on these quantitative restrictions (WT/DS91/1; WT/DS92/1; WT/DS93/1; WT/DS94/1; WT/DS96/1) on the basis of similar claims to those set forth by the United States.[1] Subsequently, Japan, the European Communities, Canada, Australia, Switzerland and New Zealand asked to join in the consultations requested by the United States (WT/DS90/2, WT/DS90/3, WT/DS90/4, WT/DS90/5, WT/DS/90/6, WT/DS/90/7). The United States and India formally consulted on these measures in Geneva on 17 September 1997, and Japan participated as an interested third party under Article 4.11 of the DSU.

1.2 On 3 October 1997, the United States requested that the WTO Dispute Settlement Body ("DSB") establish a panel to examine this dispute.[2] In its request, the United States considered that quantitative restrictions maintained by India, including, but not limited to, the more than 2,700 agricultural and industrial product tariff lines notified to the WTO in Annex I, Part B of WT/BOP/N/24 dated 22 May 1997, appeared to be inconsistent with India's obligations under Articles XI:1 and XVIII:11 of GATT 1994 and Article 4.2 of the Agreement on Agriculture. Furthermore, the import licensing procedures and practices of the Government of India are inconsistent with fundamental WTO

[1] Switzerland did not refer to Article 4 of the Agreement on Agriculture in its request.
[2] WT/DS90/8, 6 October 1997.

requirements as provided in Article XIII of GATT 1994 and Article 3 of the Agreement on Import Licensing Procedures. The DSB established the panel on 18 November 1997, with the following terms of reference:

> "To examine, in light of the relevant provisions of the covered agreements cited by the United States in WT/DS90/8, the matter referred to the DSB by the United States in that document and to make such findings as will assist the DSB in making the recommendations or in giving the rulings provided for in those agreements."

1.3 On 10 February 1998, the United States requested the Director-General to determine the composition of the Panel, pursuant to paragraph 7 of Article 8 of the DSU. On 20 February 1998, the Director-General accordingly composed the Panel (WT/DS90/9) as follows:

Chairman: Ambassador Celso Lafer

Members: Professor Paul Demaret

Professor Richard Snape

1.4 The Panel met with the parties on 7 May and 22 and 23 June 1998 and submitted its report to the Parties on 11 December 1998.

II. FACTUAL ASPECTS

A. *Consultations in the Committee on Balance-of-Payments Restrictions*

2.1 At the time the Panel was established, India maintained quantitative restrictions on imports of products falling in 2,714 tariff lines at the eight-digit level of HS96 for which it claimed balance-of-payments justification. These restrictions had been notified to the Committee on Balance-of-Payments Restrictions in May 1997 in the course of consultations being held with India. The restrictions that are within the scope of the dispute appear in Annex I, Part B of WT/BOP/N/24. A previous notification had been made in July 1996 (WT/BOP/N/11 and Corr.1) and included quantitative restrictions maintained for both balance of payments and other reasons.[3]

2.2 India had been consulting under Article XVIII:B in the Committee on Balance-of-Payments Restrictions regularly since 1957.[4] During the simplified consultations held on 15 November 1994, the Committee appreciated the courage and sagacity with which India had carried out its economic reform program. It encouraged India to continue implementing its import liberalization programme.

---

3 According to India, as of 13 April 1998, the number of items on which there were import restrictions had been reduced to 2,296 HS lines at the 8-digit level.

4 BISD 8S/74.

The Committee noted that, if the balance of payments showed sustained improvement, India's aim was to move to a regime by 1996-1997, in which import licensing restrictions would only be maintained for environmental and safety reasons. Members of the Committee welcomed the significant improvement in India's balance-of-payments situation since the last consultation but recognized that it remained volatile.[5]

2.3 Full consultations were begun in December 1995, and first resumed on 20-21 January 1997. During the consultations held on 6 and 8 December 1995, the Committees commended India for the wide-scale economic reforms and comprehensive stabilization programme over the past four years, which had resulted in robust economic recovery. The reforms, which included a considerable measure of trade and financial liberalization, exchange rate unification and a move to current account convertibility, had contributed to a large increase in the share of trade in India's GDP. The Committees noted that, since 1992, rapid export growth and capital inflows had been the source of the turnaround in India's external sector and the steady increase in the level of foreign exchange reserves. However, they took note that, in recent months, there had been a deterioration in the trade balance, investment inflows had slowed and the foreign exchange reserves had declined. In addition, the fiscal deficit and the level of indebtedness remained high. The Committees recalled India's stated aim to move, by 1996-97, to a trade régime under which quantitative restrictions are retained only for environmental, social, health and safety reasons, provided sustained improvement was shown in its balance-of-payments. They also took note of the statement by the IMF that, with continued prudent macro-economic management, the transition to a tariff-based import régime with no quantitative restrictions could reasonably be accomplished within a period of two years. The Committees noted that, since the last full consultation, there had been considerable liberalization of India's import régime, including a gradual increase in the number of consumer items which were freely importable; yet almost one-third of tariff lines at eight-digit level under the HS Classification remained subject to quantitative restrictions. The Committees noted the view expressed by India that, in the context of a deteriorating balance-of-payments situation, it would be neither prudent nor feasible to consider the general lifting of quantitative restrictions on imports at this stage. Many Members supported India's continued use of import restrictions under Article XVIII:B for balance-of-payments reasons in view of the uncertainty and fragility they perceived in India's balance-of-payments position, and they felt that liberalization and structural reform policies should continue at a pace and sequence suited to Indian conditions. Many other Members stated that India's balance-of-payments position was comfortable, that India did not currently face the threat of a serious decline in foreign exchange reserves as set out in Article XVIII, paragraph 9, and that therefore India was not justified in its continued

[5] GATT document BOP/R/221, 1 December 1994.

recourse to import restrictions for balance-of-payments reasons. Many Members stated that the continued use of quantitative restrictions was inconsistent with paragraphs 1, 2, 3, 4 and 9 of the Understanding and asked India to present a firm time-table for the phasing out of the restrictions, and further information required, before the resumption of the consultations. Others, in the light of the ongoing liberalization, did not share these views. In the light of the above considerations, the Committees welcomed India's readiness to resume the consultations in October 1996, and to notify to the WTO all remaining restrictions maintained for balance-of-payments purposes soon after the announcement of the 1996/97 Export-Import Policy.

2.4 In its resumed consultations with India, in January 1997, the Committee took note of the positive developments in India's economic situation since 1995. The Committee welcomed the Indian authorities' continued commitment to economic reform and liberalization and noted India's progressive removal of quantitative restrictions notified under Article XVIII:B. The Committee noted the statement of the IMF that India's current monetary reserves were not inadequate and were not threatened by a serious decline.[6] The IMF also expressed the view that the import restrictions could be removed within a relatively short period of time. However, India cautioned that its balance-of-payments needed close monitoring and that the abrupt removal of import restrictions notified under Article XVIII:B could undermine the stability of its economy and the reform process. The Committee agreed to resume the consultations with India at the beginning of June 1997 to consider a proposal from India on a time-schedule for the elimination of its remaining import restrictions notified under Article XVIII:B and to conclude the consultations consistently with all relevant WTO balance-of-payments provisions.[7]

2.5 On 19 May 1997, India notified the Committee of the import restrictions under Article XVIII:B that were being maintained under its Export-Import Policy for 1997-2002.[8] At the same time India notified a time-schedule for the removal of its remaining import restrictions pursuant to paragraph 11(d) of the 1994 Understanding. This plan contained a time-schedule of nine years from 1 April 1997 to 31 March 2006, divided into three equal phases. The notification also included a list of products in respect of which quantitative restrictions on imports maintained under Article XVIII:B were removed by India since its last notification of July 1996, as well as the import policy changes announced on 1 April 1997 under its annual Export-Import Policy for 1997-1998.

2.6 On 10-11 June 1997, the Committee resumed its consultations with India to discuss the plan. The representative of the IMF noted that his answers to the questions posed during the January 1997 consultation on India's balance-of-

---

[6] WT/BOP/R/22, para.15.

[7] *Ibid.*

[8] T/BOP/N/24, Annex I, Part B.

payments situation had not changed during the interim period. At that meeting all Members expressed their appreciation of India's commitment to eliminate the import restrictions over a period of time and commended India on the comprehensiveness, transparency and timeliness of the plan. Many Members however voiced concern about the length of the time-schedule; some agreed that India should adopt a cautious approach, others encouraging an acceleration of the phase out. Some Members considered that India's balance-of-payments situation no longer justified continued recourse to Article XVIII:B. In this meeting India offered to revise the phase-out plan to seven years. Since no consensus on the revised proposal on the time-schedule could be reached, the Chairman suspended the meeting to permit further reflection.

2.7 When the Committee reassembled on 30 June 1997, India submitted a plan containing a time-schedule of seven years, under which most of the import restrictions would be eliminated in two phases of a length of three years each and a number of items of high sensitivity or bound at very low rates of duty would be eliminated during the third phase, reduced from three years to one year. However, since no consensus on the revised proposal on the time-schedule could be reached, the Chairman closed the meeting on 1 July 1997, noting that the report of the Committee to the General Council would record the views expressed in the Committee.

2.8 The reports of the Committee of the consultations (WT/BOP/R/11; WT/BOP/R/22 and WT/BOP/R/32) were adopted by the General Council.

B. Quantitative Restrictions

2.9 This dispute concerns the 2,714 restrictions listed in Annex I, Part B of document WT/BOP/N/24 dated 22 May 1997. This document is a notification by India to the WTO Committee on Balance-of-Payments Restrictions ("BOP Committee"), the Council on Trade in Goods, and the Committee on Market Access.[9]

1. Legal Basis under Domestic Law for Import Restrictions and Import Licensing

2.10 Indian domestic legislation governing import licensing can be found in: (i) Section 11 of the Customs Act, 1962, (ii) the Foreign Trade (Development and Regulation) Act, 1992, (iii) the rules and orders promulgated under the Foreign Trade (Development and Regulation) Act, 1992, and (iv) the Export and Import Policy 1997-2002.

[9] T/BOP/N/24, p. 1 (including statement by India that this notification also fulfilled the notification obligations of India under the Decision on Notification Procedures adopted by the Council on Trade in Goods on 1 December 1995 (G/L/59), and that a copy of the notification had been sent to the Chairman of the Committee on Market Access).

2.11 Section 11 of the Customs Act, 1962 provides that the Central Government of India may, by notification in the Official Gazette, prohibit (absolutely or subject to conditions), as specified in the notification, the import or export of any goods. The listed purposes for such prohibition include, *inter alia:* Indian security; maintenance of public order and standards of decency or morality; conservation of foreign exchange and safeguarding of balance of payments; avoiding shortages of goods; prevention of surplus of any agricultural or fisheries product; establishment of any industry; prevention of serious injury to domestic production; conservation of exhaustible natural resources; carrying on of foreign trade in goods by the State or by a State-owned corporation; and "any other purpose conducive to the interests of the general public." Under Section 111 (d) of the Customs Act, goods imported or exported (or attempted to be imported or exported) contrary to any prohibition are liable to confiscation.

2.12 The Foreign Trade (Development and Regulation) Act, 1992 ("FTDR Act") which replaced the Imports and Exports (Control) Act, 1947, authorizes the Central Government to prohibit, restrict or otherwise regulate the import or export of goods, by Order published in the Official Gazette (Section 3(2)). Under section 3(3) of the FTDR Act, all goods to which any Order under section 3(2) applies are deemed to be goods the import or export of which has been prohibited under section 11 of the Customs Act, 1962 (and are therefore subject to confiscation under section 111(d) of the Customs Act).

2.13 The FTDR Act prohibits imports or exports by any person except in accordance with the provisions of the FTDR Act, the rules and orders made thereunder and the Export and Import Policy currently in force (Section11(1)). Under Section 11(2), when any person makes or abets or attempts to make any import or export in contravention of the FTDR Act, any rules or orders made thereunder, or the Export and Import Policy, he is liable to a penalty of up to 1,000 rupees or five times the value of the goods concerned, whichever is greater. Only persons who have been granted an Importer-exporter Code Number ("IEC Number") by the Director General of Foreign Trade (DGFT) may import or export (Section 7).[10] The Director General, who is authorized to grant, renew or deny import and export licences, under Section 9, may suspend or cancel the IEC Number of any person who has contravened customs laws.[11]

2.14 Section 9 of the FTDR Act also requires the Director General of Foreign Trade as defined in Section 2(d) of the FTDR Act (the "Director General") to record reasons in writing if he fails to grant or renew an import license. If a license is granted, it specifies both the value and the quantity of the item that may be imported. The reasons for which the Director General may deny a license are clearly set forth in Rule 7(1) of the FTR Rules, and include, among others: that

[10] Imports made in contravention of section 7 of the FTDR Act are in contravention of section 11 of the Customs Act, 1962 and may be confiscated under section 111(d) of the Customs Act: Uniflex Cables Ltd. v. Collector of Customs, Bombay - 1995 (77) EJ, T.737 (Tribunal).

[11] TDR Act, section 8(1).

an applicant is not eligible for a license in accordance with any provision of the Export and Import Policy, 1997-2002 (the "Exim Policy"); and, in the case of a license for import, that no foreign exchange is available for the purpose.[12]

2.15 Section 15 of the FTDR Act provides for an appeal against any decision or order made under the Act. This right of appeal extends to any decision to refuse a license. In the case of an order by an officer subordinate to the Director General, appeal lies to the Director General; in the case of an order made by the Director General, an appeal lies to the Central Government. In addition, although Section 15(3) of the FTDR Act states that "the order made in appeal by the Appellate Authority shall be final....", it can be challenged as violating a legal or constitutional right under Article 226 of the Constitution before the High Court of any State that is part of the Indian Union. In addition, if the alleged violation is of a fundamental right contained in Part III of the Constitution, it can be challenged under Article 32 of the Constitution before the Supreme Court of India. A challenge would lie, *inter alia*, on the ground that the decision is arbitrary, irrational or discriminatory. The decision of a High Court in turn can be challenged in an appeal to the Supreme Court of India under various provisions of the Constitution.

2.16 Section 19 of the FTDR Act authorizes the Central Government to make rules for carrying out the provisions of the Act, by notification in the Official Gazette. The Foreign Trade (Regulation) Rules, 1993 were issued under the authority of Section 19 of the FTDR Act. They provide generally for licence applications, licence fees, licence conditions, refusal, amendment, suspension or cancellation of licences, and enforcement.

2.17 Section 5 of the FTDR Act authorizes the Central Government to formulate and announce by notification in the Official Gazette the export and import policy. The first such policy, the Export and Import Policy 1992-1997, was in effect from 1992 until 31 March 1997. The policy currently in effect is the Export and Import Policy 1 April 1997 - 31 March 2002. Export and Import Policy statements have been issued once every five years, effective at the 1 April start of the government fiscal year. Revisions during the five-year period generally are published on 1 April of subsequent years during the five-year period, although changes may be made and announced in public notices at any time. The Export and Import Policy 1997-2002 includes, inter alia, the Negative List of Imports (" Negative List") found in Chapter 15 of the Export and Import Policy. The list sets forth various prescribed procedures or conditions for imports, and the eligibility requirements including export performance that must be met to qualify for Special Import Licences. Section 4.7 of the Export-Import Policy 1997-2002 provides that "[n]o person may claim a licence as a right and the Director General of Foreign Trade or the licensing authority shall have the power to refuse to

[12] Rule 7(1)(j) and (l).

grant or renew a licence in accordance with the provisions of the Act and the Rules made thereunder."

2.18 The Handbook of Procedures published on 1 April 1997 effective for the period 1997 to 2002 sets out the procedures that must be followed to export or import specific goods, and provides application forms for import licences. The ITC (HS) Classifications relates the rules set forth in the Export and Import Policy and the Handbook to the 8-digit product categories set forth in the Harmonized System of commodity classification. For each product listed at the 8-digit level, the book indicates five types of information in five columns: the 8-digit code; the item description, the applicable policy (prohibited, restricted, canalized or free); any conditions relating to the Export and Import Policy (these conditions appear either indicated with the particular item or in licensing notes at the end of the HS Chapter or section thereof); and an indication of whether the product can be imported under a Special Import Licence.

2. *Licensing Régime*

2.19 India regulates the import of goods by means of the Negative List . If an item is on the Negative List, a prospective importer must apply for a licence to the DGFT.

2.20 The Negative List classifies all restricted imports in one of three categories: prohibited items, restricted items, and canalized items. None of the prohibited items, listed in Part I of the Negative List, are listed in Annex I, Part B of document WT/BOP/N/24. In WT/BOP/N/24, Annex I, Part B, restricted items are identified with the symbol "NAL" (non-automatic licensing), "SIL" or "STR" in the column "QR symbol". Restricted items are listed in Part II of the Negative List. An item classified as "restricted" under the Negative List is only permitted to be imported against a specific import licence or in accordance with a public notice issued for that purpose.[13] The leading item on the Negative List is "all consumer goods, howsoever described, of industrial, agricultural, mineral or animal origin, whether in SKD/CKD condition or ready to assemble sets or in finished form."[14] Paragraph 3.14 of the Export and Import Policy further defines "consumer goods" as "any consumption goods which can directly satisfy human needs without further processing and include consumer durables and accessories thereof." The Negative List also lists seven product categories to be treated as consumer goods "for the removal of doubts": consumer electronic goods, equip-

---

[13] *See* Export and Import Policy, 10, para. 4.1 ("Any goods, the export or import of which is restricted through licensing, may be exported or imported only in accordance with a licence issued in this behalf). *See also* the restrictions listed in Part II of the Negative List of Imports, *id.*, para. 15.2. In a few instances, specific licences are not needed, although importation is still restricted. For instance, the import of radioactive material is allowed without a licence, subject to the recommendation of the Department of Atomic Energy.

[14] Export and Import Policy, Chapter 15, Part II "SKD/CKD" is "semi-knocked down/completely knocked down".

ments and systems, howsoever described; consumer telecommunications equipments namely telephone instruments and electronic PABX; watches in SKD/CKD or assembled condition, watch cases and watch dials; cotton, woollen, silk, man-made and blended fabrics including cotton terry towel fabrics; concentrates of alcoholic beverages; wines (tonic or medicated); and saffron.[15]

2.21 Canalized items, listed in Part III of the Negative List, may in principle be imported only by a designated canalizing (government) agency. A number of canalized items appear in Annex I, Part B of WT/BOP/N/24 (indicated by "STR" in the column labelled "QR Symbol").

2.22 A person intending to import a restricted item must submit an application for an import licence to the Director General of Foreign Trade in India's Ministry of Commerce ("DGFT"), or an officer authorized by him ("licensing authority") with territorial jurisdiction. Import licences are not transferable. Any person who imports or exports (with or without a licence) must have an Importer-Exporter Code (IEC) number, unless specifically exempted.[16] In addition, any person applying for an import or export licence must present a Registration-cum-Membership Certificate (RCMC) granted by the Export Promotion Council relating to his line of business, the Federation of Indian Exporters Organisation, or (if the products exported by him are not covered by any Export Promotion Council) the regional licensing authority.[17] The application forms for the RCMC requires the applicant to claim status as a merchant exporter or manufacturer exporter of a specific product or products.[18]

2.23 The application form for import of items covered by the Negative List requests information on the applicant's name and address, the type of unit, the applicant's registration number, the end product(s) to be manufactured with licensed capacity, details of the items applied for export, the total CIF value applied for, past production in the previous year, exports done during the previous year, and "justification for import".

2.24 Whenever imports require a licence, only the "Actual User" may import the goods, unless the Actual User condition is specifically dispensed with by the licensing authority.[19] Paragraph 3.4 of the Export-Import Policy defines "Actual User" as an actual user who may be either industrial or non-industrial. Paragraph 3.5 of the Policy defines "Actual User (Industrial)" as "a person who utilizes the imported goods for manufacturing in his own unit or manufacturing for his own use in another unit including a jobbing unit." Paragraph 3.6 of the Policy defines "Actual User (Non-Industrial)" as "a person who utilizes the imported

[15] Export and Import Policy, Chapter 15, Part II "SKD/CKD" is "semi-knocked down/completely knocked down".

[16] Export and Import Policy, section 4.9.

[17] Export and Import Policy, paras. 4.10 and 13.8 ; Handbook para. 13.3; Handbook Appendix 14.

[18] See "Form of Application for Registration cum Membership with Export Promotion Councils" and "Form of Registration cum Membership Certificate", from Handbook, App. 3A and 3B.

[19] Export and Import Policy, para. 5.2.

goods for his own use in (i) any commercial establishment carrying on any business, trade, or profession; or (ii) any laboratory, Scientific or Research and Development (R&D) institution, university of other educational institution or hospital; or (iii) any service industry." The Actual User then cannot legally transfer the imported goods to anyone except with prior permission from the licensing authority concerned, except for a transfer to another Actual User after a period of two years from the date of import.[20]

2.25 About ten per cent of tariff lines subject to import licensing may also be imported under Special Import Licences (SILs). These items are listed in WT/BOP/N/24, Annex I, Part B by the symbol "SIL" in the "QR symbol" column.

2.26 Firms receive SILs from the Indian Government in proportion to their exports or NFE (net foreign exchange) earnings. SILs are issued by the DGFT or regional licensing authorities, and are freely transferable (there are SIL brokers and a resale market for SILs).

2.27 There are various methods by which a person or firm may apply for a Special Import Licence. First, an established private or state-run exporter which meets export performance criteria set forth in Chapter 12 of the Export and Import Policy, and elaborated upon in Chapter 12 of the Handbook, can qualify to be recognized by the regional licensing authority or the DGFT as an Export House, Trading House, Star Trading House, or Super Star Trading House.[21] Such designated exporters automatically qualify for SILs on the basis of entitlement rates set out in paragraph 12.7 of the Handbook.[22] Additional bonuses are earned if a designated exporter exports specified products (products made by small-scale industries; fruits, vegetables, flowers or horticultural products; or products made in the North Eastern States) and where over 10% of such an exporter's exports are to one or more of 43 listed Central and Latin American countries and territories.[23]

[20] Handbook, para. 5.36.

[21] Status as an Export House, Trading House, Star Trading House, or Super Star Trading House is accorded by the DGFT or the regional licensing authority on the basis of the FOB/Net Foreign Exchange (NFE) value of exports of goods and services by the exporter concerned during the preceding three years or the preceding licensing year, at the option of the exporter. Export and Import Policy, para. 12.3.

[22] Super Star Trading Houses must have made Rp. 2,250 crores in exports or Rp. 1,800 crores in net foreign exchange earnings in the preceding licensing year, or averaged Rp. 1,500 crores in exports/1,200 crores in NFE earnings in the preceding three licensing years. Export and Import Policy, para. 12.5.

[23] Handbook Vol.1, para. 12.7. The countries and territories targeted are: Antigua, Argentina, Bahamas, Barbados, Belize, Bermuda, Bolivia, Brazil, British Virgin Islands, Cayman Islands, Chile, Colombia, Costa Rica, Cuba, Dominica, Dominican Republic, Ecuador, El Salvador, Falkland Islands, French Guiana, Grenada, Guadeloupe, Guatemala, Guyana, Haiti, Honduras, Jamaica, Martinique, Mexico, Montserrat, Netherlands Antilles, Nicaragua, Panama, Paraguay, Peru, St. Vincent, St. Kitts-Nevis-Anguilla, St. Lucia, Suriname, Trinidad & Tobago, Uruguay, Venezuela, Virgin Islands (U.S.). Appendix 33.

2.28 Other exporters can still receive Special Import Licences equal to 4% of the fob value of their exports, subject to certain minimum export criteria set out in paragraph 11.11 of the Handbook. SILs are also granted to exporters of telecommunications equipment and electronic goods and services;[24] to exporters of diamonds, gems and jewelry;[25] to deemed exporters;[26] and to small scale exporters holding ISO/9000-series or IS/ISO/9000-series quality certification.

III. CLAIMS AND MAIN ARGUMENTS

A. *Scope of the Complaint*

3.1 The United States requested the Panel to find that:

- the quantitative restrictions at issue violate Article XI:1 and XVIII:11 of the GATT 1994 and Article 4.2 of the Agriculture Agreement; and
- recommend that India bring its measures into conformity with the GATT 1994 and the Agreement on Agriculture.

3.2 At the request of the Panel, the **United States** clarified that it sought a ruling that India is not currently justified under the balance-of-payments exception. If India asserted that these restrictions were justified under Article XVIII:B of GATT 1994, the United States requested the Panel to accept the findings and determinations made by the IMF. It also requested that the Panel find that the additional evidence presented by the United States corroborated the IMF's determination.

3.3 The United States considered that the Panel should find that Article XVIII:B is in the nature of an affirmative defense with respect to which India bears the burden of proof and requested the Panel to make an alternative conditional finding that even if the burden of proof were on the United States to make

[24] Export and Import Policy, para. 11.9.

[25] Exports of diamond, gem, and jewelry products are counted at 50% of the actual FOB value of exports.

[26] Chapter 10, para. 10.1 of the Export and Import Policy defines "deemed exports" as transactions in which the goods supplied do not leave India and the payment for the goods is made in India by the recipient of the goods. Para. 10.2 of the Policy provides that the following categories of supply of goods by the main or sub-contractors qualify as "deemed exports" if the goods are manufactured in India: (1) Supply of goods against duty-free licences under the Duty Exemption Scheme; (2) Supply of goods to Export Oriented Units or units located in Export Processing Zones or Software Technology Parks or to Electronic Hardware Technology Parks; (3) Supply of capital goods to holders of licences under the Export Promotion Capital Goods scheme, under certain conditions; (4) Supply of goods to projects financed by multilateral or bilateral agencies under international competitive bidding where the legal agreements provide for tender evaluation non-inclusive of the customs duty; (5) Supply of capital goods and spares to fertilizer plants (up to 10% of free-on-rail value) if under international competitive bidding; (6) Supply of goods to any project for which the Ministry of Finance has permitted duty-free imports; (7) Supply of goods to approved projects in the power, oil and gas sector.

a *prima facie* case, that India no longer had any justification for maintaining the measures under Article XVIII:B, the United States would have met this burden.

3.4 The United States further requested the Panel to find that each of the four restrictions, discussed below in paragraph 3.9, constituted a quantitative restriction within the meaning of GATT 1994 and the Agreement on Agriculture in order that there be no confusion as to which measures the Panel's recommendations applied.

3.5 If the Panel did not agree to the request for the ruling on Article XI:1, Article XVIII:11 and Article 4.2 of the Agreement on Agriculture, then the United States in its second written submission, sought a ruling that the measures at issue were not applied in accordance with Article XIII:2:(a).

3.6 **India** requested the Panel to reject the US complaint. India claimed that it was clear from Article XVIII:12 and the 1994 Understanding that the conformity of import restrictions with Article XVIII:9 and 11 must be determined by the General Council and that the Member may maintain the import restrictions until it had been informed of their inconsistency with the criteria set out in Article XVIII:9 and 10 by the General Council. In the absence of such a determination by the General Council, India continued to have the right to maintain the remaining restrictions under Article XVIII:B. In India's view, acceptance of the arguments of the United States would result in making whole paragraphs of Article XVIII:B and whole sections of the 1994 Understanding redundant, altering fundamentally the negotiated balance reflected in the text of Article XVIII:B and the 1994 Understanding. It would also be a serious deviation from practices consistently followed under the GATT 1947 and result in transferring without any basis the authority to determine the legal status of import restrictions from the Committee and the General Council to the IMF and panels. Furthermore India claimed that, in light of Article XVIII:12 (d), as well as Appellate Body rulings, the United States bore the burden of demonstrating that India's restrictions were inconsistent with Article XVIII:11.

3.7 With respect to the violation of Article XI:1, India claimed that no finding was necessary since the measures at issue had been notified as quantitative restrictions within the meaning of Article XI:1 India added that Article XI:1 simply prohibited quantitative restrictions; it did not regulate how quantitative restrictions that Members were allowed to maintain under exceptions to Article XI:1 were to be administered. India claimed that the manner in which import restrictions were administered was regulated by other provisions, including Article XIII of GATT 1994 and the Agreement on Import Licensing. However, findings on the consistency of the administration of the measures should not be considered by the Panel because the requests were not made, not even subsidiarily, in the first submission of the United States.

3.8 India also claimed that Article 4.2 of the Agreement on Agriculture, as clarified in the note to this provision, did not cover measures taken under the balance-of-payments provisions of the GATT. Therefore, the restrictions maintained by India were not inconsistent with Article 4.2 of the Agreement on Agriculture.

B. Article XI:1

1. United States

3.9 The **United States** contended that India maintained quantitative restrictions consisting of import licensing requirements on thousands of products. These were the items listed in the "Negative List of Imports" in India's official Export and Import Policy. Most imports into India remained subject to an arbitrary, non-transparent and discretionary import licensing regime; formal quotas did not exist. Persons wishing to import an item on the Negative List had to apply for a license and explain their "justification for import": the authorities provided no explanation of the criteria for judging applications, and no advance notice of the volume or value of imports to be allowed. In fact, licenses were routinely refused on the basis that the import would compete with a domestic producer. The leading item on the Negative List was consumer goods (including many food items), and for many consumer goods inclusion on the Negative List had amounted to an import ban or close to it.

3.10 The United States considered that the restrictiveness of India's licensing of consumer goods imports was demonstrated by the trade statistics in the Secretariat Report for the Trade Policy Review of India. Table AI.4 (Imports by groups of products, 1980-96) shows that there have been *zero* imports of clothing since *1980.* Table AII.1 (Effective tariff and bindings, by HS chapter) shows 29 HS chapters with *zero imports for 1995/96*, including *inter alia*, meat; fish; cereals; malt and starches; preparations of meat or fish; cocoa, chocolate and cocoa preparations; nuts, canned and pickled vegetables and fruits, and fruit juices; wine, beer, spirits and vinegar; leather articles; matting and baskets; carpets; knitted fabrics; clothing; headgear; umbrellas; and furniture. The same TPR report table shows 21 other HS chapters with just US$36 million per chapter in imports for a country of over 900 million population; these include *inter alia*, dairy products and eggs; coffee; oilseeds; pasta, tapioca, breakfast cereal, and breads; cosmetics; blankets, bed linen, curtains, tents and used clothing; footwear; ceramic products; and musical instruments.[27] Thus, in many cases import licensing amounts to an import ban, or close to it.

3.11 The United States noted that where an import license was granted for an item on the Negative List, it was only granted to an "Actual User". This "Actual User condition" ruled out any imports by wholesalers or other intermediaries, and itself was a further quantitative restriction on imports. Some of the restrictions on imports were made effective through "canalization": channelling of imports

[27] Total imports for 1995/96 were US$36,053 million, according to Table A1.4; the products listed here are those listed in Table AIII.1 as having an 0.1% share of total imports (US$36 million).

through state trading operations of authorized "canalizing agencies." Where canalizing agencies restricted imports, their operations were a quantitative restriction on imports. Some of the items on the Negative List could be imported by using "Special Import Licences (SILs)." However, these items too remained under restriction. Certain exporters could receive these licenses, which could then be used to import certain designated items which were otherwise subject to the normal discretionary import licensing regime. Items importable with SILs were generally items not produced in India. and were *not* to be equated with import liberalization.

3.12 The United States requested the Panel to find that all four measures: (1) restriction of items through discretionary licensing (2) canalization; (3) restriction of items through special import licensing and (4) the "Actual User" condition, constituted quantitative restrictions within the meaning of Article XI:1

(a) Import licensing as an import restriction

3.13 The **United States** noted that the measures that were the subject of this dispute were "restrictions other than duties, taxes or charges" as defined in Article XI:1. It pointed out that the GATT had on many occasions recognized that discretionary or non-automatic import licensing constituted a quantitative restriction on trade under Article XI:1. Under the WTO, the panel on "*EC - - Regime for the Importation, Sale and Distribution of Bananas*" recognized that "Past GATT panel reports support giving the term 'restriction' [in Article XI:1] an expansive interpretation."[28]

3.14 The United States claimed that an early precedent had appeared in the 1950 Working Party Report on a "*Notification by Haiti under Article XVIII.*" The text of Article XVIII:12 as it existed in 1950 permitted a contracting party to maintain certain protective measures which would not otherwise be permitted by the GATT, if the GATT CONTRACTING PARTIES examined the measures and concurred with a release.[29] Under this provision, Haiti had notified a law which, *inter alia*, provided for discretionary import licensing of imports of various tobacco products. The working party found that "in so far as the law establishing the Régie provided that the importation of tobacco, cigars and cigarettes should be subject to licences issued by a government authority and that licences should be issued at the discretion of that authority in the light of market requirements, there was an element of restriction in the measure which was contrary to Article XI of the General Agreement".[30] The CONTRACTING PARTIES then, by a

[28] Panel Report on *EC - Regime for the Importation, Sale and Distribution of Bananas*, WT/DS27/R/USA, adopted on 25 September 1997, para. 7.154, citing Panel Report on *Japan - Trade in Semiconductors*, adopted on 4 May 1988, BISD 35S/116, 153, paras. 104-105; Panel Report on *EEC - Programme of Minimum Import Prices, Licences and Surety Deposits for Certain Processed Fruits and Vegetables*, adopted on 18 October 1978, BISD 25S/68, 98-100, para. 4.9.

[29] BISD I/46, Art. XVIII:12.

[30] GATT/CP.5/25, adopted on 27 November 1950, BISD II/87.

formal decision on 27 November 1950, granted a release from the provisions of Article XI "for the maintenance of the measure in so far as it requires importers to obtain an import permit".[31]

3.15 The United States further mentioned that in 1950, the CONTRACTING PARTIES examined the application of the GATT to quantitative restrictions used for commercial, protective or bargaining purposes. The resulting report on "*The Use of Quantitative Restrictions for Protective and other Commercial Purposes*" was approved unanimously by the CONTRACTING PARTIES acting jointly under Article XXV:1.[32] This report referred to import licensing as an import restriction.[33]

3.16 The United States stated that the 1978 Panel on "*EEC - Programme of Minimum Import Prices, Licences and Surety Deposits for Certain Processed Fruits and Vegetables*" found that a non-automatic licensing system denying licenses for imports below certain minimum prices was a "restriction" within the meaning of Article XI:1.[34] Similarly, the Panel on "*Japan - Trade in Semi-Conductors*" examined an export licensing system in the light of Article XI:1, and found that "this wording [of Article XI:1] was comprehensive; it applied to all measures instituted or maintained by a contracting party prohibiting or restricting the importation, exportation or sale for export of products other than measures that take the form of duties, taxes or other charges."[35]

3.17 The United States considered that the import licensing regime generally applicable for imports of restricted items, or for imports by private firms of canalized imports, was totally discretionary. Both the normal discretionary import licensing regime and the SIL regime were "non-automatic import licensing" as defined under the Agreement on Import Licensing Procedures (import licensing where the approval of the application is *not* granted in all cases, and/or which is administered in such a manner as to have restricting effects on imports). Approval was *not* granted in all cases; no licence was accorded by right, nor did the Indian authorities provide any criteria for how licence applications would be evaluated. Furthermore, persons who did not export could not apply for, or be granted, an import licence. The licensing procedures were administered in such a manner as to have restrictive effects on the imports in question. After all, the products in question were subject to these licensing procedures because they were listed on the Negative List of Imports.

---

31 "Release granted to Haiti under Article XVIII, Paragraph 12 relating to the Import of Tobacco", Decision of 27 November 1950, BISD II/27.

32 GATT document GATT/CP.4/33, adopted on 3 April 1950, republished as "The Use of Quantitative Restrictions for Protective and other Commercial Purposes," Sales No. GATT/1950-3.

33 *Ibid.*, p. 7, paras. 5-7.

34 Panel Report on *EEC - Programme of Minimum Import Prices, Licences and Surety Deposits for Certain Processed Fruits and Vegetables*, adopted on 18 October 1978, BISD 25S/68, 98-100, para. 4.9.

35 Panel Report on *Japan - Trade in Semiconductors*, adopted on 4 May 1988, BISD 35S/116, 153, para. 104.

(i) Restriction of items through discretionary licensing

3.18 The **United States** recalled that in India's December 1995 full consultations in the Committee on Balance-of-Payments Restrictions, several Members had specifically requested India to provide a notification explaining the administration of specific restrictions and the criteria for granting import licences.[36] To date India had provided no such notification. When the United States had asked India, during the consultations in this dispute, what criteria were used to evaluate granting a licence for a restricted product, the Indian Government had responded simply that "The applications for import licences under this category are placed before a Special Licensing Committee for consideration. The Committee consists of representatives of technical authorities and administrative Ministries and decides cases on merits."[37] Similarly, India had stated in response to a question from the EC in the Committee on Import Licensing that "The licensing authority may take the assistance and advice of a Special Licensing Committee which is headed by the DGFT and consists of representatives of technical authorities and Department(s) with administrative responsibility for the item under consideration. Applications for the granting of import licences are considered on merit. General rules, where applicable, are prescribed in a Public Notice."[38] In spite of repeated requests to the Indian Government, the United States noted that it had been unable to obtain any concrete information on which types of imports of restricted products the Indian authorities actually considered to have "merit" or what factors the Indian Government actually evaluated to determine whether a licence application had "merit".

3.19 For the United States, the Indian Government had also not provided any information on the total amount of licences or total amount of imports that would be authorized in a given future period. In years past, government experts would determine semi-annually the amount of foreign exchange available, and imports would be allocated against that amount. The United States considered that the size of India's reserves at present, and the fundamental change in the direction of India's economic, trade and development policy since 1991, had made such an approach obsolete. But the Government's withholding of any information concerning how many imports it would permit created a continuing commercial uncertainty for all importers and for India's trading partners.

3.20 Thus, according to the United States, the generally applicable import licensing process was a complete black box for the importer and for the foreign exporter. No information was provided on the Government's sectoral priorities with respect to products or on what its views of "merit" might be. All that the

36 WT/BOP/R/11, "Report on the Consultations with India," 23 January 1996, para. 20

37 Handbook paragraph 5.30 states that "The licensing committee will consist of representatives of technical authorities and Departments/Ministries concerned."

38 G/LIC/Q/IND/2, 20 January 1997.

United States knew was that the Indian licensing authority generally refused to grant import licences for "restricted" items when it was considered prejudicial to the state's interest to do so.[39]

3.21 The United States added that the broad definition of "consumer goods," and the fact that some goods were *only* restricted if they were consumer goods, created considerable confusion, commercial uncertainty and distortion of trade. For instance, monosodium glutamate (MSG) did not appear in the Negative List of Imports and was therefore freely importable under the 1992-1997 Export and Import Policy. However, on 1 November 1996 the DGFT issued a clarification that MSG was freely importable only in bulk; if it was put up in consumer packs MSG became a "consumer good" under the Negative List, and all imports were subject to discretionary import licensing.[40] Thus, arbitrarily-chosen characteristics of a product such as its package size could unexpectedly change the import regime applicable to trade in that product. The 1996 study on *Liberalisation of Indian Imports of Consumer Durables* by the Export-Import Bank of India had noted that the only two commonly-used consumer durable goods that were freely importable were cameras and nail cutters.[41]

(ii) Canalization

3.22 The **United States** noted that the import restrictions on canalized products, implemented through canalization, were among those restrictions for which India claimed balance-of-payments justification. In 1996/97, petroleum products accounted for 78% of canalized imports followed by edible oils at 12%.[42]

3.23 India's most recent notification concerning state trading noted that "Import of cereals and edible oils was undertaken on the advice of Government from time to time. Government is guided by a number of factors including the balance of payments *and domestic production and prices situation.*"[43] For the United States, this indicated that protection of domestic production was also a strong motive in maintenance of these restrictions, and that these restrictions might amount to outright prohibition of imports in some instances.

---

[39] In this connection, the United States called attention to "Consultation with India (Simplified Procedures): Background Paper by the Secretariat", GATT Document BOP/W/159, 31 October 1994, para. 8.

[40] "Grievances Column: An importer suffers due to lack of transparency in import policy," *Impex Times* 24 August 1997. The *Impex Times* is a semimonthly newsmagazine specializing in India's import licensing policy, published by a retired Joint Chief Controller of Imports and Exports. The article notes the experience of an importer who contracted for imports of MSG in consumer packs, which was shipped before the clarification letter; the import was treated as unauthorized by customs and the importer was fined an amount equivalent to the value of the goods.

[41] Export-Import Bank of India, *Liberalization of Indian Imports of Consumer Durables*, February 1996, p. 16.

[42] WT/TPR/S/33, p. 66, para. 65.

[43] G/STR/N/1/IND, 31 January 1996, para. 3 (emphasis added).

Table 1
Imports of canalized items during 1992-95
Quantity: 000 tonnes; Value: RS. Crores

S.I. No.	Name of item	1992-1993		1993-1994		1994-1995	
		Quantity	Value	Quantity	Value	Quantity	Value
1	Crude oil	27,247	10,685.36	30,822	10,688.52	27,319	10,316.03
2	Aviation turbine fuel	-	-	-	-	78	51.31
3	Furnace oil	-	-	-	-	267	91.62
4	High-speed diesel	7,159	3,691.34	7,535	4,174.97	8,637	4,360.09
5	Urea	1,863	731.68	2,755	824.3	2,951	1,546.9
6.	Cereals						
	a Wheat	2,599	n.a.	476	n.a.	-	-
	b. Rice	86	n.a.	56	n.a.	-	-

"Note: Even though canalized, no import of motor spirit and bitumen took place during the last three years. The Hundustan Vegetable Oils Corporation Ltd., even though a canalized agency for import of certain oils and oilseeds as indicated in Annex 1, was not authorized to import any of these items during the last three years. Also, since the State Trading Corporation of India (STC), the canalizing agency for import of certain oils and oilseeds, does not deal with any of these canalized items, no information on these items is included in this statement."

Source: (For table and note: G/STR/N/1/IND, Annex 2. One crore rupees = Rs. 10 million (approx. US$250,000).)

3.24 Table 1 above and the notes thereto demonstrated that canalization resulted in zero imports in 1992-95 for the edible oils and oilseeds canalized through the Hindustan Vegetable Oils Corporation, and zero imports of wheat and rice during 1994-95. While India's notification on state trading (dated January 1996) stated that "The State Trading Corporation of India Ltd., which was a major State Trading Enterprise does no longer deal with any canalized item of import/export",[44] India's notification of all quantitative restrictions including those operated through canalization (dated June 1997) still asserted that some imports were canalized through the State Trading Corporation, in some cases exclusively.[45] As the United States understood, if the STC was the sole authorized importer of a product, but was not importing (i.e. for palm stearin, excluding crude palm stearin; palm kernel oil; and tallow amines of all types), then no imports were taking place and canalization amounted to an import ban. If the STC and the Hindustan Vegetable Oils Corporation together were the sole authorized importers of a product but did not deal with it or were not authorized to import it

[44] G/STR/N/1/IND, 31 January 1996, p. 9.
[45] WT/BOP/N/24, p. 117-118: see indications with respect to symbols "MMTC, STC, IPL/BOP-XVII, XVIII:B", "STC/BOP-XVII, XVIII:B" and "STC, HVOC/BOP-XVII, XVIII:B".

(i.e. for coconut oil, RBD palm oil and RBD palm stearin), again no imports were taking place and canalization amounted to an import ban.

3.25 While the Director General of Foreign Trade was legally authorized to grant import licences for a canalized product to entities other than the designated state-trading agency,[46] such licences are only granted on the basis of a "No Objection Certificate" issued by the state-trading agency concerned.[47] The United States said it had been informed in consultations by India that from 1 April to 15 September 1997, no such licence was issued to any non-governmental entity. For this reason, although the Special Import Licence regime was in theory available for imports of certain petroleum products canalized through the Indian Oil Corporation Ltd.,[48] it did not appear to be actually utilized by non-governmental entities. Special Import Licences were otherwise not available for canalized imports.

3.26 The United States argued that the import restrictions maintained by India through "canalization" of imports through state trading ("canalizing") agencies were also "restrictions" within the purview of Article XI:1. As the Note *Ad* Articles XI, XII, XIII, XIV and XVIII stated, "Throughout Articles XI, XII, XIII, XIV and XVIII, the terms 'import restrictions' or 'export restrictions' include restrictions made effective through state-trading operations."

3.27 The United States recalled that it was well-established under the GATT 1947 that import restrictions were no less subject to Article XI:1 because they might be run through state trading. The Haitian import restrictions referred to above were maintained through a tobacco monopoly.[49] As another example, a 1961 working party examined residual import restrictions maintained by Italy; certain items were controlled by state-trading agencies operating under Article XVII. The working party report recorded: "Insofar as the State-trading operation had the effect of restricting imports, the Italian authorities fully recognized that, by virtue of the interpretative notes *ad* Articles XI, XII, etc. in Annex I to the General Agreement, it constituted an import restriction within the purview of Article XI".[50] In the 1987-88 dispute concerning Japanese import restrictions on various agricultural products, the panel firmly rejected Japan's argument that Article XI:1 did not apply to import restrictions made effective through state trading:

---

[46] Export and Import Policy, Article 4.8.

[47] WT/TPR/S/33, p. 66, para. 64.

[48] Items 271000.01 (aviation gasoline); 271000.02 and 271000.11 (jet fuel and kerosene jet fuel); ex 271000.39 (furnace oil); 271320.00 (petroleum bitumen) in WT/BOP/N/24 p. 50, where "SIL/IOC/BOP-XVII-XVIII:B" is indicated.

[49] BISD II/87, Op. Cit.

[50] Report of the Working Party under Article XXII:2 on "Italian Restrictions Affecting Imports from the United States and Certain other Contracting Parties," L/1468, adopted on 16 May 1961, BISD 10S/117, 119, para. 7. The Italian government asserted that the state monopoly on these products was protected by the Protocol of Provisional Application (recognizing that the restrictions were otherwise inconsistent with the GATT).

"The Panel examined this contention and noted the following: Article XI:1 covers restrictions on the importation of any product, 'whether made effective through quotas, import ... licences or other measures'. The wording of this provision is comprehensive, thus comprising restrictions made effective through an import monopoly. This is confirmed by the note to Articles XI, XII, XIII, XIV and XVIII, according to which the term 'import restrictions' throughout these Articles covers restrictions made effective through state-trading operations. The basic purpose of this note is to extend to state-trading the rules of the General Agreement governing private trade and to ensure that the contracting parties cannot escape their obligations with respect to private trade by establishing state-trading operations. This purpose would be frustrated if import restrictions were considered to be consistent with Article XI:1 only because they were made effective through import monopolies ... The Panel found for these reasons that the import restrictions applied by Japan fell under Article XI independent of whether they were made effective through quotas or through import monopoly operations."[51]

3.28 The United States noted that the 1988 panel report on "*Canada - Import, Distribution and Sale of Alcoholic Drinks by Canadian Provincial Marketing Agencies*" had found that practices of Canadian provincial liquor boards systematically discriminating against imported beverages "should be considered as restrictions made effective through 'other measures' contrary to the provisions of Article XI:1".[52] Furthermore, in the 1989 panel report on the U.S. complaint concerning "*Korea - Restrictions on Imports of Beef*," that panel found that the Korean import restrictions, administered through a state-trading entity, violated Article XI:1.[53] Finally, India had conceded that the "canalization" restrictions within the scope of this dispute were "restrictions" within the purview of Article XI:1, by notifying them as balance-of-payments import restrictions in WT/BOP/N/24.

3.29 The United States argued that, to the extent that the import licensing or canalization had banned or would ban imports of any product, through the refusal of the DGFT and the relevant licensing authorities to issue licences or through a ban on imports by canalizing agencies, India's import regime constituted not just a restriction but a *prohibition* on imports.

---

[51] Panel Report on *Japan - Restrictions on Imports of Certain Agricultural Products*, L/6253, adopted on 22 March 1988, 35S/163, 229, para. 5.2.2.2. For findings applying this rule to individual products see paragraphs 5.3.1.1 and 5.3.9 of the same report.

[52] Panel Report on Canada - *Import Distribution and Sale of Alcoholic Drinks to Canadian Provincial Marketing Agencies*, L/6304, adopted on 22 March 1988, BISD 35S/37, 89, para. 4.24.

[53] Panel Report on *Korea - Restrictions on Imports of Beef* (hereafter - *Korea-Beef*) L/6503, adopted on 7 November 1989, BISD 36S/268, 301-302, paras. 113, 115.

(iii) Restrictions of items through special import licensing

3.30 The **United States** contended that the Special Import Licence (SIL) regime was a non-automatic import licensing procedure as well and was equally in violation of Article XI:1. SILs were issued to Indian exporters, who could resell them at a profit to importers. But they could only be used for imports of a few products. SIL-eligible products included only 10% of the HS lines subject to restrictions, and in some cases only selected products within those lines. In the case of SILs, approval of licence applications was not granted in "all cases": only certain exporters might be granted approval for SILs, and only those exporters, or "actual users" to whom the exporters had transferred the SILs, might use them to import designated goods.

3.31 The United States referred to the Export-Import Bank of India's 1996 report on *Liberalisation of Indian Imports of Consumer Durables* which had shown that very few consumer durables could be imported through SILs; most types of consumer durables produced in India in substantial amounts were excluded from the list and were subject to the generally applicable discretionary import licensing regime (which was a *de facto* ban on imports, or close to it). For instance, household refrigerators were made in India and could not be imported through SILs; the only refrigerators that could be imported through SILs were those above 300 litres capacity.[54]

3.32 Estimates of the premium for brokered SILs ranged from 4% to 15%.[55] This premium amounted to a burden the importer must bear in addition to the tariff and, in the view of the United States, indicated that the volume of SILs granted was substantially below the pent-up demand for imports. The Export-Import Bank had found that the major determinant of additions to the SIL list had been maintenance of the resale premium for SILs as an incentive to exporters, not liberalization of consumer goods imports.[56] Even with SILs, imports of consumer durables had been extremely small: the Bank study found that in 1993/94, imports of household refrigerators amounted to only 556 units total; only 34 washing machines were imported, 29 vacuum cleaners, 10 microwave ovens,

[54] Export-Import Bank of India, *Liberalization of Indian Imports of Consumer Durables*, Occasional Paper No. 44, February 1996. Refrigerators and refrigerator-freezers: see items 8418210.00-841829.00, in ITC (HS) Classifications and WT/BOP/N/24.

[55] In meetings with a U.S. government delegation in New Delhi in 1997, DGFT officials estimated the premium at 8 to 15%. A recent article in the *Economic Times* estimates the premium at 4% (Ajoy K. Das, "Exporters in jitters over BJP stand on QRs", *Economic Times*, 9 March 1998). The U.S. Embassy in New Delhi inquired on 30 March 1998 to a local firm which purchases SILs and determined that the rate as of that date was 6 to 8% (6% for larger amounts); the SIL premium rate varies daily in this range.

[56] Export-Import Bank of India (1996), Op. Cit. p. 17-18.

100 colour TV sets, 284 motor cars, and 28 two-wheelers, for the entire population of India.[57]

3.33 The United States noted that access to SILs was also limited in many cases to high-value products, to eliminate any imports that would compete with domestic products. For instance, lipstick (item 330410.00) could be imported under SIL, but only if the c.i.f. value of each unit was US$10 or above. The availability of SILs was also selective by sector. Poultry, fish, almost all dairy products, french-fried potatoes, coffee, pet food, fresh fruit and other such agricultural products were treated as consumer goods ineligible for SIL imports, and thus imports were in effect banned or severely restricted. As of 1 April 1997, approximately 10% of total lines at the HS eight-digit level could be imported through a Special Import Licence; of the total lines eligible for import under SIL, only 14.6% were agricultural products including fisheries, 29.6% were textile and clothing products and 55.8 were other industrial products.[58] Thus, hardly any agricultural products were eligible to be imported under SIL. The severe limits on this programme largely prevented its ostensible benefits from reaching the Indian consumer.

3.34 The United States concluded that the SIL regime was trade-restrictive and trade-distorting. The United States considered that SILs were administered in such a manner as to have restricting effects on imports; the quota premium for purchase of SILs (with estimates ranging from 4% to 15%) testified to the trade-restricting effect of the SIL regime. Import licences were conditioned on export performance - even on targeting of exports toward certain parts of the world. Finally, the SIL regime certainly did not amount to an automatic import licensing procedure for the tariff items importable with SILs.

(iv) The "Actual User" condition

3.35 The **United States** argued that the "Actual User" condition attached to import licences was also a quantitative restriction on imports, and would independently violate Article XI:1 even if the licences in question were otherwise automatic import licences. As noted above (paragraph 3.16), denial of licences for imports below certain minimum import prices constituted an import restriction within the meaning of Article XI:1, and denial of permission to export below minimum export prices constituted an export restriction. Similarly, the "Actual User" condition denied a license for imports by intermediaries. This measure would eliminate most consumer goods imports into India even if those imports were not already subject to a *de facto* ban. If the "Actual User" condition was not inconsistent with Article XI:1, then any WTO Member - not just India - could limit imports by enacting similar provisions in its law.

---

[57] Export-Import Bank of India (1996), Op. Cit. Table 1.3, p. 23 (based on DGCIS Monthly Statistics of the Foreign Trade of India).

[58] WT/TPR/S/33, Op. Cit. p 65, para. 63.

3.36 The United States pointed out that while import intermediaries were treated as normal participants in the economy in all of India's developed trading partners, and in the United States and the EC such intermediaries had actively developed the market for imports from India, in India the import intermediary was excluded from importing by the government's import licensing regime. The "Actual User" condition itself constituted a quantitative restriction on imports. The WTO Secretariat had noted that the "Actual User" condition "further impede[s] foreign competition on the Indian market."[59] A 1992 World Bank study on India's trade regime observed that the "Actual User" policy would prevent most consumer goods imports even if the ban on such imports were lifted.[60]

3.37 The United States cited the example of newsprint imports which illustrated the real-world impact of the "Actual User" condition imposed on import licences. The Impex Times, a small semi-monthly newspaper specializing in news about India's import and export regime, was published in New Delhi by a retired Joint Chief Controller of Imports and Exports. Newsprint had been freely importable, but was then brought under control, and import licences were made subject to the "Actual User" restriction. The publisher of this newspaper noted "the difficulties which small actual users have to face in importing for themselves. In the first instance, they do not know the technique of import. Secondly, they do not have the financial resources to import their requirements covering a longer period because import of small quantities at a time is both uneconomical and troublesome. Moreover, it is also uneconomic to store imported quantities in go-downs and pay bank interest."[61]

2. *India*

3.38 India considered that the request of the United States for a finding on the inconsistency of India's import restrictions with Article XI:1 was a request either for a declaratory judgement or for a specific remedy and, therefore, should not be granted by the Panel.

India noted that, in its request for the establishment of a Panel, the United States had noted:

> "The United States considered that quantitative restrictions maintained by India, *including, but not limited to*, the more than 2,700 agricultural and industrial product tariff lines notified to the WTO in Annex I, Part B of WT/BOP/N/21 dated 22 May 1997, appear to be inconsistent with India's obligations under Article XI:1 and XVIII:11 of GATT 1994 and Article 4.2 of the Agreement on Agriculture. Furthermore, the *import licensing procedures and prac-*

---

[59] BOP/W/159, 31 October 1994, para. 8.

[60] M. Ataman Aksoy, *The Indian Trade Regime*, World Bank Policy Research Working Paper No. WPS 989 dated October 1992, p. 8.

[61] *Impex Times*, 10 May 1997, p. 7.

> *tices of the Government of India are inconsistent with fundamental WTO requirements as provided in Article XIII of the GATT 1994 and Article 3 of the Agreement on Import Licensing Procedures.*"

Subsequently, the United States had narrowed both the factual and legal scope of the complaint significantly by stating:

> *This dispute concerns the 2,714 restrictions or prohibitions maintained under the Export and Import Policy, 1997-2002 which are listed in Annex I, Part B of document WT/BOP/N/24 dated 22 May 1997.* The existence of these restrictions is not in dispute, as this document is a notification by India to the WTO Committee on Balance-of-Payments Restrictions ..."

The United States thus referred only to those import restrictions which India had notified to the Committee as "quantitative restrictions" subject to Article XVIII:B of the GATT.

3.39 India further noted that, in its first submission, the United States also narrowed the legal scope of its complaint. It merely requested the Panel to find that "the quantitative restrictions at issue in this dispute violate Article XI:1 and Article XVIII:11 of the GATT and Article 4.2 of the Agriculture Agreement". Findings on the consistency of the Indian licensing procedures with Article XIII of the GATT and Article 3 of the Licensing Agreement were thus no longer requested by the United States. The United States had also specifically stated that it was not invoking the provisions of the 1994 Understanding dealing with the administration of India's import restrictions.

3.40 According to India, therefore, at issue before the Panel were thus the import restrictions notified under Article XVIII:B, whose status under Article XI:1 of the GATT, as the United States correctly noted, was not in dispute. Nevertheless, the United States made in its first submission detailed allegations about the manner in which the import restrictions were administered. However, *Article XI:1 simply prohibited quantitative restrictions; it did not regulate how quantitative restrictions that Members were allowed to maintain under exceptions from Article XI:1 were to be administered.* That question was regulated in other WTO provisions, such as Article XIII of the GATT, Article 3 of the Licensing Agreement and paragraphs 1 to 4 of the 1994 Understanding. However, the United States had not invoked any of these provisions - not even subsidiarily in case the Panel were to find India's import restrictions to be covered by Article XVIII:B - , which implied that the scope of this proceeding did not include the administration of the import restrictions.

3.41 Since the United States had not requested the panel to make any findings on these matters. India, concluded that the United States invoked the dispute settlement procedures only with respect to the justification of the import restrictions and not in respect of matters arising from their application. India, therefore, reserved its position on the allegations of the United States with respect to the application of India's import restrictions, in terms of both their factual basis and their legal implications.

3.42 India recalled that the United States had explained at the first meeting why it had presented all these details as follows: "*Clarification by the panel of the prohibited nature of each of these restrictions is appropriate and necessary*. In particular, clear and unequivocal factual and legal findings in respect of each of these restrictions will greatly assist the parties *in the implementation process* of any ruling and recommendations." What the United States had described as issues related to the "prohibited nature" of the import restrictions were - as the United States pointed out itself - inconsistencies that might arise in the implementation of the findings the United States was requesting. For example, the United States had claimed that a ruling on the "actual user condition" for the grant of import licences was also necessary because: "Unless the Panel clarifies that the 'actual user' condition itself is a quantitative restriction on imports banned by Article XI:1, India may simply expand this barrier to restrict imports of every item on its so-called liberalization list." The United States had also claimed that the Panel "must rule that SILs are import restrictions banned by Article XI:1. It is important to remove any doubt that liberalization of restrictions requires automatic import licensing and nothing less."

3.43 India pointed out that, in fact, India had notified all of its import restrictions at issue in this dispute including the restrictions on imports of items subject to the "actual user" condition and SILs as "quantitative restrictions" falling under Article XI:1. Further, as compared to 1991, when more than 11,000 items at the HS 8-digit level were subject to import restrictions under Article XVIII:B, India maintains import restrictions only on 2,296 items today. The items on which import restrictions had been removed had all been made freely importable and were not subject to the "actual user" condition or to SILs. Therefore, there was absolutely no factual basis for the apprehension of the United States that India would subject items on which import restrictions were removed to the "actual user" condition or SILs.

3.44 Moreover, in India's view, in the guise of a request for findings on the "prohibited nature" of the import restrictions, the United States was in effect requesting the Panel to rule on the ways in which India was to implement an adverse finding of the Panel. However, Panels were not entitled to make declaratory judgements on potential future inconsistencies and had in practice never done so. The dispute settlement provisions of the GATT and the DSU defining the causes of action, the remedy available and the scope of the retaliation all presupposed the existence of a measure that was currently nullifying or impairing benefits and capable of being brought into conformity with the obligations under the WTO agreements.[62]

[62] Article XXIII:1(a) of the GATT, Article 19.1 of the DSU and Article 22.8 of the DSU. India referred in this connection to the arguments it presented on this issue in the *Patents* case (Panel Report on *India - Patent Protection for Pharmaceutical and Agricultural Chemical Products*, 5 September 1997, WT/DS50/R, para. 4.32)

3.45 India added that panels may also not grant so-called specific remedies under Article 19:1, first sentence, of the DSU. The only recommendation that the Panel could make under this provision, if it were to find India's import restrictions to be inconsistent with Article XVIII:B, was that India bring its import restrictions into conformity with the GATT and the Agreement on Agriculture. The background to Article 19:1 of the DSU was the following. Two adopted GATT panel reports recommended that anti-dumping or countervailing duties be repaid. However, when the panel on "*United States - Imposition of Anti-dumping Duties on Imports of Seamless Stainless Steel Hollow Products from Sweden*" submitted its report to the GATT Committee on Anti-Dumping Practices with such a recommendation, the United States objected to the "specific remedy" recommended by the panel.[63] Since then the United States had consistently taken the position that panels should only provide the general, prospective remedy which GATT panels have traditionally accorded and leave the method of implementation to the party concerned.[64] It was this view which was reflected in Article 19.1, first sentence, of the DSU.

3.46 India recalled further that, in the *Patents* case against India, the United States had also attempted to obtain a specific remedy in the guise of ruling on the nature of the inconsistency. In that case the United States had argued that India had failed to grant exclusive marketing rights in accordance with Article 70.9 of the TRIPS Agreement *and* that India had failed to grant exclusive marketing rights of a certain nature.[65] That panel had reacted to this request as follows:

> We consider a finding *on the nature of the right to be granted under Article 70.9* unnecessary to settle this particular dispute, which concerns the current non-existence of an exclusive marketing rights system in India. Rather it is sufficient for the Panel to recommend that India bring itself into conformity with its obligations under the TRIPS Agreement.[66] (emphasis added).

In India's view, the reaction of the present Panel to the United States' request for a finding on "the prohibited nature of India's restrictions" should be the same as the above ruling on the request for a finding on the "nature of the right to be granted under Article 70.9".

3.47 India noted that the United States had vigorously opposed panel rulings on how Members should implement findings on anti-dumping and countervailing duties - areas in which it resorts to trade-restrictive measures more frequently

---

[63] ADP/117 and Corr.1, 24 February 1994; ADP/M/35, p. 25.

[64] This view was for instance expressed by the United States as third party in the *Coconuts* case (Panel Report on *Brazil - Measures Affecting Dessicated Coconut*,WT/DS22/R, 17 October 1996, paras. 220 and 221).

[65] WT/DS50/R, para. 3.1(d) and (e).

[66] Panel Report on *India - Patent Protection for Pharmaceutical and Agricultural Chemical Products* (hereafter *Patents*), WT/DS50/R, para. 7.64. India noted that the United States did not appeal this ruling.

than any other Member of the WTO - but asks for rulings on how Members should implement panel findings in the fields of intellectual property rights and balance-of-payments measures- areas in which its investment and export interests were at stake. Therefore, India requested the Panel to note that the request for findings on "the prohibited nature" of India's import restrictions was the United States' second attempt to introduce specific remedies selectively into WTO jurisprudence in a manner that suited the particular interests of one Member. With respect to the allegation by the United States of discretion in India's import licensing regime, India submitted that discretionary import licensing *per se* was not prohibited under the covered Agreements. It was true that the second and third sentences of paragraph 4 of the 1994 Understanding provided that

> "in order to minimize any incidental protective effects, a Member shall administer restrictions in a transparent manner. The authorities of the importing Member shall provide adequate justification as to the criteria used to determine which products are subject to restriction".

3.48 However, the context made it clear that discretionary import licensing was not forbidden. Thus, the sixth sentence of paragraph 4 of the 1994 Understanding provided that:

> "in the administration of quantitative restrictions, a Member shall use discretionary licensing only when unavoidable and shall phase it out progressively".

3.49 India said that it needed to use discretionary licensing on a case-by-case basis, *inter alia,* for the following reasons. India's economy had been almost totally closed to imports barely 15 years ago. Because of the size and structure of the economy, it was impossible for India to estimate precisely the level of demand for imports, the import elasticity of demand for a huge number of products, as well as the elasticity of substitution of domestic products by consumers, and the effective rate of protection for all these products. Accordingly, India considered recourse to discretionary licensing to be unavoidable. Further, India was progressively phasing out its import restrictions. As part of its autonomously initiated programme of economic liberalization, India had already reduced the number of items on which there were import restrictions to just 2,296 HS-lines at the 8-digit level, as of 13 April 1998, from about 11,000 HS-lines in 1991.

3.50 India stated that it was also important to note that, in any case, the footnote to the 1994 Understanding specifically stated that:

> "nothing in this Understanding is intended to modify the rights and obligations of the Members under Articles XII or XVIII:B of the GATT 1994".

3.51 The effect of the footnote was that the 1994 Understanding could not limit a Member's right under Article XVIII:B, if any, to maintain discretionary licensing under Article XVIII:B. Article XVIII:B did not impose any restriction on a Member's right to implement import restrictions through discretionary licensing. Moreover, Article 3:3 of the Licensing Agreement specifically exempted Members implementing import restrictions through "non-automatic import licensing" from the requirement of publishing "sufficient information for other Members and traders to know the basis for granting and/or allocating licences".

3.52 Although the provisions of Article XVIII:B of the GATT 1994 and Article 3:3 of the Licensing Agreement might provide a legal basis for India not to publish the basis for allocation of licences, India sought to clarify that India's import licensing regime was a transparent, rule-based one. The basic regulatory framework for the administration of India's foreign trade had been described. Imports and exports were regulated, *inter alia*, under the Foreign Trade (Regulation and Development) Act, 1993 (the "FTDR Act"). Section 19 of the FTDR Act conferred rule-making power on the Government of India, pursuant to which the Government had notified the Foreign Trade (Regulation) Rules, 1993 (the "FTR Rules"). Section 5 of the FTDR Act authorized the Government of India to notify its policy relating to imports and exports, pursuant to which the Government had notified the Export and Import Policy, 1997-1992 (the "Exim Policy"). Pursuant to paragraph 4.11 of the Exim Policy, the Government had also notified the Handbook of Procedures, 1997-2002 (the "Handbook").

3.53 The FTDR Act not only laid down transparent criteria for grant of a licence, it also provided for an appellate process to ensure that the criteria employed in decision-making were consistent with those laid down under the FTDR Act, the FTR Rules, the Exim Policy and the Handbook. There was absolutely no basis in fact, therefore, for the allegation of the United States that India's import licensing regime was "arbitrary" or "non-transparent". Although India's import licensing regime was discretionary, the discretion conferred was not unbridled or unfettered but was guided and controlled in India's municipal law by an elaborate statutory and regulatory framework that was also overseen by the superior courts in India.

3.54 India explained that it did not announce quotas as required under Article XIII:2(a) because quotas were not practicable in the case of a relatively closed economy like India that was in the process of liberalizing its economy. As a developing country with a low standard of living, India simply did not have the financial and administrative resources to identify and administer the quotas for nearly 2,300 tariff lines. India noted that Article XIII:2(a) clearly permitted India to administer its import restrictions through import licenses or permits without specifying quotas.

3.55 India further noted that, in accordance with the general rules of treaty interpretation set forth in Article 31 of the Vienna Convention on the Law of Treaties, 1969, the terms of Article XIII:2(a) of GATT 1994 must be interpreted in good faith in accordance with their ordinary meaning as revealed by their context and in the light of the object and purpose of the GATT 1994. The context of Article XIII:2(a) made it clear that it was not intended to apply to an import licensing regime such as that of India. Article XIII:2 stated that the conditions in paragraphs (a) through (d) of Article XIII:2 are for the purpose of ensuring that trade in any product approaches "as closely as possible the shares which the various contracting parties might be expected to obtain in the absence of such [import] restrictions".

3.56 The administration of India's import licensing regime was wholly non-discriminatory. Paragraph 4.2 of the Handbook of Procedures, 1 April 1997 to 31 March 2002 applicable to exports and imports (notified in the Gazette of India pursuant to paragraph 4.11 of the Exim Policy) provided that imports would be valid to or from any country except Iraq (which was currently subject to international sanctions imposed by the United Nations). This was a legally enforceable obligation undertaken by the Government of India. If the Director-General refused to grant a licence for imports because the applicant wished to import goods from a particular country or granted a licence subject to the condition that goods must be imported from a particular country, an applicant might appeal against such a decision under Section 15 of the FTDR Act or request one of the superior courts (i.e., one of the High Courts or the Supreme Court) to invalidate such a decision.

> Responding to a question by the Panel on the grant of licences to importers and exporters and the definition of "actual users", India stated that import licences might be granted to any person including an industrial user who was engaged in production solely for the domestic market. Licences, including Special Import Licences, for items on the Negative List were accessible also to persons other than actual users.

3.57 India clarified that the focus on consumer products in its import policy alluded to by the United States was consistent with Article XVIII:10 of the GATT 1994, which explicitly recognized that a Member "may determine [the] incidence of [import restrictions] on imports of different products or classes of products in such a way as to give priority to the importation of those products which are more essential in the light of its policy of economic development". India added that in the context of permitting the selective application of surcharge for balance-of-payments reasons, paragraph 4 of the Understanding on the Balance-of-Payments Provisions of the GATT 1994 also explicitly recognized that capital goods or inputs needed for production "contribute to the Member's efforts to improve its balance-of-payments situation".

3.58 In the light of the above, India therefore concluded that, under the DSU, a panel cannot rule on inconsistencies that have not yet arisen nor on the manner in which India should implement a finding of inconsistency. India, therefore, requested that Panel not to rule on the "prohibited nature of India's restrictions".

3.59 The **United States** replied to India's contention that the FTDR Act provided judicial review of licensing decision by recalling the report of the panel in "*Argentina - Measures Affecting Imports of Footwear, Textiles, Apparel and Other Items*". That panel had found that the existence of a remedy in a domestic court did not provide a defense to the violation of an obligation under the GATT 1994.[67] India's review procedures therefore did not make its quantitative restrictions any less a violation of Article XI:1.

3. *Nullification and Impairment*

3.60 The **United States** contended that, as India was in violation of its WTO obligations, nullification or impairment of benefits was to be presumed.

> "In cases where there is an infringement of the obligations assumed under a covered agreement, the action is considered *prima facie* to constitute a case of nullification or impairment. This means that there is normally a presumption that a breach of the rules has an adverse impact on other Members parties to that covered agreement, and in such cases, it shall be up to the Member against whom the complaint has been brought to rebut the charge."[68]

3.61 India's violations of the GATT thus *prima facie* constituted a case of nullification or impairment. Moreover, past GATT panels had regarded violations of Article XI:1 in a special light with regard to nullification or impairment, because of the fundamentally trade-distorting nature of quantitative restrictions. The panel on "*Japan - Restrictions on Imports of Certain Agricultural Products*" found that "Article XI:1 protected expectations on competitive conditions . . . the presumption that a measure inconsistent with Article XI causes nullification or impairment could therefore not be refuted with arguments relating to export volumes".[69] Moreover, the earlier panel on "*Japanese Measures on Imports of Leather*" stated that it "wished to stress that the existence of a quantitative restriction should be presumed to cause nullification or impairment not only because of any effect it had had on the volume of trade but also for other reasons e.g., it would lead to increased transaction costs and would create uncertainties which could affect investment plans".[70]

3.62 The United States stated that India's quantitative restrictions and licensing regimes had damaged and continued to damage U.S. trade interests. While U.S. trade interests in the Indian market were substantial, they had been severely impaired by India's extraordinary 50 years of import restrictions. In 1996, the United States exported US$1.3 billion to India in goods subject to quantitative restrictions. However, while the ASEAN area had a population half the size of

---

[67] Panel Report on *Argentina - Measures Affecting Imports of Footwear, Textiles, Apparel and Other Items* (hereafter *Argentina - Textiles*), WT/DS56/R, 25 November 1997, paras. 6.66-6.69.

[68] DSU, Article 3.8.

[69] Panel Report on *Japan - Restrictions on Imports of Certain Agricultural Products,* Op. Cit, para. 5.4.3, citing also as support *United States: - Taxes on Petroleum and Certain Imported Substances* (BISD 34S/136, the *Superfund* case) and *Japanese Measures on Imports of Leather* (BISD 31S/94).

[70] Panel Report on *Japanese Measures on Imports of Leather,* L/5623, adopted on 15/16 May 1984, BISD 31S/94, 113, para. 55.

India's, U.S. exports to ASEAN were eight times the value of U.S. exports to India. As the panel on "*Japanese Measures on Imports of Leather*" noted, "the fact that the United States was able to export large quantities of leather to other markets [than Japan] ... tended to confirm the assumption that the existence of the restrictions [on leather imports] had adversely affected United States' exports".[71]

3.63 The nature and operation of India's import licensing regimes also damaged and continued to damage U.S. trade interests. The uncertainty and limitations imposed by India's licensing regime deterred or prevented exporters from undertaking the investments in planning, promotion and market development necessary to develop and expand markets in India for their products. No exporter would put resources into developing a product's market in India without some assurance that it would be able to export some minimum amount per year, and the Indian system provided no such assurance - only a guarantee of continuing uncertainty - if the product in question was on the Negative List of Imports.

3.64 India's restrictions had caused particularly severe damage to the trade of developing countries. The *de facto* ban on consumer goods imports hurt developing country exports most severely, since it was developing country products that would be most competitive in many consumer-goods sectors. Restricted items included many agricultural goods and among them many tropical products; since the licensing system was operated so as to protect domestic producers, these restrictions were most severe on their developing-country competitors. The canalization of imports, operated so as to subsidize and protect local agricultural producers, appears to operate as a *de facto* ban on the imports of some tropical products such as coconut oil and palm oil.

3.65 Most of all, India's restrictive import regime had damaged the export potential and economic growth of India itself. For fifty years the Indian market had been protected with limited internal competition. As the economists Joshi and Little observed: "This has proved to be a recipe for high-cost, low-quality production, and lack of innovation".[72] The incentive structure produced by a highly protectionist trade regime had produced an Indian private sector that was, with only a few exceptions, oriented toward the protected home market.[73] The Indian control regime had shifted business objectives away from competition toward rent seeking; "It became less important to compete successfully within a framework of regulation than to manipulate regulators so as to avoid competition. One consequence had been a strong nexus between businesses and politicians to create and divide monopoly rent".[74] Professor Jagdish Bhagwati had observed that Indian trade policies had produced a "dismal export performance": he noted that

[71] Panel Report on *Japanese Measures on Imports of Leather*, L/5623, adopted on 15/16 May 1984, BISD 31S/94, 113, para. 54.

[72] Vijay Joshi and I.M.D. Little, *India's Economic Reforms 1991-2001* (Oxford, 1996), p. 68.

[73] Vincent Cable, "Indian Liberalization and the Private Sector," in Robert Cassen and Vijay Joshi, *India: the Future of Economic Reform* (Oxford, 1995), p. 214.

[74] *Ibid.*, p. 212-213.

"the inward-orientation of the trade-and-payments regime, in drastically impairing India's export performance, simultaneously prevented the build-up of labour-intensive exports and hence a favourable impact on wages and employment and therefore *ceteris paribus* on poverty as well".[75]

C. *Article 4.2 of the WTO Agreement on Agriculture*

3.66 The **United States** claimed that the quantitative restrictions or prohibitions at issue violate Article 4.2 of the WTO Agreement on Agriculture.

3.67 The United States stated that, of the 2,714 HS lines listed as subject to quantitative restrictions in Annex II, Part B of India's 1997 notification of quantitative restrictions, 710 (26%) were products covered by the Agreement on Agriculture.[76] Since processed food, fresh fruits and vegetables, coffee, poultry, and many other agricultural products were "consumption goods which could directly satisfy human needs without further processing", India's ban on imports of consumer goods also served as a form of agricultural protectionism During the negotiation of the WTO Agreement on Agriculture, the participants in the Uruguay Round of multilateral trade negotiations agreed to eliminate their non-tariff barriers to trade in agricultural products and to replace them by tariffs, which would be subject to reduction over time. To safeguard this achievement, Article 4.2 of the Agreement on Agriculture provided that "[m]embers shall not maintain, resort to, or revert to any measures of the kind which have been required to be converted into ordinary customs duties ... ". Footnote 1 to Article 4.2 clarified that "These measures include quantitative import restrictions ... discretionary import licensing, non-tariff measures maintained through state-trading enterprises ... and similar border measures other than ordinary customs duties, whether or not the measures are maintained under country-specific derogations from the provisions of GATT 1947, but not measures maintained under balance-of-payments provisions or under other general, non-agriculture-specific provisions of GATT 1994 or of the other Multilateral Trade Agreements in Annex 1A to the WTO Agreement." Since the IMF had conclusively found that there was no balance-of-payments necessity for these import restrictions, with respect to these items, India was in violation of its obligations under Article 4.2. With respect to nullification and impairment, the United States considered that the points made in Section 3 above, applied equally to the Agreement on Agriculture.

3.68 **India** referred to the note to Article 4:2 which stated that:

> "These measures include import restrictions,..., whether or not the measures are maintained under country-specific derogations from the provisions of GATT 1947, *but not measures maintained under balance-of-payments provisions* or other general, non-agriculture-

---

75 Bhagwati, J. *India in Transition: Freeing the Economy* (Oxford, 1993), p. 57, 61.

76 The product scope of the Agreement on Agriculture is defined by Annex 1 thereof.

specific provisions of GATT 1994 or of the other Multilateral Trade Agreements in Annex 1A to the WTO Agreement."

This note thus made it clear that Article 4:2 did not extend to measures maintained under the balance-of-payments provisions. The question of the consistency of India's import restrictions with Article 4:2 of the Agreement on Agriculture thus depended on their consistency with Article XVIII:B of the GATT, and the legal status of India's import restrictions under the Agreement on Agriculture was consequently identical to that under the GATT. India's claim that its import restrictions were consistent with Article XVIII:B should therefore be understood by the Panel as including the claim that they were consistent with the Agreement on Agriculture.

D. *Article XVIII:B*

1. *Competence of the Panel*

3.69 India claimed that the Committee and the General Council have the exclusive authority to determine whether a time-schedule for the removal of import restrictions is consistent with Article XVIII:11 of the GATT. India argued that:

(a) according to Articles XV:2 and XVIII:12 of the GATT and paragraphs 5-13 of the 1994 Understanding the final decision on the justification of import restrictions rests with the Committee and the General Council;

(b) Articles 3:2 and 11 of the DSU do not permit panels to reach the final decision on the legal status of a time-schedule for the removal of import restrictions;

(c) the footnote to the 1994 Understanding, by its express terms, limits the right to invoke the dispute settlement procedures to mattes arising from the *application* of import restrictions and does not modify a Member's right to a determination of the *justification* of its import restrictions in accordance with the provisions of Article XVIII:B;

(d) the terms of the footnote to the 1994 Understanding and the identical terms in the Understanding on Article XXIV are designed to settle long-standing controversies on the relationship between the special review procedures of Articles XVIII:B and XXIV and the general dispute settlement procedures under Article XXIII; and

(e) decision-making authority deliberately assigned to WTO bodies composed of Members cannot be reassigned to the dispute settlement process without understanding the proper functioning of the WTO legal system."

(a) The relationship between Article XVIII:B and Article XXIII

3.70 India argued that according to Articles XV:2 and XVIII:B of the GATT and the 1994 Understanding, the main steps in the procedures for the examination of balance-of-payments measures are the following:

(a) A Member introducing or intensifying import restrictions for balance-of-payments purposes shall promptly *notify* them to the WTO.[77]

(b) The import restrictions notified are subject to *consultation* in the Committee.[78]

(c) The Committee consults with the IMF on the financial aspects of the consultations and accepts the determination of the IMF on those aspects.[79]

(d) The Committee reports on its consultations to the General Council of the WTO.[80]

(e) If the Committee and the General Council find the import restrictions to be inconsistent with Article XVIII:B they "shall indicate the nature of the inconsistency and may *advise that the restrictions be suitably modified*", and if the inconsistency is of a serious nature, they shall "*so inform* the Member applying the restrictions" and make "appropriate recommendations for securing conformity with such provisions within a *specified period*".[81]

According to India, these rules and procedures left no room for doubt that import restrictions maintained for balance-of-payments purposes do not require the affirmative approval of the General Council and that a Member having duly notified its import restrictions under Article XVIII:B may maintain them until the General Council advises the Member of the need to modify them or until the end of the period for their removal specified by the General Council.

3.71 India added that this conclusion was confirmed by the fact that the United States proposed in 1954 to amend the GATT's balance-of-payments provisions to require the affirmative approval of import restrictions by the CONTRACTING PARTIES. According to this proposal, Article XII of the GATT would have been redrafted as follows:

(a) Notwithstanding the provisions of paragraph 1 of Article XI, any contracting party may restrict the quantity or value of merchandise permitted to be imported, to the extent necessary to safeguard its

77 Paragraph 3 of the 1979 Declaration and paragraph 9 of the 1994 Understanding.

78 Paragraph 5 of the 1994 Understanding.

79 Article XV:2.

80 Paragraph 13 of the 1994 Understanding.

81 Article XVIII:12 (c)(i) and (ii).

external financial position and balance of payments, subject to the provisions of the following paragraphs of this Article.

(b) (a) Subject to sub-paragraph (b) of this paragraph, no contracting party may maintain, institute, or intensify restrictions under this Article *without the approval* of the CONTRACTING PARTIES.

(b) Any party maintaining such restrictions on [effective date] shall immediately consult with the CONTRACTING PARTIES with a view to *obtaining approval for their continuation*...[82]

However, India pointed out that the Working Party which examined the United States' proposal concluded that it would not find general acceptance[83] and it was therefore rejected. Accordingly, the United States was effectively requesting the Panel to do what it failed to get incorporated in the balance of payments disciplines of the GATT. The United States had argued before the Panel that a Member must be found to have violated Article XVIII:B unless it succeeds in demonstrating the consistency of its import restrictions with that provision. But, by arguing that the examination of the conformity of the import restrictions can be moved from the Committee and the General Council to a panel and that the burden of proof falls on the Member invoking the balance-of-payments provisions, the United States was effectively attempting to force Members resorting to Article XVIII:B to obtain the approval of their import restrictions by a panel. India summarized its views on this issue in the terms used by the United States in the *Wool Shirts* case: the Panel should reject the United States' argumentation as "a blatant attempt to effectively amend the GATT 1994 and other WTO agreements through litigation"."

3.72 India also contended that the legal claims made by the United States were not founded on the principles of interpretation of the Vienna Convention on the Law of Treaties (1969) (hereafter "Vienna Convention") applied by the Appellate Body, that is on the terms of the GATT and the Understanding on the Balance-of-Payments Provisions of the GATT 1994, (hereafter "1994 Understanding") as interpreted in their context and in the light of their objectives. The claims were also inconsistent with the principle set out in Article XVI:1 of the Marrakesh Agreement Establishing the World Trade Organization (hereafter "WTO Agreement"), according to which the Panel "shall be guided by the decisions, procedures and customary practices followed by the CONTRACTING PARTIES to GATT 1947 and the bodies established in the framework of the GATT 1947." India argued that acceptance of the arguments of the United States would result in making whole paragraphs of Article XVIII:B and whole sections of the 1994 Understanding redundant, altering fundamentally the negotiated balance reflected in the text of Article XVIII:B and the 1994 Understanding. It would also be a

---

[82] GATT 1947 document W.9/73, dated 6 December 1954 (emphasis added).

[83] BISD 3S/171.

serious deviation from practices consistently followed under the GATT 1947 and result in transferring without any basis the authority to determine the legal status of import restrictions from the Committee and the General Council to the IMF and panels. Moreover, acceptance of the arguments of the United States had serious systemic implications with respect to such highly controversial matters as the question of the proper forum for determining the consistency of regional trade agreements with Article XXIV.

3.73 According to India, Article XVIII:B and the 1994 Understanding stipulated that the final decision on the legal status of import restrictions notified under Article XVIII:B was to be made by the General Council upon a recommendation by the Committee. It was that final decision which determined the legal status of the import restrictions under the GATT and consequently the rights and obligations between Members in respect of such import restrictions. In India's view, according to Article XVIII:B, balance of payments restrictions did not require the affirmative approval of the General Council; a Member having duly notified its import restrictions under Article XVIII:B might maintain them until the General Council advised the Member of the need to modify them or until the end of the period for their removal specified by the General Council. The request by the United States to rule that the import restrictions maintained by India under Article XVIII:B were inconsistent with India's obligations was therefore essentially a request that the Panel disapprove the import restrictions and thereby render them illegal. India considered that a panel could not make such a determination because it would be beyond its competence.

3.74 India referred to Article 11 of the DSU which stated that the Panel must make "an objective assessment of the facts of the case and the applicability of and conformity with the relevant covered agreements" and, according to Article 3:2 of the DSU, the Panel "cannot add to or diminish the rights and obligations provided in the covered agreements". The Panel would have to determine the legality of the import restrictions under India's obligations as of the date on which the United States submitted this request, i.e., before the Committee had made a recommendation on India's time schedule for the removal of its import restrictions. Accordingly, the Panel could not determine that they were illegal by substituting its own ruling for the final decision referred to in Articles XV:2 and XVIII:12.

3.75 India cited numerous provisions in the WTO agreements that assigned the task of determining the legal status of a measure to WTO bodies other than panels:

> The task of determining whether a subsidy notified as a non-actionable subsidy under Article 8.3 of the Agreement on Subsidies and Countervailing Measures met the criteria under Article 8.4 and 8.5 of that Agreement had been to the Committee on Subsidies and Countervailing Measures and a special arbitration body. A finding of the Committee or the arbitration body was binding on all Members and should therefore also determine for panels whether or not

a subsidy was actionable. If a panel were to reverse or pre-empt such a finding in the normal dispute settlement procedures, it would arrogate to itself the competence of the Committee or arbitration body.

The task of determining whether a Member had a principal supplying interest within the meaning of the provisions for the renegotiation of tariffs had been assigned to the General Council in Article XXVIII:1 of the GATT. The decision of the General Council - or the failure of the General Council to take a decision on the principal supplier status of a Member - could not be reversed by a panel.[84]

According to Article V of the General Agreement on Trade in Service ("GATS") Members could enter into a regional economic integration agreement. Such an agreement must be notified. The Council on Trade in Services could establish a working party to examine such an agreement and, based on the report of the working party, "the Council may make recommendations to the parties as it deems appropriate".[85] These procedures were also designed to determine the legal status of such agreements in relation to all Members on the basis of the evaluation of a body composed of the representatives of the Members.

3.76 For India, the decision of the drafters of the WTO agreements to submit the determination of the legal status of certain measures to separate procedures and bodies specifically established for that purpose furthered the objectives of the WTO. This was because issues such as the determination of the legal status of a subsidy notified as non-actionable should be made definitively and in a manner binding for all Members by a body with expertise in that field, whose decisions should not be challengeable in disputes between two Members. Similarly, the determination as to whether a free trade area or a customs union agreement met the criteria of Article XXIV of the GATT or Article V of the GATS required a broad economic and political assessment that was best made by the representatives of the Members meeting in the Committee on Regional Trade Agreements. India believed it would be inappropriate for panels to conduct that evaluation, and the only two GATT panels that had been asked to examine such agreements in the light of Article XXIV had both refused to conduct such an evaluation.[86]

---

84 India referred to the 1992 request by Argentina for the establishment of a panel to determine its principal supplying interest in respect of soybean exports to the EC. The EC responded by stating that "Argentina's recourse to the dispute settlement mechanism in this case was inappropriate and improper" since this was not a dispute between Argentina and the EC but between Argentina and the CONTRACTING PARTIES (C/M/260, page 28). The panel was not established.

85 Article V:7(c) of the GATS.

86 India referred to: Panel Report on *European Community - Tariff Treatment on Imports of Citrus Products from Certain Countries in the Mediterranean Region*, hereafter *EC-Citrus*), GATT docu-

The decision on whether or not to approve import restrictions notified under the balance-of-payments provisions of the GATT or a time-schedule for the removal of such import restrictions was not a technical, legal matter that could reasonably be resolved through judicial fiat. The Members had agreed on provisions that assigned the task of determining the legal status of a range of politically delicate matters to specialized bodies acting under particular procedures. These provisions reflected an assessment of the WTO membership that such matters should not be decided by panels settling a dispute between two Members, and that assessment must be respected by panels.

3.77 According to India, if the arguments of the United States in the present case were to be accepted, it would lead to panels resolving all matters arising under the WTO agreements. On a correct construction of the provisions of the WTO Agreements, however, not all decisions could be taken by panels. Many decisions on trade policy matters that Members of the WTO took under their domestic law - such as the decision to impose safeguard measures or to grant adjustment assistance - were taken by specialized agencies with broad discretion. Just as the domestic courts respected the competence and discretionary powers of such agencies, so must WTO panels respect the competence and discretionary powers of the specialized bodies established under the WTO agreements. If the legal status of a subsidy, a regional trade agreement or a balance-of-payments restriction had been determined by the competent WTO body, panels could not reverse that determination; if the competent WTO body had not yet made its determination, panels could not step in and pre-empt that determination.

3.78 India further argued that, under the GATT 1947, all decision-making power, including the authority to adopt panel reports, rested with the CONTRACTING PARTIES. There was therefore no reason to fear contradictions between panel rulings and other decisions adopted by the CONTRACTING PARTIES. Under the WTO, however, panels and the Appellate Body made their findings and recommendations independently of the other organs of the WTO. If the competence assigned expressly to bodies composed of representatives of Members were assigned to the dispute settlement process, conflicting decisions could therefore easily arise. In the present case, such an inconsistency could not be excluded. According to Article IV:1 of the WTO Agreement, the General Council "shall have the authority to take decisions on all matters under any of the Multilateral Trade Agreements, if so requested by a Member". If the General Council could not arrive at a consensus, it should decide according to Article IX:1 of the WTO Agreement the matter by a majority of the votes cast. If this were to occur, a conflict between a ruling by the Panel and the determination of the General Council could occur, a conflict which could not but undermine the

ment L/5776, page 81 (circulated on 7 February 1985, not adopted); report of the Panel on *EEC - Member States' Import Regimes for Bananas*, (hereafter *Bananas I*), GATT document DS32/R, pages 80-82 (circulated on 3 June 1993, not adopted).

credibility and acceptability of the WTO legal system. This would be the inevitable consequence of accepting the arguments of the United States in this dispute.

3.79 For India, the complaint of the United States, though formally directed against India, was in substance a complaint about the failure of a WTO body to take a decision sought by the United States. However, just as Members of the WTO could not complain under the procedures of the DSU about the failure of the General Council to grant a waiver or to declare a Member a principal supplier under Article XXVIII, they could not complain about the failure of the General Council to take a decision disapproving import restrictions maintained under Article XVIII:B. The DSU served to settle disputes between Members of the WTO, not between Members of the WTO and the organs of the WTO, and that the United States' attempts to defend its "alternative routes" theory served only to hide the fact that its complaint constitutes in legal terms a complaint about the failure of a WTO body to take a decision along the lines desired by the United States. India, therefore, requested that the Panel should refrain from making its own assessment of the balance-of-payments justification of India's remaining import restrictions, and should take into account the fact that during fifty years no panel had ever decided what the United States had requested of this Panel.

3.80 According to India, there was no legal vacuum if the balance-of-payments justification was determined by bodies composed of Members rather than by panels. For fifty years balance-of-payments measures had been examined by bodies composed of government representatives and not panels. This well-established precedent had served the system well. The consulting country could not prevent a final decision on its import restrictions by the Committee because any issue that was unresolved in the Committee could be submitted to a vote by the General Council. The consensus-making process in the Committee took place in the shadow of a potential vote and had so far always succeeded. The negotiators of the 1994 Understanding rejected the proposal to empower panels to examine the balance-of-payments justification of measures notified under Articles XIII and XVIII. Their assessment was that an examination of these matters by bodies composed of government representatives was consistent with the WTO system. Panels must respect that assessment. India believed that it would not serve the WTO system well if balance-of-payments matters, which raised not only technical but also delicate political matters, were submitted to the rigidities of an adjudication process.

3.81 The **United States** countered that Members were free to resort to dispute settlement under Article XXIII with respect to any matters relating to Article XVIII:B. This conclusion followed from the text of the WTO Agreement and the decisions taken by and other practice of the GATT 1947 CONTRACTING PARTIES, and was confirmed by the limited available drafting history.

3.82 The United States recalled that the text of neither Article XII nor Article XVIII:B prohibited recourse to dispute settlement under Article XXIII. Nor did the text of Article XXIII contain any such prohibition. In fact, Article XVIII (as a part of the GATT 1994) was among the WTO Provisions that had been made subject to the DSU as set forth in Appendix I to the DSU and for which no special and additional provisions were found in Appendix 2 of the DSU. Article 1 of the DSU provided that the DSU's normal rules were to apply with respect to all disputes brought under the consultation and dispute settlement provisions of the agreements listed in Appendix 1, subject only to the "special and additional" provisions listed in Appendix 2 to the DSU. Appendix 1 listed the Multilateral Trade Agreements on Goods, which includes GATT 1994; however, the DSU's drafters, including India, did not provide the broad carve-out from dispute settlement that India now asserted existed. To the knowledge of the United States, no carve-out for BOP measures had even been discussed - let alone agreed - during the dispute settlement negotiations of the Uruguay Round. Quite the reverse was true: Footnote 1 to the 1994 Understanding confirmed the right of recourse to Article XXIII, and Appendix 2 of the DSU explicitly did not list consultations under Article XVIII:12 as a special or additional rule.

3.83 The United States recalled that the DSU provided as follows:

> "The dispute settlement system of the WTO is a central element in providing security and predictability to the multilateral trading system. The Members recognize that it serves to preserve the rights and obligations of Members under the covered agreements, and to clarify the existing provisions of those agreements in accordance with customary rules of interpretation of public international law."[87]

In the opinion of the United States, because the DSU was an "agreement to the [GATT 1994 and the 1994 Understanding] which was made between all the parties in connection with the conclusion of the [GATT 1994 and the 1994 Understanding],"[88] it was part of the context for both Article XVIII:12 and the 1994 Understanding. In that light, India's suggestion that the Committee that holds Article XVIII:12(c) consultations was the sole body able to decide the question before this Panel was an untenable interpretation of the GATT 1994.

3.84 The consultation process and dispute settlement were separate tracks serving different functions. For example, the panel in the *Korea Beef* case had pointed out that "[Article XXIII] provided for the detailed examination of the individual measures by a panel of independent experts whereas [Article XVIII:B] provided for a general review of the country's balance-of-payments situation by a committee of government representatives."[89] The function of the dispute settlement system was to "preserve the rights and obligations of Members", as provided in Article 3.2 of the DSU; the consultation process was designed to assess

[87] DSU, Article 3.2.

[88] Vienna Convention, Article 31(2)(a).

[89] Panel Reports on *Korea - Restrictions on Imports of Beef*, L/6504, adopted on 7 November 1989, BISD 36S/202, 227, para.96; L/6505, adopted on 7 November 1989, BISD 36S/234, 265, para.112; L/6503, adopted on 7 November 1989, BISD 36S/268, 303 para.118.

the situation of, and measures taken by, Members that were in fact addressing balance-of-payments difficulties. India did not have such difficulties and could not rely on the consultation process to protect measures that were no longer justified. India had an obligation to remove those measures and Article XXIII was available to preserve and enforce that obligation.

3.85 The United States noted that India had argued that if panels could rule on balance-of-payments measures, inconsistencies with decisions of the General Council might arise, an argument which would lead to the untenable conclusion that no panel had any jurisdiction over any WTO agreement, because the General Council had the authority to adopt interpretations of all the WTO Agreements.[90] Furthermore, since the General Council did not authorize restrictive measures taken for balance-of-payments purposes in advance, there was no danger of inconsistent decisions in this case.

3.86 Furthermore, according to the United States, the 1994 Understanding expressly contemplated (in paragraph 13) the possibility that the BOP Committee might not reach a decision:

> "The Committee shall endeavour to include in its conclusions proposals for recommendations aimed at promoting the implementation of Articles XII and XVIII:B, the 1979 Declaration and this Understanding.... In the absence of specific proposals for recommendations by the General Council, the Committee's conclusions should record the different views expressed in the Committee."

Therefore, exclusive allocation of competence to the Committee would leave the rights of individual members hostage to the Committee decision process, because the practice of the Balance-of-Payments Committee is that it makes recommendations by consensus. In the absence of consensus, the Committee's conclusions record the different views expressed.[91] India's position, if adopted, would effectively give all Members the right to maintain measures without balance-of-payments justification.

3.87 The United States also noted that the first of the three examples given by India was clearly mistaken because arbitration under Article 8.5 of the Agreement on Subsidies and Countervailing Measures was one of the special and additional rules listed in Appendix 2 to the DSU since Appendix 2 of the DSU provided that arbitration was a special procedure within the context of the DSU. The United States further considered that this was not the proper case to examine any of those three examples as none of the examples involved fell within the Panel's terms of reference.

3.88 In the view of **India**, the United States' claim that India had attacked the ability of the WTO dispute settlement to even examine quantitative restrictions

[90] Marrakesh Agreement Establishing the World Trade Organization, Article IX:2.

[91] Rules of Procedure for Meetings of the Committee on Balance-of-Payments Restrictions, WT/BOP/10, 12 December 1995.

for which a BOP claim had been made, and that India was seeking to open a large gap in that rule of law, was based on a complete misunderstanding - or misrepresentation - of India's position. India had not claimed that special dispute settlement procedures applied in this case. India, in fact, was in complete agreement with the United States that nothing in the DSU nor in the 1994 Understanding precluded the examination of India's import restrictions by the Panel in accordance with the normal dispute settlement procedures. However, what India had argued in fact was the following:

(i) The Panel, in accordance with the normal dispute settlement procedures, should conduct an objective assessment of India's import restrictions in light of the relevant provisions of the GATT and the 1994 Understanding, as mandated by Articles 7 and 11 of the DSU. The Panel should note that both parties agree that the import restrictions at issue fall under Article XI:1, but disagree on their justification under Article XVIII:B.

(ii) The Panel should note that, according to Articles XV:2 and XVIII:12 of the GATT and paragraph 13 of the 1994 Understanding, a Member invoking Article XVIII:B may maintain its import restrictions until the General Council, based on a recommendation of the Committee on Balance-of-Payments Restrictions, has reached its "final decision" and advised the Member that its import restrictions are inconsistent with Article XVIII:B.

(iii) The Panel should note that the footnote to the 1994 Understanding specifically confirms that nothing in the 1994 Understanding is intended to modify the above rights and obligations of Members under Article XVIII:B and that the United States has the right to invoke the dispute settlement procedures only with regard to the application of the import restrictions maintained by India.

(iv) The Panel should note that the balance-of-payments consultations with India did not conclude with a recommendation that because India's remaining import restrictions no longer have any justification, they should be eliminated. The Panel should find that India, therefore, retains the right under Article XVIII:B to progressively relax its import restrictions.

(v) The Panel should find also that it cannot rule on the manner in which the import restrictions at issue are applied because the United States has not invoked, not even subsidiarily, any of the provisions of the GATT and the 1994 Understanding relevant to the application of import restrictions a Member may maintain under Article XVIII:B.

3.89 India added that it followed from the above that India was not claiming that the United States' access to the DSU was in any way limited, but that the Panel, in examining the import restrictions at issue under the normal procedures, must take into account the rights of India under Article XVIII:B.

3.90 In response to India's argument that the WTO system allocated decisions to specific bodies because issues "should be made definitively and in a manner binding for all Members by a body with expertise in that field," and that panels lacked expertise compared to the Balance-of-Payments Committee, the **United States** argued that the WTO dispute settlement system called on panels and the Appellate Body to assess many specialized questions, such as the scientific basis for SPS measures. If India's argument were accepted, then the mere existence of any specialized body within the WTO with a review function would preclude dispute settlement under Article XXIII; for instance, the existence of the Committee on Antidumping Practices and the Committee on Safeguards would preclude review by panels of antidumping and safeguards measures. In any event, if India was concerned with ensuring that appropriate expertise be brought to bear on questions before the WTO, India should have no objection at all to having the IMF - the institution with the most expertise in balance-of-payments matters and the access to the most complete and current information - determine whether or not India had balance-of-payments difficulties within the meaning of Article XVIII:9.

3.91 The United States noted that India had also argued from an analogy to the relationship between specialized agencies and domestic courts: saying that domestic courts "respect" the agencies' expertise. But "respect" did not mean - as India intimated - that the courts had no role to play. To the contrary, India said that its courts could review decisions made by agencies to ensure that they were not arbitrary, irrational or discriminatory, a system used by many countries. For these reasons, India's analogy did not support its point.

3.92 The United States further argued that, contrary to India's assertions, India was not permitted to maintain its import restrictions until it had been informed of their inconsistency with the requirements of Article XVIII:B by the General Council. Article XVIII:11 did not say that Members "shall eliminate [their restrictions] *when informed that* conditions no longer justify their maintenance." It said that Members "shall eliminate [their restrictions] *when conditions no longer justify* their maintenance.

3.93 In addition, the United States contended that India had misread Paragraph 13 of the 1994 Understanding by claiming it entitled India to maintain balance-of-payment measures until a decision of the General Council. Paragraph 13 provided only that the Balance-of-Payments Committee might make recommendations to the General Council and the General Council might act on the recommendations of the Committee, but that in the absence of the specific proposals for recommendations by the General Council, the Committee's conclusions would record only the different views expressed in the Committee. Paragraph 13 further said that when a time schedule for the removal of restrictions has been presented, the General Council "may recommend" that a Member adhering to that time schedule shall be deemed to be in compliance with its GATT 1994 obligations. This necessarily implied that when the General Council had not made such a recommendation, the Member concerned - even if it adhered to a time schedule for removal of restrictions - could not thereby automatically be deemed to be in compliance with its GATT 1994 obligations. In this case the Committee had not made proposals for recommendations, and the General Council had therefore not made any recommendations in relation to a time schedule for removal of the challenged measures. Consequently, India's adherence to the time schedule that it unilaterally proposed did no *ipso facto* mean that it was complying with its GATT 1994 obligations.

3.94 For the United States, India's notion that it had a right to maintain measures inconsistent with the WTO Agreement until asked to remove them would undermine the legitimacy of the WTO as a rules-based institution. It also would quickly lead to an unravelling of the concessions that Members have made to one another, as Members waited to implement their own obligations until asked to do so while at the same time insisting that other Members carry out theirs. Such a result was not consistent with the terms of Article XVIII:B; it also would not be consistent with the object and purpose of the GATT 1994.

3.95 Any suggestion that a Member was entitled not to carry out its obligations to other Members - such as the obligation to remove quantitative restrictions when they were no longer justified - would be an interpretation of the GATT 1994 that contravened Article 26 of the Vienna Convention on the Law of Treaties: "Every treaty in force is binding upon the parties to it and must be performed by them in good faith." That Article stated the long-standing rule of customary international law, *pacta sunt servanda*: India was expected to carry out its obligations without waiting to be asked to do so.

3.96 The United States replied to India's argument that balance-of-payments matters were politically delicate, and therefore not to be handled by panels, by pointing out two flaws with this argument: First, this dispute was not in the least political. It had arisen because the facts were clear: India's balance-of-payments situation had improved and no longer qualified India to maintain import restrictions for balance-of-payments purposes. Second, even if this dispute could be described as, in some sense, "politically delicate", what made the justification of a balance-of-payments measure any more "politically delicate" than the justification of any trade measure that enjoyed wide domestic support, or the justification of a trade-related environmental measure? The United States noted that India's recourse to the WTO dispute settlement system in the ongoing "shrimp/turtles" dispute demonstrated that India recognizes the strength of the WTO system: it was a system of rules. The provisions of the WTO Agreement, and the rights and obligations of the Members, had been negotiated; the dispute settlement system served the purpose of enforcing those obligations and thereby protecting those rights. The fact that in "politically delicate" cases individual Members were not able to block adoption of decisions, but had to abide by the negotiated rules of the system, was one of the most important accomplishments of the Uruguay Round.

3.97 The United States added if any Member could institute a measure for balance-of-payments purposes and then prevent consensus in the BOP Committee concerning the BOP justification for the measure, the measure would be completely beyond control if it were exempt from panel review in the dispute settlement process. Such opportunistic behaviour by one Member would then shift the adjustment burden to others, who would be tempted to follow suit in a descending spiral. This example illustrated that placing measures off-limits to the rule of law, simply because a BOP claim had been made, was dangerous for the WTO system as a whole.

(b) Footnote 1 of the 1994 Understanding

> "Nothing in this Understanding is intended to modify the rights and obligations of Members under Article XII or XVIII:B of GATT 1994. The provisions of Articles XXII and XXIII of GATT 1994 as elaborated and applied by the Dispute Settlement Understanding may be invoked with respect to any matters arising from the application of restrictive import measures taken for balance-of-payments purposes."

3.98 **India** contended that the reference in footnote 1 of the Understanding to "matters arising from the application of restrictive import measures" was to import restrictions that have a valid balance-of-payments justification. In contrast, the reference to "restrictions...being applied in a manner involving an inconsistency" in Article XVIII:12(c)(ii) must be interpreted to refer to import restrictions lacking balance-of-payments justification and import restrictions administered in a GATT-inconsistent manner because the provision referred to inconsistencies with Article XVIII:B and Article XIII. If the reference to application in the footnote were interpreted to comprise all the matters in Article XVIII:12(c)(ii) merely because the terms "being applied" were used, the footnote would have the effect of implementing, in a circuitous manner, the 1990 proposal of the United States to empower panels to render import restrictions illegal through their findings. The footnote, India contended, did not modify a Member's right to a determination of the justification of its import restrictions in accordance with the provisions of Article XVIII:B. India went on to say that the Panel's examination should not modify India's rights under Article XVIII:B, including India's right under paragraph 12(c)(ii) to be informed of any serious inconsistency of its import restrictions by the General Council. In India's view, the consistency of balance-of-payments measures with Articles I, II, X, and XIII of the GATT and the provisions of other WTO agreements, such as the Agreement on Import Licensing Procedures, could be examined by a panel but the question of their balance-of-payments justification should be determined in accordance with the procedures set out in Articles XV:2 and XVIII:B, the 1979 Declaration on Trade Measures Taken for Balance-of-Payments Purposes and the 1994 Understanding.

3.99 The **United States** responded that the text of footnote 1 *confirmed* rather than denied the availability of dispute settlement. Footnote 1 did *not* say "... but the provisions of Articles XXII and XXIII may not be invoked with respect to matters relating to justification of such measures," or that Articles XXII and

XXIII "may be invoked *only* with respect to any matters arising from the application of restrictive import measures taken for balance-of-payments purposes." In the view of the United States, had the drafters of the GATT 1994 intended to impose restrictions on dispute settlement, they would have used words of prohibition or limitation, as they did in other places in the WTO Agreement,[92] not the words that they actually wrote in footnote 1.

3.100 The United States also noted that India had claimed that footnote 1 of the 1994 Understanding, for the first time, limited dispute settlement under Article XXIII in balance-of-payments matters to questions of "application" of measures. The United States replied that, even if India's interpretation of footnote 1 were to be accepted (and it should not be), this dispute would be properly before this Panel since it had "arisen" precisely because of India's "application" of quantitative restrictions that it originally instituted for balance-of-payments purposes, because India was applying the challenged measures in excess of what was necessary to address its balance-of-payments situation. The heading immediately before paragraph 1 of the 1994 Understanding, which covered paragraphs 1 to 4 of the 1994 Understanding, was "Application of Measures", and paragraph 4 included the requirement that "... measures taken for balance-of-payments purposes ... may not exceed what is necessary to address the balance-of-payments situation." Lawful application of measures taken for balance-of-payments purposes included the obligation not to apply measures in excess of what was necessary to address the balance-of-payments situation. The removal of unjustifiable measures thus was, to the drafters of the Understanding, a part of the "application" of such measures.

3.101 The United States added that a review of "restrictions[that]are being applied" (Article XVIII:12(c)(ii)) was a review of an application (footnote 1) of restrictive measures and the relationship between the two clauses confirmed that Article XVIII:12 procedures were not an exclusive means of addressing the rights and obligations of members under Article XVIII:B.

3.102 In response, **India** pointed out that the first sentence of paragraph 4 of the Understanding was not enforceable because it used "may" rather than the mandatory "shall", while every other sentence in the paragraph relating to the application of measures, except for the one exempting essential products from surcharges, used the mandatory "shall". In India's view this confirmed India's right to have justification of its import restrictions determined by the Committee in consultations.

(c) Negotiating history to footnote 1

3.103 **India** drew the attention of the Panel to the negotiating history which lay behind the 1994 Understanding and its footnote. It recalled that in June 1990,

---

92 Such as, for example, the provisions of Article 64.2 of the Agreement on TRIPS.

the delegations of the United States and Canada had formally proposed the adoption of a "Declaration on Trade Measures Taken for Balance-of-Payments Purposes.[93] The provisions of the proposed Declaration relating to dispute settlement were as follows:

> "In those cases in which the Council has approved specific recommendations by the Committee, the rights and obligations of contracting parties shall be assessed in the light of those recommendations. ...In those cases in which the Committee has been unable to agree on a specific recommendation, the question of the consistency of the measures under review with the Articles and this Declaration has not been resolved. The consulting contracting party or affected contracting parties can, if they wish, attempt to resolve the question in the Council. *Alternatively*, affected contracting parties can, if they wish, pursue the matter through *normal GATT dispute settlement procedures pursuant to Articles XXII and XXIII.* "

3.104 In India's view, the objective of the United States and Canada had been to create an alternative procedural avenue for determining the justification of balance-of-payments restrictions. This notion was rejected and was not reflected in the final text of the Understanding. Moreover, the United States and Canada proposed that access to the normal dispute settlement procedures be unqualified, as in the case of the standard references to the DSU in the WTO agreements. This proposal also was not taken over into the final text. India added that while some of the elements of the 1990 proposal of the United States found their way into the final version of the 1994 Understanding, the proposal that matters left unresolved by the Committee and the General Council be settled under the normal dispute settlement procedures was not taken over into the 1994 Understanding. On the contrary, the footnote to the 1994 Understanding left no doubt that nothing in the 1994 Understanding changed the right under Article XVIII:B to maintain the import restrictions until the General Council, based on a recommendation by the Committee, had found them to be inconsistent. According to India, the reference to "matters arising from the application of restrictive import measures" in the footnote to the Understanding had not emerged by accident but was part of carefully negotiated compromise language and should be interpreted accordingly.

3.105 India was of the opinion that the footnote indirectly confirmed that disputes arising from the other matters regulated in the 1994 Understanding, in particular the matters regulated in paragraph 13 entitled "Conclusions of Balance-of-Payments Consultations", were not meant to be resolved by panels or the terms of the footnote would not have been explicitly limited to the application of the measures. Instead, the general, all-encompassing formulation chosen in the other

---

93 *Proposal by Canada and the United States*, Multilateral Trade Negotiations, The Uruguay Round, Group of Negotiations on Goods (GATT), Negotiating Group on GATT Articles, MTN.GNG/NG7/W/72, 15 June 1990.

GATT Understandings (except that for Article XXIV, where similar issues of competence arose) and in all WTO agreements would have been chosen, or the formulation proposed by the United States in 1990. In the view of India, these considerations suggested that the drafters referred to the application of the measures because they presumed that the final decision on their justification would continue to be taken by the General Council in accordance with the procedures set out in Articles XV:2 and XVIII:12 and paragraph 13 of the 1994 Understanding.

3.106 Therefore, in India's view, the United States' claim that India's arguments were "textually baseless", in fact, was itself not supported by the terms of Article XVIII:B and the 1994 Understanding. The United States had the right to resort to the dispute settlement procedures, but these procedures did not authorize panels to ignore the rights of the defendant party under the relevant provisions of the GATT. India accordingly invoked its right to a progressive relaxation and elimination of its import restrictions pending a decision by the General Council. India argued that this right had not disappeared simply because the United States had the right to resort to the DSU with respect to the application of India's import restrictions.

3.107 The **United States** responded that India had cited no explanation for the rejection of that text, and thus the mere fact that a different text served as the basis for the 1994 Understanding rather than the text proposed by the United States and Canada proved nothing.[94]

3.108 In addition, the United States recalled that the negotiators of the 1994 Understanding (and the negotiators of the Understanding on the Interpretation of Article XXIV of the GATT 1994) were well aware of the Panel report on *European Community - Tariff Treatment on Imports of Citrus Products from Certain Countries in the Mediterranean Region*[95] (*Citrus*) and the more recently issued Panel report on *Republic of Korea - Restrictions on Imports of Beef*[96] (*Korea-Beef*) and *EEC-Member States' Import Regime for Bananas*[97] (*Bananas I),* and they were aware of the criticism of the finding in *EC-Citrus* In that context, the burden in the negotiations was on those contracting parties (such as, apparently, India) who wished to *preclude* recourse to dispute settlement. Thus, if India wished to achieve the result it now advocated - namely, that panels should be

---

[94] The United States considered that Article 32 of the Vienna Convention also required the Panel to disregard India's argument. This isolated piece of negotiating history did not confirm the meaning of the provisions in question, and the interpretation of those provisions was not ambiguous, obscure, manifestly absurd or unreasonable.

[95] L/5776, Op. Cit.

[96] Panel Report on *Republic of Korea - Restrictions on Imports of Beef*, adopted on 7 November 1989, BISD 36S/202, 227; Panel Report on *Republic of Korea - Restrictions on Imports of Beef*, adopted on 7 November 1989, BISD 36S/234; Panel Report on *Republic of Korea - Restrictions on Imports of Beef*, adopted on 7 November 1989, BISD 36S/268, 303, hereafter *Korea - Beef*.

[97] DS/32/R, Op. Cit.

prevented from deciding balance-of-payments matters - India should have negotiated an explicit exception to Article XXIII. India obviously did not obtain such an exception. Negotiators were aware of the possibilities that panels would examine quantitative restrictions for which balance of payments cover had been claimed and intentionally did not exclude them from the scope of panel review in the WTO system.[98]

(d) Relationship between Paragraph 12 of the Understanding on the Interpretation of Article XXIV and the footnote to the 1994 Understanding on the Balance of Payments Provisions of the GATT 1994

3.109 **India** went on to note that the reference to the application of measures in the text of the footnote to the 1994 Understanding was identical to that in the text of paragraph 12 of the Understanding on the Interpretation of Article XXIV of the GATT 1994. None of the other clauses giving access to the DSU in the WTO agreements and Understandings contained a similar reference to the application of measures. These limited access to the DSU in respect of import restrictions and regional trade agreements in an identical fashion and for the same reasons. In both these areas, there were longstanding and serious controversies among the contracting parties to the GATT 1947 on the appropriateness of resorting to the procedures of Article XXIII. Different views had been expressed on the relationship between the procedures under Article XXIV and Article XXIII during the GATT Council's discussions in 1982 on the United States' recourse to Article XXIII with respect to tariff preferences granted by the EC within the framework of association agreements with Mediterranean countries.[99] After a long debate and consultations, the GATT panel on "*Citrus*" had been established, and had found that:

> "In the opinion of the Panel, examination - or re-examination-of Article XXIV agreements was the responsibility of the CONTRACTING PARTIES. In the absence of a decision by the CONTRACTING PARTIES and without prejudice to any decision the CONTRACTING PARTIES might take in the future on such a matter, the Panel was of the view that it would not be appropriate to determine the conformity of an agreement with the requirements of Article XXIV on the basis of a complaint by a contracting party under Article XXIII:1(a) ... such an examination should be done clearly in the context of Article XXIV and not Article XXIII, as an

[98] In the view of the United States, footnote 1 served a function by confirming, shortly after the reports on *Citrus, Bananas*, and *Korean Beef*, the availability of dispute settlement under Article XXIII in balance-of-payments cases.

[99] GATT documents C/M/159-162.

> assessment of all the duties, regulations of commerce and trade coverage as well as the interests and rights of all contracting parties were at stake in such an examination and not just the interests and rights of contracting party raising a complaint...The Panel considered that the practice, so far followed by the CONTRACTING PARTIES, never to use the procedures of Article XXIII:2 to make recommendations or rulings on the GATT-conformity of measures subject to special review procedures was sound. It felt that the purposes served and balance of interest underlying them would be lost if contracting parties could invoke the general procedures of Article XXIII:2 for the purpose of requesting decisions by the CONTRACTING PARTIES on measures to be reviewed under the special procedures. The Panel therefore concluded that it should ... abstain from an overall examination of the bilateral agreements."[100]

3.110 India mentioned that this issue also arose in the proceedings of the panel on *"Bananas I"*, which faced the claim that tariff preferences for bananas granted by the EEC under the Lomé Convention were justified by Article XXIV interpreted in the light of Part IV of the GATT on Trade and Development. The panel recognized that it could be argued that the procedures of Article XXIV prevailed over those of Article XXIII. However, the panel did not have to rule on this issue because it found that Article XXIV was not modified by Part IV.[101]

3.111 In that dispute, the European Communities (the *EC*) argued that the review procedures for regional free trade agreements contained in Article XXIV:7 should prevail over the general dispute settlement procedures in Article XXIII of the GATT 1947 and that panels, therefore, should not examine any measures justified under a free trade agreement. The Panel was of the view that:

> [E]ven if the latter argument were accepted, the procedures of Article XXIV could reasonably be permitted to prevail over those of Article XXIII only in those cases in which the agreement for which Article XXIV was invoked was *prima facie* the type of agreement covered by this provision, i.e., on the face of it capable of justification under it.[102]

3.112 In *Bananas I*, even the *EC* admitted that the measures at issue in that dispute "was justified not by Article XXIV on its own, but by Article XXIV taken in combination with the provisions of Part IV of the General Agreement". The Panel found, however, that:

> ... the requirements of Article XXIV were not modified by the provisions of Part IV. The Panel consequently had to conclude that

[100] Panel Report on *European Community - Tariff Treatment on Imports of Citrus Products from Certain Countries in the Mediterranean Region*, Op. Cit., p. 81.

[101] DS32/R, 3 June 1993, p. 81 (not adopted).

[102] DS32/R, 3 June 1993, para 367.

> a legal justification for the tariff preference accorded by the *EC* to imports of bananas originating in the ACP countries could not emerge from an application of Article XXIV to the type of agreement described by the [*EC*] in the Panel's proceedings ...[103]

Thus, the reasoning of the *Bananas I* panel actually supported examining only whether the measure in question was *prima facie* relatable to Article XXIV. If the measure *prima facie* was covered by Article XXIV, the Panel should desist from subjecting the measure to review.

3.113 India concluded that the identical terms of the footnote to the 1994 Understanding and of paragraph 12 of the Understanding on Article XXIV represented a compromise between the conflicting positions taken by the contracting parties in these cases. On the one hand, they confirmed the right to resort to the DSU procedures; on the other hand, they limited that right to "matters arising from the application" of measures under the balance-of-payments provisions and regional agreements. That compromise ensured that the application of all such measures could be examined by a panel and that Members could not escape their obligations under the DSU merely by invoking Article XVIII:B or Article XXIV. At the same time it ensured that the justification of import restrictions and regional trade agreements would be determined by the WTO bodies that had been given the competence to make that determination.

3.114 The **United States** noted that the *Bananas I* panel realized the implications of the argument (made by the European Communities in that case and by India in this case) against permitting dispute settlement procedures under Article XXIII in a situation where Article XXIV (or, to translate the argument to India's position in this case, Article XVIII) procedures were available: the implication being that a Member's *mere invocation* of Article XXIV (or Article XVIII) would insulate that Member's actions from all other Members' rights under Article XXIII. Therefore, the *Bananas I* panel reasoned that, *at a minimum*, panels acting under Article XXIII could make decisions as to whether a measure for which Article XXIV (or Article XVIII) had been invoked was "on the face of it capable of justification under" that Article.[104] The *Bananas I* panel then went on to determine whether the agreement at issue in that case was on its face an agreement of the type envisaged by Article XXIV; the panel noted that at least one of the requirements of Article XXIV was not met by that agreement (namely the requirement that the agreement cover trade between the parties, not just into one party's territory from the others').

3.115 Addressing India's claim that - because of similar wording in the two WTO Understandings concerning balance-of-payments measures and Article XXIV - recourse to dispute settlement was not available to examine the "justification" of measures claimed to be justified under either Article XVIII or Arti-

[103] DS32/R, 3 June 1993, para 372.
[104] DS32/R, 3 June 1993, para. 367.

cle XXIV, the United States noted that India did not appear to accept that position itself; in the dispute entitled *Turkey - Restrictions on Imports of Textiles and Clothing Products*, India had recently caused the establishment of a panel to examine whether certain quantitative restrictions imposed by Turkey in accordance with the customs union agreement between Turkey and the European Union could be justified under Article XXIV.[105]

3.116 The United States also recalled its position with respect to the context within which the Uruguay Round negotiations had taken place and its position that in light of that context, the texts of the two Understandings had to be understood as confirming rather than limiting the availability of dispute settlement under Article XXIII.

3.117 **India** responded that in its request for the establishment of a Panel, India had alleged violation of only Articles XI and XIII of GATT 1994 and Article 2 of the Agreement on Textiles and Clothing (*ATC*). On the understanding that it was without prejudice to its rights in the panel proceedings involving India and Turkey, India explained that it had not sought any finding about the justification of EU - Turkey custom union under Article XXIV. When Turkey tried to defend its action by citing Article XXIV, India pointed out that Article XXIV:8(a)(ii) could not be applied in such a way as to modify the obligations of Members in respect of Article 2.4 of the ATC and Article XI:1 of GATT 1994. India therefore, considered that it had not taken a position in this dispute with the United States which contradicted its position in its dispute with Turkey. India pointed out that in the present panel proceedings, the US claim was not about the application of the measures, which was on a non-discriminatory MFN basis, but about their justification. India reiterated that according to the text, this was outside the scope of the provisions of the 1994 Understanding, which clearly state that dispute settlement provisions "may be invoked with respect to any matters arising from the *application* of restrictive import measures taken for balance-of-payments purposes".

(e) Practice under GATT 1947

3.118 **India** argued that the importance of distinguishing between the justification of the measure itself and the conformity of the application of the measure had been recognized in the jurisprudence on Article XX which established different criteria for the adoption of a measure (to be examined under the relevant subparagraph of Article XX) and its application (to be examined under the preamble). A GATT panel found that "the preamble of Article XX made clear that it was the application of the measure and not the measure itself that needed to be examined." The Appellate Body confirmed in the *"United States - Standards for Reformulated and Conventional Gasoline"* case that the preamble of Article XX

[105] WT/DS34/2, circulated 2 February 1998; WT/DSB/M/43 and Corr.1.

addresses not so much the questioned measure but rather the manner in which that measure is applied.[106] In the *Bananas* case, the Appellate Body made a clear distinction between issues arising from the application of tariff quotas (which it considered to be covered by the Licensing Agreement) and those arising from the tariff quotas themselves (which it considered to be covered by the GATT).[107] In the present case also, India was convinced that the Appellate Body would recognize as well that the footnote to the 1994 Understanding referred by its express terms only to the "application" of restrictive import measures, not the measures themselves, and interpret this provision accordingly.

3.119 The **United States** considered it was incorrect to draw a hard and fast distinction between application and justification. First, India's allusion to the *Citrus* Panel was of limited relevance. Not only had the *Citrus* panel report never been adopted, it had been criticized in the GATT Council by several contracting parties for its refusal to recognize recourse to dispute settlement pursuant to Article XXIII:1(a) with respect to those agreements.[108] Furthermore, *Bananas I* reached the opposite conclusion when it considered an argument by the defending contracting parties that the procedures available to the CONTRACTING PARTIES under Article XXIV precluded recourse to dispute settlement under Article XXIII. The *Bananas I* panel did not accept that such preclusion was possible under the GATT 1947 and went on to find that even if some form of preclusion should be considered to exist, then "the procedures of Article XXIV could reasonably be considered to prevail over those of Article XXIII only in those cases in which the agreement for which Article XXIV was invoked was *prima facie* the type of agreement covered by this provision ... ."[109] The panel further noted that "[i]f preferences granted under *any* agreement for which Article XXIV had been invoked could not be investigated under Article XXIII, any contracting party, merely by invoking Article XXIV, could deprive other contracting parties of their rights under Article XXIII."[110] The *Bananas I* panel thus clarified that a panel could indeed examine the consistency with Article XXIV of an agreement (the Lomé Agreement) for which Article XXIV cover had been claimed. That panel rejected the *Citrus* panel's *non liquet* approach and ruled that the Lomé Convention did not fulfill the basic legal requirements of Article XXIV. The United States concluded that this Panel could do the same and find that India's restrictions no longer fulfilled the basic legal requirements of Article XVIII:B.

3.120 With respect to India's citation of *Gasoline*, the United States argued that the Appellate Body in that case clearly considered that the text of Article XX,

[106] Report of the Appellate Body on *United States - Standards for Reformulated and Conventional Gasoline* (WT/DS2/AB/R), 29 April 1996, DSR 1996:I, 3, at 21.

[107] Report of the Appellate Body on *European Communities - Regime for the Importation, Sale and Distribution of Bananas* (WT/DS27/AB/R), 9 September 1997, paras. 197 and 198.

[108] GATT document C/M/186, C/M/187.

[109] DS32/R, Op. Cit., para. 367.

[110] *Ibid.*, para. 367.

which is divided into an introduction and a series of subparagraphs, required a two-part review. Following that two-part review the Appellate Body concluded that the challenged measures were not justified because they failed the test set out by the introductory clauses of Article XX - or, in the jargon that India wanted to see adopted, that the measures were not "justified" because they were improperly "applied".[111] In the view of the United States, the Appellate Body had not made the distinction that India was trying to make.

3.121 In response to India's reference to the *Citrus* and *Bananas I* panel reports, the United States drew the Panel's attention to the panel report in *Korea - Beef* , as well as to the limited applicability of the cases that India had cited. The *Korean Beef* report in particular had analyzed the text of the General Agreement and concluded that the periodic reviews conducted under Article XVIII:B constitute a separate track from dispute settlement under Article XXIII. Contrary to India's suggestion, the panel had reached and decided that issue as a matter separate from the issue of whether the Korean restrictions were justified.

3.122 The United States found the reasoning of the *Korea - Beef* panel report particularly instructive because Korea sought to raise the same "jurisdictional" bar claim that India now asserted. That panel had found that it could proceed to examine the justification of measures claimed to be justified under Article XVIII:B, notwithstanding Korea's argument that such measures were beyond the power of the panel to review.

> "In comparison [to Article XVIII:12], the wording of Article XXIII was all-embracing; it provided for dispute settlement procedures applicable to all relevant articles of the General Agreement, including Article XVIII:B. The former provided for the detailed examination of individual measures by a panel of independent experts whereas the latter provided for a general review of the country's balance-of-payments situation by a committee of government representatives … It was the view of the Panel that excluding the possibility of bringing a complaint under Article XXIII against measures for which there was claimed balance-of-payments cover would unnecessarily restrict the application of the General Agreement. This did not preclude, however, resort to special review procedures under Article XVIII:B. Indeed, either procedure, that of Article XVIII:12(d) or Article XXIII, could have been pursued by the parties in this dispute."[112]

[111] WT/DS2/AB/R, pp. 20-22, 27.

[112] Panel Report on *Republic of Korea - Restrictions on Imports of Beef*, adopted on 7 November 1989, BISD 36S/202, 227, paras. 96-97; Panel Report on *Republic of Korea - Restrictions on Imports of Beef*, adopted on 7 November 1989, BISD 36S/234, 265, paras. 112-13; Panel Report on *Republic of Korea - Restrictions on Imports of Beef*, adopted on 7 November 1989, BISD 36S/268, 303, paras. 118-19.

3.123 The Panel's reasoning in *Bananas I* was relevant only to the extent that the Panel determined that it should not follow the reasoning in *Korea - Beef*. If, for example (contrary to the position of the United States), the Panel determined that as a general matter a Member need not remove its balance-of-payments measures until requested to do so by the General Council, the Panel should follow the reasoning of *Bananas I* and determine *at a minimum* whether India's measures *prime facie* were capable of justification under Article XVIII:B. The United States submitted that, in view of the IMF's determinations with respect to India's balance-of-payments situation, as well as the other facts presented by the United States, the challenged measures were not "capable of justification" under Article XVIII:B..

3.124 However, as the *Bananas* panel found in the context of Article XXIV and the *Korea - Beef* panel found in the context of Article XVIII:B, India's argument would unnecessarily restrict the application of the WTO Agreement. If India's approach were accepted, a mere claim of balance-of-payments cover could be used to frustrate justified access to dispute settlement. The United States urged the Panel to reject India's invitation to create such a restriction not found in the text of either the DSU or Article XVIII.

3.125 In the view of the United States. contracting parties were always free to resort to dispute settlement under Article XXIII of GATT 1947 with respect to any matters relating to Article XVIII:B. The text of neither Article XII nor Article XVIII:B prohibited recourse to dispute settlement under Article XXIII; equally, the text of Article XXIII did not contain any such prohibition. As a matter of practice, during the first years of operation of the GATT, in the event *any* issue arose with respect to measures justified under Article XII, an aggrieved contracting party was able to proceed with dispute settlement under Article XXIII. This was stated expressly in the 1950 Report of the Working Party on "The Use of Quantitative Restrictions for Protective and Commercial Purposes", which said:

> "It appeared to the CONTRACTING PARTIES that insofar as these types of practice were in fact carried on for [certain protective and commercial purposes] and were not justified under the provisions of Articles XII to XIV in relation to the use of import restrictions to protect the balance of payments or under other provisions of the Agreement specifically permitting the use of import restrictions, they were inconsistent with the provisions of the Agreement, and such misuse of import restrictions might appropriately provide a basis for recourse to the procedures laid down in the Agreement for the settlement of disputes. Moreover, it was not particularly relevant to the Agreement whether such practices were

determined unilaterally or in the course of bilateral negotiations."[113]

3.126 Similarly, in 1952, at the request of the United States, a working party had been established under Article XXIII to examine the justification (including the balance-of-payments justification) for Belgium's restrictions against dollar area imports; the restrictions had been imposed to avoid a surplus in intra-European trade.[114] In short, the practice prevailing in decisions taken under the GATT 1947 before 1955 (i.e., before the Review Session adopted the present version of Article XVIII) permitted the establishment of Article XXIII panels to consider measures maintained for balance-of-payments purposes. The position had remained unchanged after the Review Session. In 1957, the Working Party on German Import Restrictions considered measures maintained by Germany for which there was no longer a balance-of-payments justification. Many delegations (including India) declared themselves ready to resort to dispute settlement on the grounds of nullification or impairment if the German restrictions remained in place:

> "[A] substantial number of delegations (Australia, Canada, Ceylon, Denmark, India, Japan, New Zealand, Norway, Pakistan, the United Kingdom and the United States of America) ... pointed out that, as the Federal Republic was no longer entitled to resort to the provisions of Article XII, the maintenance of restrictions, unless sanctioned by any other provision of GATT, would be in breach of Article XI ... .These delegations emphasized that the very structure of the Agreement would be undermined and the balance of rights and obligations between contracting parties upset if ... Germany continued to maintain restrictions inconsistently with the General Agreement .... If the Federal Government followed the policy which it now declared, it might well leave other contracting parties no choice but to take action on grounds of nullification and impairment."[115]

3.127 Subsequent decisions adopted with respect to Article XVIII, such as the two sets of consultation procedures adopted by the Council in 1970 and 1972[116] and the 1979 Declaration on Trade Measures Taken for Balance-of-Payments

---

[113] GATT/CP.4/33 (Sales No. GATT/1950-3), para. 22.

[114] GATT/IC/7; GATT/IC/SR.3, pp. 19-20; *Analytical Index / Guide to GATT Law and Practice* (6th ed., 1995), pp. 689, 702.

[115] *Report of the Working Party on German Import Restrictions*, 30 November 1957, BISD 6S/55, 56, paras. 2 and 3.

[116] *Documentation for Article XII:4(b) and Article XVIII:12(b) Consultations*, L/3388, adopted on 28 April 1970, BISD 18S/48, *and Procedures for Regular Consultations on Balance-of-Payments Restrictions with Developing Countries*, L/3772/Rev.1, adopted on 19 December 1972, BISD 20S/47.

Purposes[117], had not changed the relationship between Article XVIII:B and Article XXIII.

3.128 **India** noted that most of the authorities cited by the United States related to the period before 1957 prior to the amendment of Article XII and the introduction of Article XVIII:B, which resulted in introducing procedures for consultations on import restrictions for balance-of-payments purposes. Moreover, the 1950 Report of the Working Party on the "The Use of Quantitative Restrictions for Protective and Commercial Purposes" not only had not been a working party set up under Article XXIII but also appeared to proceed on the assumption that the import restrictions in question did not have any justification under Article XII and were inconsistent with Articles XIII and XIV.[118] Similarly, the working party established under Article XXIII to examine the justification for Belgium's restrictions on imports from the dollar area had been concerned with discriminatory import restrictions that were not directed towards controlling the general level of imports.[119]

3.129 India added that the Report on Quantitative Restrictions adopted at the Review Session recommended against stricter limits on import restrictions and the introduction instead of special consultation procedures both in Articles XII and XVIII:B.[120] After the introduction of consultation procedures in Article XII, the economic justification of import restrictions had never been determined by a dispute settlement panel though the application of import restrictions had been considered after the Committee had determined that there was no economic justification for the import restrictions of a particular contracting party. Thus, a working party was set up under Article XXIII to review import restrictions maintained by Germany under Article XII only after consultations resulted in the conclusion that Germany's import restrictions were no longer justified.[121]

3.130 India pointed out that in the case of *Korea - Beef,* the Panel did not decide on its own that import restrictions had no balance-of-payments justification but determined the legal status in light of the conclusions of the Committee. Several contracting parties had been of the view that the panel procedures could not be used as a substitute for the consultation process in the Committee and that these panels should not be established. Others considered that the resort to Article XXIII was an unconditional right. In the end, three parallel panels on *Korea - Beef* were established[122] and the controversy on this issue continued in the proceedings before them.[123] The panels avoided deciding the issue by concluding in

[117] L/4904, adopted on 28 November 1979, BISD 26S/205.

[118] GATT/CP.4/33 (Sales No. GATT/1950-3).

[119] GATT/IC/7; GATT/IC/SR.3, pp. 19-20.

[120] *Report of the Review Working Party on Quantitative Restrictions,* L/332/Rev.1, adopted on 2, 4 and 5 March 1955, BISD 3S/170, 171, para. 4.

[121] *German Import Restrictions*, BISD 6S/55, 56, Op. Cit.

[122] Panel Report on *Republic of Korea - Restrictions on Imports of Beef,* BISD 36S/268, Op. Cit.

[123] *Ibid.*, BISD 36S/279-289.

reports with identical findings that the Committee had already determined the legal status of the import restrictions imposed by Korea and they could therefore base their decision on the determination made by the CONTRACTING PARTIES. The panel which examined the United States complaint ruled:

> "The Panel considered the various arguments of the parties to the dispute concerning past deliberations by the CONTRACTING PARTIES on the exclusivity of special review procedures under the General Agreement. However, the Panel was not persuaded that any of these earlier deliberations in the GATT were directly applicable to the present dispute ... The latest full consultation concerning Korea's balance-of-payments situation in the Balance-of-Payments Committee had taken place in November 1987, the report of which had been adopted by the CONTRACTING PARTIES in February 1988 ... The Panel considered that it should take into account the conclusions reached by the Balance-of-Payments Committee.[124]

3.131 The panel then examined the conclusions in the Committee, noted that the prevailing view had been "that the current situation and outlook for the balance of payments was such that import restrictions could no longer be justified under Article XVIII:B", noted that the balance-of-payments situation had improved since the consultations and found on that basis that the import restrictions were not justified by Article XVIII:B. The remainder of the panel's findings dealt with matters arising from the application of the import restrictions, in particular their consistency with Articles II, X and XIII. The panel thus did not arrogate to itself the competence of the Committee and the CONTRACTING PARTIES but based its ruling on the conclusions that had already been reached by these bodies."

3.132 However, India noted that the United States' claimed that the *Korea Beef* case supports its position on dispute settlement being available even in the absence of a finding on justification of import restrictions by the Committee after consultations. India referred to the finding of that Panel, under the heading "*Procedural aspects*", that contracting parties had the right to resort to Article XXIII in respect of measures for which Article XVIII:B was invoked, thereby rejecting the argument of Korea that the panel could examine neither the application nor the justification of the measures because the procedures set out in Article XVIII:B were *lex specialis* in relation to those set out in Article XXIII. Under the heading "*Justification for restrictions*" that Panel had found that:

> The latest full consultation concerning Korea's balance-of-payments situation in the Balance-of-Payments Committee had taken place in November 1987, the report of which had been adopted by the CONTRACTING PARTIES in February 1988... The Panel considered

[124] BISD 36S/302-304.

> that it should *take into account the conclusions reached by the Balance-of-Payments Committee.*[125]

3.133 India stated that that Panel had then examined the conclusions in the Committee, noted that the prevailing view had been "that the current situation and outlook for the balance of payments was such that import restrictions could no longer be justified under Article XVIII:B" and that this view had been adopted by the CONTRACTING PARTIES, and found on that basis that the import restrictions were not justified by Article XVIII:B. The remainder of that Panel's findings dealt with matters arising from the application of the import restrictions, in particular their consistency with Articles II, X and XIII. That Panel thus did not decide on its own that Korea's import restrictions had no balance-of-payments justification; it determined the legal status of the import restrictions in the light of the action the CONTRACTING PARTIES had taken on them.

3.134 When the panel actually examined the justification for Korea's beef import restrictions, it did not initiate a *de novo* review of the justification under Article XVIII:11 for Korea's import restrictions. Instead, it looked to the results of the previous consultations in the Committee to determine the justification of Korea's import restrictions on beef. It found that the consensual decision-making procedure of the Panel had been frustrated by Korea because the report of the Committee had indicated that the prevailing view in the Committee was that Korea's import restrictions could no longer be justified. Thus, the *Korea - Beef* panel took a nuanced and carefully-reasoned approach to the issue of how to reconcile the special responsibility for examining the justification of import restrictions under Article XVIII:11 expressly assigned to the Committee with the general dispute-settlement procedures in Article XXIII. The report of the *Korea - Beef* ruling on this central issue in this dispute was especially important because it was adopted by the CONTRACTING PARTIES.

3.135 In the present dispute, however, India noted that the Committee's Report on Consultations with India reflected that a significant proportion of the Committee found that India's import restrictions were justified. Therefore, India clearly had not abused the procedures of the Committee. Subsequently, India reached agreement with all the dissenting members of the Committee except the United States on its time-schedule. Therefore, effectively there was a consensus (barring only the United States) within the Committee on approving India's time-schedule. Accepting the arguments of the United States in this case, therefore, could result in frustrating the ability of the Committee to exercise its responsibility in the future. A single member could frustrate a consensus on approving the legal status of the import restrictions of a Member invoking Article XVIII:B in the future and then take recourse to dispute settlement on the basis that the legal status of the import restrictions remained in doubt.

[125] BISD 36S/302-304.

3.136 The **United States** noted that India's settlements with other Members had not been notified to the Committee, had in any event not been signed until after the United States made its request for the establishment of this Panel, and were irrelevant to the questions before this Panel.

2. *Burden of Proof*

3.137 **The United States** considered that it was up to India to provide evidence that it met all the provisions of XVIII:B and that the only burden on the United States to sustain its complaint under Article XVIII:11 was that there was no balance-of-payments justification for the measures maintained. In the view of the United States, a party invoking the balance-of-payments exception of Article XVIII:9 had the burden of establishing that the requirements of this exception were fulfilled. The only GATT panel that had examined an Article XVIII:B claim, the 1989 panel on *Korea - Beef*, had found explicitly that "Article XI:1 did not permit the use of either import restrictions or import prohibitions; exemptions from this general proscription had to be specifically justified under other provisions of the General Agreement."[126] Thus, if India wished to rely on Article XVIII:9 to excuse itself from the general prohibition on quantitative restrictions in Article XI:1, it was up to India to put forward evidence and legal argument sufficient to demonstrate that all the requirements of Article XVIII:9 had been met. If India wished to invoke Article XVIII:B to claim justification of the quantitative restrictions at issue, it must make such a claim as an affirmative defense. To sustain such a defense India would have to put forward evidence and legal argument sufficient to demonstrate *inter alia*, that its import restrictions did not "exceed those necessary" to "forestall the threat of, or to stop, a serious decline in its monetary reserves" or (if India's monetary reserves were in fact inadequate) to "achieve a reasonable rate of increase in its reserves".

3.138 The United States requested the Panel to make a finding that India had not furnished factual material that met India's burden of proof.

[126] L/6503, adopted on 7 November 1989, BISD 36S/268, 301, Op. Cit., para. 112. See also Appellate Body Report on *United States - Measure Affecting Imports of Woven Wool Shirts and Blouses from India,* DSR 1997:I, 323 at 337 ("Articles XX and XI:(2)(c)(i) are limited exceptions from obligations under certain other provisions of the GATT 1994, not positive rules establishing obligations in themselves. They are in the nature of affirmative defences. It is only reasonable that the burden of establishing such a defence should rest on the party asserting it."); *United States - Section 337 of the Tariff Act of 1930*, BISD 36S/345, adopted November 7, 1989, para. 5.9 ("Article XX(d) thus provides for a *limited and conditional exception* from obligations under other provisions."); *United States - Prohibition on Imports of Tuna and Tuna Products from Canada*, BISD 29S/91, adopted February 22, 1982, para. 4.8; *United States - Restrictions on Imports of Tuna*, BISD 39S/197, para. 5.22 ("previous panels had established that Article XX was a limited and conditional exception from obligations under other provisions of the General Agreement, and *not a rule establishing obligations in itself*. Therefore, the practice of panels has been to interpret Article XX narrowly ..."); *Canada - Administration of the Foreign Investment Review Act*, L/5504, adopted on 7 February 1984, BISD 30S/140, 164, para. 5.20; *Japan - Restrictions on Imports of Certain Agricultural Products,* L/6253, adopted 2 February 1988, BISD35S/163, 227, para. 5.1.3.7.

3.139 **India** cited the WTO dispute on *United States - Measure Affecting Imports of Wool Shirts and Blouses from* India *(Wool Shirts),* in which India had argued that the United States, as the party invoking Article 6 of the Agreement on Textiles and Clothing ("ATC"), had to prove that its safeguard action was consistent with Article 6 because the provision was an exception from the general prohibition of import restrictions contained in Article XI of the GATT. The United States had opposed India's contention, arguing that it constituted nothing but "a blatant attempt to effectively amend the GATT 1994 and other WTO agreements through litigation". The Appellate Body had ruled in favour of the United States on the issue as follows:

> The transitional safeguard mechanism provided in Article 6 of the *ATC* is a fundamental part of the rights and obligations of WTO Members ... Consequently, a party claiming a violation of a provision of the *WTO Agreement* by another Member must assert and prove its claim. In this case, India claimed a violation by the United States of Article 6 of the *ATC*. We agree with the Panel that it, therefore, was up to India to put forward evidence and legal argument sufficient to demonstrate that the transitional safeguard action by the United States was inconsistent with the obligations assumed by the United States under Articles 2 and 6 of the *ATC*.[127]

3.140 In India's view, the United States could not claim in these proceedings that the principle it defended so vigorously in the *Wool Shirts* case did not extend to GATT balance-of-payments provisions. The distribution of the burden of proof could not be different when Article 6 of the ATC was invoked by developed country Members than when Article XVIII:B of GATT 1994 was invoked by developing country Members. India's point was that the burden of proof issues in the *Wool Shirts* case and the present case were the same and that the principle applied by the Appellate Body in *Wool Shirts* should govern the Panel's consideration of the present case.

3.141 In response to India's arguments based on the *Wool Shirts* case, the **United States** stated that Articles XX and XVIII:B were similar in that both constituted affirmative defences to a general prohibition on quantitative restrictions in Article XI:1. As the Appellate Body had pointed out in the *Wool Shirts* case, a Member relying on Article XX or Article XI:(2)(c)(i) as a basis for not complying with its obligations under Article XI:1 bore the burden of establishing that its non-compliance was justified under those Articles.[128] A quantitative restriction sought to be justified under Article XVIII:B was a quantitative restriction that "deviate[s] temporarily"[129] from the requirements of Article XI:1 and that - apart

[127] Appellate Body report on *United States - Measure Affecting Imports of Wool Shirts and Blouses from India, (*hereafter *Wool Shirts),* WT/DS33/AB/R, 25 April 1997, pp. 337-338

[128] WT/DS33/AB/R, Op. Cit. p. 337.

[129] Article XVIII:4(a).

from the affirmative defense provided by Article XVIII:B - would otherwise be in violation of Article XI:1. Article 6 of the Agreement on Textiles and Clothing ("ATC") was negotiated as a integral part of the carefully drawn balance of rights and obligations contained in that agreement. As a result, the Appellate Body held that with respect to Article 6 of the ATC, the burden of proof rested with the Member alleging a violation of that Article.[130]

3.142 **India** recalled that the Appellate Body had noted that Article 6 was "carefully negotiated language ... which reflects an equally carefully drawn balance of rights and obligations of Members ..." and "that balance must be respected".[131] India noted further that the provisions of the GATT permitting a WTO Member to impose import restrictions to safeguard its external financial position were a fundamental part of the rights and obligations of WTO Members. They contained carefully negotiated language reflecting a carefully drawn balance of rights and obligations of Members, and that balance must also be respected. India contended that the ruling of the Appellate Body on Section 6 of the ATC which permits import restrictions to safeguard the textiles industry applied equally to the provisions of Article XVIII:B which permit import restrictions to safeguard the external financial position of developing country Members.

3.143 India argued that the United States must assert and demonstrate that India's plan was inconsistent with India's obligations under Article XVIII:11 of the GATT. Article XVIII:B itself clarified on whom the burden should be cast. The Committee had never made a finding that India's import restrictions were inconsistent with Article XVIII:B or that India's import restrictions did not have any justification under Article XVIII:B. In this situation, the special dispute settlement provisions set out in Article XVIII:12(d) provided that a Member could bring a complaint only if it "can establish a *prima facie* case that the restrictions are inconsistent" with Article XVIII:B. India saw no reason to distribute the burden differently under the general dispute settlement provisions of Article XXIII. For India, the burden of proof was an academic issue in light of Article XVIII:12(d) which specifically placed the burden of establishing a *prima facie* case on the complainant. India's import restrictions were consistent with Article XVIII:B until the General Council found otherwise. The only way for the United States to meet its burden of proof was to demonstrate that the General Council did so. According to Article XVIII:11 and the note thereto, India could progressively relax its import restrictions as long as their sudden removal would not jeopardize its external financial position within the framework of its existing policies. The United States had provided no evidence that these conditions were met. In India's view, the IMF statement did not support the United States' position because the elimination of import restrictions "within a relatively short time-period" according to the IMF would only be possible if India were to change

[130] WT/DS33/AB/R, Op. Cit. p. 1337.

[131] *Ibid.*, p. 337.

simultaneously its macro-economic policies, which India was clearly not obliged to do given the proviso in Article XVIII:11. Nor did the competence of the IMF extend to all matters required to be taken into account by the Committee.

3.144 Therefore, the Panel should reject the United States' assertion that India bore the burden of proving that its import restrictions were consistent with Article XVIII:B.

3.145 As far as the **United States** was concerned, whether India or the United States had the burden of proof was, in this case, a moot point; the facts conclusively established that India did not meet the requirements for continuing to maintain the challenged measures. The International Monetary Fund had found and determined that India's monetary reserves were not only adequate but "comfortable", and had found that India was not faced with a threat of serious decline in its monetary reserves. Under Article XV:2, these findings must be accepted by the Panel. It followed that India's quantitative restrictions on imports were not "necessary" to achieve a reasonable rate of increase in India's reserves. Therefore India legally could not demonstrate its conformity with the conditions for invocation of Article XVIII, and India's import restrictions were not excused from the prohibition on import restrictions in Article XI:1.

3.146 The United States requested the Panel to make an alternative conditional finding that even if the burden of proof were on the United States to make a *prima facie* case that India no longer had any justification for maintaining these measures under Article XVIII:B, the United States would have met this burden.

3.147 **India** noted that the United States had claimed, as a matter of law, it did not have to prove that the removal of India's restrictions would not produce conditions justifying the reintroduction of import restrictions as required by the interpretative note A*d* Article XVIII:11. According to the United States, this was because an analysis of the ordinary meaning of the Article XVIII:11, the note to Article XVIII:11, and Article XVIII:9, read in their context and in the light of the object and purpose of Article XVIII:B showed that the note to Article XVIII:11 imposed no requirements apart from those already contained in paragraphs (a) and (b) of the proviso to Article XVIII:9. India maintained, however, that the United States was required, as a matter of law, to establish a *prime facie* case that India's balance-of-payments and monetary reserves situation would not be adversely affected by the removal of its restrictions in a manner that might require it to reintroduce import restrictions under Article XVIII:B.

3.148 India contended that this interpretation accorded by the United States to the second sentence of Article XVIII:11 and the interpretative note was fundamentally inconsistent with the customary rules of treaty interpretation contained in Article 31 of the Vienna Convention on the Law of Treaties. The context of the term "conditions" in the second sentence of Article XVIII:11 were intended to refer both to the limitations contained in Article XVIII:9 and the condition relating to equilibrium in its balance of payments on a sound and lasting basis referred to in the first sentence of Article XVIII:11. This approach to interpreting the term "conditions" was consistent with Article XVIII:9 which provided that a

Member might impose import restrictions in order to safeguard its balance of payments. In addition, it was also consistent with the overall object and purpose of Article XVIII:B as set forth in Article XVIII:2, i.e., to facilitate the economic development of less-developed country Members.

3.149 India argued that both the Committee and the panel in *"Korea Beef"* took exactly the same approach to interpretation of the requirement of the second sentence of Article XVIII:11 "when conditions no longer justify such maintenance". Thus, the report of the panel recorded that:

> "At the full consultation in the Balance-of-Payments Committee with Korea in November 1987, "[t]he prevailing view expressed in the Committee was that the current situation and outlook for the balance of payments was such that import restrictions could no longer be justified under Article XVIII:B"."

According to the *Korea Beef* panel, therefore, the term "conditions" referred not only to (i) the monetary reserves situation, and (ii) the balance-of-payments situation, but also to (iii) other economic indicators. The requirements of the Note *Ad* Article XVIII:11 were not at issue in *"Korea Beef"*. The note to Article XVIII:11 made it clear that the requirement of removal of the import restrictions also requires a determination that "*the removal of the import restrictions themselves would not lead to a fresh threat to its reserves or balance of payments situation*". However, subparagraphs (a) and (b) of the proviso to Article XVIII:9 plainly contemplate threats or conditions that pre-exist and are independent of the institution of import restrictions. Based on the above analysis, India considered that the United States was required to advance evidence proving each of the following:

(i) Under the second sentence of Article XVIII:11, India's balance-of-payments situation no longer justifies the maintenance of import restrictions.

(ii) Under Article XVIII:9(a), India's monetary reserves currently do not face a serious decline or a threat of one at least in the medium term. Unlike in the case of Article XII:2(a), even a medium term threat is sufficient in the case of Article XVIII:9(a) because the latter omits the word "imminent".

(iii) Under Article XVIII:9(b), India's monetary reserves are not inadequate in relation to its programme of economic development.

(iv) Under Article XVIII:11, the immediate elimination of India's import restrictions will not produce conditions requiring it to institute import restrictions again under Article XVIII:9.

3.150 Based on the Appellate Body rulings in *Wool Shirts* and again in *EC Hormones*, in order to make a *prime facie* case, the complaining party must adduce evidence (as well as arguments) that would require the Panel to rule, as a matter of law, in its favour.[132] In this case, this meant that the United States must adduce evidence that would require the Panel to conclude that India's balance of payments and reserves situation did not meet each of the criteria set forth above. India considered that the evidence submitted by the United States, as a matter of law, could not discharge its burden of meeting the above four legal criteria in Article XVIII:11 to prove that India's balance of payments and reserves situation no longer entitled India to maintain import restrictions in accordance with its time-schedule.

3.151 India added that this evidence must be sufficient to overcome three presumptions in favour of India's residual import restrictions arising out of the text of Article XVIII:B:

> First, Article XVIII:8 presumes that less-developed country Members "tend, when they are in rapid process of development, to face balance of payments difficulties..."
>
> Second, Article XVIII:12(f) required the CONTRACTING PARTIES to take into account the factors referred to in Article XVIII:2 which includes the presumption that (I) the import restrictions of a less-developed country Member invoking Article XVIII:B "may be necessary... in order to implement programmes and policies of economic development designed to raise the general standard of living of [its] people and that such [import restrictions] are justified insofar as they facilitate the achievement of the objectives of the [GATT 1994]" and (ii) the less-developed country Member invoking Article XVIII:B "should enjoy additional facilities to enable them... to apply [import] restrictions for balance of payments purposes in a manner which takes full account of the continued high level of demand for imports likely to be generated by their programmes of economic development."
>
> Third, Article XVIII:12(b) placed an affirmative obligation on the CONTRACTING PARTIES to review its import restrictions during consultation and, under Article XVIII:12(c), to inform a Member it its import restrictions were inconsistent with Article XVIII:B and advise or recommend how to bring its import restrictions into conformity with Article XVIII:B. In the case of India, the Committee's Report on Consultations with India reflected that the CONTRACTING PARTIES had, in fact, held these consultations and that they had not concluded that India's import restrictions lacked justification under Article XVIII:11. This raised a pre-

[132] WT/DS33/AB/R, p. 14; *also* Appellate Body Report, *EC Measures Concerning Meat and Meat Products (Hormones)*, WT/DS26/AB/R, para. 104.

sumption that India's import restrictions were consistent with Article XVIII:11.

India submitted that the evidence adduced by the United States could not overcome these presumptions in India's favour.

3.152 The **United States** did not agree that India had correctly described what needed to be shown. For the United States, Article XVIII:9, Article XVIII:11 and the Note Ad Article XVIII:11 set out the relevant issues. The United States considered that the evidence it had presented addressed the four points made by India in paragraph 3.149. The IMF determinations addressed each of those points. For example, the IMF's determinations clearly included a consideration of the medium term. Both the IMF and the Reserve Bank of India were well-informed about India's development program, and their views that reserves were adequate and not under threat of serious decline must be understood to include a consideration of that program. However, if the Panel did not agree that the IMF's statements were sufficient with respect to the factual question of whether India had balance-of-payments difficulties within the meaning of Article XVIII:B, the United States requested a conditional alternative finding that the additional evidence the United States had presented corroborated the IMF's determinations. It made this request in light of a possible appeal of the Article XV:2 issue.

3. *Article XVIII:9, XVIII:11 and the Note Ad Article XVIII:11*

3.153 The United States claimed that India had no balance-of-payments justification under Article XVIII:B for the maintenance of import restrictions and India was required to remove the measures at issue based on an analysis of the relevant text of Article XVIII:B.[133]

3.154 The United States recalled that the basis for invocation of Article XVIII:B was Article XVIII:4 of the GATT: "a contracting party, the economy of which can only support low standards of living and is in the early stages of development, shall be free to *deviate temporarily* from the provisions of the other Articles of this Agreement [the GATT] as provided in [Article XVIII:B]." Thus, Article XVIII:B was a narrow and temporary exception to the general prohibition on quantitative restrictions in Article XI:1. The Appellate Body had recognized the exceptional nature of Article XVIII, finding that "certain provisions of the GATT 1994, such as Articles XII, XIV, XV and XVIII, permit a WTO Member, in certain specified circumstances relating to exchange matters and/or balance of payments, *to be excused* from certain of its obligations under the GATT 1994."[134]

---

[133] Article 31(1) of the Vienna Convention on the Law of Treaties (the "Vienna Convention") provides that "[a] treaty shall be interpreted in good faith in accordance with the ordinary meaning to be given to the terms of the treaty in their context and in the light of its object and purpose."

[134] Appellate Body Report on *Argentina - Measures Affecting Imports of Footwear, Textiles, Apparel and Other Items*, AB-1998-1, WT/DS56/AB/R, para. 73 (emphasis added).

The temporary nature of the Article XVIII:9 exception was demonstrated by the large number of disinvocations of Article XVIII:B which had taken place in recent years.[135] This exception allowed WTO members to impose such measures on a temporary basis, in a very limited set of circumstances. It did not provide *carte blanche* for India to continue fifty years of protectionist import restrictions particularly after the IMF had determined that India has "no threat of a serious decline in its monetary reserves".

3.155 The United States recalled the provisions of Article XVIII:9:

> ... a contracting party coming within the scope of paragraph 4(a) of this Article may, subject to the provisions of paragraphs 10 to 12, control the general level of its imports by restricting the quantity or value of merchandise permitted to be imported; *Provided* that the import restrictions instituted, maintained or intensified *shall not exceed* those necessary:
>
> (a) to forestall the threat of, or to stop, a serious decline in its monetary reserves, or
>
> (b) in the case of a contracting party with inadequate monetary reserves, to achieve a reasonable rate of increase in its reserves.[136]

The proviso in Article XVIII:9 made clear that any measures taken for balance-of-payments reasons must meet two tests. The first test was that there must be balance-of-payments difficulties that fall within the requirements of subparagraph (a) or subparagraph (b). That is, there must be a serious decline in reserves; or the threat of a serious decline in reserves; or inadequate monetary reserves that were increasing at less than a reasonable rate. The second test was that the balance-of-payments measure must be *"necessary"* to meet the particular balance-of-payments difficulties that the Member concerned was facing.

3.156 The United States contended that Article XVIII:B did not give India the right to "phase out" its quantitative restrictions beyond the time when its balance-of-payments difficulties had ended. Article XVIII:11 allowed for progressive relaxation of balance-of-payments measures as the balance-of-payments situation improved; but this progressive relaxation was required to take place only during the period when the conditions of Article XVIII:9 were still met, not afterwards. The concept of a "phase out" *after* that period was entirely absent from Article XVIII:B. Article XVIII:11 provided that:

> "[The contracting party concerned] shall progressively relax any restrictions applied under this Section as conditions improve,

[135] The *Analytical Index/Guide to GATT Law and Practice* (1995 ed.) lists disinvocations by Argentina, Brazil, Colombia, Ghana, Greece, Korea, Peru and Portugal (p. 395) and Spain (p. 431). In addition, since 1995 Egypt, Turkey and the Philippines have disinvoked Article XVIII and Israel and South Africa (which did not specify whether they consulted under Article XII or XVIII) have also disinvoked the GATT balance-of-payments provisions.

[136] Article XVIII:9 (emphasis added).

> maintaining them *only to the extent necessary under the terms of paragraph 9* of this article and *shall eliminate them when conditions no longer justify such maintenance.*[137]

3.157 The text of Article XVIII:11 closely paralleled that used in Article XII:2(b) for developed countries. The term "phase-out" appeared nowhere in the text of either provision. Once there was no balance-of-payments justification for restrictions, they must be "eliminated." The "progressive relaxation" provided under Article XVIII:11 and Article XII:2(b) was for those measures which were still justified by balance-of-payments needs.

The Note Ad Article XVIII:11 (the "Ad Note") stated:

> The second sentence in paragraph 11 shall not be interpreted to mean that a contracting party is required to relax or remove restrictions *if such relaxation or removal would thereupon produce conditions justifying the intensification or institution, respectively, of restrictions under paragraph 9 of Article XVIII.*[138]

3.158 The United States contended that this Ad Note was explicitly tied to the requirements of Article XVIII:9 .

3.159 In the view of the United States, the text of Article XVIII:9, 11 and the Ad Note confirmed that India must remove its quantitative restrictions based on a balance-of-payments justification when that justification no longer existed. The phrases "shall not exceed" in paragraph 9 and "shall eliminate them when conditions no longer justify such maintenance" in paragraph 11 must be read together since "such maintenance" referred to the words "maintaining them only to the extent necessary under the terms of paragraph 9". Similarly, paragraphs 9 and 11 must be read with the Ad Note, which provided instruction on how these two paragraphs should *not* be interpreted. The Ad Note would not *require* the immediate removal or elimination of restrictions if such relaxation would cause conditions set forth in paragraph 9, *i.e.,* either a *threat* or an *actual* serious decline in monetary reserves, or prevent a contracting party with inadequate reserves from achieving a reasonable rate of increase in its reserves. These three provisions of Article XVIII:B stated an absolute obligation on the part of India to correlate its measures to its reserve position: *if* its reserve situation met either subparagraph (a) or (b) of the proviso in paragraph 9 *and* quantitative restrictions were *necessary* to address that situation, then India might institute and maintain quantitative restrictions. But even in such a case, India might institute and maintain such quantitative restrictions only *to the extent* that they were necessary to meet subparagraph (a) or (b) of the proviso. Whenever India's reserve situation was not in one of the situations described in subparagraph (a) or (b) of the proviso to paragraph 9, then quantitative restrictions could not be "necessary" to address the situation.

137 Article XVIII:11 (emphasis added).

138 Note Ad Article XVIII:11 (emphasis added).

3.160 India's continued maintenance of these quantitative restrictions also violated India's obligations under paragraph 11 of Article XVIII. Reflecting the limited and temporary nature of the exception provided in Article XVIII:B for developing members with balance-of-payments difficulties, paragraph 11 provided that WTO Members using this exception maintain quantitative restrictions only to the extent necessary under the terms of Article XVIII:9, and obligated Members to eliminate such restrictions when they were no longer necessary. Because the IMF had stated clearly that India's reserve position no longer satisfied the conditions laid out in Article XVIII:9(a) and (b), and this determination must be accepted by the WTO and the Panel, the "terms of paragraph 9" were not satisfied and Article XVIII:11 required immediate elimination of the restrictions in question. The IMF had made it clear that India was not experiencing a serious decline in its monetary reserves; that there was no threat of such a decline; and that India's monetary reserves were not inadequate.[139] Therefore, quantitative restrictions could not be "necessary" in the sense of Article XVIII:9; *any* quantitative restrictions must "exceed those necessary." The IMF's factual determinations made clear both that there was no balance-of-payments justification for maintenance of the challenged measures and that removal of the challenged measures would not produce conditions justifying the institution of such measures. Therefore, India could not establish that its balance-of-payments situation met the requirements of either Article XVIII:9 or of the Ad Note, and it therefore could not maintain the challenged measures.

3.161 The United States considered that an important context for interpreting the provisions of Article XVIII:B was the Understanding on the Balance-of-Payments Provisions of the General Agreement on Tariffs and Trade 1994 (the "1994 Understanding"). The 1994 Understanding reinforced India's obligation to remove the challenged measures at the time when the justification for those measures lapsed. In the terminology of the Vienna Convention, the 1994 Understanding was an "agreement relating to [Article XVIII:B of the GATT 1994] which was made between all the parties in connection with the conclusion of [the GATT 1994]", and it therefore formed part of the context for the interpretation of Article XVIII:B.[140]

---

[139] *Report on the Consultation with India,* WT/BOP/R/22, 3 March 1997, para. 8.

[140] Vienna Convention, Article 31(2)(a). The United States had noted India's repeated references to the first sentence of Footnote 1 of the 1994 Understanding: "Nothing in this Understanding is intended to modify the rights and obligations of Members under Articles XII or XVIII:B of GATT 1994." To India, this sentence apparently meant that even when the 1994 Understanding mentioned such rights and obligations, it could not have an effect on them. This was not so. To give one example, the first sentence of the 1994 Understanding plainly said that the 1994 Understanding "*clarifies*" the provisions of those Articles. Uncertainties about the rights and obligations of Members under Articles XII and XVIII:B might be able to be resolved by reference to the Understanding. To give another example, it was also clear that provisions of the 1994 Understanding could qualify the exercise by Members of their Article XVIII:B rights; for example, in paragraph 3, Members' use of quantitative restrictions was conditioned on their justifying why price-based measures were inadequate.

3.162 The 1994 Understanding was relevant to the application of balance-of-payments measures where there was a balance-of-payments justification. Paragraph 4 of the Understanding stated, in part:

> "Members *confirm* that restrictive import measures taken for balance-of-payments purposes may only be applied to control the general level of imports and *may not exceed what is necessary to address the balance-of-payments situation*."[141]

These words were similar to those used in Articles XVIII:9, 11, and the Ad Note to paragraph 11. Measures taken for balance-of-payments purposes may not exceed what is *necessary*. This notion, however, presupposed that *any* measures were necessary; if there were no balance-of-payment problem as defined by Article XVIII:9 and 11, then no measures could be deemed necessary.

3.163 The United States considered that paragraphs 1 and 11 of the 1994 Understanding also shed light on the meaning of Articles XVIII:9, 11, and the Ad Note. These paragraphs addressed, *inter alia*, the requirement for members invoking balance-of-payments provisions to provide a time schedule for the removal of restrictive import measures taken for balance-of-payment purposes. Paragraph 11 stated that Members invoking the balance-of-payments exceptions of the GATT 1994, at the first consultation after so doing, should provide the Balance-of-Payments Committee a "plan for the elimination and progressive relaxation of remaining restrictions". Similarly, paragraph 1 stated that Members invoking the balance-of-payments exceptions should make a *public* announcement of time-schedules for the removal of restrictive import measures "as soon as possible", and if no such announcement was made they should provide a justification as to why this was not possible. These provisions demonstrated that any phase-out should begin *while* a member was still experiencing balance of payments problems, or at a minimum as the balance-of-payments crisis was lessening.

3.164 For the United States, these paragraphs did not support India's argument that it was entitled to phase out restrictions taken for balance-of-payments reasons years after there was no longer *any* balance-of-payments problem. Rather, they were consistent with the United States' reading of Article XVIII:B that India must remove *all* quantitative restrictions when there was no longer any threat of or actual serious decline in a Member's monetary reserves.

3.165 The United States noted also that GATT practice demonstrated that contracting parties had been requested to remove their restrictions as their balance-of-payments improved. The Vienna Convention rules of interpretation provided for the examination of subsequent practice of parties to a treaty as an aid to the interpretation of that treaty.[142] The practice of the CONTRACTING PARTIES to

---

[141] 1994 Understanding, paragraph 4 (emphasis added).

[142] Article 31(3)(b). Article XVI:1 of the Marrakesh Agreement Establishing the World Trade Organization also provides that the WTO shall be guided by the decisions, procedures and customary practices followed under the GATT 1947.

the GATT 1947 subsequent to the adoption of Article XII and the present text of Article XVIII:B demonstrated that contracting parties had been required to remove their quantitative restrictions as their balance-of-payments positions improved. The examples of Germany, Italy and Spain were instructive.

3.166 In 1957, the IMF concluded that Germany's restrictions on imports were no longer necessary to safeguard Germany's monetary reserves and balance of payments.[143] In light of this finding, Germany was requested by the CONTRACTING PARTIES to remove those restrictions. Germany objected to doing so; Germany made the argument that it would liberalize certain products over a two-year period, and would remove or relax certain discriminatory measures with respect to other products.[144] The *Report of the Working Party on German Import Restrictions* records contracting parties' response to this argument:

> "A number of delegations (Australia, Canada, Ceylon, Denmark, *India*, Japan, New Zealand, Norway, Pakistan, United Kingdom, United States) pointed out that under paragraph 2 of Article XII, restrictions should be eliminated when they are no longer justified under that paragraph. *While the application of a liberal licensing policy was welcome in circumstances where restrictions could be legitimately maintained, it was no substitute for the elimination of restrictions required under the Agreement.*"[145]

Germany ultimately agreed to disinvoke Article XII and obtained a waiver of its obligations under Article XI:1 from the CONTRACTING PARTIES.[146]

3.167 The United States referred to a similar result involving Italy. In 1959, Italy's proposal to phase out gradually its quantitative restrictions was rejected by the Committee.[147] The IMF made a statement at the November committee meeting stating its factual determination that Italy's balance of payments and reserve position no longer justified restrictions on imports. It further stated that Italy was in a position to make "rapid progress in the elimination of such restrictions."[148] Italy argued that the complete elimination of quantitative restrictions would aggravate the structural disequilibrium of its economy, but it would do so progressively. The Committee disagreed, and said it would not hold further consultations under Article XII with Italy. Similarly, in 1973, the IMF concluded that quantitative restrictions maintained by Spain could no longer be justified on balance-of-payments grounds. Spain argued that it was undertaking various liberalization measures during the course of that year, and that Spain needed to follow a course

---

[143] Results of the International Monetary Fund Consultations, QRC/4/Add.2, 17 June 1957.

[144] *Report of the Working Party on German Import Restrictions*, BISD 6S/55, Op. Cit. page 11 (statement by the representative of the Federal Republic of Germany).

[145] *Ibid.*, para. 5 (emphasis added).

[146] *German Import Restrictions*, Decision of 30 May 1959, BISD 8S/31.

[147] Report of the Committee on Balance-of-Payments Restrictions on Consultation Under Article XII:4(b) with Italy, L/1088, 3 November 1959, adopted at SR.15/13.

[148] *Ibid.*, Annex I, para. 5.

of gradual liberalization. The Committee rejected the Spanish arguments in light of the IMF's findings and invited the Spanish Government to reconsider its position with regard to its remaining import restrictions.[149]

3.168 **India** argued that its time-schedule for the removal of its import restrictions was consistent with Article XVIII:11 of the GATT and invoked its right to a progressive relaxation and elimination of its import restrictions pending a decision by the General Council.

3.169 India contended that an analysis of the provisions of Article XVIII:B confirmed that import restrictions maintained by a Member in good faith could not be considered inconsistent with Article XVIII:11 until the Committee determined that these import restrictions lacked justification. Under Article XVIII:9, a Member might impose import restrictions in order to safeguard its balance of payments without prior authorization by the WTO subject to the limitations contained in the proviso to paragraph 9 and paragraphs 10 and 11 of Article XVIII:B. The drafting history of Article XVIII:B recorded in the context of Article XII that:

> After a detailed consideration of the various proposals put forward with a view to establishing stricter rules for the introduction and maintenance of quantitative restrictions through the institution of fixed time limits and approval by the CONTRACTING PARTIES, the Working Party came to the conclusion that such proposals would not find general acceptance among the contracting parties, but that, on the other hand, the general opinion was in favour of strengthening and widening the scope of consultations under Article XII, as well as under Article XIV.[150]

3.170 Article XVIII:11, second sentence, stated that import restrictions shall be eliminated when conditions no longer justified their maintenance in terms of the criteria set out in Article XVIII:9. An interpretative note to this provision made it clear that a WTO Member was not

> "required to relax or remove restrictions if such relaxation or removal would thereupon produce conditions justifying the intensification or institution, respectively, of restrictions under paragraph 9 of Article XVIII".[151]

In arguing that:

> "The text of Article XVIII:11 ... closely parallels that used in Article XII:2(b) for developed countries. The term "phase-out" appears

[149] *Report on the 1973 Consultation with Spain*, BOP/R/63, 20 July 1973, adopted by the GATT Council on 19 October 1973 (C/M/90, page 2).

[150] *Report of the Review Working Party on Quantitative Restrictions*, BISD 3S/170, 171, para. 4.

[151] Note Ad Article XVIII:11, General Agreement, 1947.

> nowhere in the text of either provision. Once there is no BOP justification for restrictions, they must be "eliminated" ... India now has no BOP problem justifying restrictions. If India should have a BOP problem in the future, it remains free to reinvoke Article XVIII:B ..." .

India considered that the United States overlooked two important differences between Article XII and Article XVIII:B. The first was that, Article XII:2(a) stipulated that a developed country Member's import restrictions "shall not exceed those necessary ... to forestall the *imminent* threat of ... a serious decline in its monetary reserves ..." while there was *no such requirement in Article XVIII:B*. The GATT Working Party which drafted Article XVIII explained:

> ... paragraph 9 [of Article XVIII] recognizes that the reserve problems for [developing] countries is one of adequacy of the reserves in relation to their programme of economic development, that for this reason the word "imminent" which occurs in paragraph 2 (a) is inappropriate in this context, and that in order to safeguard their external financial position these countries may need over a period of time to control the general level of their imports in order to prevent that level from rising beyond the means available to pay for imports as the progress of development programmes creates new demands.[152]

The second important difference was that Article XVIII:11, unlike the corresponding provision in Article XII:2(b), was subject to the proviso that no developing country Member:

> "... is required to relax or remove restrictions if such relaxation or removal would thereupon produce conditions justifying the intensification or institution, respectively, of restrictions under paragraph 9 of Article XVIII."

The term "thereupon" in the text of this note left no doubt that it referred to a situation in which the sudden removal of the import restrictions would produce conditions justifying their reintroduction. The note thus made it clear that developing countries were not required to engage in a "stop-and-go" policy of the type suggested by the United States, immediately eliminating all import restrictions as soon as their reserve situation had improved and reinvoking Article XVIII:B after the removal gave rise to new balance-of-payments difficulties; rather, they might remove them gradually over time so as to avoid renewed balance-of-payments difficulties.

3.171 In India's view, Article XVIII:11 was intended to ensure that a Member had a right to maintain import restrictions even when there was no immediate

[152] Note Ad Article XVIII:11, General Agreement, 1947, BISD 3S/183.

balance-of-payments need in terms of Article XVIII:9 if their relaxation or removal would produce conditions justifying their intensification or reintroduction in terms of Article XVIII:9. Under the terms of Article XVIII:9, developing country Members might introduce, maintain or intensify import restrictions in order to forestall the threat of, or to stop, a decline of their reserves to a level that was inadequate for the implementation of their programmes of economic development. Consequently, irrespective of whether or not its import restrictions were currently necessary to address an existing crisis in its balance of payments, India was entitled to remove them gradually within a time-schedule designed to avoid balance-of-payments difficulties that would result in a serious decline in its monetary reserves and, thereby, jeopardize its programme of economic development.

3.172 In response to a question from the Panel as to what level or composition of reserves India would consider "adequate", India noted that as the drafters of Article XVIII:B had pointed out, this provision recognized that "the reserve problem for developing countries is one of adequacy of reserves in relation to their programme of economic development" and that these countries "need over a period of time to control the general level of their imports in order to pay for imports as the progress of development programmes creates new demands".[153] In terms of Article XVIII:9, the adequacy of the level of reserves held by India thus would vary with its development policies and it was therefore not possible to indicate one level of reserves that would be adequate in all circumstances. For the reasons which India explained in detail to the Committee, and which all but one member of that Committee found convincing, a sudden removal of import restrictions covering one-third of imports would create considerable economic uncertainty and political opposition, which in turn would adversely affect India's investment climate and the external financial position. The schedule had not been drawn up with a particular target for the level of India's reserves in mind; its purpose was rather to ensure that the liberalization, by itself, did not generate the risk of balance-of-payments problems difficult to resolve in the Indian context with macro-economic policies alone. According to Article XVIII:11, India was not required to withdraw its import restrictions on the ground that a change in its development policies would render them unnecessary. The issue raised by the argumentation of the United States thus was whether India's current external financial position was such as to permit a sudden removal of all the remaining import restrictions affecting one third of imports without a change in other economic policies. India believed that its current reserve level was inadequate for that purpose.

3.173 For India, Article XVIII:11 and the note thereto specifically permitted the progressive relaxation rather than immediate elimination of import restrictions when their sudden removal would produce conditions justifying their intensifica-

[153] BISD 3S/183.

tion. India's phase-out plan was nothing but a preannounced time-schedule for progressive relaxation and elimination of its remaining import restrictions designed to avoid such conditions. India did not claim that its balance-of-payments situation was such that it could simply maintain its import restrictions at their existing level; India claimed that its external financial constraints were such that it must relax its import restrictions progressively so as to avoid the creation of conditions jeopardizing its development policies and that its time-schedule for progressive relaxation and elimination of its remaining import restrictions was for this reason consistent with Article XVIII:11. India's remaining import restrictions could therefore only be evaluated against India's proposed time-schedule for progressive relaxation and elimination of its remaining import restrictions. In India's view, the United States bore the burden of proving that the time-schedule currently being followed by India did not meet the conditions set out in the note to Article XVIII:11.

3.174 India was of the view that its economic and external financial position at the present time was such that the prompt removal of import restrictions on 2,714 HS tariff lines covering about one-third of total imports would produce conditions justifying their reintroduction in terms of Article XVIII:9, particularly when its programme of economic liberalization included liberalization measures in other sectors of its economy that could also have an adverse impact on its balance of payments. Accordingly, India considered that the progressive relaxation and elimination of its import restrictions within the remaining five years of its six-year time-schedule for removal of its import restrictions would avoid producing such conditions and that this plan, therefore, met the requirements of Article XVIII:11.

3.175 In response to a question from the Panel as to how India was addressing the first sentence of Article XVIII:11, India pointed out that the obligation under the first sentence of Article XVIII:11 was not absolute and unqualified. The first sentence of Article XVIII:11 did not state that a less-developed country Member "shall employ domestic policies that restore equilibrium in its balance of payments ...". Rather, it enjoined that the Member "shall pay due regard to the need for restoring equilibrium in the balance of payments ... and the desirability of assuring an economic employment of productive resources". Thus, it was clear that this obligation must be read in the context of the other provisions of Article XVIII:B and its object and purpose. In addition, the first sentence of Article XVIII:11 required a Member to pay due regard to two separate elements: (i) the need for restoring equilibrium in their balance of payments on a sound and lasting basis and (ii) the desirability of assuring an economic employment of productive resources. Both elements must be taken into account in interpreting the obligation imposed by the first sentence of Article XVIII:11.

3.176 India considered that the term "economic employment of productive resources" was capable of two interpretations. On one interpretation, the term could refer to the need to avoid the inefficient use of productive resources through indiscriminate protection of domestic industries from import competition. However, Article XVIII:11 did not refer to "economically efficient employment of productive resources". Therefore, it could also be interpreted to mean that policies designed to ensure balance-of-payments equilibrium could not be policies that cause contraction of a Member's economy, resulting in unused industrial capacity as well as high unemployment.

3.177 Theoretically, India continued, it was always possible to bring about a long term equilibrium in the balance of payments through macroeconomic policies such as currency devaluation, high interest rates and fiscal policies to lower government spending. The result, however, would be inconsistent with the ordinary meaning of the first sentence of Article XVIII:11 as well as the object and purpose of Article XVIII:B. First, such policies would severely retard economic growth. Not only would industrial capacity be left idle because of the resulting economic contraction but unemployment would also rise. This would be inconsistent with the second element of the first sentence of Article XVIII:11 which was to ensure the economic employment of productive resources. This was also clearly inconsistent with the purpose of Article XVIII:B, which was to facilitate the economic development of less-developed country Members. Second, such policies in general and, currency devaluation, in particular, would place an undue burden of restoring equilibrium in the balance of payments on a long-term basis on international trade. This was because the less-developed country Member in question would be unable to procure both essential goods that it deemed essential for economic development as well as non-essential goods. Accordingly, the first sentence of Article XVIII:11 could not be interpreted as requiring policies that would restore long-term equilibrium in the balance of payments at the cost of a significant decline in economic growth. India drew the attention of the Panel to the paper entitled "Proposals for a Review of GATT Article XVIII: An Assessment" by Frances Stewart, published in the *Uruguay Round, Papers on Selected Issues* by the United Nations, New York, 1989, a copy of which was made available to the Panel at its request on 23 June 1998.

3.178 Against this background, India wished to demonstrate that it was following responsible domestic policies that pursue long-term equilibrium in its balance of payments without placing the burden of adjustment on the trading interests of its fellow Members. In this connection, India referred to its Basic Document dated 8 January 1997 which it had presented to the Committee for the 1997 consultations with India.[154] As discussed there, India had undertaken major economic reforms in 1991-92 designed to remove internal and external barriers to competition in the Indian economy. India began its economic reforms in 1991 with a substantial package of economic reforms consisting both of macroeconomic stabilization measures as well as structural reforms. For convenience, India would summarize the relevant reforms under the same heads as its 1997 Basic Document while updating them to take account of more recent developments: (i) in-

[154] WT/BOP/16, pp. 3-6.

dustrial policy; (ii) exchange rate related reforms; (iii) fiscal reforms; and (iv) trade policy reforms. (The summary is attached as Annex 1).

3.179 In response to India's argument that, pursuant to the Ad Note, (1) it had the right to phase its import restrictions out gradually, and (2) because it had submitted a schedule for phasing out the challenged measures, it "need not comply with the criteria set forth in the proviso to Article XVIII:9", the **United States** stressed that this was not what the Ad Note said. What it said was that developing country Members were not "required to relax or remove restrictions if such relaxation or removal would thereupon produce conditions justifying the intensification or institution" of balance-of-payments measures. The Ad Note clarified that a developing country Member invoking balance-of-payment justification might continue to impose those restrictions which continued to be necessary to avoid, *inter alia*, a threat of a serious decline in monetary reserves. However, the corollary of the Ad Note was that where no such threat of or actual serious decline in monetary reserves existed, the provisions of paragraph 11, *i.e., "shall eliminate them when conditions no longer justify such maintenance"*, required the immediate elimination of the restrictions. The Ad Note applied in only one possible case: if, and only if, removal of India's import restrictions would result in balance-of-payments conditions meeting the specific criteria of the proviso in paragraph 9. Otherwise, India could not rely on the Ad Note to maintain its restrictions.

3.180 India had referred to the Ad Note 11 and alleged that Article XVIII:11 gave a Member a "right" to maintain import restrictions "even when there is no immediate balance-of-payments need in terms of Article XVIII:9". This interpretation would eviscerate Article XVIII:11 of any content. The Note Ad XVIII:11 referred only to the provisions in Article XVIII:9 concerning action to "forestall the threat of, or to stop, a serious decline in its monetary reserves, or in the case of a contracting party with inadequate monetary reserves, to achieve a reasonable rate of increase in its reserves". In other words, the Ad Note applied only when relaxation of restrictions would cause a "serious decline in monetary reserves". The IMF had already dealt with this issue, by finding that India could eliminate its import restrictions without creating any balance-of-payments problems or indeed any adjustment burden. Indeed, the IMF's conclusion had been that elimination of import restrictions would only *strengthen* India's balance-of-payments position. India now had no balance-of-payments problem justifying restrictions. If India were to have a balance-of-payments problem in the future, it remained free to reinvoke Article XVIII:B and impose price-based measures consistent with the provisions of the Understanding on the Balance-of-Payments Provisions of the GATT 1994. But India could not keep its existing, highly-restrictive import licensing scheme in the absence of any *present* balance-of-payments justification. If accepted, India's interpretation of Article XVIII:11 would render the phrase "shall eliminate them when conditions no longer justify such maintenance" a nullity and any Member could claim it needed decades to phase out restrictions after its balance-of-payments justification had ended. Under India's interpretation, it would never be possible to establish whether or not the test of the Ad Note had been met.

3.181 In the view of the United States, in order to rule that India had met the conditions set forth in the Ad Note, the Panel would need to make certain factual findings about India's economy, such as a finding that India's reserve position would be threatened with a serious decline. It was the position of the United States that India had the burden of proof on this issue and that India had not even established a *prima facie* case (let alone overcome the proof that the United States had submitted). In the event the Panel were to rule that the United States had the burden to make a *prima facie* case on the absence of such a threat from the removal of the restrictions, the United States would point, *inter alia*, to the findings of the IMF delivered at the January 1997 Committee consultation and the statements by India. India had provided no factual evidence from which the Panel could make findings that India was faced with such a threat or actual serious decline in its monetary reserves from the removal of the restrictions. India's mere unsubstantiated assertions about the facts could not substitute for proof of the actual facts.[155]

3.182 With respect to India's invocation of an alleged right to progressive relaxation pending a decision by the General Council, the United States countered that Article XVIII:11 stated, with no ambiguity, that India "shall eliminate [its measures] when conditions no longer justify their maintenance." Article XVIII:11 did *not* say that India "shall eliminate [its measures] when advised to do so by the General Council." The absence of any textual support for India's position meant that, in the words of Article 31 of the Vienna Convention, India's position could not be supported by "the ordinary meaning to be given to the terms of the treaty in their context and in the light of its object and purpose."

4. *Removal of Restrictions According to Article XVIII:11, Article XVIII:12(c)(ii) and Paragraph 13 of the Understanding*

3.183 At the request of the Panel, the Parties provided their views on the question of whether there should be a differentiation in legal terms between: on the one hand,

> gradual relaxation which might be legal under Article XVIII:11 and the Note Ad Article XVIII:11, and, on the other hand
>
> gradual removal of restrictions as provided for in Article XVIII:12(c)(ii) and paragraph 13 of the 1994 Understanding.

3.184 The **United States** argued that when measures were justified under Article XVIII:B, a time period in which to remove them - for as long as those balance-

[155] The United States referred to p. 335 of *Wool Shirts*, WT/DS33/AB/R, Op. Cit, DSR 1997:I, 323.

of-payments difficulties continued - was also justified by Article XVIII:B. With respect to measures for which there was no balance-of-payments justification the United States was of the view that Article XVIII:B did not apply, nor did Article XVIII:12(c) and Paragraph 13 of the 1994 Understanding.[156] To the extent that a Member wished to retain measures for which there was no balance-of-payments justification, that Member must either meet the requirements of provisions of the GATT 1994 other than Article XVIII:B, or must obtain the consent of the WTO pursuant to the appropriate waiver provisions of the WTO Agreement (e.g., Article XXV:5 of GATT 1994 or Article IX:3 of the WTO Agreement).

3.185 India submitted that there were actually three separate situations with distinct legal consequences covered by the Panel's question:

(a) Progressive relaxation and elimination of import restrictions maintained under Article XVIII:B in accordance with Article XVIII:11 of the GATT prior to a determination of an inconsistency by the Committee;

(b) Gradual removal of import restrictions within a period specified by the Committee under Article XVIII:12(c)(ii); and

(c) Progressive relaxation and elimination of import restrictions in accordance with a time-schedule presented pursuant to paragraphs 1 and 13 of the 1994 Understanding.

(a) Progressive relaxation and elimination under Article XVIII

3.186 **India** argued that an analysis of the provisions of Article XVIII:B confirms that import restrictions maintained by a Member in good faith cannot be considered inconsistent with Article XVIII:11 until the Committee determines that these import restrictions lack justification.

(i) Under Article XVIII:9, a Member may impose import restrictions in order to safeguard its balance of payments without prior authorization by the WTO subject to the limitations contained in the proviso to paragraph 9 and paragraphs 10 and 11 of Article XVIII:B. Thus, the agreed drafting history of Articles XVIII:B records in the context of Article XII that:

> After a detailed consideration of the various proposals put forward with a view to establishing stricter rules for the introduction and maintenance of quantitative restrictions through the institution of fixed time limits and approval by the CONTRACTING

[156] Accordingly, because the United States considered that India did not have balance-of-payments problems justifying the challenged measures, the United States did not invoke these provisions in its request for the establishment of a panel in this dispute.

> PARTIES, the Working Party came to the conclusion that such proposals would not find general acceptance among the contracting parties, but that, on the other hand, the general opinion was in favour of strengthening and widening the scope of consultations under Article XII, as well as under Article XIV.[157]

3.187 The only mechanism specifically referred to in Article XVIII:B for enforcing the limitations on import restrictions for balance-of-payments purposes (in the proviso to paragraph 9 and in paragraphs 10 and 11 of Article XVIII:B) was the consultation mechanism provided in Article XVIII:12. Under subparagraphs (c)(i) and (c)(ii) of Article XVIII:12, the Committee was under an affirmative obligation to inform the Member if it determined during consultations that its restrictions were inconsistent with Article XVIII:B or Article XIII.

3.188 A Member always ran the risk that the Committee would find that its import restrictions were inconsistent with Article XVIII:11 because they lacked balance-of-payments justification. As a result, a Member invoking Article XVIII:B had an incentive to progressively relax and eliminate its import restrictions as its balance-of-payments difficulties lessened. However, the Note *Ad* Article XVIII:11 provided that the Committee should not require relaxation or elimination of import restrictions where such relaxation or elimination could result in conditions justifying the intensification or introduction of import restrictions. Thus, the Note Ad Article XVIII:11 required the Committee to take considerations of prudence and precaution into account prior to requiring elimination.

3.189 In the case of India's import restrictions, a significant proportion of the membership of the Committee had found that India's time-schedule was justified precisely because they took into account the considerations referred to in the Note Ad Article XVIII:11. As a result, *the Committee had not determined that India's residual import restrictions were inconsistent with Article XVIII:11* which the Committee was obligated to do either under sub-paragraph (i) or sub-paragraph (ii) of Article XVIII:12(c) if it found that India's residual import restrictions were not justified during consultations. India believed that the Panel must take this into account when reviewing the legal status of India's import restrictions after consultations. As the Appellate Body pointed out in *EC Hormones*, a precautionary principle cannot be introduced into a treaty provision on the ground that it is a customary principle of international law in the absence of a clear textual directive to do so.[158] However, the Note Ad Article XVIII:11 definitely constituted such a clear textual directive. Accordingly, India should be

---

[157] *Report of the Review Working Party on Quantitative Restrictions*, L/332/Rev.1 and Addenda, adopted on 2, 4 and 5 March 1955, BISD 3S/170, 171, paragraph 4.

[158] *EC Measures Concerning Meat and Meat Products (Hormones)*, WT/DS26/AB/R, para. 124.

permitted to phase out its import restrictions in accordance with its time-schedule for the progressive relaxation and elimination of its import restrictions.

(b) Article XVIII:12(c)(ii)

3.190 The **United States** considered that there were two reasons why Article XVIII:12(c)(ii) did not provide a basis for a gradual reduction of measures without balance-of-payments justification. First, Article XVIII:12(c)(ii) related to measures that were balance-of-payments-justified but impermissibly applied (e.g., in violation of Article XIII or Article XVIII:10). This interpretation was consistent with the text of the first sentence of Article XVIII:12(c)(ii) which used the phrase "restrictions are being *applied* in a manner involving an inconsistency of a serious nature with the provisions of *this* section or with those of Article XIII ... ." (emphasis supplied). Second, as a matter of GATT practice, the consultations provisions of Article XII:4(c) (the counterpart in Article XII to Article XVIII:12(c)) had not been applied when Germany and Italy were required to remove their balance-of-payments restrictions. In both those cases, the Balance-of-Payments Committee had taken the view, when the IMF declared that those countries' balance-of-payments situations no longer justified restrictions, that it would not be appropriate to continue consultations under Article XII.[159]

3.191 **India** contended that the periodic consultations process under Article XVIII:12 was intended to monitor issues relating to justification under Article XVIII:11 and Article XVIII:9 as well as application under Article XVIII:10 and Article XIII. Thus, paragraph (b) of Article XVIII:12 provided for periodic consultations - of the type envisaged by Article XVIII:12(a) - at roughly two-year intervals to review import restrictions maintained by each Member under Article XVIII:B. The issues to be reviewed included "the nature of [the Member's] balance of payments difficulties, alternative corrective measures which may be available, and the possible effect of the restrictions on the economies of other contracting parties". Paragraph (c) of Article XVIII:12 provided for the actions that the Committee might take in the course of and after consultations. When the Committee determined that the import restrictions involved a "minor or a technical"[160] inconsistency, subparagraph (i) of Article XVIII:12 (c) provided that the Committee "shall indicate the nature of the inconsistency and may advise that the restrictions be suitably modified". Where the Committee determined that the import restrictions "are being applied in a manner involving an inconsistency of a serious nature with the provisions of [Article XVIII:B] or with those of Article XIII ... and that damage to the trade of any contracting party is caused or threatened thereby", subparagraph (ii) provided that it "shall so inform the [Member invoking Article XVIII:B] and shall make appropriate recommendations for se-

[159] L/644, approved 22 November 1957, para. 45 (Germany); L/1088, approved 17 November 1959 (Italy).
[160] *Report of the Review Working Party on Quantitative Restrictions*, Op. Cit. 1, para. 9.

curing conformity with such provisions within a specified period". Thus, regardless of whether the inconsistency was of a minor or a serious nature, the Committee was under an affirmative obligation to inform the Member invoking Article XVIII:B of the inconsistency and to advise it how to bring its import restrictions into conformity with the relevant provision of Article XVIII:B or Article XIII.

3.192 India noted that the United States had argued that the power of the Committee under Article XVIII:12(c)(ii) to secure conformity with the provisions of Article XVIII:B "within a specified period" extended only to cases of inconsistency with Article XVIII:10 and Article XIII and not to cases where import restrictions lacked justification under Article XVIII:11. Therefore, according to the United States, a Member whose import restrictions lacked justification must eliminate its restrictions immediately. India presumed that the argument by the United States was because Article XVIII:12(c)(ii) referred to "restrictions ... being *applied in a manner* involving an inconsistency of a serious nature with the provisions of this Section ...". On the other hand, the United States had firmly denied that there was any distinction between "application" and "justification" with respect to the second sentence of the footnote to the 1994 Understanding. India expressed the view that the United States should be consistent in its arguments: either there was a distinction for purposes of both the footnote to the 1994 Understanding *and* Article XVIII:12(c)(ii) or there was none.

3.193 According to India, the United States' interpretation of Article XVIII:12(c)(ii) was not consistent with its context or the object and purpose of Article XVIII:B. Clearly, Article XVIII:12(b) - read with Article XVIII:12(a) - contemplated consultations with a Member on the justification of its import restrictions. However, on the United States' interpretation of Article XVIII:12(c)(ii), if the Committee determined during consultations that the Member's import restrictions lacked justification under Article XVIII:11, there were two possibilities: either the Committee could treat it as a minor inconsistency under Article XVIII:12(c)(i); alternatively, the Committee was not empowered to take action on justification issues under either of the sub-paragraphs of Article XVIII:12(c). The second was clearly not a plausible interpretation. The United States had admitted in this dispute that working parties and the Committee had been examining the justification of Members' import restrictions under Articles XII and XVIII:B for decades and had been requiring the elimination of restrictions. Moreover, this interpretation was inconsistent with the purpose of consultations as defined in the agreed drafting history of Article XVIII:B.

3.194 India suggested that the apparent view of the United States, that lack of justification under Article XVIII:12(c) was a minor inconsistency meriting action by the Committee only under Article XVIII:12(c)(i), would hardly be a credible legal characterization of the seriousness of the inconsistency. In any case, even under Article XVIII:12(c)(i), the Committee could still authorize a Member to "modify" its import restrictions over time rather than eliminating them immediately. The purpose of permitting a specified period to eliminate restrictions under Article XVIII:12(c)(i) would be the same as under Article XVIII:12(c)(ii), i.e., to take account of the need to mitigate the balance of payments effects of immediate elimination by permitting it to be done over time. India suggested that another plausible policy-based reason for giving a Member "a specified period" under Article XVIII:12(c)(ii) even in the case of a serious inconsistency with Article XIII, for example, was that domestic adjustment difficulties might render it extremely difficult for a Member to eliminate its import restrictions overnight. (India added that only the former consideration should apply when considering the justification of import restrictions under Article XVIII:11.)

3.195 India considered there were good reasons why Members should be permitted to eliminate their import restrictions over a period of time even in the case of a minor inconsistency. Whether the issue of justification fell under subparagraph (i) or (ii) of Article XVIII:12(c), the Committee had the power to recommend that the import restrictions be eliminated over a specified period rather than immediately even after determining that the import restrictions at issue lacked justification.

(c) Paragraph 13 of the 1994 Understanding

3.196 The **United States** argued that paragraph 13 of the 1994 Understanding related to measures that were balance-of-payments-justified at the time of consultations in the Committee but for which the balance-of-payments situation was improving. The United States considered that the text of the 1994 Understanding made clear that the Understanding applied only to measures for which a balance-of-payments justification was still present. Paragraph 4 made that point: "restrictive import measures taken for balance-of-payments purposes ... may not exceed what is necessary to address the balance-of-payments situation." Similarly, the text of Paragraph 11(a) provided that the plan for consultations should include "an overview of the balance-of-payments situation *and prospects* ... and the domestic policy measures taken in order to *restore* equilibrium on a sound and lasting basis." These words in paragraphs 4 and 11(a) would not have been used if measures were to be applied and consultations held *after* the end of a balance-of-payments "situation". Footnote 1 to the 1994 Understanding provided that the Understanding could not modify India's rights; therefore, the 1994 Understanding could not provide India with a right to phase out its restrictions gradually because that right did not exist under Article XVIII:12(c) (or any other provisions of Article XVIII:B). Paragraph 13 did provide that, if a consensus was reached with respect to a balance-of-payments situation that was easing, the Member applying balance-of-payments measures could be "deemed to be in compliance with its GATT 1994 obligations". That provision applied when a Member with *current* balance-of-payments difficulties proposed a plan to remove its restrictions over time; if the plan was accepted by a consensus within the Balance-of-Payments Committee and approved by the General Council, that Member might then carry out that plan even if its balance-of-payments difficulties came to an end *sooner*.

3.197 In **India**'s view, the right to a time-schedule for the removal of import restrictions that did not meet the criteria set out in Article XVIII:9 within a period specified by the Council was reflected in paragraph 13 of the 1994 Understanding, which provided:

> "In those cases in which a time-schedule has been presented for the removal of restrictive measures taken for balance-of-payments purposes, the General Council may recommend that in adhering to such a time-schedule, a Member shall be deemed to be in compliance with its GATT 1994 obligations. Whenever the General Council has made specific recommendations, the rights and obligations of Members shall be assessed in the light of such recommendations."

3.198 India considered that the 1994 Understanding represented an attempt by the Uruguay Round negotiators to introduce new disciplines with respect to balance-of-payments restrictions in the GATT 1994, and that paragraphs 1 and 11(d) of the 1994 Understanding appeared to impose an obligation on Members to publicly announce a time-schedule and to submit it to the Committee as a part of the consultations process. However, this obligation might not be legally enforceable because the first sentence of the footnote to the 1994 Understanding provides that "[n]othing in this Understanding is intended to modify the rights and obligations of Members under ... Article XVIII:B ...". Nevertheless, a Member could not refuse a request from the Committee to provide it with a time-schedule because the Committee could always recommend disinvocation of Article XVIII:B. For example, in the context of Sri Lanka's failure to properly notify its import restrictions under Article XVIII:B, the *Analytical Index* noted that:

> "In its Report on the simplified consultation held with Sri Lanka in 1994, the Committee came to the following "interim conclusion": 'In the absence of precise information on import restrictions maintained for balance-of-payments purposes, the Committee was unable to conclude the simplified consultation with Sri Lanka. The Committee requested Sri Lanka to notify, by tariff line, import restrictions, if any, maintained for BOP purposes, or to disinvoke Article XVIII:B....' Sri Lanka made the requested notification in October 1994."[161]

3.199 Further, Members had an incentive to submit a time-schedule under paragraph 13 of the 1994 Understanding regardless of whether their import restrictions were currently justified under Article XVIII:B. The third sentence of this paragraph provided that in accepting a favourable recommendation from the Committee on a Member's time-schedule under paragraph 13, the General Council "... may recommend that in adhering to such a time-schedule, a Member shall be deemed to be in compliance with its GATT 1994 obligations". Under para-

[161] *Analytical Index: Guide to GATT Law and Practice*, Vol. I, p. 381.

graph 13, a Member's rights and obligations would have to be assessed in the light of any of the General Council recommendation[s]. The effect of this provision was that, unlike under Article XVIII:12(c), a Member's time-schedule could be insulated against potential challenges in the Committee on the basis of lack of justification under Article XVIII:11 for the period specified in the time-schedule regardless of its current balance-of-payments situation or changes therein. The only limitation on this legal protection was if the Member failed to adhere faithfully to its time-schedule.

3.200 India considered that paragraphs 1 and 13 of the 1994 Understanding represented an incentive to a Member maintaining import restrictions under Article XVIII:B to present a time-schedule regardless of its current balance-of-payments situation. Thus, the language of the third sentence of paragraph 13 could also be interpreted as providing immunity in cases where there might not be any current balance-of-payments justification. Therefore, as in the case of Article XVIII:12(c)(ii), paragraph 13 could be interpreted also as providing a period to eliminate import restrictions under Article XVIII:B in order to encourage Members to submit a time-schedule.

3.201 In India's view, paragraph 13 of the 1994 Understanding also clarified the legal status of different proposals for recommendations by the Committee to the General Council. The Committee was required to make "proposals for recommendations aimed at promoting implementation of Articles XII, XVIII:B, the 1979 Declaration and the 1994 Understanding". A proposal for a favourable recommendation by the General Council with respect to a Member's time-schedule would give the Member immunity from all challenges, current and future, to its import restrictions. However, the last sentence of paragraph 13 contemplated the possibility that there would be a divergence of opinion within the Committee resulting in the absence of a proposal from the Committee for a recommendation by the General Council. It was important to note that paragraph 13 specified the legal consequences only of explicit approval of a Member's time schedule - not of absence of approval of a Member's time-schedule. Clearly, in such a situation the legal consequences would have to be based on an analysis of the provisions of Article XVIII:B. This was confirmed by the first sentence of the footnote to the 1994 Understanding which provided that nothing in the 1994 Understanding was intended to modify a Member's rights and obligations under Article XVIII:B. Under Article XVIII:B, a Member's import restrictions could be considered inconsistent with Article XVIII:B only if the Committee affirmatively determined that its residual import restrictions were inconsistent with its obligations under Article XVIII:B or Article XIII of the GATT 1994.

3.202 In this dispute, India stated that it clearly fell in the category of a divergence of opinion within the Committee on approval of its time-schedule. India gave the Committee a time-schedule in response to a request from the Committee. That request from the Committee was not premised on a finding of lack of justification for India's residual import restrictions under Article XVIII:11. Rather, India viewed the request of the Committee as based upon the provisions of paragraphs 1 and 11(d) of the 1994 Understanding and submitted a time-schedule in the light of the incentive available in paragraph 13 for time-schedules which are approved by the General Council. After considering India's proposed time-schedule, the Committee did not either explicitly approve or disapprove India's time-schedule under Article XVIII:B. Therefore, no specific proposal for a recommendation of the General Council resulted. The General Council in turn did not make any specific recommendations in the light of which India's rights or obligations could be assessed.

3.203 Accordingly, India contended that the legal status of its residual import restrictions at this time must be assessed in light of the provisions of Article XVIII:B. Based on an analysis of India's obligations under Article XVIII:11, the Note *Ad* Article XVIII:11, Article XVIII:12(c) and the provisions of the 1994 Understanding, it was clear that the divergence of opinion within the Committee on proposing that the General Council favourably recommend India's time-schedule could not adversely affect the legal status of its residual import restrictions under Article XVIII:B. Under Article XVIII:12(c), if the Committee found that import restrictions were not justified under Article XVIII:11, the Committee was under an obligation to inform the Member of this inconsistency. The Committee had not done so in this case. In fact, a significant proportion of the Committee had found that India's residual import restrictions were justified. Therefore, in accordance with the reasoning of the *Korea - Beef* panel, India submitted that the Panel also should find that India's residual import restrictions were consistent with Article XVIII:B.

3.204 India added that Articles 19:1 and 21 of the DSU required that a Member must bring an illegal measure promptly into conformity with its obligations. This requirement applied to measures the Member concerned should never have introduced and it was only reasonable that Members should eliminate such measures promptly. In contrast, Article XVIII:12 and paragraph 13 of the 1994 Understanding provided that a Member having notified import restrictions under Article XVIII:B might be required to eliminate such measures within a period specified by the Council or a time-schedule approved by the Council. These rules and procedures applied to import restrictions that have been maintained legally. It would not be reasonable to require Members, in such a situation, to remove measures within the time-frame envisaged in Articles 19.1 and 21 of the DSU.[162]

---

[162] India considered that it was worth noting in this context that time-schedules for the gradual removal of restrictive import measures maintained for many years were negotiated in the Uruguay Round in the following areas:

- The Agreement on Textiles and Clothing provides a time-schedule of ten years divided into three phases for the elimination of import restrictions on textile and clothing products;
- the Agreement on Agriculture provides for a time-schedule of six years for the reduction commitments on market access, domestic support and export subsidies, with the flexibility of a time-schedule of ten years for developing country Members;
- the Marrakesh Protocol to the GATT 1994 provides for a time-schedule of five years for the implementation of tariff reductions;

5. *Article XVIII:B: Special and Differential Treatment*

3.205 According to **India**, Article XVIII:B was the most important expression of the principle of special and differential treatment of less-developed countries in the GATT. Article XVIII:9 permitted a less-developed country Member to resort to import restrictions in order to safeguard its balance of payments and to ensure adequate reserves to implement its programme of economic development. In assessing the reserves, or need for reserves, of a Member, Article XVIII:9 also required certain special factors to be taken into account including the availability of "special external credits or other resources...; and, the need to provide for the appropriate use of such credits or resources".

3.206 India noted that the above criteria in Article XVIII:9 were linked to the criteria prescribed in Article XVIII:11 for the progressive relaxation and removal of restrictions. The first sentence of Article XVIII:11 required a Member imposing import restrictions to keep in mind two objectives: first, the restoration of "equilibrium in its balance of payments on a sound and lasting basis"; and, second, "an economic employment of productive resources". However, as external and domestic conditions improved, a Member must progressively relax its import restrictions, maintaining them only to the extent necessary under the terms of Article XVIII:9, and must eliminate them when conditions no longer justified such maintenance. Thus, the right to maintain import restrictions under Article XVIII:11 was tied to the larger problem of balance-of-payments difficulties and the economic development needs of less-developed country Members but, at the same time, the extent of import restrictions was dependent upon the criteria for monetary reserves laid down in clauses (a) and (b) of Article XVIII:9.

3.207 India stated that Article XVIII:B provided explicitly for special and differential treatment of developing countries, in particular by permitting them to phase out their import restrictions gradually in accordance with the note to Article XVIII:11, an option not available to developed countries. Article XVIII:B recognized indirectly the applicability of the precautionary principle to the balance-of-payments policies of developing countries because, unlike Article XII, it did not require an *imminent* threat to the reserves and therefore permitted a progressive relaxation designed to forestall a more distant threat to the reserves.

3.208 India considered that the provisions of Article XVIII:B of the GATT 1994 embodied a presumption that less-developed country Members would face balance-of-payments difficulties on account of economic development. Thus, Article XVIII:2 explicitly recognized that less-developed country Members might need to apply import restrictions "... in order to implement programmes and policies of

---

- the Agreement on Trade-Related Investment Measures provides for a time-schedule for the elimination of notified TRIMs of two years for developed country Members, five years for developing country Members and seven years for least-developed country Members.
- the Understanding on the Interpretation of Article XXIV of the GATT 1994 grants WTO Members the flexibility of a time-schedule of 10 years normally to form a free-trade area or customs union.

economic development designed to raise the general standard of living of their people". Further, Article XVIII:8 of the GATT 1994 explicitly recognized that less-developed country Members tend, during a "... rapid process of development, to experience balance-of-payments difficulties arising mainly from efforts to expand their internal markets as well as from the instability in their terms of trade". Moreover, the sequence of the terms of Article XVIII:11 suggested that there was a dynamic linkage between domestic policy reform and improvements in the balance of payments and that such improvements would enable Members to progressively relax and eliminate import restrictions as the balance-of-payments situation improved. Therefore, Article XVIII:11 was premised upon the notion that trade liberalization must follow upon improvements in the balance-of-payments situation and not *vice versa*. Again, although the preamble to the 1979 Declaration recognized the inefficiency inherent in import restrictions, it also emphasized the right of a less-developed country to maintain import restrictions to be evaluated in the context of its "individual development, financial and trade situation". Accordingly, there was no requirement in Article XVIII:B that a Member must provide evidence that maintaining import restrictions would result in improvements in its balance-of-payments or, conversely, that the removal of import restrictions would cause deterioration in its balance of payments. In view of the presumption underlying Article XVIII:B, the burden was on the United States to establish that maintaining import restrictions would not result in improvement, or would cause a deterioration, in India's balance of payments.

3.209 In response, the **United States** noted that the text of Article XVIII (which contained provisions that Article XII did not) reflected the special and differential treatment that the negotiators of that Article agreed upon, and the 1955 Report made explicit that balance-of-payments measures under Article XVIII were to be used sparingly and within a legal framework of rights and obligations reflected in the text of Article XVIII. For example, within this legal framework, Article XVIII:C recognized policies such as protection for infant industries (as long as compensation was made available to other Members in accordance with the requirements of that Section), while Article XVIII:B was intended to address specific problems related to a Member's balance-of-payments situation. India had both the benefits as well as the obligations that the text of Article XVIII reflected.

3.210 The United States noted that India had referred to the provisions of Article XVIII:2 and 8, which describe the special considerations applicable to developing country Members. There was no doubt that - *if a balance-of-payments basis for trade measures existed* - then those factors applied in assessing the measures adopted in response. This did not mean, however that India, or this Panel, could ignore the fundamental limitation on balance-of-payments measures: namely, that the proviso in Article XVIII:9 be met. The United States considered that one could see that this was the correct interpretation of Article XVIII:2 and 8 by considering the object and purpose of Article XVIII:B, as expressed in Article XVIII:8: to the extent that developing country Members tend to experience balance-of-payments difficulties in the course of development, and therefore Article XVIII:B is intended to provide a response *to those difficulties*. However, for a country such as India which did not have balance-of-payments difficulties, the question of *how* balance-of-payments measures should be applied did not arise.

3.211 With respect to India's argument about a precautionary principle, the United States considered that on the facts of this case - that India's balance-of-payments position was excellent in January of 1997, had remained excellent since that time, and in the view of the IMF would in fact be better if the quantitative restrictions under challenge were removed; and that there was no threat of a serious decline in India's monetary reserves - India was not a candidate for any "prudential or precautionary" measures.

3.212 As to India's argument that Article XVIII:11 set forth a "dynamic linkage" in which progressive relaxation of import restrictions led to an improvement in a Member's balance-of-payments position, which in turn led to more relaxation, which in turn led to balance-of-payments improvements, and so on, the flaw with this argument was that the IMF repeatedly had concluded that India *could* and *should* eliminate the restrictions at issue in this dispute in a short period of time. In fact, Article XVIII:11 expressly contemplated that a Member applying measures for balance-of-payments purposes would both relax them - as India had been doing - and would eliminate them. The IMF's determinations meant that the liberalizations initiated by India in 1991 had now led to a point where India no longer had balance-of-payments difficulties or the threat of them, and India's GATT 1994 obligations to its fellow Members, developed and developing, required that India take the step of eliminating its measures now.

6. *Article XVIII:10 and the 1994 Understanding*

3.213 **India** requested the Panel not to rule on the consistency of India's import restrictions with Article XVIII:10 of the GATT 1994 or any of the provisions of the 1994 Understanding. as the United States had not referred to these or any other provisions of GATT 1994 in its request.

3.214 India referred to *India-Patent Protection for Agricultural and Pharmaceutical Chemical Products* case (*Patents*) in which the Appellate Body found that a claim must be included in the request for establishment of a Panel.[163] In this case, the Appellate Body found that the failure of the United States to refer specifically to Article 63 of the Agreement on Trade-Related Intellectual Property Rights (the "TRIPS Agreement") in its request for establishment of a panel disentitled it from raising this provision later. In that case, the Appellate Body also noted that a general reference by the United States in its request to the inconsistency of India's legal regime with "the obligations of the TRIPS Agreement including but not necessarily limited to Articles 27, 65 and 70" was not sufficient

[163] Appellate Body Report on *India-Patent Protection for Agricultural and Pharmaceutical Chemical Products*, WT/DS50AB/R, 19 December 1997, Op. Cit.

to permit it to challenge the measures at issue in that case as being inconsistent with Article 63. The Appellate Body reasoned that:

> "With respect to Article 63, the convenient phrase, "including but not necessarily limited to", is simply not adequate to "identify the specific measures at issue and provide a brief summary of the legal basis of the complaint sufficient to present the problem clearly" as required by Article 6.2 of the DSU."

3.215 In the present case, the United States' request for the establishment of a panel cited specifically only Article XI:1 and Article XVIII:11 of the GATT and did not even contain the phrase "including, but not limited to, other provisions of the GATT". In the *Patents* case, the Appellate Body pointed out that even inclusion of such a phrase in the request for establishment of a panel did not authorize the panel to deal with claims not covered by the terms of reference. Accordingly, the United States could not make a legal claim that India's import restrictions were inconsistent with provisions of Article XVIII:B other than Article XVIII:11 or of any of the provisions of the 1994 Understanding.

3.216 India contended that the provisions of the 1994 Understanding were not mentioned in the terms of reference. According to the Appellate Body the request for the establishment of a panel must refer to the specific provisions on which the legal claims were based; otherwise it did not meet the requirement in Article 6:2 of the DSU that such a request identify the specific measures at issue.[164] More importantly, the United States had, at the first meeting of the Panel, explicitly stated that it was *not* invoking the provisions of the 1994 Understanding. The provisions of the 1994 Understanding thus clearly did not form part of the complaint submitted by the United States. In this connection, India pointed out again that the Appellate Body recognized that panels could not make findings beyond those requested by the parties to the dispute.[165]

3.217 In response to a question from the Panel, India pointed out that the requirement to give preference to price-based measures was set out in paragraph 3 of the 1994 Understanding. The issue of the use of import restrictions on selected products was addressed in Article XVIII:10 and paragraph 4 of the 1994 Understanding. India noted that the United States had not only not referred specifically to any of these provisions in its request for establishment of a panel, it had not sought any findings on any of these provisions in its submission for the first meeting of the Panel. Therefore, India requested the Panel not to address these issues. India nevertheless wished to point out the following: all of India's remaining import restrictions predated the 1994 Understanding. Therefore, none of them were "new" import restrictions within the meaning of paragraph 3 of the 1994 Understanding. According to paragraph 3 of the 1994 Understanding, the

[164] Appellate Body Report on *India-Patent Protection for Agricultural and Pharmaceutical Chemical Products*, WT/DS50AB/R, 19 December 1997, para. 90, Op. Cit.

[165] Appellate Body Report on EC *Hormones*, WT/DS26/AB/R; WT/DS48/AB/R, paras. 155-156.

obligations to give preference to price-based measures applied only when "new" import restrictions were imposed. The context suggested that import restrictions that were in place on 1 January 1995 were not "new" import restrictions within the meaning of that provision. This provision therefore did not apply to India's import restrictions.

3.218 India recalled that it had explained its use of price-based measures to the Committee on Balance-of-Payments Restrictions (the "Committee") as follows: "Quantitative restrictions are inefficient, but guarantee, in the Indian context, a level of certainty which price-based measures cannot."[166] In any case, the policy of India was to phase out the import restrictions progressively, replacing them by macro-economic policies rather than by price-based import controls which was in the interest of all Members. India had consistently pursued this policy since 1991 irrespective of its balance-of-payments situation.

3.219 To the knowledge of India, none of the restrictive regimes examined by the Committee applied across-the-board to all products. There was therefore nothing unusual about the product-selective nature of India's import restrictions. About ten years earlier, Indian import restrictions had applied to most imports; at present, however, they covered only about one fourth of the HS-lines that were subject to import restrictions at that time. In any case, the product-selective nature of India's import restrictions was mainly a consequence of the decision of the Indian Government to progressively liberalize its import regime. Despite being product-selective, the import restrictions were nevertheless designed to control the level of total imports. The first part of India's movement from a policy of import-substitution industrialization to export-driven growth was based on structural reforms that required India to liberalize imports of capital goods and industrial intermediates and raw materials. Simultaneous liberalization of consumer goods imports would have detracted from India's ability to sustain its structural reforms on the balance-of-payments front. India also wished to place on record that, despite this dispute initiated by the United States, India continued to adhere to the time-schedule for progressive relaxation and elimination of its remaining import restrictions that it had proposed and negotiated with its trading partners.

3.220 The focus on consumer products was consistent with Article XVIII:10 which explicitly recognized that a Member "may determine [the] incidence of [import restrictions] on imports of different products or classes of products in such a way as to give priority to the importation of those products which are more essential in the light of its policy of economic development". In fact, in the context of permitting the selective application of surcharges for balance-of-payments reasons, paragraph 4 of the 1994 Understanding also explicitly recognized that capital goods or inputs needed for production "contribute to the Member's efforts to improve its balance-of-payments situation".

[166] WT/BOP/R/22/ pp, 7 and 8.

3.221 The **United States** pointed out that it had not claimed violation of Article XVIII:10 because the import restrictions were not restrictions with valid balance-of-payments justification. It considered that under Article 7.1 of the DSU, the terms of reference of the Panel were "to examine, in light of the relevant provisions in ... the covered agreement(s) cited by the parties to the dispute ... ". The United States cited the GATT 1994 in its request for establishment of a panel in this matter.[167] Pursuant to the "Incorporation Clause," the 1994 Understanding formed an integral part of the GATT 1994 and was therefore part of the Panel's terms of reference. The United States considered that the 1994 Understanding applied to measures in force on or after 1 January 1995. The GATT 1994 Incorporation Clause provided for only one general exemption from the GATT 1994, the exemption in paragraph 3 of the Incorporation Clause, which did not apply to the challenged measures. Furthermore, where drafters of the WTO Agreement wished to exempt measures, or to establish transitional arrangements, they had been able to do so expressly.

7. *Arguments Drawn from Consultations in the Committee on Balance-of-Payments Restrictions*

3.222 The **United States** recalled that one of the fundamental principles of the GATT was that imports from WTO Members shall be free from prohibitions or restrictions other than duties, taxes and other charges. This rule, provided in Article XI:1 of the GATT 1994, applied to all prohibitions or restrictions, whether made effective through quotas, import licences or other measures. Article XVIII:4 and Article XVIII:B permitted a WTO Member "the economy of which can only support low standards of living and is in the early stages of development" to deviate temporarily from Article XI:1, if that Member satisfies certain substantive and procedural conditions. Any Member applying balance-of-payments import restrictions must consult in the WTO Committee on Balance-of-Payments Restrictions ("the Committee"); consultation and other procedural requirements were provided in GATT Articles XII and XVIII:B, the 1979 Declaration on Measures Taken for Balance-of-Payments Purposes, and the 1994 Understanding on the Balance-of-Payments Provisions of the GATT 1994.

3.223 The United States recalled that, at the time of India's simplified consultations with the Committee in 1994, India maintained the same highly restrictive import licensing system as it did at the time of the Panel proceedings, restricting (and effectively banning) imports of almost all consumer goods.[168] Recognizing the contradiction between the increasing strength of India's reserve position and balance-of-payments restrictions, the Committee encouraged India to continue import liberalization: "The Committee noted that, if the balance of payments showed sustained improvement, India's aim was to move to a regime by 1996/97,

---

[167] WT/DS90/8.

[168] "Background Paper by the Secretariat, BOP/W/159, 31 October 1994, paras. 10-12.

in which import licensing restrictions would only be maintained for environmental and safety reasons."[169] The balance of payments had indeed showed sustained improvement since 1994, but India still maintained thousands of tariff lines under licensing restrictions not maintained for environmental or safety reasons.

3.224 During the next full consultations with India in the Committee, held in December 1995, the Committee invited the IMF to participate in the consultation in accordance with Article XV:2 of GATT 1994. The IMF reiterated the call for India to phase out its import restrictions in light of its improved level of monetary reserves. In an official statement approved by the Fund's Executive Board and presented to the Committee, the IMF representative noted that India's medium-term balance-of-payments prospects looked sound, and

> "On the external front ... the quantitative restrictions on imports of consumer goods need to be eliminated, and replaced by tariffs at moderate levels. Excessive protectionism has hindered the development of this important sector of the economy. Some phasing of this process may be appropriate in view of recent exchange market pressures, the potential volatility of private capital inflows, and the need to provide adequate time for adjustment of certain domestic industries. *Nevertheless, the transition to a tariff-based import regime with no quantitative restrictions could reasonably be accomplished within a period of two years.*"[170]

In the 1995 consultations, "[m]any Members expressed concerns about the consistency of the system and methods of India's restrictive measures with the balance-of-payments provisions of GATT 1994. They had concerns about the sectoral scope of the measures in place, particularly the selective application of restrictions to consumer products". They asked for a consolidated notification of the restrictions at the HS 8-digit level.[171] The Committee "recalled India's stated aim to move, by 1996/97, to a trade regime under which quantitative restrictions are maintained only for environmental, social, health and safety reasons, provided sustained improvement was shown in its balance of payments. They also took note of the statement by the IMF that, with continued prudent macroeconomic management, the transition to a tariff-based import regime with no quantitative restrictions could reasonably be accomplished within a period of two years."[172] Statements by India concerning the purported need for import restrictions failed to convince the Committee, which did not conclude that India's im-

[169] GATT document BOP/R/221, 1 December 1994, para. 4.
[170] Report on the Consultation with India, WT/BOP/R/11, 23 January 1996, Annex II (Statement by the IMF Representative) (emphasis added).
[171] *Ibid.*, para. 17.
[172] *Ibid.*, para. 25.

port restrictions were justified under Article XVIII:B. The Committee decided to resume full consultations with India in October 1996.[173]

3.225 The United States added that, during the January 1997 full consultations, the Committee again invited the IMF to participate, in accordance with Article XV:2 of GATT 1994. In a formal statement officially approved by the Executive Board of the Fund, the IMF representative stated the IMF's finding that India's balance-of-payments and reserve positions were sound, and that import restrictions were no longer needed:

> "Early action and a clear timetable for removing the continuing QRs [quantitative restrictions] on consumer goods imports ...would help reduce distortions to investment incentives and encourage the emergence of an efficient, export-oriented consumer goods industry. Moreover, in the Fund's judgment, the external situation can be well managed using macroeconomic policy instruments without recourse to QRs. *The Fund's view, therefore, is that QRs should be removed over a relatively short period ...*"[174]

In the Committee, the IMF representative elaborated further on these comments in response to questions concerning the strengthening of India's balance-of-payments and reserves positions. Using the language of Article XVIII:B, the IMF representative stated the IMF's findings of fact:

> "(i) there had not, over the past year, been a serious decline in India's foreign exchange reserves: from end March 1996 to end December 1996 they had increased by US$2.7 billion and, in relation to imports, had remained relatively constant at around five months of import coverage;
>
> "(ii) US$19.8 billion in reserves appeared a comfortable level in relation to imports and to the stock of short-term debt (US$5 billion), rather than an inadequate or very low level; with continued broadly sound macroeconomic policies, India should be able to meet all external payment requirements without difficulties, and to weather the consequences of possible external shocks without undue disruption;
>
> "(iii) India was not faced with a threat of a serious decline in its monetary reserves; on the contrary, barring major unforeseen shocks India's reserves should continue to increase in 1997 and in the medium term, and the balance of payments could be expected to benefit from a steep decline in amortization of the exceptional financing obtained to meet the 1990-91 crisis. While the current account

[173] Report on the Consultation with India, WT/BOP/R/11, para. 27, 23 January 1996, Annex II (Statement by the IMF Representative) (emphasis added).

[174] "Report on the Consultation with India," WT/BOP/R/22, 3 March 1997, Annex II, Statement by the IMF Representative, para. 12 (emphasis added)..

deficit might widen as a result of import growth related to investment, this should be comfortably financed by rising private capital inflows;

"(iv) current quantitative restrictions imposed by India were not necessary to achieve a reasonable rate of increase in reserves; indeed, the removal of quantitative restrictions, in conjunction with other measures, could be expected to strengthen the external position over the medium term, reduce distortions to investment and encourage the emergence of an efficient consumer goods industry;

"(v) the replacement of quantitative restrictions by moderate tariffs would contribute to stability and economic success by providing revenue for deficit reduction, since the government would capture rents that now accrue to those able to obtain import licenses or bring goods into India illegally. Though the long run aim should be for Indian tariffs to fall to international levels, in the short run the replacement of quantitative restrictions by tariffs could be expected to help the revenue position."[175]

3.226 The United States added that, during the June 1997 consultations, the Committee again consulted with the IMF. The Fund representative "noted that his answers to the questions posed during the January 1997 consultations on India's balance-of-payments situation had not changed during the interim period".[176] In a formal statement officially approved by the Executive Board of the Fund, the IMF representative noted that "[f]or 1997/98, the balance of payments is expected to register another sizable surplus ... Gross official reserves are expected to increase by a further US$5 billion to over US$27 billion (six and a half months of imports)".[177] Based on these and other facts, the IMF statement again specifically found: "It remains the Fund's view that the external situation can be well managed using macroeconomic policy instruments alone; quantitative restrictions are not needed for balance-of-payments adjustments and should be removed over a relatively short time period".[178]

3.227 On these facts, the United States was of the opinion that the provisions of Article XVIII:B therefore did not entitle India to continue to maintain the challenged measures.[179]

3.228 **India** submitted that the Committee's Report on Consultations with India recorded that a significant proportion of the membership of the Committee was not convinced by the IMF "factual determinations" that the United States had

---

175 "WT/BOP/R/22, Op. Cit, p. 2, para. 8 (emphasis added).

176 "Report on the Consultations with India," WT/BOP/R/32, 18 September 1997, para. 4.

177 *Ibid.,* Annex IV, Statement by the Representative of the International Monetary Fund, para. 10.

178 *Ibid.*, para. 13.

179 India also noted that the proviso in Article XVIII:9 (unlike its counterpart in Article XII) did not require an "imminent" threat of a serious decline in reserves. It did of course still require a *threat of a serious decline* in reserves. In India's case no such threat exists or is expected.

presented before the Panel. After considering the IMF's statement, there had been a divergence of opinion within the Committee on whether India's time-schedule was no longer justified under Article XVIII:11. India submitted, therefore, that this Panel should not treat the views of the IMF expressed in its statement before the Committee as conclusive on the issue of whether India's import restrictions did not meet the requirements of Article XVIII:11. In fact, there should be a presumption against giving it any probative value in this dispute.

3.229 India submitted that the IMF's views as expressed in its statement to the Committee were not consistent with the criteria set forth in Article XVIII:11 and, therefore, could not discharge the burden of the United States under Article XVIII:B. As noted above, the first sentence of Article XVIII:11 stated that a Member imposing import restrictions under Article XVIII:B "shall pay due regard to the need to restore equilibrium in its balance-of-payments" in carrying out its domestic policies. The words "shall pay due regard to the need" indicate that this obligation to carry out particular domestic policies is not mandatory or enforceable. To impose an enforceable obligation, the first sentence of Article XVIII:11 would have used mandatory language such as "shall adopt domestic policies". Thereafter, the second sentence of Article XVIII:11 imposed the requirement that a Member must eliminate import restrictions when conditions no longer justify their maintenance. However, the proviso to this sentence made it clear that a Member could not be required to withdraw its import restrictions on the ground that a change in its development policy would render its import restrictions unnecessary. The findings of the IMF referred to by the United States were clearly inconsistent with this requirement because it stated that "the external situation can be well-managed using macroeconomic policy instruments without recourse to [import restrictions]". Macroeconomic instruments included a variety of development policy instruments such as interest rates and external policy instruments such as exchange rates. Paragraph 13 of the IMF Statement for the Committee in January 1997 contained a number of other developmental policy changes that alone would make it possible to manage India's external situation without import restrictions. Under the terms of Article XVIII:11, the determination that must be made to require elimination of QRs could not be made conditional on such changes in India's development policies. The penultimate sentence of the IMF Statement concluded that "[import restrictions] are not needed for balance-of-payments adjustment and should be removed over a relatively short time-period". Again, this did not constitute an unqualified determination that India could immediately eliminate its import restrictions without suffering any harm.

3.230 As far as India was concerned, India’s time-schedule for the progressive relaxation and elimination of its remaining import restrictions was designed to avoid renewed balance-of-payments difficulties. As India's representative explained in the Committee in January 1997, the progressive relaxation and elimination of India's remaining import restrictions was important for three reasons:

> "First, the balance-of-payments situation needs to be monitored, and the phasing should be done in a careful manner to avoid a bal-

ance-of-payments crisis ... Second, the fiscal stance of policies is still somewhat loose, and creates pressure on monetary policy as well as exchange markets. Trade liberalization has to be done in step with our fiscal consolidation. Third, there is popular democratic consensus behind reforms in India, and a gradual phase out without any risk of adverse fall out is the best guarantee for continuity of the popular support base for reforms ... Quantitative restrictions are inefficient, but guarantee, in the Indian context, a level of certainty which price-based measures cannot ... Any precipitous action on removal of quantitative restrictions which may undermine the stability of the Indian economy or the reform process itself, cannot only do great harm to India, but as well to the foreign investors and major trading partners who have a stake in the sustainable development of the Indian economy."[180]

3.231 When India presented its plan for the progressive relaxation of its import restrictions to the Committee, all members, including the United States, had accepted the principle of a progressive relaxation. The difference of views related only to the length of the phase-out period. When the Committee resumed consultations on 30 June - 1 July 1997, while other developed country Members of the Committee appeared to be willing to accept a six-year phase-out plan, the United States insisted on a shorter time-frame, suggesting that five years would be acceptable. The Committee was therefore unable to reach a consensus on India's time-schedule for the removal of its remaining import restrictions, and could not conclude the consultations with a finding on the legal status of India's import restrictions under Article XVIII:B and a recommendation to the General Council on the time-schedule for the removal of its remaining import restrictions in accordance with paragraph 13 of the 1994 Understanding. It was for this reason that a multilateral accommodation of India's phase-out plan has not yet occurred. At the origin of the dispute before the Panel was thus the insistence of a single member of the Committee that import restrictions maintained for almost 50 years be removed within a period of five rather than six years.[181]

3.232 India contended that the United States claim that the IMF had already disposed of the issue of the appropriate length of the phase-out period was both factually and legally incorrect. At the meeting of the Committee in June 1997, the representative of the IMF had made the following comments on the length of the phase-out period:

> It remains the Fund's view that the external situation can be well managed using macroeconomic policy instruments alone; QRs are

[180] WT/BOP/R/22, Op. Cit., pp. 7 and 8.
[181] WT/BOP/R32, Op. Cit., para. 33.

> not needed for balance-of-payments adjustment and should be removed over a relatively short time period.[182]

For India, this statement was an economic truism. Of course, import restrictions were not "needed" for balance-of-payments adjustment, in a technical, economic sense. Trade controls were only one instrument among many that governments use to respond to an external financial constraint. Import restrictions could always be replaced by macro-economic policy instruments. If the abstract possibility to turn from import restrictions to macro-economic policy instruments determined the right to resort to import restrictions, Members could never resort to import restrictions, and if the speed of progressive relaxation and elimination of import restrictions were determined in this manner, import restrictions would always have to be eliminated immediately. However, this approach was clearly inconsistent with Article XVIII:11, which made it clear that

> no [Member] shall be required to withdraw or modify restrictions on the ground that a change in its development policy would render unnecessary the restrictions which it is applying.

In the context of Article XVIII:11, the appropriate duration of India's time-schedule must thus be judged against the economic policies actually pursued by India, not in terms of a hypothetical change in those policies. The IMF had not provided views on that issue, wisely so because this was essentially a trade matter best judged by the Committee. India recalled that Article XVIII:11 provided that:

> In carrying out its domestic policies, the contracting party concerned shall pay due regard to the need for restoring equilibrium in its balance of payments on a sound and lasting basis and to the desirability of assuring an economic employment of productive resources. It shall progressively relax any restrictions applied under this Section as conditions improve, maintaining them only to the extent necessary under the terms of paragraph 9 of this article, and shall eliminate them when conditions no longer justify such maintenance.

3.233 For India, the context of the term "conditions" in the second sentence made it clear that it was intended to refer both to the limitations contained in Article XVIII:9 and the condition relating to equilibrium in its balance of payments on a sound and lasting basis referred to in the first sentence of Article XVIII:11. This approach to interpreting the term "conditions" was consistent with Article XVIII:9 which provided that a Member might impose import restrictions in order to safeguard its balance of payments. In addition, it was also consistent with the overall object and purpose of Article XVIII:B as set forth in Arti-

[182] WT/BOP/R32, Op. Cit., p. 29.

cle XVIII:2, i.e., to facilitate the economic development of less-developed country Members.

3.234 According to Article XVIII:11 and the Ad Note thereto, India might progressively relax its import restrictions as long as their sudden removal would jeopardize its external financial position within the framework of its existing policies. The United States had provided no evidence that these conditions were not met. The IMF statement did not support the United States' position because, the elimination of the import restrictions "within a relatively short time period" according to the IMF would only be possible if India were to change simultaneously its macro-economic policies, which India was clearly not obliged to do given the proviso in Article XVIII:11. Moreover, the competence of the IMF did not extend to all of the matters required to be taken into account by the Committee and the General Council under Article XVIII:11 and Article XVIII:9.

3.235 India noted that the IMF considered that India could remove the import restrictions in a relatively short period of time because the import restrictions could be replaced by macro-economic policy measures. However, the appropriate length of the phase-out period could not possibly be determined in that manner. Import restrictions were but one of many instruments governments used to adjust the balance-of-payments and could, in a technical or economic sense, always be replaced by macro-economic policies. If the abstract possibility to replace import restrictions with macro-economic policies were the criterion, import restrictions could never be imposed and existing import restrictions could not be progressively removed but would have to be eliminated immediately. However, both Article XII:3(d) and Article XVIII:11 made it clear that import restrictions might be maintained even if they could be replaced by other policies.

3.236 For India, the body competent to decide whether India's time-schedule met the requirement set out in the note to Article XVIII:11 was the Committee on Balance-of-Payments Restrictions. All members of that Committee except the United States had, in effect, agreed with India's time-schedule. However, even the United States accepted the principle of a progressive relaxation and elimination of restrictions. At one stage, in informal consultations of the members of the Committee, the United States indicated that a five-year phase-out period would be acceptable. India considered that the prevailing view in the Committee created a presumption that the time-schedule for the progressive relaxation and elimination of its remaining import restrictions proposed by India was consistent with Article XVIII:11. It was obvious, and therefore hardly required proof, that India could not maintain its existing development policies and eliminate, in one stroke, import restrictions affecting one-fourth of its HS-lines at the 8-digit level without a threat to its reserves. A sudden removal of the remaining import restrictions, applied mainly to consumer goods, would lead to an immediate surge of imports; the redeployment of resources for export production, however, inevitably took time because it depended on structural adjustments in India and the development of export markets. The United States still needed to explain the factual basis for the position now taken in these proceedings that India could eliminate all import restrictions immediately without a threat to its reserves.

3.237 India pointed out that all members of the Committee, including the United States, accepted the principle of a progressive removal of India's import restrictions; the differences of view concerned only the appropriateness of the duration of the time-schedule. And all members, except the United States, agreed that India's time-schedule was acceptable. India believed that the near universal view among the members of the Committee created a presumption that the schedule of progressive relaxation met the requirements of the note to Article XVIII:11.

3.238 As a result, the Committee had not determined that India's residual import restrictions were inconsistent with Article XVIII:11 which the Committee was obligated to do either under sub-paragraph (i) or sub-paragraph (ii) of Article XVIII:12(c) if it found that India's residual import restrictions were not justified during consultations. India argued that the Panel must take this into account when reviewing the legal status of India's import restrictions after consultations. As the Appellate Body pointed out in *EC - Measures Concerning Meat and Meat Products,* a precautionary principle cannot be introduced into a treaty provision on the ground that it is a customary principle of international law in the absence of a clear textual directive to do so.[183] However, the Note *Ad* Article XVIII:11 definitely constituted such a clear textual directive. Accordingly, India should be permitted to phase out its import restrictions in accordance with its time-schedule for the progressive relaxation and elimination of its import restrictions.

3.239 The **United States** countered that with respect to the Indian allegation that the United States joined in a consensus in January of 1997 to request a phase-out plan, in fact: the consultations began in 1995, at which time India anticipated removing these restrictions within two years. Furthermore, the 1997 report was clear that there was no consensus that a phase-out plan would be acceptable. Some Members (including the United States) made clear that India's restrictions should be eliminated immediately.[184] Furthermore, the report of that meeting also did not support India's allegation that a majority of the Committee were "not convinced" by the IMF's factual presentation. The Committee in fact took note of the IMF's determinations, nor did the report of the June 1997 meeting, which summarized individual Members' views, reflect that any Member challenged the findings of the IMF.[185] The Committee had not made proposals for recommendations, and the General Council had therefore not made any recommendations in relation to a time schedule for removal of the challenged measures. Consequently, India's adherence to the time schedule that it unilaterally proposed did not *ipso facto* mean that it was complying with its GATT 1994 obligations.

3.240 The United States also pointed out that it was not asking the Panel to consider the proper phasing-out period of the challenged measures. The United States considered that, under Article 19.1 of the DSU, the Panel was required, if

---

[183] *EC Measures Concerning Meat and Meat Products (Hormones),* WT/DS26/AB/R, 16 January 1998, para. 124.

[184] WT/BOP/R/22, Op. Cit., para. 9.

[185] WT/BOP/R/32, Op. Cit..

it concluded that India's measures were inconsistent with the covered agreements, to recommend that India bring its measures into conformity with that agreement.

3.241 With respect to India's arguments regarding the first sentence of Article XVIII:11, the United States contended that these provisions had to be considered in the context of Article XVIII:B, which addressed the concerns of a developing country Member faced with temporary balance-of-payments difficulties. More general development issues, such as the development of infant industries, were addressed by the entirely different provisions of Article XVIII:C. The words of Article XVIII:11 made clear that the ability to impose the restrictions authorized by Article XVIII:B was linked to an obligation to remove those restrictions.

3.242 With respect to India's arguments regarding the proviso of Article XVIII:11, the United States was not suggesting that India should change its development policies. The point was that India did not have balance-of-payments difficulties, and, given its *current* policies, was not faced with the threat of such difficulties. India was in fact utilizing a set of macroeconomic tools to carry out a development policy of trade and investment liberalization. It was the existence of those policies and India's use of those tools - tools such as the introduction of current account convertibility, the reduction of the level of its short-term debt, and the use of measures to attract foreign direct investment - that had made it possible for India to emerge from the chronic balance-of-payments crises of the past.

3.243 Moreover, the IMF's statements were not suggestions for changes in India's development policy, but expectations that India would continue along its current policy of liberalization. To quote the IMF:

(a) "With *continued* prudent macroeconomic management, India's medium-term balance-of-payments prospects look sound."

(b) "With *continued* broadly sound macroeconomic policies, India should be able to meet all external payment requirements without difficulties."

(c) "In January of 1997: "For 1996/97 as a whole, ... [g]ross international reserves *are expected* to increase ... [to] a comfortable 5 months of imports and a level that is sizable in comparison to the stock of short-term debt ... and the cumulative stock of portfolio inflows. The *present* level of the exchange rate would seem to be broadly appropriate for current circumstances, but flexibility in exchange rate management, in close coordination with other macroeconomic policy instruments, should be *maintained*." In June of that year, the same point was expressed in slightly different words.

(d) "With *continued* prudent macroeconomic policies - and especially significant fiscal adjustment - a current account deficit rising to 3-4 per cent of GDP would be consistent with the authorities' target of maintaining a debt service ratio below 20 per cent." This appeared to be one basis for the Fund's view that "the external situation can be well managed using macroeconomic policy instruments alone."

8. *Additional Evidence*

(a) The use of trade restrictions under flexible exchange rates

3.244 In response to a question from the Panel regarding the appropriateness of trade restrictions in the context of flexible exchange rates, **India** referred to the "1979 Declaration on Measures Taken for Balance-of-Payments Purposes" in which the CONTRACTING PARTIES decided that "restrictive trade measures are in general an inefficient means to maintain or restore balance-of-payments equilibrium". However, the preamble also recognized that the less-developed countries:

> "must take into account their individual development, financial and trade situation when implementing restrictive trade measures taken for balance-of-payments purposes ...".

3.245 For India, the 1979 Declaration was premised on the belief that the special and differential treatment of the less-developed countries incorporated in Article XVIII:B continued to be important despite the introduction of flexible exchange rates. Even during the Uruguay Round, the fact that CONTRACTING PARTIES decided not to tamper with this special status of the less-developed countries demonstrated convincingly that import restrictions for balance-of-payments reasons could not be judged against considerations of economic efficiency alone. The balance-of-payments exception in the GATT 1994 reflected the fact that governments faced economic, institutional, structural and political constraints that did not always allow them to opt for the most efficient policy instrument. For example, exchange rate adjustment was subject to political constraints in less-developed countries because while the benefits of exports did not cover the entire Indian economy, the rise in domestic prices of essential imports such as petroleum products could result in increases in inflation that hit the poor the hardest. The recent economic crisis in at least one South-East Asian country was a good example of this and the logic and lesson provided were also relevant to India. Particularly in the context of India's attempt to liberalize its economy simultaneously across a number of economic sectors, the increased flexibility on the balance-of-payments front made possible by import restrictions was necessary to gain increased public and political support for economic liberalization. Accordingly, if Article XVIII:B did not exist, or if its use were subjected to rigid, legalistic procedures, the constraints on exchange-rate adjustments that were applicable to the less-developed countries could not be appropriately taken into account in WTO law, and the effectiveness of that law would be jeopardized. Departures from economic efficiency, of course, were not limited only to balance-of-payments policies. Most economists were of the view that anti-dumping measures were an inefficient instrument of competition policy and that safeguard measures, including those incorporated into the Agreement on Textiles and Clothing, were an inefficient means to promote adjustment. Nevertheless, such measures might be imposed under the WTO agreements. Each of the WTO agreements constituted a compromise between high aspirations and political realities. The finely-drawn balance of rights and obligations that the negotiators of these agreements arrived at when reaching these compromises must be respected by panels, whose function was - as the Appellate Body has repeatedly found - to help enforce the results of past negotiations reflected in agreed texts.

3.246 The **United States** responded to the same Panel question by arguing that under conditions of volatile capital flows and flexible exchange rates, trade restrictions could have perverse effects on external accounts by undermining market confidence and, at best, could provide only short-term relief from balance-of-payments pressures.[186] Since it took time for the markets to react and contract prices to adjust to exchange rate changes, trade restrictions attempted to adjust the prices of imported goods or limit their availability more directly. This increase in imported goods price, or the prohibition on their importation, would decrease their consumption, and at a given exchange rate, reduce a current account deficit, stabilizing a balance-of-payments imbalance.

3.247 However, with a flexible exchange rate, imported goods prices could adjust, leading to a resumption of pressures on the current account. Further, when kept in place for extended periods, restrictions diverted resources from potential export sectors to import-competing lines of production and retarded development via the lost benefits from trade. In this case, such restrictions served as a palliative and did not remedy fundamental imbalances.[187] Instead, they could actually prolong the adjustment process.

3.248 In addition, the United States wished to point out that in paragraph 44, the 1955 Report of the Review Working Party mentioned that developing nations may need to impose controls on "the general level of their imports." However, India did not maintain restrictions on the general level of imports. Instead, India targeted 2,700 line items, most of which were consumer goods.

3.249 In the 1955 Report, the authors were writing in a world of fixed exchange rates, global capital controls, low levels of international trade resulting from generally high trade barriers, and capital markets disrupted by two World Wars and a worldwide depression. These conditions no longer prevailed, and experience with

[186] Precisely, the question was: "To what extent are trade restrictions an appropriate response to balance-of-payments difficulties in a context of flexible exchange rates and volatility of capital flows? Is the reasoning advanced in the 1955 Report of the Review Working Party on "Quantitative Restrictions" relevant in the context of more flexible exchange-rate arrangements that have been adopted in more recent years?"

[187] The United States pointed out that in India's case, the quantitative restrictions fall on consumer goods. Hence, resources are being diverted to develop domestic, consumer goods industries at the expense of exports that could generate foreign exchange.

macroeconomic management and economic development strategies in the intervening years had shown trade barriers, especially quantitative restrictions, to be inadvisable. Some developing countries might still face current account difficulties, but they had policy tools other than trade restrictions by which to expand economic growth. In most cases, a developing country could ameliorate current account crises with the appropriate mix of fiscal, structural, and monetary policies. While these direct remedies might not move a country to a current account surplus, they permitted the country to remain open to the well-developed international capital markets, thereby increasing growth rates above levels sustainable with domestic savings.

(b) The effect of trade liberalization on the balance of payments

3.250 In response to questions from the Panel regarding the pressure exerted on the balance-of-payments or international reserves by trade liberalization, the **United States** considered that even though import growth had been outpacing export growth in India, it was not fair to say that India's balance of payments had been under pressure. Due to higher net transfers from abroad, and rapid growth in the export of nonfactor services, India's current account deficit had not expanded markedly, staying below 1.5% of GDP since 1993/94 (except for 1995/96 when the deficit reached 1.7% of GDP). India's foreign exchange reserves increased steadily from US$9.8 billion at the end of 1993 to US$26.6 billion in October 1997 (a 30% annual increase). The Indian authorities sold 8.4% of their reserves in intervening to support the rupee between the end of October 1997 and the end of February 1998. However, this intervention was necessitated primarily by concerns about the Asia crisis, not trade liberalization.

3.251 Some part of import growth was undoubtedly due to the reduction of import restrictions. However, there were several other factors which deserved the bulk of the responsibility for rapid increase in the value of imports: rapid economic growth (real GDP growth has been accelerating since 1991, reaching 7.5% in FY 1996/97): a depreciating rupee (the rupee fell 25% against the dollar between the end of 1993 and the end of 1997); and climbing oil prices (in local currency).

3.252 In fact, trade liberalization tended to promote increased efficiency. The recent effort by the Indian Government to open the Indian economy had led to improved economic growth. The IMF, in its report to the WTO Balance-of-Payments Committee identified the quantitative restrictions in India as a significant impediment to efficiency.[188] The IMF staff had conveyed the view that eliminating the quantitative restrictions and establishing appropriate tariff levels would simultaneously open India's economy, raise additional tariff revenue, re-

---

[188] WT/BOP/R/22, Op. Cit., para. 8, sub-paras. iv - v.

duce the government dissavings, and increase India's already sizable foreign exchange reserve. From this assessment, the United States concurred with the IMF that India could liberalize its quantitative restriction regime in a timely fashion.

3.253 As a general point, trade liberalization and greater integration benefited developing countries. For example, after experimenting with trade restrictive import substitution policies, many Latin American countries began to open their economies up after the 1980s, leading to higher growth rates. Nevertheless, trade and capital liberalization also carries greater exposure to exchange rate and capital market volatility, so balance-of-payments pressures might arise at the same time. Their correlation, however, did not imply causation. Instead, such balance-of-payments crises might arise when a country had misaligned macroeconomic fundamentals. The appropriate response, though, to these imbalances was to address them directly instead of relying on trade restrictions. Further, there was no guarantee that maintaining trade restrictions would prevent a country from experiencing a balance-of-payments crisis. As private capital flows were orders of magnitude larger than any one country's foreign exchange reserves, it was much more important for a country to have a credible and sound macroeconomic regime. Trade restrictions could signal a country's attempt to skirt market forces. To the extent that a country was already in poor macroeconomic health, the restrictions might actually increase the likelihood of a balance-of-payments crisis, not decrease it.

3.254 **India** considered that although the statistical link between trade liberalization and the trade deficit could not be proved, available trade data, contained in the *Economic Survey of India, 1996-97* indicated the need for caution in assessing the impact of removal of import restrictions on India's balance of payments. India considered, therefore, that the central economic issue in this dispute was whether India was entitled to a time-schedule for the progressive relaxation and elimination of its restrictions as required by Article XVIII:11.

3.255 India was particularly concerned about the potential adverse effects of immediate elimination of its remaining import restrictions on a significant number of tariff-lines in the context of its overall programme of macro-economic stabilization measures and structural reforms. Thus, in the context of the linkages between trade policy reforms and other reforms, an influential World Bank study of economic liberalization in about 40 less-developed countries entitled *Best Practices in Trade Policy Reform*, noted that:

> Tariff reform may cause revenue losses, devaluation may increase inflation and liberalization may aggravate balance of payments problems. Does this mean that trade liberalization is inconsistent with stabilization efforts? Indeed, there is little doubt that macroeconomic stability makes trade policy (and some other) reforms more difficult to implement successfully. For this reason, some

> analysts have argued that the fiscal deficit and inflation should be reduced before trade policy reforms are introduced.[189]

On the experience of developing countries with the sequencing of reforms, the study noted that:

> In general, the benefits of trade policy reforms are greater when accompanied by domestic economic reforms. Hence, trade policy and domestic reforms are best carried out simultaneously. But in practice not all actions can be taken at the same time and so the issue of sequencing becomes relevant. Initiating trade policy reforms often exposes the need for domestic reforms and investments ... It also exposes unforeseen infrastructural needs of industries that are based almost entirely on foreign demand ... And sometimes domestic reforms should be deferred until the business and financial communities clearly understand that the protection against imports will be reduced. Otherwise, when investment or price controls are removed in highly protected sectors, increased investment and production might be encouraged in the wrong sectors. At other times, trade policy reforms may need to wait until a domestic control is relaxed. For example, a processed product (such as textiles) may see its effective protection vanish or become negative if its tariffs are reduced while the price of its basic input (cotton) which is set by a monopolistic parastatal, remains high.[190]
>
> ...
>
> Experience suggests that substantial and comprehensive liberalization can be completed in less than five to seven years from the start of the adjustment program, although the decision on the pace of reform ultimately depends on the specific circumstances of the country involved. This should allow time for quantitative restrictions to be phased out and for tariffs to be reduced to, say, 15 to 25 percent.[191]

In India's view, the conclusions of this study were particularly noteworthy:

> If all reforms cannot be carried out simultaneously, careful sequencing of the reforms can usually avoid conflicts among them. With respect to macroeconomic stability, it is necessary to consider the likely consequences of trade liberalization for the fiscal deficit and ways to offset adverse effects, if they are judged likely to be serious. When the inflation rate is very high and variable, stabilization efforts can precede other reforms.

---

[189] Vinod Thomas, John Nash, *et al*, *Best Practices in Trade Policy Reform*, (World Bank, 1991), pp. 204-205.

[190] *Ibid.*, p. 206.

[191] *Ibid.*, p. 207.

> Greater emphasis on complementary policies, investments, and institutional reform will improve the payoff to trade policy reform. Where domestic market problems are severe, deregulation, infrastructural improvements, and institutional reforms are essential for the success of trade policy reforms.[192]

3.256 India assured the Panel that India supported trade liberalization and believed that it brought benefits in terms of economic growth. The issue in this area, was not so much whether trade liberalization improved the balance of payments in the long run, but the manner in which trade reforms should be carried out. In accordance with Article XVIII:11, India considered that it should progressively relax and eliminate its import restrictions in a manner that did not result in producing conditions that would compel it to reinstitute import restrictions to manage its balance of payments.

3.257 In response to a request from the Panel that India identify the concrete reasons why the immediate removal of its remaining import restrictions would thereupon lead to a balance-of-payments problem, **India** pointed to the behaviour of India's trade account since India began its programme of economic liberalization in 1991. The following table from the Economic Survey of India, 1997-98 (published by India's Ministry of Finance prior to the presentation of the annual budget in Parliament) contained data on India's trade deficit between 1991 and 1997.

Table 1

Years	**1990-91**	**1991-92**	**1992-93**	**1993-94**	**1994-95**	**1995-96-**	**1996-97**
Trade Balance (US$ million)	-9,348	-2,798	-5,448	-4,056	-9,049	11,359	-1,429
Trade Balance (% of GDP)	-3.2	-1.1	-2.4	-1.6	-2.9	-3.4	-4.0

3.258 The table showed that the trade deficit had deteriorated continuously since 1992-93, increasing to nearly US$14.3 billion in 1996-97 or to 4.0% of GDP. Significant deterioration on the trade account began in 1994-95 after a three-year phase between 1991-92 and 1993-94 when the trade deficit was relatively low. By 1996-97, however, the trade deficit had already reached an alarming 4% of GDP and was provisionally assessed to have worsened further in fiscal 1997-98. India noted also that by 1995-96 itself, the deficit on the trade account had increased to above that recorded in 1990-91 when India was forced to turn to the IMF for emergency loans. Projections by the Planning Commission for the me-

[192] Vinod Thomas, John Nash, *et al*, *Best Practices in Trade Policy Reform*, (World Bank, 1991), p. 215.

dium term indicated that imports were likely to increase further if the import restrictions that were currently in place were eliminated immediately.[193]

3.259 The dramatic change in the behaviour of imports in the reform period came out far more clearly if import volumes were considered. In the period 1992-93 to 1995-96, import volume grew, on the average, at 22.1%.[194] Import volume growth during this period stood in sharp contrast to its behaviour during the decade of the eighties. During the periods 1980-81 to 1985-86 and 1985-86 to 1990-91, import volume grew at the more sedate pace of 6.6% and 5.7% respectively.

3.260 India's Planning Commission had also carried out an analysis to estimate the likely impact of immediate elimination of India's import restrictions on its balance of payments. It noted, however, that the standard econometric techniques for predicting the impact on India's balance of payments of the immediate removal of India's residual import restrictions could not be readily used in the case of commodities subject to import restrictions because continuity assumptions are isolated. Therefore, its analysis was based on inferences from the behaviour of commodities which were not under import restrictions. The basic analysis was presented in the following table.[195]

Table 2
Domestic production and imports of tradable commodities in India
(Rs million)

	1989-90	1996-97

[193] The Planning Commission has estimated that import elasticity in the Ninth-Plan period is expected to be 1.75 without the removal of the existing import restrictions.

[194] To put this in the proper context, it is perhaps useful to mention that export volume over the same period grew at the significantly slower pace of 16.8%.

[195] The assumptions on which the analysis was based are as follows:

(i) Since imports are measured in terms of the value of the product, it is not proper to relate them to the value added in different sectors. Rather, they should be related to the gross value of output. The latter data are not generally available in the National Accounts. Therefore, they have been collated separately.

(ii) The analysis is limited to tradable commodities, which include products originating in agriculture, mining and quarrying and manufacturing. All non-traded goods and services have been excluded. The tradable commodities have been classified on the basis of whether their imports are subjected to import restrictions or not. Although such categorization cannot be entirely water-tight, the broad orders of magnitude indicated are relatively accurate. As is evident from the table above, the gross value of output of commodities subject to import restrictions has declined from almost 60% in 1989-90 to below 55% in 1996-97.

(iii) Imports have also been categorized on the same basis as domestic production. Thus, imports subject to import restrictions are estimated to be 18% of total imports in 1989-90 and 16% in 1996-97.

(iv) The total value of consumption has been defined as the gross value of domestic output plus the value of imports on a commodity basis. No correction has been made either for exports or for changes in stocks because this is unlikely to make any substantive difference.

		1989-90	1996-97
I.	Gross value of domestic output		
	(a) Total	4,713,609	13,428,860
	(b) Under import restrictions	2,799,826 (59.4%)	7,340,765 (54.7%)
	(c) Not under import restrictions	1,913,783 (40.6%)	6,088,095 (45.3%)
II.	Value of Imports		
	(a) Total	367,266	1,639,530
	(b) Under import restrictions	65,801 (17.9%)	260,222 (15.9%)
	(c) Not under import restrictions	301,465 (82.1%)	1,379,308 (84.1%)
III.	Total value of consumption (I+II)		
	(a) Total	5,080,875	15,068,390
	(b) Under import restrictions	2,865,627 (56.4%)	7,600,987 (50.4%)
	(c) Not under import restrictions	2,215,248 (43.6%)	7,467,403 (49.6%)
IV.	Share of imports in total value of consumption (II / III)		
	(a) Total	7.23%	10.88%
	(b) Under import restrictions	2.30%	3.42%
	(c) Not under import restrictions	13.61%	18.47%

Note: Figures in brackets are percentages to total.
Source: The Government of India.

3.261 As was evident, the share of imports in the "total value of consumption" differed substantially between products subject to import restrictions and those which were not. In 1996-97, these figures were 3.42% and 18.47% respectively. Thus, the removal of import restrictions would certainly lead to an increase in the share of imports of such products, although the magnitude of the increase would depend on a number of factors such as the level of tariff protection, the relative international competitiveness of products subject to import restrictions relative to those that were not subject to import restrictions, the relative domestic supply possibilities, etc. Therefore, it was not possible to pinpoint exactly the likely magnitude of increases in imports.

3.262 As an initial indication, upon the removal of import restrictions, if the percentage share of imports of products that are currently subject to import restrictions rises to the level reached by products that are no longer subject to such restrictions, the *additional* import bill from the removal of import restrictions would have been approximately US$30.6 billion in 1996-97, as compared to the total merchandise import bill for that year of US$43.5 billion. The above figures, however, could be disputed, and a sensitivity analysis of the removal of import restrictions was presented in the table that follows. The sensitivity analysis showed that depending upon the assumption made about the likely percentage share of imports in total value of consumption of 5.00 per cent, net addition to imports, in terms of 1996-97 values, would range upwards of US$3 billion.

Table 3
Sensitivity analysis of QR removal, 1996-97
(Percent share and US$ billion)

Percentage share of imports in total value of consumption	Net addition to imports (US$ billion)
3.42	0.0
5.00	3.2
7.50	8.3
10. 00	13.3
12.50	18.4

Note: Exchange rate US$ = Rs. 37.50.
Source: The Government of India.

3.263 Another important factor that was likely to affect the behaviour of the trade deficit was the marked deceleration in export growth over the last two years.[196] This deceleration had been caused by a number of factors including the following: a slowdown in the expansion of world trade;[197] and an inability to switch export production in response to changes in the pattern of world demand. The prospects of recovery of world trade appeared particularly remote after the South-East Asian currency crisis. The South-East Asian currency crisis also almost certainly would affect India's export competitiveness, especially because the South East Asian economies were direct competitors with respect to both commodities and markets for Indian exports.

3.264 Besides the anticipated low growth of exports, an analysis of the evolution of Indian imports pointed to some potential areas of concern on the trade account. As would be expected with any process of global integration, both export-to-GDP and import-to-GDP ratios had shown secular increases. Merchandise exports which accounted for 6.2% of GDP in 1990-91, had grown to account for 9.9% of GDP in 1995-96. The import-to-GDP ratio over the same period had risen from 9.4 to 13.3%. But these averages understated the growing importance of foreign trade in the economy. A more accurate picture would be obtained if these ratios were calculated using the annual change in exports and imports as a proportion of the annual change in GDP. The annual change in exports as a proportion of the annual change in GDP had increased from 15.3% in 1991-92 to 18.6% in 1995-96. Over the same period, however, the same ratio for imports increased far more steeply, from 6.2% to 25.7%.

3.265 India's rising trade deficit has not resulted in a significant deterioration of its current account deficit only because of the steady improvement in the invisibles account. After registering a nominal surplus of US$1.6 billion in 1991-92

[196] In fact preliminary data for the current year, i.e. 1997-98, would suggest that export growth had actually turned negative.
[197] World trade experienced a halving of growth rate in 1996 compared to the preceding year.

amounting to 0.7% of GDP, the surplus on the invisibles account went up to US$5.7 billion in 1994-95 and further to US$8.5 billion in 1996-97, amounting to 1.7 and 2.4% of GDP respectively. Perhaps the most significant aspect of this improvement had been the sharp increase in net private transfers. This form of inflow which was US$3.8 billion or 1.7% of GDP in 1991-92, had by 1996-97, risen to more than US$11.5 billion, amounting to 3.3% of GDP. However, it was believed that unexpectedly high private transfers in 1996-97 were largely due to the inflow of a large part of the redemption proceeds of India Development Bonds (issued during the balance-of-payments crisis in 1991) on maturity. Consequently, it was unlikely that private transfers will be as high in subsequent years.

3.266 The influence of private transfers on the overall invisibles balance was significant because of the relative stagnation of the other major components on the invisibles account. Thus, improvement in the invisibles account was attributable to net private transfers, which were highly unpredictable. In particular, recent increases in net private transfers had been attributed to terminal repatriation by Indian workers abroad. This implied that such transfers were likely to decline steeply in the future. *Therefore, private transfers could not be depended on to finance India's trade deficit.* This was corroborated by the Planning Commission's estimates for the Ninth Plan period which indicated that the balance on the invisibles account was likely to be just half the present level. It was this feature of India's current account deficit during the 1990s, *i.e.*, where a large and growing trade deficit was financed essentially through private transfers, that raised serious doubts about the sustainability of the current account deficit. Thus, even the IMF had indicated that in the next few years, India's current account deficit could increase to about 3% to 4% of the GDP from the present level of 1.1%. The Ninth Plan projections also indicated a widening of the current account deficit.[198]

3.267 In recent years, India had been able to finance its current account deficit largely because of increases in portfolio and FDI flows. However, net portfolio flows had declined substantially from US$3.31 billion in 1996-97 to US$1.61 billion in 1997-98 on a balance-of-payments basis. In addition, there had been a net outflow of investment by foreign institutional investors to the extent of US$448.90 million in the first quarter of fiscal 1998-99 based on data from the Securities and Exchange Board of India. There were a number of factors that could adversely affect these flows:

(i) In the wake of the South-East Asian financial crisis, capital issues abroad by Indian companies had been adversely affected.

(ii) The legislatively mandated imposition of economic sanctions on India by the United States and other steps taken by some industrialized countries in regard to postponement of fresh approvals of

[198] Ninth Plan projections indicate that for the period as a whole, the current account deficit as a percentage of the GDP is expected to be about 2.1%.

bilateral and multilateral assistance to India would also affect inflows of foreign capital.

(iii) Moody's Investors Service ("Moody's"), one of the leading international private credit rating agencies, had lowered India's foreign currency country ceiling for long term debt and notes to Ba2 from Baa3 and had downgraded the foreign currency country ceiling for short term debt to Non-Prime from Prime-3. Moody's had also lowered the long term foreign currency deposit ceiling to Ba3 from Ba1. Other private international private credit rating agencies were likely to follow. Such downgrading would adversely affect the ability of Indian corporate entities to borrow abroad. It would also affect other types of foreign investment in India.

3.268 Since independence in 1947, India had faced serious balance-of-payments crises in the late 1950s, the mid-1960s, the late 1970s and the early 1990s. India currently faced significant infrastructural bottlenecks that were hindering it in maintaining a reasonable rate of economic growth. A significant proportion of the necessary investment would need to come from foreign sources both to cover the savings gap and to finance the necessary imports. In addition, analysis of India's balance-of-payments outlook even for the short term indicated that India was likely to face simultaneous pressures on the external front from a number of sources. According to the latest figures, the foreign currency assets held by the Reserve Bank of India had already declined by US$1.87 billion in the first quarter (June 26, 1998) of fiscal 1998-99. For all these reasons, India believed that the immediate elimination of its import restrictions would create a serious balance-of-payments problem.

(c) The balance-of-payments situation

3.269 The **United States** considered that even if (contrary to the views expressed in Section III(D)(9) below) the IMF's findings were insufficient to establish that India did not meet the requirements of Article XVIII:B, additional evidence from public sources, including Indian Government sources, settled the question.

3.270 On the basis of IMF data, from the US$2.1 billion low, Indian foreign reserve holdings have increased to US$ 4.2 billion in 1991, US$6.3 billion in 1992, US$10.7 billion in 1993, US$20.3 billion in 1994, US$20.8 billion in 1996 (a slight dip to US$18.6 billion occurred in 1995), US$25.0 billion in 1997 and US$26.9 billion in March 1998.[199] The United States emphasized that India had moved to overall balance-of-payments surplus in the 1990s as it had simultaneously taken strong action to open its market to imports and experienced rapid economic growth. Again, on the basis of latest publicly available data from the

[199] *International Financial Statistics*, International Monetary Fund Statistics Department.

IMF, India's real gross domestic product rose at an average annual compound rate of 6.6 per cent in the five years between 1991 and 1996. Nominal goods exports have been rising at an annual compound rate of 13.7 per cent between 1991 and 1997 (annualized from first three quarters) rising from US$17.6 billion to an annualized US$38.1 billion.[200]

3.271 In the view of the United States, import-market opening measures by India in the 1990s had undoubtedly reduced product market distortions in India and helped improve the efficiency of production and investment. In turn, a more open and successful Indian economy had helped support growing international confidence in management of the Indian economy and in India's successful economic future. Such confidence had, of course, been important, not only to India's healthy economic performance in the 1990s, but also to its balance-of-payments surplus position in recent years. Against the background of India's economic performance in this decade, the United States found it difficult to understand on what grounds India could suggest that the additional market opening represented by withdrawal of import restrictions that were no longer justifiable on balance-of-payments grounds would necessarily threaten a balance-of-payments crisis.

3.272 The United States also quoted statements made by India's new Finance Minister, Yashwant Sinha, during his visit to the United States. On 13 April, the Finance Minister had stated that "the macroeconomic fundamentals were strong. Our foreign exchange reserves were substantial, our currency markets orderly, our external debt well under control and *the East Asian crisis did not engulf India*"[201] On 15 April, Mr. Sinha stated "India has a strong foreign exchange reserve position and the process of economic reforms is on. It is because of these strong economic fundamentals that *while the rest of East Asia is experiencing a financial meltdown, India has remained largely untouched*"[202] A press release of the Reserve Bank of India dated 1 April, announced that during the year 1997-98, the foreign currency assets of the RBI increased by US$3.5 billion, including a US$2.5 billion increase since 16 January 1998.[203] Since 1990, as a consequence of the strength of the Indian balance-of-payments position and government actions to deal with that strength, India's foreign reserve holdings had risen dramatically.

3.273 The United States considered that even if the IMF's findings were insufficient to establish that India did not meet the requirements of Article XVIII:B, additional evidence from Indian sources settled the question. In addition to the press releases cited above, other Indian government sources, addressed to the world financial community and to actual and potential investors, confirmed the strength of India's balance-of-payments position. The Government of India's

---

200 *International Financial Statistics*, International Monetary Fund Statistics Department.

201 Press Release, Consulate General of India, New York, "Finance Minister Addresses the Asia Society In New York", Monday, 13 April 1998.

202 Press Release, 15 April 1998, Indian Embassy.

203 Press Release, Reserve Bank of India, April 1998.

Basic Document for the January 1997 consultations in the Balance-of-Payments Committee confirmed the strength of India's balance-of-payments position and showed that the previous increase in the trade deficit occasioned by the removal of quantitative restrictions had in fact been accompanied by a substantial *increase* in India's reserves:

> "India's external balance of payments have improved since the crisis in 1991. After registering a decline in the dollar value of exports in 1991-92, the country has witnessed an annual export growth of about 20 per cent in dollar terms during 1993-96. Imports, in dollar terms, have also increased at a rapid pace by 22.9 per cent in 1994-95 and by 26.8 per cent in 1995-96. *In spite of an increasing trade deficit, buoyant invisible receipts and capital inflows allowed foreign exchange reserves to grow from a low of one billion dollar to almost $ 21 billion at end-March 1995.* Reserves declined to $17 billion at end March 1996 and recovered partially by increasing to a level of $19.5 billion by end-November, 1996."[204]

3.274 The United States cited a statement entitled "Monetary and Credit Policy for the First Half of 1998-99," in which Dr. Bimal Jalan, Governor of the Reserve Bank of India, noted the success of using macroeconomic policy instruments to manage India's external position in the wake of the Asian financial crisis. Specifically, Dr. Jalan noted:

> "The developments in some of the Asian currencies gave rise to significant pressures on the exchange rate of the rupee in the second half of the year. Keeping these developments in view, a package of monetary measures was introduced on January 16, 1998. ...
>
> "The impact of January measures on the external position of the country has been favourable. During 1997-98, the foreign currency assets of the Reserve Bank increased by US$3.6 billion - from US$22.4 billion on March 31, 1997 to US$26.0 billion on March 31, 1998. Inclusive of gold and SDR, the total foreign exchange reserves stood at US$29.4 billion on March 31, 1998, representing an increase of US$2.9 billion over March 31, 1997. Since January 16, 1998, the foreign currency assets have increased by US$2.5 billion up to March 31, 1998."[205]

3.275 The United States added that the Reserve Bank of India had taken the same position. In the "Assessment and Prospects" chapter of its 1996/97 Annual Report, the Reserve Bank of India had written:

---

[204] WT/BOP/16, 8 January 1997, para. 40.

[205] Statement by Dr. Bimal Jalan, Governor, Reserve Bank of India on "Monetary and Credit Policy for the First Half of 1998-99," 29 April 1998, at paras. 11, 12.

"The distinct strengthening of the balance of payments since 1991-92 has resulted in a healthy build-up of foreign exchange reserves. The level of foreign exchange reserves (including gold and SDRs) rose to US$ 29.9 billion by August 14, 1997 equivalent to seven months of imports and well above the conventional thumb rule of reserve adequacy (three months of imports). In the context of the changing interface with the external sector and the importance of the capital account, reserve adequacy needs to be evaluated in terms of indicators other than conventional norms. *By any criteria, the level of foreign exchange reserves appears comfortable.* They are equivalent of about 25 months of debt service payments and 6 months of payments for imports and debt service taken together. Thus, even if exchange market developments accentuate the leads and lags in external receipts and payments, the *reserves would be adequate to withstand both cyclical and unanticipated shocks.* Furthermore, in the context of fluctuating capital flows, it is useful to assess the level of reserves in terms of the volume of short-term debt which can be covered by the reserves. At the end of March 1997, the ratio of short-term debt to the level of reserves amounted to a little over 25 per cent. The strength of our foreign exchange reserves can be gauged from the fact that the ratio of short-term debt to reserves was 220 per cent for Mexico, 150 per cent for Indonesia, 64 per cent for Argentina, 50 per cent for Thailand and 30 per cent for Malaysia at the end of 1995. Furthermore, the level of reserves exceeds the total stock of short-term debt and portfolio flows which taken together, constitute a little less than 75 per cent of the level of reserves. It is necessary to keep these different criteria in view while determining the desired level of reserves.

"The recent strengthening of India's balance of payments has enabled the country to accept the obligations of Article VIII of the International Monetary Fund which prohibits all restrictions on payments in relation to current account transactions."[206]

3.276 In summary, in the view of the United States, the facts overwhelmingly confirmed that India had not been experiencing a serious decline in its reserves; that India had not been faced with the threat of a serious decline in its monetary reserves; that India's reserves had not been inadequate or at a very low level; and that the removal of the quantitative restrictions would not subject India to a situation in which it would be threatened with or experience a serious decline in the level of its monetary reserves.

[206] The Annual Report on the Working of the Reserve Bank of India (for the year July 1, 1996 to June 30, 1997), Chapter VII "Assessment and Prospects," paras. 7.23 and 7.24 (emphasis added).

3.277 The United States recalled that although India had argued that it required time to *plan* for adjustment to the removal of the challenged measures, India had been well-aware of the concerns of many of its trading partners concerning these massive restrictions since at least 1994. India's response, made in 1994, is recorded as follows:

> "The [Balance-of-Payments] Committee noted that, if the balance of payments showed sustained improvement, India's aim was to move to a régime by 1996/97, in which import licensing restrictions would only be maintained for environmental and safety reasons."[207]

3.278 The United States added that India's reserves had increased from US$20.3 billion in 1994 to US$25.0 billion in 1997. India had had three years to plan for the elimination of the measures. However, by 1997, the measures had not been eliminated. Furthermore, the IMF advised India in a Committee meeting in January of 1997, of its factual determination that India lacked any balance-of-payments justification for the restrictions now at issue in this dispute.

3.279 Finally, the United States noted that, as India itself pointed out, Article 21 of the DSU provided that if it was impracticable to comply immediately with the recommendations and rulings of the DSB the Member concerned was to have a reasonable period of time in which to do so.[208] Article 21, however, also provided that this period was to be determined by the Dispute Settlement Body, the parties to the dispute, or as a last resort by an arbitration - not by the Panel. The issue of the amount of time that India should or should not have to implement the rulings and recommendations of a panel was a separate procedure.

3.280 **India** argued, with respect to the evidence submitted by the United States in the press releases, that the objective of the statements of the Finance Minister had been to provide an assurance to businessmen, investors and opinion-makers in the United States that his Government supported the process of economic reforms initiated in India in 1991, and that his Government would give the reform process itself a further boost. The presumption underlying this advocacy of the reforms process was that India had seen gains from the economic reforms carried out thus far. However, the Finance Minister himself in these statements cautioned that problem areas remained and that India's economic development and restructuring process had as yet not run its course. In recognition of the complementarity between domestic policies and trade reforms, the Finance Minister had pointed out the need for a carefully calibrated approach on globalization. The progressive elimination of import restrictions by India in the recent past, and India's commitment to phase out import restrictions over a period of time, had been specifically noted by the Finance Minister. India submitted that a Finance Minister was the steward of his nation's finances and was required to emphasize the

[207] GATT document BOP/R/221, 1 December 1994.

[208] DSU, Article 21.3.

positive approach of the new Government with respect to foreign inflows and the balance-of-payments situation. Finance markets would react adversely if a Finance Minister emphasized the negative aspects of the balance-of-payments situation. Accordingly, the statements of the Finance Minister should be read in the above context and not literally. Moreover, they also related to a situation existing at a particular point of time.

3.281 Similarly, according to India, in the press release of India's Central Bank, the Reserve Bank of India (the "RBI") simply announced that India's foreign currency assets had increased as a result of "a number of monetary measures to stabilize the forex market". This statement must be read in its proper context. It revealed both the extreme volatility in the foreign exchange market and the beneficial impact on India's reserves of a number of monetary measures designed to address this volatility. India wished the Panel to note that the monetary measures included increases in interest rates that necessarily had an impact on economic growth and development. Further, India's time-schedule was premised upon such improvements in its monetary reserves and balance of payments. In India's view, the United States had not shown in what way these statements by the Finance Minister and the RBI had a bearing on the criteria specified in Article XVIII:11 and the interpretative note thereto. Accordingly, India urged the Panel to put the United States to strict proof that India's balance of payments and reserves situation did not meet the criteria laid down in Article XVIII:11 read with the interpretative note thereto.

3.282 India noted that in support of its claim that India no longer met the conditions under Article XVIII:11 for maintenance of its import restrictions the United States had produced evidence from publicly available data from the IMF that, according to the United States, confirmed the strength of India's reserves and balance of payments position. India considered that such data could not rise, as a matter of law, to the level of the determinations required to be made by the Committee under Article XVIII:11. The fact that India's reserves situation had improved did not necessarily mean that India's monetary reserves did not face a threat of a serious decline in the medium term or that its monetary reserves were adequate over the medium term in relation to its programme of economic development. Such "publicly available data from the IMF" did not quantify or evaluate potential threats to India's balance of payments that in turn could result in a drawdown of reserves. Further, such data also did not in any way reflect the determination required to be made under Article XVIII:11 that removal of import restrictions would not result in a recurrence of a threat of a serious decline in its balance of payments.

3.283 India commented that all the statements quoted by the United States referred to the recent foreign exchange reserves position. These figures did not relate to medium- and long-term perceptions of the threat to India's monetary reserves or balance of payments or India's medium- and long-term economic development needs. Earlier, India had included evidence relating to its trade balance figures after 1991. The latest figures, as indicated in the Economic Survey of 1997-98 indicated that the trade deficit, as presently estimated, were as high as

US$11,359 million, representing 3.4 % of GDP in 1995-96 and US$14,299 million, representing 4% of GDP in 1996-97. It was almost impossible to predict accurately the effect on India's trade deficit of immediately eliminating import restrictions on items in the remaining HS-lines at the 8-digit level that constitute a large proportion of India's total annual consumption. Rules of thumb about the adequacy of India's current monetary reserves with respect to current imports became instantly irrelevant in light of the impossibility of making such predictions.

3.284 India contended that the current account deficit had remained within manageable proportions only because of a substantial increase in basic capital inflows on private account. According to the *Economic Survey of India, 1996-97*, net flows on private account rose from about US$2.2 billion in 1992-93 to an average of US$6.3 billion during the period between 1993-94 and 1995-96, and further to US$10.4 billion in 1996-97. In a developing economy, excessive reliance on private capital inflows posed a serious danger of a balance-of-payments crisis. Recent experience in the East Asian economies had clearly shown the disastrous effect on the entire process of economic growth of a balance-of-payments crisis. The United States had quoted a work by former economic advisor to the GATT Secretariat, Dr. Jagdish Bhagwati, on India's regulatory regime for international trade. India invited the Panel's attention to a recent article entitled "The Capital Myth: the Difference between Trade in Widgets and Dollars" by Dr. Jagdish Bhagwati, which appeared in the journal *Foreign Affairs*, May/June, 1998. Dr. Bhagwati had pointed out in this article that in 1996, total private capital inflows to Indonesia, Malaysia, the Republic of Korea and the Philippines were US$93 billion, up from US$41 billion in 1994. In 1997, that suddenly changed to an outflow of US$12billion. According to Dr. Bhagwati:

> "Each time a crisis related to capital inflows hits a country, it typically goes through the wringer. The debt crisis of the 1980 cost South America a decade of growth. The Mexicans, who were vastly overexposed through short term inflows, were devastated in 1994. The Asian economies of Thailand, Indonesia and South Korea, all heavily burdened with short-term debt, went into a tailspin nearly a year ago, drastically lowering their growth rates."

3.285 India also quoted the 7-13 March 1998 issue of *The Economist*:

> "The financial crisis might seem to be over: currencies have steadied and stock markets are recovering. But the economic crisis has barely begun."

3.286 Given the recurring trade deficit, India considered that it must necessarily follow a policy of great caution while progressing steadily towards its ultimate goal of total economic liberalization. A large country such as India with a huge population and a potentially huge market could run into a serious economic crisis unless the march towards liberalization was carefully calibrated. It was vital to note, therefore, that, when the Finance Minister of India and the Governor of the Reserve Bank of India talked about the adequacy of levels of foreign exchange reserves, they were talking in the context of the present situation - a situation in which quantitative restrictions on consumer goods and controls on capital mobility exist. Nowhere had they made any statement regarding the adequacy of reserves in a situation in which such controls were dramatically removed overnight. On the other hand, the latest official publication of the Ministry of Finance, which was placed before the Indian Parliament in the last week of May 1998, clearly brought out the view of the Government of India. According to the *Economic Survey of India, 1997-98*:

> "While India's current level of reserves appears comfortable by traditional yardsticks, it is important to recognize that with an increasingly open economy, on both current and capital accounts, the need for reserves to cushion orderly development of the economy from changes in the external environment rises. Furthermore, the recent crisis in East and South East Asia has brought into sharper focus the need to maintain high levels of reserves to counter the increased volatility in short term capital flows. Inflows and outflows need to be carefully monitored and calibrated at all times to forestall the threat of a serious decline in resources."

3.287 The **United States** noted that India had argued that Members should not be compelled to replace import restrictions taken for balance-of-payments measures with other macro-economic policies, because such policies always could, "in a technical or economic sense," replace import restrictions, and Article XVIII:11 did not permit a developing country Member to be required to change its development policies. However, India had said to the Balance-of-Payments Committee, this Panel, to the financial community and to potential investors that its Government was in fact utilizing a full set of macroeconomic tools to carry out a development policy of trade liberalization. Furthermore, India was implying that the IMF was not able to make judgements about whether a particular country, such as India, had a full range of macroeconomic tools actually available to it. This was incorrect; the IMF had responsibility to review and assess every Fund member's economy once a year. As the IMF had determined, India did not have a serious decline or a threat of a serious decline in its balance-of-payments situation and there was no basis for the Panel to find that it would be in difficulty if the challenged measures were removed. Therefore, the point was that, in a *real* sense, not a technical sense, India did not now have balance-of-payments difficulties.

3.288 The United States further considered that the material laid before the Indian Parliament in May of 1998 as referred to in paragraph 3.286 above did not change the analysis. For example, the quoted statement conceded that the level of reserves appeared comfortable by the traditional yardsticks. Although it said that the level needed to be carefully monitored, the United States had not argued that India should not monitor its external position. Nothing in the quoted material suggested, however, that there had been a serious decline in reserves, that they were inadequate by any measures (including for India's development program), or that there was any threat to them. The fact that a Member monitored its reserves did not establish the existence of a threat to its reserves.

3.289 The United States went on to note that India had suggested that its trade deficit was a reason for "caution," and presumably meant to imply that the challenged measures should be maintained out of "caution." That was not the legal standard in Article XVIII:B. In any event, India's own Basic Document to the Balance of Payments Committee had made it clear that over the last five years India's balance-of-payments situation had been well managed *despite a growing trade deficit:*

> "In spite of an increasing trade deficit the favourable trends on invisible transactions resulted in improvements in the current account deficit from 3.2 per cent of GDP in 1990-91 to 1.7 per cent in 1995-96. During 1993-94 and 1994-95, the improvements in the current account were reinforced by favourable trends in the capital account, and foreign exchange reserves grew from a low of US dollar one billion in 1991 to almost US dollars 21 billion at end March 1995."[209]

3.290 In fact, contrary to India's arguments, it was India, not the United States, that was arguing from a technical and theoretical position. India seemed to be suggesting that it would *never* be possible to establish whether or not the test of the Note *Ad* Article XVIII:11 is met. That would render the *Ad* Note a nullity, and therefore could not be the correct interpretation. No guarantee could be given that the economy of any country - developed or developing - would remain free of balance-of-payment difficulties forever. The Note Ad Article XVIII:11 could not be interpreted to require such a guarantee. The Ad Note must instead be interpreted to require an examination of the actual circumstances: is there a threat of a serious decline now? are reserves inadequate now? The IMF had answered these questions: reserves are adequate, and there is no such threat. The Reserve Bank of India agreed:

> "By any criteria, the level of foreign exchange reserves appears comfortable. ... Thus, even if exchange market developments accentuate the leads and lags in external receipts and payments, the reserves would be adequate to withstand both cyclical and unanticipated shocks."[210]

3.291 In short, the evidence the United States had provided about India's particular situation met any reasonable burden that the *Ad* Note could have been intended to contain.

3.292 The United States also noted that India had stated that this Panel should not take the statements of the Indian Minister of Finance or the Reserve Bank of

[209] WT/BOP/16, Op. Cit., para. 3.

[210] The Annual Report on the Working of the Reserve Bank of India (for the year July 1, 1996 to June 30, 1997), Chapter VII "Assessment and Prospects," paras. 7.23 and 7.24 (emphasis added).

India literally, according to India, because they were responsible for talking up the economy. The United States considered that assertion extraordinary, particularly if India was suggesting that their statements could not be relied upon by others. No one questioned the fact that Indian and world financial markets listened very closely to what the Minister of Finance and the Reserve Bank said. The consequence of that fact, however, was that the Minister and the Reserve Bank must speak with particular care and precision, *not* that what they said should be treated as unreliable. If the financial markets could depend on what they said, so could this Panel.

3.293 With respect to India's quotation of Dr. Bhagwati's article in *Foreign Affairs*, the United States pointed out that Dr. Bhagwati's had said nothing about *India's* debt situation causing difficulties. Dr. Bhagwati had mentioned Mexico, Thailand, and Indonesia, the first three of which had been discussed in the Reserve Bank of India's assessment submitted to the Panel by the United States. The Reserve Bank had said:

> "Furthermore, in the context of the fluctuating capital flows, it is useful to assess the level of reserves in terms of the volume of short-term debt which can be covered by the reserves. At the end of March 1997, the ratio of short-term debt to the level of reserves amounted to a little over 25 per cent. The strength of our foreign exchange reserves can be gauged from the fact that the ratio of short-term debt to reserves was 220 per cent for Mexico, 150 per cent for Indonesia, 64 per cent for Argentina, 50 per cent for Thailand and 30 per cent for Malaysia at the end of 1995. Furthermore, the level of reserves exceeds the total stock of short-term debt and portfolio flows which taken together, constitute a little less than 75 per cent of the level of reserves."

(d) Article XXII consultations

3.294 **India** made reference to the Article XXII consultations held subsequent to the impasse in the Committee. Canada, Switzerland, European Communities, Australia, New Zealand and the United States had initiated action against India under the dispute settlement procedures and requested consultations with India. Japan had been a third party in these consultations. During these consultations, India had arrived at a mutually agreed solution with all the Members that had initiated consultations under Article XXII of the GATT except the United States on the basis of a six-year time-schedule for removal of its import restrictions, by suitably front loading some of the products of interest to these Members of the WTO and thereby improving its phase-out plan.

3.295 In July 1997, the United States[211], Australia[212], Canada[213], New Zealand[214], Switzerland[215] and the European Communities[216] requested consultations with India under Article 4 of the DSU regarding the import restrictions notified under Article XVIII:B. Japan requested to be joined as an interested third party in the consultations with the United States[217] as well as with each of the other Members that requested consultations. India agreed in letters bilaterally exchanged in November 1997 with Australia, Canada, European Communities, Japan, New Zealand, and Switzerland to a time-schedule of *six years*, divided into three phases covering the periods 1 April 1997 to 31 March 2000, 1 April 2000 to 31 March 2002 and 1 April 2002 to 31 March 2003. Each of the agreements contains a clause according to which "India intends, upon reaching bilateral solutions with the trading partners which have requested consultations under GATT Article XXII, to seek multilateral accommodation for its revised phase out plan" and that the Member concerned "will cooperate with India in this regard". The time-schedule for the removal of India's remaining import restrictions according to the phase-out plan announced originally, and as further improved through these mutually agreed solutions, is summarized in the following table.

Phase	Dates	Number of HS-items to be removed	Percent of HS-items to be removed
I	1 April 1997 to31 March 2000	1,143	42
II	1 April 2000 to 31 March 2002	1,147	43
III	1 April 2002 to 31 March 2003	424	15
TOTAL		2,714	100

3.296 India said that in the consultations preceding the establishment of this Panel as well as subsequent to the establishment of the Panel it had attempted to achieve a settlement with the United States, just as it did with some of its other trading partners, by adjusting the six-year time-schedule in such a way as to front-load a number of products of interest to the United States and by reducing the number of items that would be liberalized in the third phase (i.e. the sixth year) to a minimum. India also pointed out that the United States would also benefit from the mutually agreed solutions India had arrived at with other trading partners. However, the United States insisted on more and more "front-loading"

[211] WT/DS90.
[212] WT/DS91.
[213] WT/DS92.
[214] WT/DS93.
[215] WT/DS94.
[216] WT/DS95.
[217] WT/DS90/2. Such requests were also made by the European Communities (WT/DS90/3), Canada (WT/DS90/4), Australia (WT/DS90/5), Switzerland (WT/DS90/6) and New Zealand (WT/DS90/7).

of items of export interest to United States enterprises without clearly indicating the final goal post. During the final stages of bilateral contacts, it became clear to India that the United States, while showing some flexibility by not rejecting outright the idea of a six-year time-schedule, was not agreeing to the actual six-year phase-out plan proposed by India with a structure of 3+2+1 years, even after it was further front-loaded as desired by the United States (i.e. in addition to the front-loading done as a result of mutually agreed solutions with other trading partners, which was obviously available to US also because of MFN principle). India believed that this was because of the United States' assumption that even India's improved six-year phase-out plan would result in the bulk of the priorities of the United States being liberalized on a longer time-line than what the United States thought it could achieve through dispute settlement. India felt that the United States approach implied that the length of the time-schedule for the removal of import restrictions that had been maintained legally for almost 50 years would be determined by the provisions of the DSU which relate to illegal measures and consequently envisage prompt removal of illegal measures, rather than by the Committee on Balance-of-Payments Restrictions and the General Council. India stated that it could not either agree to or acquiesce with this approach.

3.297 India concluded that in the light of the deliberations of the Committee on Balance-of-Payments Restrictions, as well as the agreement that India had reached with those WTO Members who had requested consultations with it under the dispute settlement procedures (other than the United States), the Panel could presume safely that the prevailing view in the Committee on Balance-of-Payments Restrictions would be that India's phase-out plan was consistent with its obligations under Article XVIII:B of the GATT. India also believed that the vast majority of the WTO's General Council could be expected to approve India's phase-out plan for removing its import restrictions as required under paragraph 13 of the 1994 Understanding.

3.298 The **United States** argued that India had presented a picture of its consultations with the United States and other Members which was irrelevant and inadmissible in any panel proceeding, outside the terms of reference of this Panel, and factually distorted. The United States considered that all material concerning dispute settlement consultations between India and any other WTO Members - including the United States-should be excluded from the record of the Panel proceedings and should not be used as the basis for the Panel's findings. The Panel should reject India's attempts to impose on this Panel and on the dispute settlement process a settlement it alleged to have reached with other Members not part of this dispute.

3.299 The United States contended that by citing material concerning the bilateral negotiations that took place between it and Australia, Canada, the EC, Japan, New Zealand and Switzerland regarding India's import restrictions notified under Article XVIII:B, India had behaved in the same manner as Costa Rica in the dispute concerning restrictions on imports of underwear by the United States. The United States referred to paragraph 7.27 of the Panel report in that dispute:

> "Costa Rica submitted to the Panel information concerning the bilateral negotiations that took place between Costa Rica and the United States before and after the imposition of the restriction. More specifically, Costa Rica submitted information relating to settlement offers made by the United States concerning the level of the restriction to be imposed. In this respect, we note that Article 4.6 of the DSU reads as follows:
>
> > 'Consultations shall be confidential, and without prejudice to the rights of any Member in any further proceedings.'
>
> "In our view, the wording of Article 4.6 of the DSU makes it clear that offers made in the context of consultations are, in case a mutually agreed solution is not reached, *of no legal consequence to the later stages of dispute settlement*, as far as the rights of the parties to the dispute are concerned. Consequently, *we will not base our findings on such information.*"[218]

3.300 The United States considered that India's attempts to bring in alleged settlements with third parties were also contrary to the basic principle of international law, *pacta tertiis nec nocent nec prosunt*, which was found in Article 34 of the Vienna Convention on the Law of Treaties: "A treaty does not create either obligations or rights for a third State without its consent." The United States was certain that India would agree with the proposition that a settlement with one WTO Member could not excuse a violation that impaired the rights of another. The alleged phase-out schedules were never agreed with the United States and had never been notified to the Committee on Balance-of-Payments Restrictions. Only three of the five "mutually agreeable solutions" with other countries had even been notified to the DSB; the three notified stated that they were all signed *after* the date of establishment of this Panel. Indeed, other WTO Members might have decided to settle with India simply because they knew that this Panel had been established and they would be able to benefit from the outcome of the Panel proceeding. However, any speculation about the intentions of third parties-by either India or the United States-remained just speculation which was irrelevant to the task facing the Panel, and should be excluded from the Panel's deliberations.

3.301 In response, **India** noted that the United States took the position that:

> all material concerning dispute settlement consultations between India and any other WTO Members - including the United States - should be excluded from the record of this Panel proceeding and should not be used as the basis for the Panel's finding. The Panel should reject India's attempt to impose on this Panel and the dis-

[218] Panel Report on *United States - Restrictions on Imports of Cotton and Man-made Fibre Underwear*, (hereafter *Underwear*), WT/DS24/R, para. 7.27 (emphasis added).

pute settlement process a settlement it alleges to have reached with other Members not part of this dispute.

3.302 The United States then accused India of behaving like Costa Rica in the *Underwear* case by submitting information on bilateral consultations held in the context of dispute settlement proceedings between the United States and Costa Rica. The United States also accused India of violating the principle that a treaty does not create either obligations or rights for a third State without its consent.

3.303 India had submitted information to the Panel on the settlement reached with Australia, Canada, the EC, Japan, New Zealand and Switzerland in the course of bilateral consultations, and not information on the manifestly unsuccessful consultations held with the United States. India had followed the common practice of explaining the background and origin of the dispute and why prior consultations with the United States had failed while other consultations had resulted in agreements. The information submitted by India was relevant to the Panel's examination because it substantiated India's argument that all members of the Committee except the United States had been ready to support the multilateral accommodation of India's time-schedule.[219] Unlike the United States in the *Patents* case,[220] India was not asking the Panel to endorse an agreement reached with a third Member. India argued that the prevailing view in the Committee created a presumption that its time-schedule was consistent with the requirements of the note to Article XVIII:11.

3.304 Recalling that the United States had stated that "India alleges that the objective of the US complaint is simply to shorten to five years a six-year phase-out plan which India agreed to with other countries. This is fundamentally wrong", India wished to clarify that it was the United States' objective that was fundamentally wrong. India noted that, in the context of the balance-of-payments consultations (not the confidential consultations under the DSU), the United States had suggested that a five-year phase-out period would be acceptable. The objective of the United States in the present proceedings appeared to be to confuse the issue by mixing up two different periods, namely, the phase-out period which India was entitled to under Article XVIII:11 for the removal of the import restrictions maintained legally for about 50 years and the time-period foreseen in the DSU for the removal of illegal measures, which was normally 15 months.

---

[219] India noted that the Panel was facing two requests to strike material submitted to the Panel from the record. India requested in its first submission that the factual allegations on which the United States based no legal claims be struck from the record. The United States demanded that the parts of procedural history leading up to the dispute be struck. India considered that there was a qualitative distinction between the two requests and hoped that this would be reflected in the report of the Panel.

[220] In that case the United States requested the Panel to suggest that India implement its obligations under Article 70.8 of the TRIPS Agreement in the same manner as the United States had agreed with Pakistan (WT/DS50/R, para. 4.36).

9. *Consultations with the International Monetary Fund*

(a) Introduction

3.305 Although the **United States** was of the opinion that the Panel had before it sufficient evidence, if there were any doubts, the Panel should consult with the IMF. The United States claimed that since Article XV:2 required the WTO to consult the IMF, in all cases where the WTO is called on to consider matters concerning monetary reserves, balance of payments or foreign exchange arrangements, the Panel must also do so, and since the WTO must accept the IMF's findings on the matters specified in Article XV:2, the Panel must also do so. Although Article XV:2 did not mention panels, *per se*, an interpretation of WTO would include panels. Although the Appellate Body had found in *Argentina - Measures Affecting Imports of Footwear, Textiles, Apparel and Other Items* that the dispute did not involve "problems concerning monetary reserves, balance of payments or foreign exchange arrangements", it had found with respect to panel proceedings that Article XV:2 "*requires* the WTO to consult with the IMF when dealing with 'problems concerning monetary reserves, balance of payments or foreign exchange arrangements"[221] The Appellate Body had also found that the Panel had ample authority to consult with the Fund under Article 13.1 of the DSU, which provides that "Each panel shall have the right to seek information and technical advice from any individual or body which it deems appropriate".[222]

3.306 **India** noted that the text of Article XV:2 required Contracting Parties, not the Panel, to accept the determinations of the IMF on specific matters. Under Article XVIII:B, it was the Contracting Parties which must accept the determination of the Fund on certain aspects of the criteria relating to a Member's monetary reserves set forth in Article XVIII:9(a) and (b), as it was for the Contracting Parties to reach a final decision referred to in Article XV:2 on whether India's import restrictions exceeded those necessary to meet the criteria relating to its reserves in Article XVIII:9(a) and (b). India considered that the competence of the IMF did not extend to all the matters required to be taken into account by the General Council in making the final decision on whether India's balance of payments and reserves situation met the criteria of Article XVIII:9(a) and (b). A comparison of the plain text and context of Articles XV and XVIII:B, as well as the object and purpose of the GATT , bore this out. Article XV:2 limited the role of the IMF in determining the justification of import restrictions under Article XVIII:B to rendering statistical findings and financial determinations relating to monetary reserves and balances of payments. On the other hand, the Commit-

[221] Appellate Body Report, *Argentina-Measures Affecting Imports of Footwear, Textiles, Apparel and Other Items*, WT/DS56/AB/R, 27 March 1998.

[222] On 26 February 1952, the Intersessional Committee of GATT 1947 established a working party under the complaint procedures of Article XXIII to examine Belgian restrictions on imports from the dollar area. The terms of reference of the working party provided for the working party to consult as necessary with the Fund in accordance with Article XV. GATT/IC/SR.3, p. 18-21, cited in *Analytical Index/Guide to GATT Law and Practice* (6th ed. 1995), p. 689.

tee and the General Council were under an obligation to take into account the economic development and trade aspects of the balance-of-payments situation and the adequacy of reserves of less-developed countries under the criteria specified in Article XVIII:9. India argued that Article XVIII:B and the 1994 Understanding clarified that the WTO, in its relations with the IMF, must act through the Committee and the General Council. It was these bodies that had the task of consulting with the IMF and of "reaching their final decision" on the basis of the IMF's determination on certain financial aspects of the balance-of-payments consultations. The United States' argument that the reference to the WTO included a reference to a WTO panel failed to take into account this distribution of competence among the organs of the WTO.

3.307 India added that, most importantly, the issues of whether a time-schedule for the progressive relaxation and removal of import restrictions met the criteria set out in the Article XVIII:11 read with the interpretative note and whether the Committee should recommend the endorsement of a time-schedule for the removal of the import restrictions proposed by the consulting Members were outside the IMF's competence. The appropriate duration of a time-schedule for removal of import restrictions were clearly a trade and economic developmental issue and not a statistical or financial issue. Accordingly, under Article XVIII:12(c) and paragraphs 5 to 13 of the 1994 Understanding, the responsibility for endorsing a time-schedule proposed by a Member rested with the Committee and the General Council.

3.308 Furthermore, India argued, the ruling of the Appellate Body in *Argentina Textiles* must be confined to the facts of the dispute. in which Argentina had cited an arrangement with the IMF as a reason for imposing the statistical tax at issue in the dispute. The Appellate Body observed that it "might perhaps have been useful for the Panel to have consulted with the IMF on the legal character of the ... arrangement between Argentina and the IMF in this case...". , In this case, the Committee had already consulted with the IMF.

3.309 The **United States**, in turn, noted that the original intention of Article XV:2 had been to ensure that decisions made by the CONTRACTING PARTIES took proper account of the determinations of the IMF, the institution to which the architects of the post-war economic order gave the responsibility of overseeing balance-of-payments matters. Acceptance of India's position would effectively mean that panels would be less constrained by the rules of GATT 1994 than other bodies of the WTO and would introduce inconsistency between panels and the rest of the WTO. The United States also remarked that India had said that the Committee must accept the determinations of the IMF under Article XV:2, even though the Committee was not mentioned in the Article.

(b) Views on the competence of the International Monetary Fund

(i) "...shall accept the determination of the Fund..."

3.310 The **United States** considered that the Panel must accept as dispositive the determination of the Fund concerning whether the facts of India's balance of payments and reserve situation placed India within the criteria listed in Article XVIII:9(a) and (b). In the Balance-of-Payments Committee, the IMF had determined that India had no balance-of-payments problem and that there was no threat to or inadequacy of India's foreign exchange reserves which would merit imposition of such restrictions.[223] The concrete significance of Article XV:2 was that the WTO, and the present Panel, must accept all findings of statistical and other facts presented by the Fund in the Balance-of-Payments Committee or to this Panel relating to India's foreign exchange, monetary reserves and balances of payments. In reaching its final decision as to whether India's measures were consistent with India's obligations under Article XVIII:9 of GATT 1994, the text of Article XV:2 required the Panel to accept the determination of the Fund as to whether there was a "serious decline in [India's] monetary reserves", or what would be a "reasonable rate of increase in [India's] monetary reserves."

3.311 The United States stated that Article XV:2 expressly allocated to the IMF the authority for making certain specific determinations within the scope of its particular expertise. Allocation of that authority to the IMF had been the intent of the drafters of Article XV:2, and that intent was carried out in the practice of the CONTRACTING PARTIES. On the matters of fact specified in Article XV:2, the WTO and its bodies were required to accept the determinations of the IMF. The WTO and its bodies were free, however, to draw conclusions from, and take decisions on the basis of, the facts determined by the IMF. In other words, Article XV:2 provided that the WTO must accept the IMF's determinations with respect to whether there was a serious decline (or a threat of a serious decline) in a Member's monetary reserves, whether a Member's reserves were inadequate, and whether a Member's rate of increase of inadequate reserves was reasonable.

3.312 For the United States, the IMF's determination that India was not facing, or threatened with, balance-of-payments difficulties was a *factual* finding for consideration by the Panel. The IMF essentially acted as an "expert" that panels must consult in disputes involving issues arising under Article XVIII:B. However, this factual determination by the IMF took nothing away from the efficacy of the "final decision" phrase in Article XV:2. In the view of the United States, the sentence containing those words simply meant that *whenever* the WTO or its bodies considered the eligibility of a Member to take measures for balance-of-

[223] WT/BOP/R/22, Op. Cit.

payments purposes, they *must* accept the IMF's determination on the factual issues specified in that clause. In other words, the "final decision" clause did not prevent the IMF's determination from being *factually dispositive* of the matters to which those determinations related. Any other reading would render meaningless the requirements that the WTO "shall accept" the IMF's determination on the specified factual issues.

3.313 **India** considered that the text of Article XV:2 made it clear that the Committee and the General Council must accept certain determinations of the IMF "in reaching their final decision"; in contrast, the argument of the United States allowed the determination of the IMF on the financial aspects of the consultations to determine the legal status of a restriction notified under Article XVIII:B. Article XVIII:12(c)(ii) also clearly stated that the Committee and the General Council determined the inconsistency of the import restrictions with Article XVIII:B. In India's view, Articles XV:2 and XVIII:12 left no doubt that the IMF did not take the final decision on the legal status of the import restrictions under the WTO. Moreover, Article XV:1 affirmed that jurisdiction over "quantitative restrictions and other trade measures" remain with the CONTRACTING PARTIES although it acknowledged the jurisdiction of the IMF over exchange issues.

3.314 In India's opinion, the drafting history confirmed that the final decisions of the Committee and the General Council did not necessarily have to follow the determinations of the IMF regarding the financial aspects of the balance-of-payments consultations. During the discussions of paragraphs 2 and 3 of the corresponding Havana Charter Article (Article 24) at the Havana Conference it was stated that:

> "If the provisions of Article 24 were considered with Article 21 [XII], there was no basis for the fears that the ITO would be subservient to the Fund. The provisions of paragraphs 2(a)(ii) and (3(a) of Article 21 [XII] made it clear that the final decision as to whether restrictions would be instituted or maintained rested with the ITO, notwithstanding determinations made by the IMF."[224]

3.315 India considered that it was important to note that "balance of payments difficulties" in Article XVIII:12 reflected the obligation of the Committee and the General Council to take the economic development needs of less-developed countries into account when assessing the justification for import restrictions. Article XVIII:8 recognized that the less-developed country Members suffered from balance-of-payments difficulties because of efforts to expand internal markets as well as from instability in their terms of trade. In addition, in arriving at any determinations under Articles XVIII:12(c) or (d), the Committee and the General Council must consider certain special factors referred to in Article XVIII:2. Article XVIII:2 also emphasized the special responsibility of the

[224] WTO, *Analytical Index: Guide to GATT Law and Practice*, Vol. 1, p. 431.

Committee and the General Council to consider economic developmental issues affecting less-developed country Members. Thus, it recognized that import restrictions might be necessary to help less-developed country Members implement their economic development programmes and that such import restrictions "*are justified insofar as they facilitate the attainment of the objectives of the [GATT]*". It also required the Committee to take "full account of the continued high level of demand for imports likely to be generated by the economic development programmes of [less-developed Members]". There was little doubt, therefore, that as between the Committee and the General Council, on the one hand, and the IMF, on the other, it was the Committee and the General Council that had a special obligation to look after the trade related economic development needs of less-developed country Members.

3.316 India noted that the IMF staff shared this understanding of the relationship between it and the WTO. A paper entitled *The Relationship of the World Trade Organization with the Fund - Legal Aspects* explained:

> "It is also important to note that "acceptance" by the CONTRACTING PARTIES of the Fund's factual findings or determinations does not preclude the right of the CONTRACTING PARTIES to make their own independent "final decision" on the balance of payments exception to the GATT. The legal effect of this consultation obligation is that the decisions of the CONTRACTING PARTIES under the balance of payments provisions of the GATT should be made *on the basis of, or having regard to*, the Fund's findings and determinations."[225]

3.317 As further evidence, India noted that the views of the CONTRACTING PARTIES had sometimes deviated from those of the IMF. For instance, when the United States imposed a surcharge for balance-of-payments reasons in 1971, the IMF reported in the GATT consultations that "in the absence of other appropriate action and in the present circumstances the import surcharge can be regarded as being within the bounds of what is necessary to stop a serious deterioration in the United States' balance-of-payments position" and it further stated that it had "no alternative measures to suggest at this time".[226] By contrast the CONTRACTING PARTIES found "that the surcharge, as a trade-restrictive measure, was inappropriate given the nature of the United States balance-of-payments situation and the undue burden of adjustment placed upon the import account ..."[227] India concluded that the Committee, in arriving at its final determination on the consistency, or otherwise, of a Member's import restrictions under Article XVIII:B, was not bound by the determinations of the IMF under Article XV:2.

[225] IMF document SM/94/303, 20 December 1994, p. 23.
[226] *Report of the Working Party on the United States Temporary Import Surcharge*; BISD 18S/214.
[227] *Ibid.*, p. 222.

3.318 The **United States** pointed out, with reference to the discussions at the Havana Conference, that India's reference was to a statement made by an individual delegation at Havana which had never been incorporated into the text of the General Agreement. and had no legal status with respect to the WTO. In addition, delegations at Geneva had considered, but not adopted, a proposal to replace the words "shall accept the determination" of the Fund with the words "shall give special weight to the opinions" of the Fund. The proposal had been made by Australia "on the main ground that since the [ITO] has the responsibility for action under [what became Article XII of the GATT 1994], it should also retain the right of final decision as to whether the criteria of para. 2(a) have been met."[228]

3.319 With respect to the *Report of the Working Party on the United States Temporary Import Surcharge*, the IMF had made a finding that the United States was in balance-of-payments difficulties. While the CONTRACTING PARTIES did not approve the particular measure chosen by the United States to respond to those difficulties, their decision did not call into question the determination by the IMF that the United States was facing balance-of-payments difficulties.

3.320 With respect to India's argument that because Article XVIII:B had an economic development dimension, the IMF's determinations could not be dispositive of the factual matters before this Panel, the United States replied that India's conclusion did not follow from its premise. Nothing suggested that the IMF was incapable of considering the development program of a Member in making its determinations about that Member's reserves. The IMF conducted a review and assessment of every Fund member's economy once a year. Furthermore, the text of Article XV:2 did not distinguish between Article XVIII:B (in which economic development played a role) and Article XII (in which it did not). Article XV:2 treated Article XII and Article XVIII:B identically. The United States also considered that this issue was essentially a theoretical one: India had provided no facts from which the Panel could conclude that the IMF's analysis of India's balance-of-payments situation was wrong.

3.321 The United States considered that IMF document SM/94/303, when read more fully, said only that while the WTO must accept a determination that a country has, for instance, a serious problem with monetary reserves, the WTO retained the right to determine whether a particular trade measure exceeded what was necessary to address the problem. The United States had not claimed otherwise.

3.322 **India** contended that the Report of the Working Party on *The United States - Temporary Import Surcharge* did not support the U.S. argument on the role of the IMF. The Working Party in that case obviously looked into both justification and application aspects. This was clear from the fact that the Working Party first "took note of the findings of the IMF" and then separately "recognized

[228] E/PC/T/163, 11 August 1947, p. 20, item 7.

that the United States had found itself in a serious balance-of-payments situation which required urgent attention". In India's view, the language used by the Working Party clearly brought out the distinction between consideration of the inputs provided by the IMF and the final decision of the CONTRACTING PARTIES on whether there was a balance-of-payments problem that justified import restrictions. In this context, India did not dispute that the Committee must consult the IMF, consider such factual inputs as they were permitted to give under Article XV:2, and then come to a conclusion that struck a balance between the rights and the needs of a country in the process of development and their fellow Member countries.

(ii) "...what constitutes a threat of a serious decline"

3.323 **India** considered that the competence of the IMF did not extend to all the matters required to be taken into account by the General Council in making the final decision on whether India's balance of payments and reserves situation met the criteria of Article XVIII:9 (a) and (b). A comparison of the plain text and context of Articles XV and XVIII:B, as well as the object and purpose of the GATT, bore this out. Article XV:2 limited the role of the IMF in determining the justification of import restrictions under Article XVIII:B to rendering statistical findings and financial determinations relating to monetary reserves and balances of payments. While taking a final decision, the Committee and the General Council were required to accept the following findings and determinations of the IMF:

(a) IMF findings of statistical and other facts relating to monetary reserves and balances of payments; and

(b) IMF determinations "as to what constitutes":

- a serious decline in monetary reserves,
- a very low level of monetary reserves,
- a reasonable rate of increase in monetary reserves; and
- the financial aspects of other matters covered in consultations.

3.324 On the other hand, according to India, the Committee and the General Council were under an obligation to take into account the economic development and trade aspects of the balance of payments situation and the adequacy of reserves of less-developed countries under the criteria specified in Article XVIII:9. The IMF determination with respect to Article XVIII:9(a) and (b) was only one component of the larger consultations process in the Committee pursuant to Article XVIII:12 which was premised upon a reconciliation of the economic development needs of an individual less-developed country Member imposing import restrictions with the interests of its trading partners.

3.325 Even on issues relating to monetary reserves, India considered that there were various omissions from the competence of the IMF with respect to monetary reserves under Article XV:2. These omissions reflected the intention of the CONTRACTING PARTIES to reserve issues relating to the economic development of the less-developed country Members for themselves. In particular, the IMF could only determine what "constituted" a serious decline in monetary reserves not whether there was one. That is, with respect to a particular Member, the IMF could only determine how much of a decline in reserves would render it a serious decline; it could not make the final decision on whether there was a serious decline in monetary reserves. If the intention behind Article XVIII:9(a) had been to permit import restrictions only after a serious decline had already occurred, then the language of Article XVIII:9(a) would have read "to forestall a threat of, or to reverse, a serious decline in monetary reserves," not to stop it. Moreover, there would be no distinction between the two situations with respect to monetary reserves contemplated by Article XVIII:9(a) and (b); presumably, after a serious decline had already occurred as determined by the IMF, the less-developed country Member concerned would already be facing a situation of inadequate reserves. The second situation covered by Article XVIII:9(b) would then be redundant or merely a reiteration in a different manner of Article XVIII:9(a). Accordingly, the role of the IMF under Article XV:2 must be limited to the words intentionally chosen by the drafters; the IMF could only specify the criteria for judging what constituted a serious decline in monetary reserves under Article XVIII:9 and not whether there was a serious decline in monetary reserves.

3.326 India considered that Article XV:2 did not entrust the determination of whether there was a threat of a serious decline in monetary reserves to the IMF. The fact that almost none of the multilateral financial institutions or the private credit rating agencies accurately predicted the recent balance-of-payments crisis in South East Asia suggested that mathematical precision was impossible in estimating the magnitude or probability of a threat to the balance of payments situation. Accordingly, it appeared to be a subject more amenable to determination within the consultations process in the Committee. In this context, it was important to note that, in contrast to Article XII:2(a) which required an "imminent threat" of a serious decline in monetary reserves before developed country Members could impose import restrictions, Article XVIII:9(a) required just "a threat". In addition, even in the context of the "imminent threat" in Article XII:2, at the Geneva session of the Preparatory Committee, one representative noted that:

> "matters to be taken into consideration may be almost entirely trade questions, such as, for instance, the imminent threat to Australia's balance of payments through the failure of her wheat crop. I say nothing about what would happen if all the sheep died. Equally there might be, in the case of another country, some financial as-

pect of the imminent threat on which I should have thought the assistance of the [IMF] would be extremely useful to the ITO."[229]

3.327 In India's view, there were trade aspects to the determination of a threat of a serious decline in monetary reserves that were solely within the competence of the Committee.

3.328 In the view of the **United States**, the question of whether a Member's balance-of-payments situation met the criteria of Article XVIII:9(a) and (b) was an exchange and financial question and therefore, in accordance with Article XV:1 and 2, for the IMF to determine. When the IMF assessed India's reserves movements, it was assessing whether these constituted a serious decline, i.e., "is there a serious decline or is one threatened?".

(iii) "... adequacy of reserves ..."

3.329 **India** also argued that Article XV:2 did not give the IMF the competence to determine whether the reserves of a less-developed country Member were "inadequate" as required by Article XVIII:9(b). The adequacy of the reserves of a developing country Member for purposes of Article XVIII:9 had to be assessed in relation to the demands of its programme of economic development over a period of time. In this regard, the Report of the Review Working Party on "Quantitative Restrictions", the main source of the drafting history of Articles XII and XVIII:B, C and D, noted that:

> "... [P]aragraph 9 [of Article XVIII], although modelled on paragraphs 1 and 2 of Article XII, recognizes that the reserve problem for these countries is one of the adequacy of the reserves in relation to their programme of economic development, that for this reason the word 'imminent' which occurs in paragraph II(a) is inappropriate in this context, and that in order to safeguard their external position these countries may need over a period of time to control the general level of their imports ..."[230]

3.330 India considered that Article XV:2 specifically omitted the determination of the adequacy of reserves of a less-developed country Member from the competence of the IMF under Article XV:2 because Article XVIII:B had an economic developmental dimension - as opposed to a purely financial one - that the Committee had a special responsibility to take fully into account as required by Article XVIII:12(f), Article XVIII:2 and Article XVIII:8.

3.331 The **United States,** noting that Article XV:2 applied equally to Article XII and Article XVIII:B, considered that the issue under subparagraph (b) of Article XVIII:9 was whether a Member with inadequate reserves was achieving a reasonable rate of increase; Article XV:2 did require the WTO to accept the

---

[229] EPCT/A/PV/41, pp. 69-70.

[230] L/332/Rev.1 and Addenda, BISD 3S/183.

IMF's determination of what constituted a reasonable rate of increase of reserves. It also required that the WTO accept the IMF's determination on financial matters generally, in addition to those specifically mentioned in Article XV:2. The United States considered that, while Article XVIII:9 also referred to the existence of "inadequate monetary reserves," this reference was clearly covered by the reference in the final sentence of Article XV:2 to "the financial aspects of other matters covered in consultation in such cases." Nor was there anything that suggested that the IMF was incapable of considering the development program of a Member in making a determination about that Member's reserves, since it reviewed and assessed each Fund member's economy annually. In the view of the United States, the IMF's determination on the adequacy of reserves should be considered as binding.

3.332 The United States considered that the *Report of the Review Working Party on Quantitative Restrictions* also recognized the interests of the trading partners of developing countries. The Report recognized that because the measures to be authorized by Article XVIII:B would have effects on other contracting parties, such measures must be restrained by rules and safeguards:

> "The general concept of the new Article is that economic development is consistent with the objectives of the General Agreement ...
>
> "[T]he new Article contains a number of safeguards to ensure that the exercise of the right to deviate from an obligation under the Agreement would be strictly limited to cases where no other alternative measure consistent with the Agreement would be available... ."[231]

This statement explained the object and purpose of Article XVIII: to achieve a balance between the rights and needs of both a country in the process of development and that country's fellow Members. The right of a developing country member to utilize the provisions of Article XVIII:B was therefore qualified by the right of other Members to protect their interests by insisting on compliance with the strict limitations that had been built into that Article. Article XVIII was a negotiated text that, like many other agreements in the trading system, took account of different Members' interests and concerns. Its drafters appreciated that point, and made sure that their Report expressed it. India was entitled to rely on measures authorized by Article XVIII:B when they were justified: India's trading partners - developed and developing - were entitled to rely on India not to exceed the limits of that authorization. In this case, that meant that India's trading partners were entitled to have India respect the limitations contained in Articles XVIII:9 and 11 that required India to eliminate the challenged measures. With respect to India's point that Article XVIII:9 (unlike its counterpart in Article XII) did not require an "imminent" threat of a serious decline in reserves, the United States noted that it did still require a *threat of a serious decline* in reserves. In India's case no such threat existed or was expected.

[231] BISD 3S/170, paras. 35-36.

(iv) "...financial aspects of other matters covered in consultation..."

3.333 In **India**'s view, although the IMF had a residual competence with respect to "the financial aspects of other matters covered in consultations", the term "financial" also delimited precisely the area of the IMF's competence. For example, the financial aspects of other matters clearly included one of the special factors specifically mentioned in Article XVIII:9, i.e., the availability of special external credits or other resources. India contended that only the CONTRACTING PARTIES and not the IMF would be able to assess the economic developmental aspects of the need to put these special credits or resources to proper use. This interpretation was also consistent with Article XV:2 which limited the competence of the IMF to questions relating to exchange, monetary reserves and balance of payments. The term "financial aspects of other matters" could not be used to extend the scope of IMF determinations with respect to the criteria set forth in the proviso to Article XVIII:9 beyond the determinations specifically mentioned in the last sentence of Article XV:2. Any such interpretation would render the words "of other matters" superflous in this sentence. India noted further that GATT working parties had also interpreted the term "the financial aspects of other matters" as covering matters other than those mentioned in the proviso to Article XVIII:9.[232]

3.334 In conclusion, India stated that an analysis of the provisions of Articles XV and Article XVIII:B made it clear that there were both economic developmental and trade aspects to the final decision to be made under Article XVIII:9 that the Committee and the General Council - not the IMF - were uniquely qualified to make. Therefore, a determination by the IMF that import restrictions lacked economic justification under Article XVIII:B was clearly outside its competence and could not bind the Committee and the General Council. It followed that the determination by the IMF that India's import restrictions did not have any justification under Article XVIII:9 was not "dispositive" .

3.335 In the view of the **United States**, the words "...and as to the financial aspects of other matters covered in consultations in such cases" were a broad text and should be construed to include statements by the Fund with respect to financial matters connected with balance-of-payments matters but not explicitly referred to in Article XV:2. The United States cited a Balance-of-Payments Committee Note from 1975:

> ..."the Fund's determinations have generally gone beyond merely stating what constitutes a serious decline in reserves...but have compared the overall level of import controls with the reserve position. During the past five years, the Committee has accepted in all

[232] *Analytical Index of the GATT*, pp. 432-433, Section II.A.4(b) under the chapter on Article XV, where the reports of the working parties on "United Kingdom Import Deposits" and "United States Temporary Import Surcharge" are discussed.

> cases the Fund's broad determinations. In one case the consulting country disagreed with the Fund's assessment and the Committee's decision to follow the Fund's determination"[233]

(v) Matters outside the scope of XV:2.

3.336 **India** cited a letter from the head of the Legal Department of the IMF provided in July 1997 in response to India's request for clarification as to whether the WTO had to accept the IMF views on matters not mentioned in Article XV:2, which mentioned that:

> "...With respect to expressions of the Fund's views outside the scope of Article XV, these are not legally required to be accepted by the Committee on Balance-of-Payments Restrictions. The report of the Committee to the WTO for its "final decision" as to whether a trade restriction is justified under the GATT must also take into account the criteria applicable to these restrictions stated in Article XVIII. Thus, for example, in the course of a consultation, the Fund may have made a determination that a contracting party has a "serious problem with its monetary reserves"; while they are obliged to accept that determination, the CONTRACTING PARTIES may nevertheless decide that the particular import restrictions or other trade measures applied by that contracting party "exceed" those "necessary" to correct its balance of payments problem as provided for under Article XII, Section 2(a) or Article XVIII, Section 9…In practice, however, there have been only rare cases in which a reviewing committee reported that a restriction was inappropriate although the Fund had identified a balance of payments problem. Additionally, a practice has developed over time whereby the Fund's statement to the Committee has become broader than that articulated in Article XV, primarily to provide a fuller context within which to assess the trade-restrictive measures... This established practice, although significant, does not change the legal point that the final decision on whether the measure is justified under the WTO agreements ultimately rests with the Committee on Balance-of-Payments Restrictions…"

3.337 For India, this confirmed that, while the IMF in practice offered views on matters other than those referred to in Article XV:2, the WTO was not required to base its final decision on these views.

[233] L/4200, 18 July 1975, paras.18-19. The country referred to was Spain: the report of the Committee, in which it followed the Fund's determination, was however adopted by the GATT Council on 19 October 1973 (C/M/90, page 2).

3.338 The **United States** noted that, as India had pointed out, in the first years of IMF-GATT cooperation on balance-of-payments matters, a question arose among the CONTRACTING PARTIES (as they were preparing for the Fifth Session, at Torquay, in 1950) whether the IMF was expected to transmit to the GATT an evaluation of the facts it accumulated on the balance-of-payments situation of countries concerned, or merely the facts themselves.[234] Although no formal decision was taken then, the practice developed under GATT 1947 to accept the conclusions provided by the IMF. The former Director of the Secretariat Legal Affairs Division had provided his views in an article:

> "GATT is institutionally not equipped to collect and evaluate data on financial matters. To arrive at meaningful conclusions, it therefore relies on the Fund's advice not only for facts on monetary matters, but also for their evaluation. Although the question as to exactly what GATT is obliged to accept from the Fund has been raised from time to time after the Torquay controversy - in particular by contracting parties dissatisfied with the Fund's findings - a formal decision to settle the issue has never proved necessary because the Fund's conclusions have, even in the controversial cases, always been accepted in the end."[235]

3.339 The United States recalled that two individual examples of this practice of following the IMF's determination included the consultations with Germany beginning in 1957, and the 1973 consultations with Spain. In each case the CONTRACTING PARTIES acted on the basis of judgments by the IMF about the reserve position of the country in question. The case of Spain was particularly noteworthy, because Spanish objections to acceptance of the IMF's conclusions were simply not accepted by the CONTRACTING PARTIES. The IMF statements to the Balance-of-Payments Committee in the 1997 consultations concerning India were another instance of this practice. They should be found to be dispositive of the factual question of whether India was faced with a threat of or serious decline in its monetary reserves, or whether the removal of the quantitative restrictions at issue in this dispute would result in a threat of or serious decline in such reserves.

3.340 In **India's** view, GATT practice was authoritative only in the context of dispute settlement cases brought under Article XXIII that were approved by the

---

[234] The United States stated that as India had pointed out, the IMF side of this story had been told by Margaret G. DeVries. What India failed to mention was the outcome: "Eventually these questions had to be answered by vote. The Board decided that the Fund was to supply to the GATT not only relevant statistical data but also conclusions as to the current need for restrictions." "Collaborating with the GATT," in J. Keith Horsefield, ed., *The International Monetary Fund 1945-1965: Twenty Years of International Monetary Cooperation* (IMF, 1969), vol. II, p. 332.

[235] Frieder Roessler, "Selective Balance-of-Payments Adjustment Measures Affecting Trade: The Roles of the GATT and the IMF," *Journal of World Trade*, Vol. 9, page 622, 648 (November-December 1975).

CONTRACTING PARTIES. Thus, the so-called GATT practice in the Committee of accepting the IMF's views on whether a Member's import restrictions had justification was no basis for according finality to the IMF's opinion if Article XV:2 did not render the IMF's opinion final. It was impossible to discern from the Committee's reports on consultations whether the members of the Committee did so because they considered themselves bound by the IMF's views or whether they did so because they independently arrived at the same conclusion. Therefore, the so-called GATT practice within the Committee could not give the IMF's determination a more binding character than warranted by the text of Articles XV:2 and XVIII:B. Accordingly, India respectfully submitted that the IMF's "determination" that India's import restrictions lacked justification could not bind this Panel.

3.341 The **United States** considered that, for the following reasons, the WTO and this Panel were required to accept factual findings and determinations by the IMF with respect to whether the removal of the quantitative restrictions at issue in this dispute would result in a serious decline (or threat thereof) in India's reserves. The Note Ad Article XVIII:11 provided that India was not required to remove the restrictions at issue in this dispute "if such removal ... would thereupon produce conditions justifying the ... institution ... of restrictions under paragraph 9 of Article XVIII." The Ad Note was therefore explicitly linked to Article XVIII:9. A link to Article XVIII:9 was also explicitly made in the final sentence of Article XV:2, by which the WTO was bound to accept the determinations of the IMF with respect to, *inter alia*, what constituted a serious decline. Article XV:2, final sentence, therefore should be read as explicitly applying to the IMF's factual findings and determinations with respect to matters arising under the Ad Note. Further textual support for this view was found in the second sentence of Article XV:2, which provided that the WTO "shall accept all findings of statistical and other facts presented by the Fund relating to ... balance of payments ... ." Additionally, Article XV:2, final sentence, also contemplated that the WTO must accept determinations of the IMF concerning "the financial aspects of other matters covered in consultation in such cases." which, in the view of the United States, would encompass factual determinations related to the Ad Note to Article XVIII:11. Thus, the United States considered that, based on the text of these provisions, the Panel must accept the IMF's factual determinations related, *inter alia*, to the existence of a serious decline in reserves or threat thereof following removal of the quantitative restrictions at issue in this dispute. The United States considered that the object and purpose of Article XV:2 is to allocate jurisdiction to the IMF for determination of factual questions, concerning, *inter alia*, foreign exchange, monetary reserves, balance of payments and other financial matters in such cases. The IMF's determination of whether removal of quantitative restrictions would lead to a serious decline was therefore a factual finding that the WTO and this Panel must accept. The United States added that even if the Panel did not agree that the IMF's determination was binding, the determinations of the IMF would provide evidence that the Panel should consider about

India's balance-of-payments situation following removal of the challenged measures.

3.342 While Article XV:2 provided that the WTO must accept the IMF's determination with respect to the matters within the scope of that Article, the United States agreed that the WTO did not, however, need to accept the IMF's determinations whether a particular trade measure exceeded or did not exceed what was necessary, or whether a particular measure otherwise complied with the requirements of Article XVIII:B or XII. Those determinations were for the WTO and its bodies to make.

3.343 **India** contended that the issues of whether a time-schedule for the progressive relaxation and removal of import restrictions met the criteria set out in the Article XVIII:11 read with the interpretative note and whether the Committee should recommend the endorsement of a time-schedule for the removal of the import restrictions proposed by the consulting Members were clearly outside the IMF's competence. The appropriate duration of a time-schedule for removal of import restrictions was clearly a trade and economic developmental issue and not a statistical or financial issue. Accordingly, under Article XVIII:12(c) and paragraphs 5 to 13 of the 1994 Understanding, the responsibility for endorsing a time-schedule proposed by a Member rested with the Committee and the General Council.

3.344 With respect to the letter from the Head of the IMF's Legal Department, the **United States** saw no conflict with its own position. The United States agreed with the points made that "the WTO is required to accept not only the Fund's findings of statistical and other facts specifically mentioned in [Article XV:2], but also the determinations under the two provisions quoted above [including the requirements in the proviso to Article XVIII:9]." and that the WTO was not required to accept the IMF's determination on matters "outside the scope of Article XV:2". Finally, The *Relationship Between the World Trade Organization and the Fund - Legal Aspects*[236] said only that while the WTO must accept a determination that a country has, for instance, a serious problem with monetary reserves, the WTO retained the right to determine whether a particular trade measure exceeded what was necessary to address the problem. In the view of the United States, the IMF had made the factual determination that India was not in any of the balance-of-payments difficulties described in Article XVIII:9; consequently, no trade measures of any kind were necessary to address India's balance-of-payments situation.

[236] IMF document SM/94/303, dated 20 December 1994.

(c) The Panel's consultations with the IMF

(i) Parties comments on the questions to the IMF

3.345 The Panel, having regard to Article 13 of the DSU and to Article XV:2 of the GATT 1994, decided to consult the IMF. It so informed the Parties and circulated its proposed set of questions for comment by the Parties on 24 June. On 30 June, the Parties comments were received and taken into consideration in redrafting the Panel's questions. (Where the full comments are not reflected the views are reflected elsewhere in the text.) The questions were sent to the IMF on 3 July, and the replies received on 22 July, as requested.

3.346 In its comments on the proposed questions, the **United States** considered that 15 July 1997, the date of request for consultations, was the date as of which the Panel should determine whether India's measures were justified under Article XVIII:B; or, at the latest, 18 November 1997, the date of the establishment of the Panel, a point with which India had agreed. Changes in India's balance-of-payments situation since then were not relevant to the current dispute.

3.347 **India** pointed out that it was relevant to ask the IMF for its views on developments since that date since much of the evidence that the United States had submitted related to the period following the establishment of the Panel.

3.348 With respect to the question regarding the IMF's views on the effect of the removal of restrictions, the **United States** considered these should focus on the balance-of-payments effect.

3.349 Both parties agreed that whether the import restrictions "exceeded" what was "necessary" to meet the criteria of paragraph 9(a) and (b) was a trade issue within the purview of the WTO.

3.350 **India** reiterated its points regarding the limited competence of the IMF, that *inter alia*, the WTO was the institution that had the responsibility of assessing the balance-of-payments situation in relation to a Member's economic development needs. Nor did India believe that the Panel should seek the IMF's opinion on whether the removal or relaxation of the restrictions would lead to conditions justifying their introduction or intensification, an evaluation which only the WTO could provide. In India's view, the IMF's role was restricted to specifying the criteria of "what constituted" a threat of serious decline, "inadequate" or a reasonable rate of increase in reserves, not whether there was.

3.351 India considered that the WTO had an obligation to consult the IMF only with respect to specific points mentioned above. However, only the WTO can apply the findings and determinations of the IMF and make determinations on whether (i) for purposes of Article XVIII:9(a), a decline in reserves will turn into a serious one or, in the absence of a decline, whether a threat of serious decline exists, and (ii) for purposes of Article XVIII:9(b), reserves are inadequate. In other words, the WTO must evaluate the likelihood of the threat of a serious decline in a Member's monetary reserves, its adequacy and whether the rate of increase in reserves exceeds what is reasonable. This followed because only the

WTO was competent to factor in the trade aspects of a threat to the balance-of-payments and monetary reserves. The trade aspect of a threat to the balance of payments was especially important when evaluating the impact of the removal of import restrictions in terms of the Note *Ad* Article XVIII:11.

3.352 Further, India reiterated its view that the WTO must assess the balance-of-payments and reserves situation of a Member invoking Article XVIII:B in relation to its programme of economic development over a period of time. This followed from a structural nature of the balance-of-payments problems of a Member under Article XVIII:B as compared to the temporary, cyclical nature of the balance-of-payments problem under Article XII:2(a). In addition, various provisions of Article XVIII:B, including paragraphs 1 through 3, 5, 8, 11 and 12(c) and (f) of Article XVIII, assigned the responsibility for assessing the economic development needs of a Member to the WTO - not the IMF.

3.353 India noted that the United States had been unable to rebut India's arguments on the competence of the IMF or to provide any textual basis for its view that the IMF's decision was final for purposes of Article XVIII:9 on the likelihood of a threat of serious decline in a Member's reserves or on the adequacy of its reserves relative to its programme of economic development.

3.354 India elaborated further stating that other decisions, declarations and understandings of the WTO relating to the balance-of-payments provisions of the GATT 1994 demarcated the respective roles of the WTO, the IMF and the Members invoking Article XVIII:B during consultations and confirm the limited role of the IMF. These WTO documents included:

(i) Procedures and Arrangements for Regular Consultations on Balance-of-Payments Restrictions, 1970[237] (the "1970 Full Consultations Procedures");

(ii) Procedures for Regular Consultations on Balance-of-Payments Restrictions with Developing Countries, 1972[238] (the "1972 Simplified Procedures");

(iii) Declaration on Trade Measures Taken for Balance-of-Payments Purposes, 1979 (the "1979 Declaration"); and

(iv) Understanding on the balance-of-Payments Provisions of the General Agreement on Tariffs and Trade 1994 (the "1994 Understanding").

3.355 In describing the full consultations procedures under Articles XII and XVIII:B, in India's view, the 1970 Full Consultations Procedures suggested a limited role for the IMF. Paragraph 6 provided that the time schedule for consultations must be drawn up in "light of the ... progress of consultations of the [IMF] with the governments concerned so as to ensure that the *most up-to-date*

[237] BISD 18S/48-53.
[238] BISD 20S/47-49.

and meaningful possible data form part of the Fund's contribution ..." [Emphasis added.] Paragraph 8 delimited the role of the IMF in consultations: "Under paragraph 2 of Article XV, the CONTRACTING PARTIES are required to consult with the IMF on the points specified in that paragraph."

3.356 In addition, Annex I to the 1970 Full Consultations Procedures contained the "Plan of Discussion for Consultations Under Articles XII:4(b) and XVIII:12(b). The heading, "Balance-of-Payments Position and Prospects", presumably covered the issue of a threat of serious decline in monetary reserves and the adequacy of reserves. The fourth item under this heading was "Factors, either external or internal, affecting the various elements of the balance-of-payments, such as exports and imports". The fifth item was "Effects of the restrictions on the balance-of-payments and expected duration of the restrictions". The sixth item was "Prospects of relaxation or elimination and likely effect of such action on the balance-of-payments". Clearly, as trade issues, these were entirely within the purview of the WTO and, therefore, the CONTRACTING PARTIES under the GATT had never intended to give the final word on the possibility of a threat of a serious decline to the IMF. India considered that this analysis was confirmed by the structure of regular consultations by developing countries under the 1972 Simplified Procedures. Under paragraph 3(b) of these simplified procedures, the Member invoking Article XVIII:B submitted a concise written statement of its balance-of-payments difficulties. Under paragraph 3(d), the IMF merely submitted balance-of-payments statistics. Under paragraph 3(c), the Committee decided whether to require the Member to invoke full consultations. Effectively, therefore, it was the Committee that determined whether a Member's balance-of-payments difficulties had lessened to the point where full consultations were necessary in the absence of an IMF determination on whether the conditions in Article XVIII:9 were met. As stated in paragraph 2, the 1972 Simplified Procedures represented a "solution which would both meet the legal requirements of the General Agreement and lessen the burden of the CONTRACTING PARTIES and the developing countries concerned without detracting from the basic objective of fostering understanding of the balance-of-payments problems of the developing countries and providing opportunities for exploring constructive solutions to them".

3.357 Nor, India commented, did the 1979 Declaration accord a greater role to the IMF than the 1970 Full Consultations Procedures and the 1972 Simplified Consultations Procedures. It provided for a basic document to be provided to the Committee by the consulting Member that had invoked Article XVIII:B, a background paper by the WTO Secretariat and a paper on "Recent Economic Developments" by the IMF. Paragraph 11 of the 1994 Understanding provided that the Basic Document should include "an overview of the balance-of-payments situation and prospects, including a consideration of the internal and external factors having a bearing on the balance-of-payments situation.". Again, this aspect of the basic document would be unnecessary if the IMF had the power to make a determination binding on the WTO as to whether a Member's balance-of-payments and monetary reserves situation justified import restrictions under Article XVIII:B. Therefore, the 1970 Full Consultations Procedures, 1972 Simplified Consultations Procedures, 1979 Declaration and the 1994 Understanding confirmed that the role of the IMF in this proceeding should be limited, as a matter of law, to the specific findings and determinations provided for in Article XV:2.

3.358 India considered that India's economic development and the effect of the progressive liberalization of India's import regime, *prima facie*, were not matters on which the Panel should seek the views of the IMF. The competence of the IMF under Article XV:2 did not extend to economic development or trade issues. Under the 1970 Full Consultations Procedures, the Member invoking Article XVIII:B must furnish to the Committee its own assessment of its economic development needs. The GATT Secretariat furnished the background paper that permitted the Committee to assess the trade issues that were involved. Accordingly, India considered that, as provided in the 1970 Full Consultations Procedures, the 1979 Declaration and the 1994 Understanding, the Panel should make its own assessment of India's economic development needs and its own assessment of how to reconcile India's trade interests with those of its trading partners after going through all the relevant material. Therefore, it would be appropriate for the Panel to ask the IMF *to explain how* it took India's economic development needs as well as risks and prudence into account, while answering each question. This would enable the Panel to determine the weight to be accorded to the IMF's views.

(ii) Questions to and replies from the IMF

1(a)(i) *As of 18 November 1997, the date of establishment of the Panel, was India experiencing a serious decline in its monetary reserves, or facing a threat thereof?*

3.359 Foreign currency reserves of India's monetary authorities (the Reserve Bank of India, RBI) stood at US$25.1 billion (excluding gold) on 21 November 1997.[239] This level represented an increase of US$5.6 billion from a year earlier, and of US$2.8 billion from end-March 1997.[240] Net of forward liabilities, foreign currency reserves stood at US$23 billion at end-November 1997.

3.360 The establishment of the WTO panel coincided with a period of turbulence in the foreign exchange market in India, with increased fears of further contagion from the financial crisis in east and southeast Asia. The facts are as follows: the rupee faced periodic bouts of downward pressure beginning in August 1997. These pressures intensified in November 1997. The RBI initially

[239] Data on official reserves are published weekly by the RBI. On 13 November 1997, foreign currency reserves were at US$26 billion. Data on the RBI's outstanding net forward sales or purchases are published monthly.

[240] India's financial years runs from 1 April to 31 March.

intervened heavily in spot and forward markets to prevent large daily fluctuations in the exchange rate that could have provoked bandwagon effects. Faced with a reserve loss of about US$2.6 billion (including forward obligations) during November 1997, and continued pressure on the rupee, the RBI subsequently abandoned active intervention and tightened monetary policy. Thus, with an appropriate macroeconomic policy response and the containment of contagion, India's foreign currency reserves on 18 November 1997 did not appear to be under a threat of a serious decline. Therefore, the question of whether an imminent threat existed is moot.

1(a)(ii) *Was India experiencing an inadequate, or a very low, level of monetary reserves?*

3.361 At about six months of imports of goods and non-factor services, India's reserves appeared to provide sufficient external liquidity and a reasonable degree of protection against unforeseen external shocks. In particular, reserves were sufficient to deal with debt service payments and potential outflows of portfolio investment, covering 2½ times the amount of maturing debt obligations in the next twelve months and 1½ times the stock of short-term debt and cumulative inflows of portfolio investment. Therefore, it is the Fund's view that the level of foreign currency reserves on November 18, 1997 was adequate.

1(a)(iii) *Was India experiencing a reasonable rate of increase in its monetary reserves?*

3.362 Gross foreign currency reserves fell by US$1.9 billion in November 1997. (Net of the RBI's forward obligations, foreign currency reserves fell by US$2.6 billion that month.) From a broader perspective, however, there has been a reasonable rate of accumulation of reserves since India's balance-of-payments crisis in 1991. For example, at end-November 1997, reserves were up US$5 billion from a year earlier. (Net of forward obligations, this increase was US$4.5 billion.)

1(b) *In connection with responding to these questions, could the IMF indicate what would have constituted a serious decline in India's monetary reserves, what would have constituted an inadequate, or a very low, level of monetary reserves for India, and what would have constituted a reasonable rate of increase in India's monetary reserves?*

3.363 A considerable degree of subjective judgment is involved in an assessment of the adequacy of the level and rate of change of reserves. The Fund's view on this question is based on the size of existing and potential claims on reserves, examined in the context of the country's economic circumstances. In the case of India, policy has prudently aimed at ensuring that reserve coverage is ahead of the sum of outstanding short-term liabilities (by remaining maturity) and potential outflows of portfolio investment. As of November 1997, short-term liabilities (by remaining maturity) and the stock of portfolio investment (after marking-to-market) were estimated at about US$16 billion. Hence, a decline in reserves to significantly below this level would be considered serious, and such levels could be deemed inadequate or very low. In case reserves were deemed to be inadequate at this threshold, any increase in reserves that would bring them above this level should be considered reasonable.

2(a) *Could the IMF provide the Panel with any statistical and other factual information relating to India's balance of payments and monetary reserves which might be relevant in order to enable the Panel to determine whether, as of 18 November 1997, the quantitative restrictions notified by India as being maintained for balance-of-payments reasons did, or did not, exceed those necessary to forestall the threat of, or to stop, a serious decline in its monetary reserves, or, in case its monetary reserves were inadequate, to achieve a reasonable rate of increase in its reserves?*

3.364 India's overall balance of payments recorded sizable surpluses in 1996/97 and 1997/98, while the current account deficit remained in the range of 1-1½ of GDP (see attached table). However, export performance in dollar terms has weakened. Exports grew by 2½% in dollar terms in 1997/98, compared with 4½% in the previous year, markedly below the growth rates recorded in recent years. In contrast, measured in volume terms the performance of exports has been better. Although the performance of exports is partly explained by weaker demand in world markets and sector-specific factors that are expected to be temporary, it has also reflected structural problems such as infrastructure constraints and the lack of reforms in the small-scale sector.[241] Imports rose by 5% in dollar terms in 1997/98 (compared with 10% in 1996/97). Declining oil imports (both in volume and dollar terms) were offset by an increase in non-oil imports (up 12½% for the year), partly in response to the relaxation of some controls on consumer goods imports.

3.365 Despite the slowdown in exports, the external position has remained manageable. Strong inflows of private capital (both portfolio investment and foreign direct investment) boosted foreign currency reserves in 1996/97 by US$5.3 billion to US$22.4 billion (5½ months of imports of goods and non-factor services) at end-March 1997. In 1997/98, robust inflows of portfolio investment in the first half of the year turned to modest net outflows in the second half, responding to changes in investor sentiment toward emerging markets following the Asian crisis. Moreover, higher premia for debt issued overseas by Indian corporations discouraged foreign borrowing. However, rising foreign direct investment, driven by longer term considerations, helped maintain a comfortable reserve position.

[241] Small-scale units are defined as manufacturing units in which investment in plant and machinery is less that Rs 30 million (about US$700,000). These units enjoy special protection from both domestic and international competition. About 800 products are reserved for production by small-scale units. The small-scale sector's products account for roughly half of all exports.

2(b) *Were there any special factors, within the meaning of GATT Article XVIII:9, affecting India's reserves and its need thereof, that the IMF considers relevant?*

3.366 With respect to special factors, within the meaning of GATT Article XVIII:9, the Fund understands the following factors to be relevant. With the exception of net forward liabilities totalling US$1.4 billion at end-November 1997, there were neither contingent liabilities nor any unusually high obligations affecting India's reserves. With regard to prospective developments in debt-service payments, amortization and interest payments in 1997/98 and 1998/99 were expected to return to lower levels after peaking in 1995/96 and 1996/97.

3. *Noting that these restrictions relate mainly to consumption goods, would relaxation or removal of the restrictions, as of 18 November 1997, have been likely to produce thereupon "conditions justifying the intensification or institution, respectively, of restrictions under paragraph 9 of Article XVIII" (Ad Note to Article XVIII:11)?*

3.367 The Fund's view remains as indicated in the statement to the WTO Committee on Balance-of-Payments Restrictions (10-11 June 1997), namely that the external situation can be managed using macroeconomic policy instruments alone. Quantitative restrictions (QRs) are not needed for balance-of-payments adjustment and should be removed over a relatively short period of time. The tariffs applied to previously restricted consumer goods imports could initially be kept close to the top of the existing tariff structure, but should be scaled back according to a pre-announced timetable. A time-bound programme for eliminating the remaining QRs over a relatively short period would reduce distortions to investment and promote an efficient, export-oriented consumer goods sector. The macroeconomic policy instruments would need to be complemented by structural measures such as scaling back reservations on certain products for small-scale units and pushing ahead with agricultural reforms.

4. *Have there been any external or internal developments affecting the Indian economy since the date of establishment of the Panel that could lead to a modification of the IMF's answers to questions 1 to 3?*

3.368 There has been a deterioration in the economic outlook and market sentiment over the past few months, and short-term risks have increased. This deterioration stems from both domestic and external factors. The growth momentum has continued to weaken, the Central Government's fiscal position worsened in 1997/98, and investor confidence has abruptly eroded. At the same time the external environment has become more uncertain. A deeper and more prolonged recession in East Asia could reduce external demand and make an export recovery more difficult. The imposition of sanctions following the nuclear tests in May 1998 and continued financial turbulence in the region have also resulted in greater external vulnerability, including from changes in market sentiment, although foreign currency reserves remained at a relatively comfortable

US$24.1 billion (over 5½ months of imports) at end-June 1998. These uncertainties undoubtedly add to near-term risks and will require especially close monitoring while the impact of the sanctions and regional developments work their way through the economy. In sum, on the basis of developments thus far, the balance of payments situation is expected to worsen and a decline in reserves (US$2½-4 billion) is anticipated for 1998/99. Nevertheless, it remains the Fund view that the external situation can be managed using macroeconomic policy instruments and that quantitative restrictions are not needed for balance-of-payments adjustment.

5(a) *If India immediately removed the remaining quantitative restrictions referred to above, would India need to change its development policy in order not to experience a serious decline in its monetary reserves or the threat of a serious decline in its monetary reserves, or (if India were to have inadequate monetary reserves) in order to achieve a reasonable rate of increase in its reserves?*

3.369 Some problems in import substituting sectors and a temporary decline in reserves cannot be ruled out in the event India immediately removed the remaining QRs. As noted in response to question 2 (a), the recent increase in non-oil imports is partly in response to the relaxation of some of the controls on consumer goods imports over the last year. However, there would also be considerable benefits to such a move, if it were implemented in a phased manner over a relatively short period. First, increased customs revenue from the tariffs applied to previously restricted consumer goods imports would contribute toward deficit reduction and could provide the necessary resources for essential spending in infrastructure and the social sectors. Second, a more competitive, efficient, and quality-conscious consumer goods sector could contribute strongly to export growth. Finally, the structural measures advocated in response to question 3 would improve the allocation of investment, promote efficiency, and enhance the growth prospects of the economy.

5(b) *Would serious structural adjustment problems, other than balance of payments problems, be likely to result from the removal of these restrictions?*

3.370 It is the Fund's judgment that removal of the QRs on consumer goods imports would enhance competitive forces and efficiency in the economy, thus promoting trade and growth. Nevertheless, there would be some inevitable adjustment in protected industries, the consequences of which could be exacerbated by existing rigid labor laws for the organized sector. The removal of import restrictions, however, would also provide fresh impetus for reforms in other areas as the existence of certain controls on the domestic economy (such as for small-scale units) would become less meaningful.

India: Balance-of-payments 1994/95-1997/98[a]
(US$ million)

	1994/95	1995/96	1996/1997	Est. 1997/98
Current account balance	-3,369	-5,899	-3,661	-6,100
Trade balance	-9,049	-11,359	-14,299	-15,600
Exports, f.o.b.	26,855	32,311	33,764	34,700
Imports, c.i.f[b]	35,904	43,670	48,063	50,300
Oil	5,928	7,526	10,036	7,600
Non-oil	29,976	36,144	38,027	42,700
Non-factor services balance	602	-186	2,407	1,263
Receipts	6,135	7,357	8,615	8,947
Payments	5,533	7,543	6,208	7,684
Net investment income	-3,431	-3,205	-3,250	-4,173
Credits	886	1,429	1,073	1,100
Debits	4,317	4,634	4,323	5,274
Interest	4,099	4,315	4,172	4,829
Dividends	218	319	151	444
Transfers, net	8,509	8,851	11,481	12,410
Private transfers, net	8,093	8,506	11,071	12,060
Grants	416	345	410	350
Capital account balance	9,156	4,678	10,456	10,615
Direct investment, net	1,343	2,133	2,524	3,075
Portfolio investment, net	3,579	2,661	3,310	1,600
FII and other, net	1,742	2,009	1,945	955
GDR issues	1,837	652	1,365	645
External assistance	1,526	833	1,109	1,000
Disbursements	3,191	2,933	3,056	3,058
Amortization	1,665	2,050	1,947	2,058
Commercial borrowing	1,030	1,275	1,009	3,500
Disbursements	4,152	4,252	5,732	5,595
Amortization	3,122	2,977	4,723	2,095
Short-term credit, net	393	49	838	-50
NRI deposits, net	172	1,103	3,536	1,140
Rupee debt	-983	-952	-727	-750
Other capital (including errors and omissions)	2,096	-2,474	-1,143	1,100
Overall balance	5,787	-1,221	6,795	4,515
IMF, net	-1,143	-1,715	-977	-615
Increase in gross reserves (-)	-4,644	2,936	-5,818	-3,900
Memorandum items:				
Foreign exchange reserves	20,809	17,044	22,367	25,975
In months of imports	7.0	4.7	5.6	6.2
Export value (in US$ terms; per cent change)	18.4	20.3	4.5	2.3
Import value (in US$ terms; per cent change)	34.3	21.6	10.1	5.2
Exports (in volume terms; per cent change)	13.1	12.7	9.0	11.2
Imports (in volume terms; per cent	29.2	13.4	12.1	14.8

	1994/95	1995/96	1996/1997	Est. 1997/98
change)				
Current account (per cent of GDP)	-1.1	-1.8	-1.0	-1.6
External debt (per cent of GDP)	32.6	27.6	25.6	24.8
Debt service ratio (per cent)	26.2	24.2	22.2	22.7

a India's financial year runs from 1 April to 31 March.
b Includes interest on trade finance. Excludes personal imports of gold, silver and jewellery.
Source: Data provided by the Indian authorities; and International Monetary Fund estimates.

(iii) Comments of the Parties on the Replies of the IMF to the Panel's Questions[242]

1. United States

3.371 The United States considered that the IMF's answers to the Panel's questions corroborated the evidence that the United States had previously presented to the Panel and established that India's balance-of-payments situation does not meet the requirements of Article XVIII:B.

"(i) India's Reserves Are Adequate, Not Seriously Declining, and Not Threatened with Serious Decline

3.372 The IMF's replies make it clear that India's balance-of-payments position does not meet the criteria of the proviso to Article XVIII:9. The IMF has found that, as of 18 November 1997, India was neither experiencing nor threatened with a serious decline in its monetary reserves; had adequate reserves; and was achieving a reasonable rate of accumulation of reserves.[243] These determinations match those made by the Fund during the consultations in the Committee on Balance-of-Payments Restrictions in January and June 1997.[244] As previously explained, these factual determinations are binding on the Panel pursuant to Article XV:2. In the alternative, even if these determinations were not binding on the Panel, they would constitute evidence that India has not rebutted.

3.373 Indeed, the IMF's determinations are fully consistent with the other evidence (including evidence from Indian sources) that the United States has furnished to the Panel. For example, the IMF stressed in particular that at the end of 1997 the Government of India utilized macroeconomic tools appropriately to manage its reserve situation, and that therefore India's currency reserves did not seriously decline nor were they under threat of serious decline in November of 1997. The IMF's analysis matches exactly the analysis of Dr. Bimal Jalan, Gov-

[242] The comments are presented *in extenso*.

[243] In addition, because the IMF found that India was not threatened with a serious decline in its reserves, it concluded *a fortiori* that the question of whether India might be threatened with an "imminent" decline was moot.

[244] WT/BOP/R/22, 3 March 1997 Op. Cit., para. 8, and WT/BOP/R/32, Op. Cit., paras. 10, 13 (IMF statement).

ernor of the Reserve Bank of India, who has explained that India made a successful decision to manage its external financial position through a package of monetary policy measures. The IMF also explained that, as of 18 November 1997, India's reserves appeared to provide sufficient external liquidity and a reasonable degree of protection against unforeseen external shocks. The IMF reached this conclusion by considering the number of months of import cover represented by India's reserves; the coverage of short-term debt; and the coverage of portfolio investment. Once again, the analysis of the IMF matches the analysis that the Reserve Bank of India applied when it concluded that the level of reserves in August of 1997 was "by any criteria ... comfortable".

3.374 India argued that in its current economic situation, it was threatened with a return of balance-of-payments difficulties, but the IMF's answers to the Panel's questions make clear that India is incorrect.[245] The IMF found explicitly that in its current situation, India is not threatened with a serious decline in its reserves justifying restrictions under Article XVIII:B. In particular, the IMF explained that, on the basis of developments thus far, a decline in India's reserves of up to US$4 billion is expected for 1998/99. Such a decline would put India's reserves at approximately US$20 billion at the end of 1998/99. However, the IMF has also explained that, given India's current economic circumstances, including the level of India's short-term liabilities and the potential outflows of portfolio investment, a decline in reserves below US$16 billion would be considered serious (and, if reserves did decline below US$16 billion, any increase above that amount would be a reasonable increase). In this connection it is also worth recalling that India declined to advise the Panel what level of reserves India considers adequate; India is therefore in no position to dispute the IMF's position on this matter.

3.375 The IMF's analysis of India's balance-of-payments situation is more complete than the analysis presented by India. India focused mostly on India's trade account.[246] The trade account is only one element of the balance of payments, however, and therefore analysis of the trade account in isolation from the other elements, as India has done, does not allow conclusions to be drawn about the balance-of-payments situation as a whole. In the final two pages of its answer, India did turn to the other components of the balance of payments. In doing so, India suggested that it is possible that private transfers and portfolio flows might decline in the future (and presumably that they might therefore not be adequate to cover India's trade deficit), but it is important to note that India did not quantify

[245] As a separate matter, the United States has previously explained its position that this Panel should only consider India's balance-of-payments position as of July 1997, when the United States initiated this dispute by requesting consultations with India. Alternatively, the Panel should look only at the situation on the date this Panel was established, 18 November 1997. The comments in this paragraph should not be interpreted as a change in the United States' position.

[246] India inexplicably returns to this argument about its trade deficit even though the United States pointed out that India's currency reserves have grown over the last several years *despite* an increasing trade deficit.

or otherwise relate any possible decline in those flows to the trade account or other aspects of its balance of payments. By contrast, the IMF analyzed the entire balance-of-payments situation, and its conclusions are contrary to India's assertions. In particular, the IMF considered not only the Indian trade account and existing and likely private transfers and portfolio flows, but, unlike India, the IMF also examined and considered the rise in foreign direct investment into India. On the basis of that analysis the IMF made estimates about the overall expected change in India's reserve position, which (as described in the preceding paragraph) led the IMF to conclude that the change in India's reserve position would not amount to a serious decline or an inadequate level of reserves. In summary, therefore, the IMF's answers contradict India's assertions and provide a more thorough exploration of the factors relevant to India's current and projected balance-of-payments position.

(ii) Removal of India's Quantitative Restrictions Would Not Thereupon Produce Conditions Justifying the Institution of Such Restrictions

3.376 India has claimed that the provisions of the Note Ad Article XVIII:11 preclude it from having to remove the restrictions at issue in this case. The IMF's replies to the Panel's questions refute India's claim.

3.377 The IMF was asked specifically whether removal of the restrictions would have been likely thereupon to produce conditions justifying the institution of restrictions. It answered by explaining once again that, given India's economic circumstances, India's external financial situation can be well managed without quantitative restrictions by using macroeconomic policy instruments alone.[247] This means that elimination of the quantitative restrictions will not result in balance of-payments conditions under which such restrictions would be necessary to meet any of the conditions described in the proviso to Article XVIII:9.

3.378 The IMF's answers to the Panel's questions also explained that removal of India's quantitative restrictions would bring specific benefits to the Indian economy, including increased tariff revenue and a more efficient, quality-conscious and export-oriented consumer goods sector. The IMF had previously made the same point during the 1997 consultations.[248] These benefits confirm the IMF's conclusion that the quantitative restrictions at issue in this case can be removed without thereupon producing balance-of-payments conditions that would justify the reintroduction of such restrictions.

3.379 In this connection, the IMF has also said that if India removed its quantitative restrictions, India would not need to change its development policy in order not to experience a serious decline in reserves or the threat thereof (or to ensure a reasonable rate of increase if its reserves were inadequate, which the IMF

[247] The IMF made similar determinations during the January and June 1997 consultation. WT/BOP/R/22, p. 11, para. 12; and WT/BOP/R/32, p. 29, para. 13.

[248] WT/BOP/R/32, p. 29, para. 13.

has already found they are not). The IMF stated that at most a *temporary* decline in reserves might take place if the restrictions are removed.

3.380 Apart from the temporary effect on India's reserves, the IMF also recognized (in answers 5(a) and (b)) that structural adjustments will be required in import substituting sectors, as these industries are currently protected from import competition. Such adjustments are a normal consequence of a process of trade and investment liberalization such as the one on which India embarked in 1991.[249] India has in any case already made the choice to pursue development by liberalizing its economy (including through removal of other quantitative restrictions) and has made this choice known to world markets.[250] Moreover, as the United States had pointed out, India has had ample warning that its quantitative restrictions no longer are justified by its balance-of-payments situation and that it must prepare for their elimination. For example, the IMF said 18 months ago, at the consultations held in January of 1997, that all such restrictions should be eliminated in a very short time.[251] None of the adjustments mentioned by the IMF in its replies to the Panel's questions amounts to a "change in development policy that would render unnecessary" India's restrictions. Instead, the structural consequences of removal of the quantitative restrictions that the IMF mentioned are simply a continuation of changes that are consistent with India's current development policy and, as the IMF points out, will be beneficial to India's balance of payments. They do not constitute a basis under Article XVIII:B for retaining the restrictions at issue in this case.

3.381 In summary, the United States considered that the IMF had confirmed that India was not experiencing, or threatened with, a serious decline in its currency reserves or inadequate reserves. The IMF has also confirmed that while removal of the quantitative restrictions at issue in this case might lead to adjustments in

---

[249] This is also implied in the first sentence of Article XVIII:11. As India's answer (dated 6 July 1998) to question 5 of the Panel's second set of questions to the parties acknowledges, Article XVIII:11 addresses the question of domestic policies to be undertaken by a Member that has imposed restrictions for balance-of-payments purposes. In the view of the United States, Article XVIII:11, first sentence is to be read as providing that Members imposing restrictions for balance-of-payments reasons are to structure their domestic policies so as to minimize the incidental protective effects of the restrictions and thereby to lessen the adjustments required when the restrictions are removed.

[250] For example, in 1995 India advised the Balance-of-Payments Committee that "to deal with [Indian economic crisis] and to lay the basis for sustained growth of output and employment, Government initiated wide ranging economic reforms in industrial, fiscal, financial, trade, exchange rate and foreign investment policies." *Report on the Consultation with India,* WT/BOP/R/11, page 7 (statement by the representative of India). See also WT/BOP/R/22, page 5 (statement by the representative of India).

[251] The United States notes that the IMF has repeated that India should eliminate these restrictions in a very short time; in view of the time that has passed for India to make preparations for the adjustment effects of elimination, the United States considers that India should eliminate its restrictions immediately. In any event, as the United States has explained before, the length of time that India may take to comply with the Panel's decision will be decided during the implementation phase of this dispute.

the Indian economy, removal of those restrictions would not lead to conditions justifying the institution of such restrictions.

3.382 Whether the Panel chooses to treat the IMF's replies as binding pursuant to Article XV:2, or as evidence obtained pursuant to Article 13 of the DSU, the United States respectfully submits that the replies of the IMF to the Panel's questions support the positions taken by the United States with respect to the facts at issue in this dispute. The IMF's answers certainly lend no support to India's assertions about its need to retain the challenged restrictions. In fact, apart from the speculations by India, which the IMF answers refute, India has provided no factual basis for its claims. The United States therefore respectfully renews its requests for findings and recommendations set out in its previous submissions."

2. India

3.383 "First, India considers that the events described by the IMF in its answer to question 1(a)(i) constitute recognition by the IMF of the threat of a serious decline in India's reserves. The IMF acknowledges that only the efforts of the Reserve Bank of India (the "RBI") to insulate the rupee from the "contagion" effects of the South-East and East Asian financial crisis staved off the threat. The IMF notes that the downward pressure on the rupee attributable to the Southeast Asian crisis commenced in August 1997 and intensified in November 1997. According to the IMF, this forced the RBI to "intervene heavily" in the foreign exchange market leading to a reserve loss of US$2.5 billion. The RBI subsequently abandoned intervention and chose to use monetary policies to stabilize the value of the rupee. Despite the fact that on 21 November 1997 India's foreign currency reserves (excluding gold) stood at US$25.1 billion, which the IMF has elsewhere termed as adequate, the loss of US$2.5 billion, in trying to defend the value of the rupee, brought it far too close to the RBI's own assessment of comfort levels to continue using reserves to support the currency. After this massive intervention failed to stabilize the value of the rupee, the RBI clearly foresaw continued haemorrhaging of reserves and therefore chose to change its policy instrument in defending the rupee. Second, the tightening of interest rates and the increase in the cash-reserve-ratio (the "CRR") which followed in December 1997 and January 1998 certainly helped stabilize the value of the rupee. But it meant the reversal of the RBI's monetary policy goals for fiscal 1997-98. Faced with sluggish industrial demand, the RBI had until then followed a policy of interest rate cuts and reductions in the CRR to inject some liquidity and dynamism into the economy. However, faced with sustained pressure on the value of the rupee, it was forced to abandon its policy goal and change tack by raising both the CRR as well as interest rates. Clearly the RBI would not have been forced to abandon a policy goal if it did not feel that it faced the threat of a serious decline in foreign currency reserves which it had been unable to control using other policy instruments. Finally, it should be remembered that the economy paid a price because of the use of monetary policy. Tighter monetary policies contributed to the postponement of an industrial recovery and caused a loss in output and employment.

3.384 India, therefore, considers that in November 1997, it did face a threat of a serious decline in its reserves in terms of paragraph (a) of the proviso to Article XVIII:9.

Questions 1(a)(ii) and 1(b)

3.385 The IMF has commented in (1)(a)(ii) that India's foreign currency reserves in November 1997 were adequate. In its reply to question 1(b), however, the IMF observes that "a considerable degree of subjective judgement is involved in an assessment of the adequacy of the level and rate of exchange reserves". India notes that there has been a fairly long debate on what constitutes adequate levels of foreign exchange reserves which spans almost the entire period since the adoption of the floating exchange-rate system. One of the early initiatives in this regard was taken at the behest of the IMF itself through the establishment of the Committee of Twenty in 1972. The Committee in its report on the International Monetary Reform considered many alternative indicators of reserve adequacy, namely, gross or net reserves; reserve holdings of the monetary authorities and those of semi-official and private institutions; reserves adjusted for seasonal and/or cyclical variations; gross levels or deviations from a base; bands around a base; reserves adjusted for potentially reversible capital movements; stock of reserves or flow of reserves; price or cost indicators of international competitiveness; a composite index derived from several indicators; currency composition of reserves, etc. The report of the Committee thus clearly indicated that the adequacy of reserves could not be evaluated using simple yardsticks such as the one applied by the IMF currently.

3.386 In this context, it is important to note that experts have suggested alternative indicators in the Indian context for evaluating the adequacy of foreign exchange reserves. They have suggested that adequacy of reserves should be measured in terms of (i) import coverage; (ii) realization of exports and imports augmented for leads and lags and debt service payments; (iii) short-term debt and portfolio stock; and (iv) net foreign assets to currency ratio. These four indicators take into account the liabilities both on the current account as well as on the capital account for assessing reserve adequacy. India considers that all these methods should be applied when assessing the adequacy of reserves position because each addresses a vital aspect of external payments viability. This approach is, therefore, more appropriate than the standard measure used by the IMF, which takes only the liabilities on the trade account into consideration. This becomes all the more important because, over time, transactions on the trade account have become relatively less important in comparison with the rapidly growing service sector and capital account transactions.

3.387 The first measure proposed stipulates that reserves should not be less than six months of imports. According to this formulation, in November 1997, reserves should have been about US$22 billion. The second measure stipulates that reserves should not be less than three months' imports plus 50% of debt service payments plus one month's imports and exports to account for leads and lags. On this basis, the reserves requirement would have had to be more than

US$22 billion. The third measure advocates that short-term debt and portfolio stock should not exceed 60% of reserves and that incremental short-term debt and portfolio liabilities should be accompanied by equivalent increase in reserves. According to this measure, reserves should have been in excess of US$27 billion. The fourth measure stipulates that the foreign currency assets to currency ratio should be not less than 40% and a desirable level of 70%. At 40%, required reserves would be US$16 billion and at 70% they would be US$28 billion. It is important to note that by at least two of the above criteria, the stock of foreign currency reserves, which stood at US$24 billion in November 1997, was inadequate.

3.388 In the context of reserve adequacy, it is also important to note that even though reserves may appear adequate on the basis of import coverage, the overnight removal of India's remaining quantitative restrictions on imports for balance-of-payments reasons (the "import restrictions") would immediately render reserves inadequate. India had already pointed out that, if the import restrictions were removed immediately, there would be a substantial increase in the import bill. India's reserves would then be inadequate even if the IMF's yardstick of import coverage were used.

Question 1(a)(iii)

3.389 It is misleading on the part of the IMF to use 1990-91 as the base year for comparison while discussing the trends in India's foreign exchange reserves. First, as is well known, India's foreign exchange reserves were at an all time low in 1991. Therefore, comparisons using 1991 as the base year necessarily overstate the recovery in India's reserves. Second, given the dramatic liberalization of the Indian economy thereafter, in part as a response to this crisis, the nature of capital inflows into the economy were both qualitatively and quantitatively very different from the preceding periods. Therefore, the initial rapid increase in foreign exchange inflows in the early 1990s were more in the nature of a one-shot adjustment in reserve levels as a result of global capital market investors making portfolio adjustments in response to the opening-up of the Indian capital markets. Finally, both the external and internal situation facing the Indian economy today is vastly different from the early 1990s. On the external front, India is coping with the fallout of the Southeast Asian currency crisis. On the internal front, market sentiment has been bearish as a result of sluggish domestic demand, which itself, at least in part, is the result of the tight monetary policies used to defend the rupee. Therefore it is difficult to be as sanguine as the IMF about the growth in India's reserves. Indeed the behaviour of India's reserves over the last year only underlines this point.

3.390 India's foreign currency reserves peaked in October 1997 when it reached US$26.2 billion. Thereafter, there have been at least two periods of sustained reserve loss. Equally important, reserve levels have exhibited marked volatility since then. Between October and December 1997, gross foreign currency reserves declined by US$2.3 billion. After fluctuating in the range of US$24 and US$25 billion in the first three months of 1998, reserves increased to

US$26.2 billion in April 1998, after which there was a decline of US$1.8 billion in June 1998. It is incorrect to conclude, therefore, that India was "experiencing a reasonable rate of increase in monetary reserves", particularly in the period since November 1997.

Question 2(a)

3.391 At the outset, India would like to point out that according to the latest figures available, exports grew by 5.3% in 1996-97 and by 1.5% in 1997-98 in dollar terms, which is indicative of a very sharp decline in export performance.

3.392 The Government of India has repeatedly emphasized, and the IMF concurs, that India's external trade performance has deteriorated significantly in the last three years as a result of both a marked slow down in export performance and continued robust growth in non-oil imports. As a result, the trade deficit went up from 1.6% of GDP in 1993-94 to 4% in 1996-97. Both the Government of India and the IMF are also agreed that the latter phenomenon, i.e., the continued robustness of non-oil imports is partially attributable to the easing of restrictions on imports of certain consumer goods.

3.393 As India has repeatedly emphasized, the marked deterioration in trade performance has not been reflected in the behaviour of the current account because of a steady improvement in the behaviour of the invisibles account. Within the invisibles account, there has been a sharp increase in inflows on account of private transfers, especially over the last three years. In 1996-97, for example, private transfers increased by more than 30% from the already high levels of the previous year to reach US$11.5 billion or 3.3% of GDP. However, private transfers are in the nature of a windfall and cannot be considered a reliable source of inflows. For example, a substantial proportion of these flows is final repatriation by returning migrant workers. In fact, in recent months, there has been an appreciable decline in inflows on this account. Therefore, even under *ceteris paribus* assumptions, there is reason to expect deterioration on the current account. And if, as anticipated, the trade account deteriorates further, then it would put significant pressure on the current account. The IMF's own estimates that the current account deficit could, in the near term, rise to between 3% and 4% of GDP concurs with the above analysis.

3.394 As far as financing of the current account deficit is concerned, 1997-98 has already seen a reversal of the trends in portfolio investment noted in the earlier two years. Foreign capital inflows have, however, slowed down in more recent months. Direct investment flows during April-May 1998 were approximately half of the levels in April-May 1997: US$485 million in the former period as opposed to US$866 million in the latter. Further, as the IMF itself has noted, portfolio investment has seen net outflows for the period April-May 1998. The imposition of sanctions and the subsequent devaluation of the rupee have muddied the waters further. It is important to note that even prior to the imposition of sanctions, credit rating institutions such as Moody's Investor Services

("Moody's") had already put India on a credit watch. Subsequently, Moody's downgraded India's credit rating.

3.395 India considers, therefore, that its external situation needs a close watch and that the transition to an open regime needs to be carefully calibrated through, among other things, a phased removal of quantitative restrictions. Specifically, India has consistently argued before the Panel that the six-year phase-out plan (commencing from 1 April 1997) submitted by India seeks to achieve the appropriate balance between its long-term interests and the risk involved in eliminating its remaining import restrictions immediately.

Question 2(b)

3.396 The reply of the IMF does not take into account the special factors in Article XVIII:9 to which the panel has drawn its attention.

3.397 In the current phase of its development, India requires substantial volumes of foreign exchange to meet the demands of critical sectors of the economy. It is well accepted that one of the critical bottlenecks facing the Indian economy is underdeveloped infrastructure. This sector requires large amounts of foreign exchange within a relatively short period of time. It is estimated that the foreign-exchange requirements to build adequate infrastructural facilities to sustain economic growth in India would be about US$20 billion over the next five years. In the light of the above, India needs to exercise prudence in the management of its foreign exchange transactions. This can be achieved only through a gradual (as opposed to immediate) elimination of India's remaining import restrictions. Rapid removal of import restrictions could lead to a substantial increase in foreign exchange outflows, which would affect India's programme of economic development adversely.

Question 3

3.398 The IMF states that India does not require import restrictions to manage its external sector and that policies of macroeconomic adjustment complemented by structural adjustment measures would suffice. India notes, however, that the IMF has stated in its answer to question 5 that "a temporary decline in reserves cannot be ruled out" as a result of immediate elimination of import restrictions. Consequently, even the IMF does not recommend immediate elimination of India's remaining import restrictions as demanded by the United States. Rather, it states that "they should be removed over a relatively short period of time".

3.399 India considers that a rapid removal of import restrictions on consumer goods will adversely affect India's balance of payments. As the IMF has noted in its response, the robust growth of non-oil imports in the past couple of years is partially attributable to the surge in consumer goods imports as a result of the removal of import restrictions on some consumer goods. As noted above, it has been estimated that there would be a substantial increase in the import bill as a result of the removal of import restrictions. It is keeping all this in view that India has proposed a six-year phase-out for its remaining import restrictions which has already effectively been accepted by all members of the WTO except the United States.

3.400 The IMF also states that "macroeconomic policy measures *would need to be complemented* by structural measures...". Structural adjustment policies of the type recommended by the IMF to address problems arising from the removal of import restrictions, namely, agricultural reforms, de-reservation of items for small scale sectors and changes in labour laws, etc., amount to changes in development policy. The proviso to the second sentence of Article XVIII:11 makes it clear that:

> "[N]o Contracting party shall be required to withdraw or modify restrictions on the ground that a change in its development policy would render unnecessary the restrictions which it is applying under this Section."

3.401 India has been autonomously engaged in a programme of economic reforms. Given that development policy changes of the type recommended by the IMF are particularly time-consuming to implement because of India's size and the democratic and federal nature of its polity, the pace of change cannot be forced. In India's assessment, based on its economic performance in the post-reform period, a period of transition is necessary for structural reforms of this nature. India has, therefore, sought a transition period for phasing out its remaining import restrictions.

3.402 Finally, by recommending scaling back of tariffs according to a pre-announced time-table, the IMF has, in fact, raised a matter that is clearly outside the purview of Article XVIII:B and the mandate of the IMF under Article XV.2.

Question 4

3.403 The IMF repeatedly stresses in its response that India is going through a difficult economic situation. This diagnosis appears to be fairly close to that of the Government of India.

3.404 The IMF notes that India's economic performance over 1997-98 was very weak on almost all fronts. Given the deepening crisis in East Asia and the imposition of economic sanctions, the performance of the economy on the external front is likely to worsen in 1998-99.

3.405 The IMF also notes that the country's balance-of-payments situation is likely to worsen in 1998-99, a period during which the foreign currency reserves could decline by as much as US$4 billion. In this context, it is useful also to remember that the rupee has faced renewed downward pressure in 1998-99 leading to a devaluation of more than 10%, over and above a devaluation of a similar magnitude in 1997-98. Equally important, the rupee continues to remain under pressure despite significant downward correction, primarily because of the "contagion" effects of the Southeast Asian crisis.

3.406 While the IMF is entirely correct in its assessment of India's difficult economic condition, particularly on the external account, it has not provided any justification for its assertion that the external situation can be managed using macroeconomic policy instruments, and that "quantitative restrictions are not needed for balance-of-payments adjustment". This conclusion of the IMF, therefore, appears to be at best a subjective judgement with little relationship with the facts that the IMF itself has presented. It is also worth noting that this disjunction between the facts presented and the conclusions based thereon runs right through the IMF response and is not limited to the reply to this question. The IMF has not presented any analysis or reasons to support its conclusions.

3.407 Consequently, India considers that this conclusion of the IMF is based on a normative judgement that import restrictions are *never* necessary for balance-of-payments adjustment. In this context, India invites the attention of the Panel to para. 141, sections (III) and (IV) of the paper entitled "Proposals for a Review of GATT Article XVIII: An Assessment" by Frances Stewart published in *Uruguay Round, Papers on Selected Issues* by the United Nations, New York in 1989, a copy of which was submitted to the Panel on 23 June 1998. India would also like to submit that such a normative judgement is clearly inconsistent with the text of Article XVIII:9 which permits a less developed country to impose import restrictions "in order to safeguard its external financial position and to ensure a level of reserves adequate for the implementation of its programme of economic development ...". It is also inconsistent with the object and purpose of Article XVIII:B as set forth in Article XVIII:2(b), that less-developed country Members "... should enjoy additional facilities to enable them ... to apply quantitative restrictions for balance-of-payments purposes in a manner which takes full account of the continued high level of demand for imports likely to be generated by their programmes of economic development".

Question 5(a)

3.408 There are two points that the IMF makes here, both of which are contentious. First, the argument that tariffs can be used as a revenue-generating mechanism does not take into account the fact that most countries are decreasing their dependence on this source of revenue. In any case, this is hardly the ideal method of generating government revenue. Further, the additional investment required for essential spending on infrastructure and the social sector is of a magnitude that would completely dwarf anything that is raised through tariffs. Second, the development of an efficient and competitive domestic consumer-goods sector requires a period of transition, which is what India has sought through the proposed phase out of the quantitative restrictions. This period of transition would also allow the adjustment process initiated by India to run its full course, and not run the risk of reversal through disequilibrating tendencies that a sudden deterioration of the external payments position will engender, consequent upon a rapid dismantling of quantitative restrictions.

Question 5(b)

3.409 As stated in the IMF's reply to question 5(a), the domestic consumer goods sector can be put on a firm footing only if it is permitted the space within which to make the transition from operating in a closed to an open economy. The IMF has also indicated that the removal of quantitative restrictions would necessitate not only macroeconomic policy measures but some structural reforms as well. It is important to note that India does have a reform process underway. The structural reforms suggested by the IMF would require changes in laws relating to, among other things, small-scale industries and labour. Because India is a federal, pluralistic and democratic polity where a consensual approach is the cornerstone of the decision-making process, any changes in legislation would necessarily be time consuming, primarily because a fine balance needs to be maintained amongst various segments of society, mainly the disadvantaged and the poor. For example, given the labour-intensive nature of small-scale production, rapid adjustment in this sector would lead to massive loss of employment that could be socially and politically unmanageable. It is for this reason that India has adopted the path of gradualism in economic reforms, which is generally accepted as the basis for the success hitherto achieved."

E. Article XIII:2(a) and the Import Licensing Agreement

3.410 In the event that the Panel disagreed with the request to find that India's quantitative restrictions violated Article XI:1, Article XVIII:11 and Article 4.2 of the Agreement on Agriculture, then the **United States** sought a finding that the challenged measures were not applied in accordance with the requirements of Article XIII:2(a).

3.411 **India** acknowledged that the legal claims of the United States were within the terms of reference of the panel, because, in its request for establishment of a panel in this dispute, the United States had claimed that it considered the import restrictions maintained by India inconsistent with, among other provisions, Article XIII of the GATT 1994 as well as Article 3 of the Agreement on Import Licensing Procedures (the "Import Licensing Agreement").

3.412 India argued, however, that the Panel should not permit the United States to raise any legal claims in its second submission that it had not raised in its first submission because doing so would be inconsistent with India's due process rights. The United States had not made any request for legal findings under these provisions in its first submission. India, therefore, considered that the United States had withdrawn or waived its legal claims under these provisions because India would not now have an opportunity to respond to any arguments that the United States might make in support of its legal claims under these provisions in its second written submission.

3.413 India recalled that the provisions of the DSU were based on the general premise that fairness and respect for the due process rights of *both* the complaining party and the responding party were essential to its over-riding objective "... providing security and predictability to the multilateral trading system ..." specified in Article 3:2 of the DSU. More specifically, the provisions of Article 12 of the Understanding on Rules and Procedures Governing the Settlement of Disputes (the "DSU") and the Working Procedures in Appendix 3 of the DSU (the "Working Procedures") also made it clear that the due process rights of the responding party as much as the complaining party must be respected. Article 12:6 of the DSU required the complaining party to submit its first submission in advance of the responding party. Thereafter, although the last sentence of Article 12:6 of the DSU required both parties to submit subsequent written submissions simultaneously, the procedural sequence for submissions and hearings described in paragraphs 4 to 7 of the Working Procedures in Appendix 3 made it clear that this provision was not intended to deprive the responding party of its opportunity to respond in its own written submission to the arguments of the complaining party in support of its legal claims. Paragraph 4 provided that both parties must transmit their written submissions in which they present facts and arguments in support of their case. Paragraph 5 of the Working Procedures provided that the first substantive meeting which took place after the first submissions of both parties required the complaining party to "present its case first" followed by the responding party. Paragraph 6 set out the procedural requirements to be followed in the case of third parties. Paragraph 7 required the second substantive meeting of the panel to be devoted solely to "formal rebuttals".

3.414 India noted that paragraph 12 of the Working Procedures set forth a proposed timetable for panel work that provides for written *rebuttals* of the parties approximately one to two weeks before the second substantive meeting of the panel. Paragraph 12 item c, made it clear that the second submission was a rebuttal submission implying that legal claims not mentioned in its first written submission could not be made. In light of this, India contended that any procedure that might permit the complaining party to raise in its second written submission legal claims that it had not mentioned at all in its first written submission or made at the first substantive meeting of a panel clearly violated the due process rights of the responding party. Likewise, any procedure that might permit the complaining party to raise in its second submission legal claims in respect of which it had not sought any finding in the first submission would clearly violate the due process rights of the responding party.

3.415 India submitted, further, that the ruling of the Appellate Body in *Bananas* did not absolve the United States of its duty to present arguments in support of all of its legal claims by the end of the first substantive meeting of the Panel.[252] In that dispute, the panel had ruled that the complaining parties could not introduce in their second submissions arguments in support of legal claims that they had not taken up in their first submission even if these claims were within the panel's terms of reference. The Appellate Body reversed the panel's ruling on the basis that "[a]ny omissions in the arguments contained in the first written submissions of Mexico or Guatemala and Honduras were rectified in their joint representations with the other Complaining Parties made at the first meeting of the parties with the Panel ... ."

[252] WT/DS27/AB/R, Op. Cit., paras. 145 to 147.

3.416 In the present dispute, however, the United States had not even referred to its legal claims under Article XIII of the GATT 1994 or Article 3 of the Import Licensing Agreement either in its first written submission or at the first substantive meeting of the panel. Accordingly, India requested the Panel not to render a finding on any legal claim that the United States made in its second written submission that was not mentioned in its first written submission.

3.417 The **United States** noted that India had confirmed that it did not utilize quotas in the administration of the challenged measures by asserting that it would not be practicable for India to administer quotas. In the view of the United States, it was hardly credible that a country that for decades administered a command economy - i.e., an economy in which all domestically consumed goods had to be planned and tracked[253] - would not now have the ability to manage a quota system for the smaller number of imported goods.

[253] See, e.g., the description of the Indian trade and planning regime in J. Bhagwati and P. Desai, *India: Planning for Industrialization; Industrialization and Trade Policies Since 1951,* Oxford University Press, 1971.

ANNEX 1

(i) Industrial Policy

1. After 1991, India had focused on bringing about a more competitive industrial structure by eliminating a number of regulatory barriers to internal competition at the entry, operational and exit stages in the life-cycle of an industrial unit. At the same time, India was also trying to increase infrastructural investment to break supply bottlenecks. The first and most important step consisted of limiting the number of industries in which an industrial licence was required from the Government of India under the Industrial (Development and Regulation) Act, 1951, prior to commencing a new industrial venture. At present, an industrial licence was required only in defence, strategic or environmentally hazardous industries. Industrial location policies were also administered more flexibly now. In addition, the Monopolies and Restrictive Trade Practices Act, 1969 had been amended to permit large companies to establish new units or expand existing ones without governmental permission. This Act was now oriented more towards the model of antitrust regulation common in developed economies where regulators focus on monopolistic, restrictive and unfair trade practices in particular industries. India was also opening up areas of the economy formerly reserved exclusively for the public sector to competition while simultaneously divesting its shareholding in public sector companies. The private sector had been permitted to invest in the provision of infrastructural services formerly restricted to the public sector.

2. India had also substantially liberalized the regulatory regime for FDI. Automatic approval was now available in an extended list of industries for up to 51% foreign equity shareholding and up to 74% in some industries. Up to 50% foreign equity in the mining sector was also permitted under the automatic approval route. The Government of India had delegated to the governments of the States the power to approve wholly foreign-owned power generation subsidiaries in which total investment did not exceed Rs.1,500 crore. Automatic approval for technology transfer arrangements with foreign companies was also available today in all industries including service industries as long as the proposal fell within specified limits, i.e., the royalty was limited to 5% of gross revenues (either inclusive of or net of taxes) and a lump-sum fee of US$2 million. The Reserve Bank of India had also dispensed with the requirement of prior approval of foreign share purchases in Indian companies under the automatic approval route.

(ii) Exchange Rate Related Reforms

3. In August 1994, India accepted the obligation under Article VIII of the Articles of Agreement of the International Monetary Fund to abolish exchange control restrictions for all transactions on the current account. The system of multiple exchange rates and the foreign exchange budget had been abolished in March 1993 and all restrictions on the trade account lifted. A committee set up by the Government of India under the chairmanship of a retired governor of In-

dia's central bank (the Reserve Bank of India) to examine the issue of putting India on the road to capital account convertibility has given its report. In accordance with the report, the capital account was being opened up in a phased manner to carefully balance the need for increasing external finance to support domestic investment while also ensuring that the volatility attached to these flows did not make the balance-of-payments situation excessively vulnerable and the monetary management of the economy difficult.

(iii) Fiscal Reforms

4. India had been attempting to reduce the high fiscal deficits of the national and state governments in order to reduce state preemption of domestic savings and to increase the proportion of government revenues that was available for development expenditure. In the case of India, large fiscal deficits usually involved government borrowings from the Reserve Bank of India which in turn was forced to allow the money supply to expand. This fuelled inflation thereby making exports less competitive and encouraging outflows of capital abroad. Accordingly, the Government of India had made determined efforts to achieve fiscal balance, mainly by pruning unproductive revenue expenditure, while also maintaining caution on public borrowings to avoid a slide into a debt trap. However, it had also lowered tax rates to increase the incentives for higher productivity and growth.

5. The 1997-98 national budget continued the tradition of lowering personal and corporate income tax rates. The highest marginal rate for personal income taxes was 30% and for domestic corporate taxes was 35%, thus approaching the levels prevalent in South-East Asian economies. Profits from exports were exempted from the minimum alternative tax and the tax on dividends had been abolished.

6. The 1997-98 national budget also slashed peak levels of tariffs from 50% to 40% which brought India's tariff structure significantly closer to the levels of the ASEAN economies. Simultaneously, customs duties had been reduced considerably on a large number of inputs, raw materials and intermediates to make domestic production more competitive in power, chemicals, textiles and information technology. The duty on capital goods had been further reduced from 25% to 20%.

7. Excise duties had been reformed to reduce the diversity of duty rates while radically simplifying the scheme of excise duty concessions for small scale industries. The ambit of the service tax had been widened to include a number of service industries including transportation of goods by road, consulting engineers, shipping and air travel agents.

8. Although the Government of India had planned to reduce the fiscal deficit of the national government to 4.5% of GDP by this year, the deficit had actually deteriorated to 6.1% of GDP for the fiscal year 1997-98. The main causes were a major shortfall in indirect tax revenues such as customs and excise duties which fell because of slower growth in industrial output and an inability to divest gov-

ernment-held equity in public sector corporations as a result of the weak performance of the capital markets over the last year.

(iv) Trade Policy Reforms

9. Trade policy reforms had been a significant component of the reforms process since 1991. To achieve long-term sustainability in the balance of payments, the draft Ninth Five Year Plan prepared by India's Planning Commission estimated that Indian exports would need to grow two percentage points faster than imports in order to keep the trade balance within control and to make adequate provision for future payments streams necessary to service external debt and investment obligations. In order to achieve such a growth rate in exports, the relative prices within the country would need to be reoriented in favour of tradables and away from non-tradables and within tradables, in favour of exportables and away from import substitutes. Such reorientation of relative prices, however, took time to effect particularly if major economic disruptions were to be avoided.

10. Since 1991, the reforms process had been based on reducing tariff barriers, progressively eliminating non-tariff barriers and introducing greater transparency in import and export procedures. As noted above, the 1997-98 budget reduced peak tariff levels from 50% to 40%. In addition, duties were lowered on inputs, raw materials and intermediates to make domestic production more competitive in power, chemicals, textiles and information technology. Duties on capital goods were further reduced from 25% to 20%. The underlying trend of import duties and excise duties had been maintained in the annual budget 1998-99.

11. With respect to the reduction of import restrictions, the reforms concentrated initially on easing access to capital and intermediate goods. More recently, they had focused on easier access also to raw materials and consumer goods. Between 1 April 1996 and 1 April 1997, India had removed 488 items from the restricted list and made them freely importable. In accordance with the time-schedule that India had agreed upon with its trading partners in the WTO, India had removed import restrictions on 460 HS tariff lines at the eight-digit level since 1 April 1997 until 13 April 1998. These covered a wide range of products, namely vegetables, flowers and fruit, dairy products, semi-processed and processed foods, marine products, chemicals and chemical-based products, paper and paper products, textiles and clothing products, metal and metal products, glass and glassware, and mechanical and electrical machinery, equipment and instruments, as well as domestic appliances. By lowering tariffs and removing non-tariff barriers, India hoped to introduce greater dynamism into its domestic industries, so that only internationally competitive industries would flourish.

12. To facilitate international trade, especially exports, India had also introduced a number of supply side reforms including the following:

(i) streamlining of customs and banking procedures and facilities with a view to reducing transaction costs related to foreign trade;

(ii) implementing Electronic Data Interchange facilities for export facilitation services like banking, insurance, air cargo, shipping, import licensing and customs;

(iii) strategic support to exporters to upgrade marketing and information skills, budgetary resources. standardization of quality and building common facilities for research, development and training;

(iv) developing new instruments specifically for export finance and insurance schemes for various tradable commodities;

(v) enhancing existing and building new international trade-related infrastructure including ports and air terminals and constructing access roads and railway lines to these facilities.

13. To conclude, India was making determined efforts to restore equilibrium in its balance of payments and to ensure that greater competition was introduced in its domestic and external sectors. At every consultation since the initiation of the economic reforms process, the Committee had consistently expressed its satisfaction with India's progress. India hoped that the Panel too would conclude that India had not violated its obligations to its trading partners under the first sentence of Article XVIII:11.

IV. INTERIM REVIEW[254]

4.1 The interim report of the Panel was issued to the parties on 11 December 1998. On 14 December, India requested additional time to review the interim report, in accordance with Article 12.10 of the Understanding on Rules and Procedures Governing the Settlement of Disputes (hereafter "DSU"). On 15 December, the Panel informed the parties that it had decided to extend the due date for the comments on the interim report from 22 December 1998 to 12 January 1999. On 12 January 1999, the United States and India submitted comments regarding the interim report in accordance with Article 15.2 of the DSU. India also requested the Panel to hold a meeting with the parties to discuss the issues raised in its comments. We met with the parties on 15 February 1999, reviewed the entire range of arguments they presented, and finalized our report, taking into account the specific aspects of the parties' arguments we considered to be relevant.

4.2 During our interim review meeting with the parties, we recalled that we had specified cut-off dates for the submission of new material and new arguments. We also specified that we were of the view that the purpose of the interim review stage was not to provide the parties with an opportunity to introduce new legal issues and evidence or to enter into a debate with the Panel. The purpose of

[254] According to Article 15.2 of the DSU, "the findings of the final report shall include a discussion of the arguments made at the interim review stage". The following section entitled "Interim Review" is therefore part of the findings of our report.

the interim review stage is to consider specific and particular aspects of the interim report. Consequently, the Panel addressed the entire range of such arguments presented by the parties which it considered to be sufficiently specific and detailed. In practice, this meant that the parties should limit their comments to the precise aspects raised in the request for review and refrain from introducing new legal issues and evidence.

A. *Comments by the United States*

4.3 With respect to the comments made by the United States on the descriptive part of the report, most of them were essentially of a clarifying nature. We took them into account and accordingly modified paragraphs 2.6, 3.82, 3.108 (footnote 98), 3.137, 3.152, 3.279.

4.4 Regarding the findings, we took into consideration the US suggestions which improve the clarity of our findings and accordingly modified paragraphs 5.53, 5.172, 5.178 and 5.179. We also revised our reasoning on burden of proof in paragraphs 5.116 to 5.121 to make it more explicit. We also made minor changes in paragraphs 5.191 and 5.197. Furthermore, we clarified paragraphs 5.206, 5.207, 5.209, 5.210, 5.211, 5.214 and 5.218 to 5.223. With respect to the footnote to paragraph 5.231, we made it clear that we meant a vote in the General Council, not in the BOP Committee. Finally, we slightly amended paragraphs 5.233, 5.234 and 5.235. In reaching our findings, we did not find it necessary to address the request of the United States that we determine which party had the burden of proof in relation to Article XVIII:B in general. The Panel applied the principle recalled by the Appellate Body in the case on *United States - Measure Affecting Imports of Woven Wool Shirts and Blouses from India*,[255] according to which each party had to support each of its particular claims.

4.5 We declined to expand the scope of our conclusions on the level of India's monetary reserves beyond the date of establishment of the Panel, and we did not follow the US suggestions that paragraphs 5.180 and 5.183 should contain conclusions as to whether India's measures exceeded those that were necessary within the meaning of Article XVIII:9, since these conclusions are contained in paragraph 5.184.

4.6 Regarding our suggestions in paragraphs 7.1 to 7.7, we agree with the United States that the parties did not address explicitly the phase-out issue in terms of the implementation period provided for in Article 21 of the DSU. However, Article 19.1 of the DSU allows panels to "suggest ways in which the Member concerned could implement the recommendations", and it does not seem that such suggestions are dependent on whether they were discussed as such by the parties. While the term "ways" may be interpreted as referring to specific actions that would ensure an appropriate implementation of the recommendations, it can-

[255] WT/DS33/AB/R, DSR 1997:I, 323, adopted on 23 May 1997.

not be limited exclusively to that. The Panel did not consider that it fell within its role to suggest particular measures which might accompany the removal of the quantitative restrictions at issue, but it feels justified in suggesting that a certain period of time should be granted to India in order to implement the recommendations.

B. Comments by India

4.7 India made both general and specific comments on the descriptive part and the findings of the interim report. India also made comments of a procedural nature during the interim review meeting with the Panel.

4.8 With respect to the comments made by India on the descriptive part of the report, India wished to add further information regarding its BOP Committee consultations, including selective references to consultations held in 1992, although these points were not included in the arguments presented to the Panel. The Panel considered that ample history of discussions held in the Committee was provided as of 1994. India also wished to add to paragraph 2.6 that "others agreed that India's residual import restrictions were justified under Article XVIII:B". However, the paragraph refers to the June 1997 consultation and the report of those consultations (WT/BOP/R/32), which records the different views expressed, does not include any such citation; rather, three delegations - including one with observer status - suggested that India had fulfilled its obligations. India also considered that a description of the licensing regime that gives effect to the quantitative restrictions under dispute should not be included under the "Factual Aspects" section. However, the Panel considered that a factual description should be included in this section. It nevertheless took into account some of India's suggestions on that part of the descriptive part of the report and modified paragraphs 2.14, 2.15, 2.18, 2.19, 2,.20, 2.21, 2.23, 2.24, 2.25, 2.26, 2.28. On the other hand, India wished to include a specific section on consultations under Article XXII of GATT 1994 held with other trading partners, during which mutually agreed solutions were reached, as "Procedural Events Leading to the Dispute". We deemed that these consultations were not facts directly related to this panel procedure; a full account of these consultations is included in the Section III.D.8(d). India also wished that its basic legal claims be presented in more details in reply to the presentation of the US claims found in Section III.A of the interim report called "Scope of the Complaint". In order to accommodate India's request, we added a summary of India's claims as found in its submissions in paragraphs 3.5, 3.6, 3.7 and 3.8. Finally, we also added paragraph 3.39 and modified paragraph 3.70.

4.9 During the interim review meeting with the parties, India also claimed that, after the IMF had, in the view of India, predicated removal of India's quantitative restrictions on specific changes in India's development policies, India had had no opportunity to present any facts with respect to these aspects of its development policy for purposes of the proviso to Article XVIII:11. India claims that only after the IMF gave its response to the questions from the Panel could India complain that it was being forced to remove its restrictions on the ground that a change in its development policy would render its restrictions unnecessary. However, at that time, the Panel had explicitly instructed the parties that they could not introduce new facts in their comments. We recall that, at the organization meeting, we had reserved our right to set a cut off date for the submission of evidence. At that time, we had considered that the date for receipt of rebuttals would be the cut off date. We also recall that, when we communicated to the parties the replies of the IMF to our questions, we specified that "Parties shall not include in their comments any material or reference that is not yet part of the record". Moreover, we cannot agree with India that it could address this issue only after the IMF replied to the Panel. The IMF's answers on the removal of the measures and the suggestions made in its replies to the Panel were not new to India. During the consultations that took place in January 1997, the representative of the IMF had already presented the Fund's view in terms similar to those used in the replies to the Panel.[256] India also claims that it addressed the issue of development policy as early as its first written submission and its replies to the second series of questions from the Panel. We therefore consider that India had several opportunities to address the question of the impact of the removal of the measures on its development policy and was not denied an opportunity to introduce any facts on its development policy in relation to the proviso to Article XVIII:11.

4.10 Regarding the findings, India's general comments emphasize two themes. Firstly, India objects to the Panel's conclusion that the Panel is competent to review the balance-of-payments justification of India's quantitative restrictions under Article XVIII:B. Secondly, it claims that the Panel is wrong in making a finding that would require the immediate removal of the measures at issue by India.

1. *Review of the Balance-of-Payments Justification of India's Measures*

4.11 India argues that the Panel's interpretation of footnote 1 to the Understanding on the Balance-of-Payments Provisions of the General Agreement on Tariffs and Trade 1994 (hereafter the "1994 Understanding on Balance-of-Payments Provisions" or the "1994 Understanding") is incorrect, essentially focusing on four issues. Firstly, India challenges the interpretation of the Panel based on the ordinary meaning of the terms. Secondly, India also considers that the Panel misconstrued the preparatory work of the 1994 Understanding. Thirdly, it considers that the Panel misconstrued the practice under GATT 1947. Finally, India claims that the Panel's interpretation creates an imbalance between the BOP Committee procedures and the dispute settlement system.

[256] WT/BOP/R/22, Annex II, paragraph 12.

(a) Interpretation of the terms of footnote 1

4.12 Footnote 1 to the 1994 Understanding on Balance-of-Payments Provisions provides that the WTO dispute settlement provisions "may be invoked with respect to any matters arising from the application of restrictive measures taken for balance-of-payments purposes". India claims that our interpretation of the footnote deprives the term "application" of any useful effect. We disagree. We identified the ordinary meaning of the terms which is confirmed by their context and the object and purpose of the WTO Agreement, whereas India's interpretation could be considered rather to support a special meaning (within the meaning of Article 31.4 of the Vienna Convention on the Law of Treaties of 1969 - hereinafter the "Vienna Convention"), in respect of which it has not proved that there was an agreement of the negotiators.

4.13 India also contests our interpretation of the context of the footnote, arguing that we failed to address explicitly its arguments concerning the use of the term "application" in the Understanding on the Interpretation of Article XXIV of the GATT 1994 (hereinafter the "1994 Understanding on Article XXIV"). We have expanded our discussion of this issue in paragraphs 5.70 to make it clear that the use of the term "application" in the 1994 Understanding on Article XXIV, if anything, supports our interpretation.

4.14 India further claims that the Panel does not acknowledge the fact that the terms "the application of" appear only in two references to the DSU, namely the 1994 Understandings on Balance-of-Payments Provisions and Article XXIV, that only in these areas was recourse to Article XXIII at issue in GATT cases, and that the terms "the application of" therefore must have been intended to qualify the right to resort to the DSU. We note, however, that the terms "the application of" appear in several other dispute settlement provisions of the WTO Agreement (such as Article XXIII:1(b) of GATT 1994 and Article XXIII:3 of GATS), but are not used in any of these provisions in a way that would lead us to imply a limitation on the availability of dispute settlement. Thus, we cannot accept the claim that the use of the terms "the application of", as such, implies a limitation on the availability of dispute settlement. Moreover, the different phrasing of the two Understandings argues against India's interpretation, as we explain in paragraph 5.70. Indeed, in the 1994 Understanding on Article XXIV, the terms at issue seem to serve the opposite purpose, that of confirming the full applicability of the DSU to Article XXIV agreements in cases where it was once disputed.

4.15 India also complains that the Panel gave inadequate attention to its examples of where it is accepted that dispute settlement procedures do not apply. We have expanded our discussion of this issue (paragraph 5.87, footnote 310). However, even if we were to accept India's point that it could be inappropriate for certain issues to be resolved by dispute settlement panels, that observation in itself does not shed light on whether footnote 1 to the 1994 Understanding on Balance-of-Payments Provisions confirms the availability of dispute settlement in cases such as this one.

(b) Practice under GATT 1947

4.16 India claims that the Panel's analysis of the practice under GATT 1947 is misleading. While we have made minor adjustments in paragraphs 5.39 to 5.46, we maintain our analysis. We do not agree that, with the exception of the Panel Report on *Republic of Korea - Restrictions on Imports of Beef, Complaint by the United States*,[257] there has never been a request for the examination of the balance-of-payments justification of restrictions under Article XXIII (see paragraphs 5.37-5.38 and the footnotes attached thereto). The existence of these cases is at variance with India's contention that the question of justification has always been reserved exclusively to the BOP Committee and that no resort to dispute settlement is possible in relation to the justification of measures under Article XVIII:B.

4.17 India also argues that the Panel misinterpreted the finding of the *Korea - Beef* report. Firstly, India claims that we speculate when we state in paragraph 5.45 that we find no evidence that the panel would have refused to review the claims of the complainants as to the justification of the balance-of-payments measures if the BOP Committee had not issued a report. We believe our statement is correct. In the *Korea - Beef* case, the BOP Committee had issued a report, but the panel found it relevant to seek confirmation that the situation was still that which had led the BOP Committee to reach its conclusions. Such a verification, involving the review of additional data published by the Korean authorities and advice from the IMF, would not have been justified if the panel had considered the Committee's opinion to be decisive and had not considered itself competent to review the justification of the Korean measures. No other interpretation can reasonably be given to the analysis found in paragraph 123 of the *Korea - Beef* report. The panel itself reached its conclusion that there was a "continued improvement in the Korean balance-of-payments situation", a conclusion which could not be based solely on the Committee report, which dated back to 1987.

4.18 India also argues that the *Korea - Beef* panel declared itself competent to look at the justification of the measures only because its terms of reference had been agreed by the complaining parties and Korea. However, its terms of reference did not expressly address the Article XVIII:B issue. The panel was directed "to examine [the Korean measures] in light of the relevant GATT provisions". In response to a request from Korea for a ruling on the admissibility of the claim under Article XXIII, the panel made an initial ruling that it clearly had a mandate to examine the merits of the case in accordance with its terms of reference.[258] In its findings, it then proceeded to consider "whether the consistency of restrictive

---

[257] Adopted on 7 November 1989, BISD 36S/268 (hereinafter the "*Korea - Beef* case"). Two other complaints were addressed by the same panel, but led to separate reports. See Panel Reports adopted on 7 November 1989, *Republic of Korea - Restrictions on Imports of Beef, Complaint by Australia*, BISD36S/202 and *Complaint by New Zealand*, BISD 36S/234.

[258] Op. Cit., para. 10.

measures with Article XVIII:B could be examined within the framework of Article XXIII". While the panel did, in its findings, refer to its terms of reference, it did so *after* it had considered the arguments of the parties concerning past deliberations by the CONTRACTING PARTIES on the exclusivity of special review procedures under the GATT and had decided that these earlier deliberations were not directly applicable in the present dispute. Then, the panel added a paragraph on the drafting history of Articles XVIII and XXIII and an analysis of their terms and functions. The panel considered that, by accepting its terms of reference, Korea had agreed to the competence of the panel to review the matter in the light of the relevant GATT provisions. From this general competence, the panel deduced its competence to review the justification of the measure under Article XVIII:B, which is part of the "relevant GATT provisions". Thus the panel's competence under Article XVIII:B was the result of its reasoning, not that of an express acceptance by Korea. This is the meaning of the first reference to Korea's acceptance of the panel's mandate, in paragraph 117. In its context, the sentence cannot be read as meaning that the panel relied on a specific acceptance by Korea of its competence under XVIII:B, and even less that it relied *exclusively* on Korea's acceptance of its mandate to look at the justification of the measures under Article XVIII:B.[259] The reference to the fact that "the parties have chosen to proceed under Article XXIII" is obviously based on the same reasoning. We therefore consider that India's references in the *Korea - Beef* case do not support its argument according to which the panel in that case did not conduct its own analysis of the justification of the measure and only reviewed the justification of measures essentially because Korea had accepted that it do so.

(c) Preparatory work

4.19 India further claims that we did not properly address the preparatory work of the 1994 Understanding. As mentioned in paragraph 5.110, we did not need to look at the preparatory work since the meaning resulting from our analysis under Article 31 of the Vienna Convention was neither ambiguous or obscure, nor did it lead to a manifestly absurd or unreasonable result. It is a well established principle of interpretation of international law not to refer to the preparatory work if the ordinary meaning of the text, taken in its context and in the light of the object and purpose of the treaty, is clear. On the other hand, recourse to the preparatory work must always be undertaken with caution and prudence.[260] The purpose of paragraphs 5.106 to 5.111 was to show that limited use could be made of the document invoked by India, since India could not provide evidence that the US-Canada proposal was rejected specifically because of the part of the proposal that dealt with recourse to Article XXIII. Indeed, several other reasons could have

[259] This is consistent with Korea's later contention on justification: Korea could challenge the competence of the panel to look at the justification without negating its consent to the terms of reference.
[260] Ian Sinclair, *The Vienna Convention on the Law of Treaties* (1980), p. 142.

contributed to the rejection of the proposal, which makes relying on it problematic. In any event, we have expanded our discussion of the preparatory work in paragraphs 5.106-5.111 to make those points more clearly.

(d) Allocation of decision-making in balance-of-payments matters

4.20 In respect of its argument that the interim report improperly allocates decision-making authority in balance-of-payments matters between panels and the BOP Committee, India first contends that, in application of the principle *lex specialis derogat legi generali,* the general provisions according to panels the right to make legal findings cannot override the specific provisions giving the BOP Committee and the General Council the power to make specified determinations. India did not really present its argumentation in terms of *lex specialis* during the Panel's proceedings and the Panel considers that this concept does not apply in the present case. While the two procedures may be said to apply to the same subject matter, the second condition for the application of the principle of *lex specialis,* i.e. the existence of a conflict between the two, is not met. The objective of the Committee procedure under Article XVIII:12(b)[261] is a general review of a Member's policy by the BOP Committee and the General Council, whereas the DSU applies in case of a dispute between two Members related to specific measures. Moreover, the Panel in its analysis of the operation of the two procedures found no circumstances where, in practice, those procedures would conflict (see paragraphs 5.92-5.97). In any event, the principle of *lex specialis* is only subsidiary. If the treaty provides for the relationship between the two "conflicting" rules, the principle no longer applies.[262] In the present case, footnote 1 to the 1994 Understanding on Balance-of-Payments Provisions clearly confirms the application of the DSU to balance-of-payments matters.

4.21 As to the argument of India that our findings lead to the anomalous result that the power to make the same decision is accorded to two different organs, we consider that it is based on an inappropriate assumption. As explained above, the two procedures (that under Article XVIII:12(b) and that under the DSU) fulfill two different and complementary objectives. One is meant to allow the review of a policy by the WTO, the other one is meant to preserve the rights of Members under the WTO Agreement. As explained in paragraphs 5.92-5.97, which we have modified slightly, we see no problem of conflicts. India also argues that it is a denial of due process to have dispute resolution available to an aggrieved Member only. We disagree. In our view, a Member invoking Article XVIII:B to justify its restrictions has nothing to complain about since it may maintain its restrictions until the Committee recommends that they should be removed. Com-

[261] In the course of which inconsistent measures may be identified by the BOP Committee, pursuant to Article XVIII:12(c).

[262] Sinclair, Op. Cit., p. 97, Daillier and Pellet, *Droit international public* (1994), pp. 263 and 265.

paratively any other Member may have reasons to complain at any time that the measures for which Article XVIII:B is invoked are not, or no longer, justified. We do not agree either that the Panel declares itself competent only to take decisions that are potentially adverse to the Member imposing balance-of-payments measures. If balance-of-payments measures are found to be justified, a panel will not find against that Member on that aspect. Moreover, while that Member may not be able to block adverse findings by a panel, as a practical matter it can do so with Committee recommendations. In light of this, the Panel considers its conclusion as to the availability of dispute settlement concurrently with the Committee procedures more in compliance with the basic principles of procedural justice than an interpretation that would allow measures not in conformity with Article XVIII:B to be maintained at the will of the Member imposing them.

4.22 India also claims that we failed to address its argument that "the transfer to panels of the competence explicitly assigned in Article XV:2 and XVIII:12 to the General Council would eliminate the procedural rights which Article XVIII:B and the Balance-of-Payments Understanding accord to Members in balance-of-payments difficulties". India's reasoning that it would be deprived of its procedural rights is based on the fundamental assumption that (i) Members have a right to "an assessment of their difficulties and corrective policies by peers" and (ii) that if a panel decides on the issue before the BOP Committee has completed its own examination, the BOP Committee will be bound by the findings of the panel. Nowhere in our report do we say this. The initiation of a dispute settlement procedure with respect to certain measures does not prevent the examination of their justification in the BOP Committee. Moreover, the BOP Committee is not constrained by the aspects of due process which require that a panel set a cut-off date for the facts on which it will rely. In other words, the Committee may always decide on the basis of new facts. Thus, just as the panel in *Korea - Beef* made its own assessments of the facts that followed the BOP Committee's decision, the BOP Committee can make its own assessment of the facts subsequent to the date of establishment of the Panel. India's arguments are of course concentrated on its position as a consulting Member. However, the situation of the Members whose rights under the WTO Agreement are affected by India's measures should not be forgotten. If one were to follow India's arguments, pursuant to which a Member can maintain measures as long as no decision to the contrary has been taken by the General Council, even when there is no longer any balance-of-payments justification, the rights of other Members under the Agreement would be unduly affected, with no effective means of redress, as noted in paragraph 4.21.

2. *Immediate Removal of the Measures and Consequence Thereof*

4.23 India claims that the Panel's finding that the Note Ad Article XVIII:11 requires India to remove all its import restrictions at once lacks any basis in law and facts. The Panel addresses the arguments of India in relation to this issue in paragraphs 5.201 to 5.215. We were required to determine whether a given measure was consistent with the provisions of Article XVIII:B. We concluded that India was in violation of Article XVIII by still maintaining in November 1997 measures that were no longer justified under Article XVIII:B. The fact that the Panel found that, as from November 1997, the measures were not justified does not mean that they should be removed immediately.[263] We could not rule on a phase-out period, but we suggested that the reasonable period of time to implement the DSB recommendations on this matter be considered in the light of a number of factors listed in paragraph 7.5. For that reason, we think that our decision is consistent with the facts and the applicable norms.

4.24 India also claims that our interpretation of the word "thereupon" in the Note Ad Article XVIII renders that provision inoperative in practice. We disagree. We consider that our interpretation of the word "thereupon" is consistent with the principles of interpretation of the Vienna Convention and is the only one that could give a useful meaning to that term. As shown in paragraphs 5.196 to 5.198, the interpretation suggested by India (*inter alia:* "by direct agency" in English, "sans intermédiaire" in French) would make the word "thereupon" redundant, since the causal link in the Ad Note is clear without that word. Moreover, saying that the relaxation or removal of the measures would "directly" (in the sense of not indirectly) produce the conditions foreseen in Article XVIII:9 would also simply restate the causal link, which is not necessary.

4.25 India comments at length on the nature of its development policy and the fact that the Panel did not address this central issue. We note first that India has submitted new data at the interim review stage. There is no trace either in the record of the Planning Commission's estimate that India faces an additional threat to its reserves from an increase in the trade deficit and a fall in its foreign exchange reserves to "significantly below" US$16 billion in a period ranging between a few months and one year. We agree with the United States that this submission of additional information is untimely. We consequently decided not to take it into account. Secondly, we remain unconvinced that India "has argued in detail and at length" regarding the changes that an immediate removal of the measures at issue would require in India's development policy. We do not disagree that India discussed the first sentence and the proviso of Article XVIII:11, or the impact of the removal of the measures on its development policy. Accordingly, we revised the part now corresponding to paragraphs 5.216 to 5.223. However, we do not agree that India produced sufficient evidence to support a claim that the removal of the measures at issue actually would require a change in its development policy. Nor can we share India's view as to the risks entailed by India's economy as a result of the removal of the measures. In paragraph 5.204, we note the IMF views that the restrictions should be removed over a relatively short period of time, not immediately, but we also note that this period has noth-

[263] Article 21.3 of the DSU does not require immediate compliance with DSB recommendations and rulings if it is impracticable to do so.

ing to do with a gradual phase-out accompanying a reduction of balance-of-payments difficulties. This is why we suggest that they should be removed within a reasonable period of time.

4.26 We note in this regard that India, in support of its contention that immediate removal of its measures would immediately lead to balance-of-payments difficulties, refers to a potential surge in imports. India does not always take into account the distinction between a projected change in imports and a projected change in its reserves. The removal of the measures at issue will most probably lead to an increase in imports, but showing that imports will increase, even substantially, does not demonstrate that balance-of-payments difficulties within the meaning of Article XVIII:9 will occur *ipso facto*. For instance, India does not take into account in its assessment the positive effects that would result from the removal of import restrictions. In relation to this, we clarified our own statements in paragraph 5.207.

3. *Other Specific Comments*

4.27 India claims in relation to paragraphs 5.159-5.163 that the Panel should not use the date of its establishment as the date at which India's balance-of-payments and reserve situation should be reviewed. Rather, India claims that "The respondent party must be able to prepare its defence as from the request for the establishment of the Panel." We first recall that our terms of reference were set as of the date of establishment and added practical reasons for using this date, as contained in paragraph 5.161-5.162. Our decision on this issue is also consistent with past practice under GATT 1947.[264] Secondly, we note that India was, during the course of the proceedings, in favour of taking into account the latest economic developments possible, i.e., using a date *after*, not *before*, the date of establishment of the Panel. The Panel therefore finds no reasons to modify paragraphs 5.159 to 5.163.

4.28 India claims that the Panel presents in paragraph 5.232 and 5.235 "speculations on the scope of the authority of the BOP Committee and the General Council under paragraph 13 of the Understanding". The Panel addressed this matter in reply to India's arguments related to its alleged right to a phase-out period. It finds it appropriate to keep this discussion.

4.29 Finally, in light of the comments by India, we also modified paragraphs 5.34, 5.47, 5.53, 5.84, 5.114, 5.244, 5.245.

[264] Panel Report on *United States - Section 337 of the Tariff Act of 1930*, adopted on 7 November 1989, BISD 36S/345, para. 5.2.

V. FINDINGS

5.1 The United States requests the Panel to find that the challenged measures, notified by India in Annex I, Part B of document WT/BOP/N/24, are quantitative restrictions subject to Article XI:1 and are not justified under the provisions of Article XVIII:11 of GATT 1994. The United States also claims that the measures are in violation of Article 4.2 of the Agreement on Agriculture. India requests the Panel to note that both parties agree that the import restrictions at issue fall under Article XI:1, but disagree on their justification under Article XVIII:B.

5.2 In the event that the measures are found not to be in violation of Article XVIII:11, the United States also requests a finding that the challenged measures violate Article XIII of GATT 1994. The United States also identified in its request for establishment of the Panel a violation of Article 3 of the Agreement on Import Licensing Procedures.

5.3 In the course of the proceedings, the Panel made a preliminary ruling and consulted the International Monetary Fund. These actions are addressed first (in Part B). We then clarify the scope of the complaint to be addressed by the Panel (Part C). In its defence, India raised issues relating to the extent of the competence of this Panel to address issues relating to the justification of import restrictions taken for balance-of-payments purposes under Article XVIII:B of GATT 1994. We consider these arguments and determine the scope of our competence in this dispute in Part D, before addressing the issue of burden of proof in Part E. In Part F, we address the claim of violation of Article XI:1 of GATT 1994, and then in Part G, we consider the claim of violation of Article XVIII:11 and the possible justification of the measures under Article XVIII:B. The claim of violation of Article 4.2 of the Agreement on Agriculture is then addressed in Part H. The claim of violation of Article XIII of GATT 1994 is addressed in Part I.

5.4 Before proceeding further in our examination, it is useful to recall the main events which preceded the establishment of this Panel.

A. *Facts Leading to the Dispute*

5.5 India has, for the past fifty years, applied quantitative restrictions justified for balance-of-payments reasons. These were applied under Article XII of GATT 1947 between 1950 and 1957 and, since, under Article XVIII:B. India has been consulting regularly under Article XVIII:B since 1957. After a serious crisis in 1990-1991 where India's monetary reserves were depleted, its balance-of-payments situation has gradually improved and it has implemented economic reforms and import liberalization programmes, including reduction of its quantitative restrictions. At the conclusion of the 1994 simplified consultations with the Committee on Balance-of-Payments Restrictions (hereafter the "BOP Committee" or the "Committee"), the Committee noted that, if the balance of payments of India showed sustained improvement, India's stated aim was to move by 1996/97 to a regime in which import licensing restrictions would only be maintained for environmental and safety reasons. Members of the Committee welcomed the significant improvements in India's balance-of-payments position but recognized that it remained volatile. The Committee concluded that a full consultation in the second half of 1995 was desirable.[265]

5.6 During the 1995 full consultations, the Committee invited the International Monetary Fund (IMF) to participate in the consultations in accordance with Article XV:2 of GATT 1994. In an official statement to the Committee, the IMF representative noted that, with continued prudent macroeconomic management, the transition to a tariff-based import regime with no quantitative restrictions could reasonably be accomplished within a period of two years. The Committee also noted the view expressed by India that, in the context of a deteriorating balance-of-payments situation, it would be neither prudent nor feasible to consider the general lifting of existing quantitative restrictions on imports at this stage. Many Members supported India's continued use of import restrictions under Article XVIII:B for balance-of-payments reasons in view of the uncertainty and fragility they perceived in India's balance-of-payments position. Many other Members stated that India's balance-of-payments position was comfortable, that India did not currently face the threat of a serious decline in foreign exchange reserves as set out in Article XVIII:9 and that therefore India was not justified in its continued recourse to import restrictions for balance-of-payments reasons. Many Members asked India *inter alia* to present a firm time-table for the phasing out of the restrictions. The Committee did not reach any conclusions and welcomed India's readiness to resume consultations in October 1996.[266]

5.7 During the resumed consultations which were held in January 1997, the BOP Committee took note of the IMF's statement that India's current monetary reserves were not inadequate and that there was no threat of a serious decline in India's monetary reserves. The Committee agreed to resume consultations in June 1997 to consider a plan to be presented by India to eliminate the measures notified under Article XVIII:B and to conclude the consultations consistently with all relevant WTO balance-of-payments provisions.[267] On 19 May 1997, India presented a new notification in document WT/BOP/N/24, including a nine year phase-out plan for removal of the measures. At the June 1997 consultations, the IMF representative stated that the views of the IMF as expressed during the January 1997 consultations on India's balance-of-payments situation had not changed during the interim period. In the course of consultations, India proposed a phase-out period of six years, plus one year for a limited number of products. A number of Members were of the view that the phase-out period for the existing measures should not exceed five years.[268] The BOP Committee concluded its

[265] BOP/R/221, 1 December 1994, para. 4.

[266] WT/BOP/R/11, 23 January 1996.

[267] WT/BOP/R/22, 3 March 1997.

[268] Finally, a period of six years was proposed by India in bilateral consultations.

consultations with India by recording the different views on the issue, without reaching a consensus on a Committee recommendation to the General Council.[269]

B. *Rulings Made by the Panel in the Course of the Proceedings*

1. *Request by India for Sufficient Time to Prepare and Present its Argumentation, Pursuant to Article 12.10 of the DSU*

5.8 On 7 April 1998, the Panel received a letter from the Permanent Mission of India requesting, pursuant to Article 12.10 of the Understanding on Rules and Procedures Governing the Settlement of Disputes (hereinafter "the DSU"), that India be granted up to 12 May 1998 to prepare and present its first written submission. India claimed that the case was of a systemic importance and covered a wide range of issues. The case occurred at a time when a new government had recently assumed office. The post of Attorney General, associated with disputes of this type, had not yet been filled and other administrative difficulties made it virtually impossible for India to adhere to the time-limit originally set for India to present its first submission.

5.9 In a letter dated 8 April 1998, the United States opposed the granting of additional time to India. The request was untimely. The WTO rules imposed very strict deadlines to which all Members had agreed. The United States would face administrative constraints if the proceedings had to be re-scheduled. In any event, the United States' first submission was straightforward and India had the necessary expertise available in Geneva to deal with it.

5.10 On 15 April 1998 we ruled as follows:

> "The Panel has carefully reviewed the arguments of the parties. The Panel notes that India could have raised several of the reasons mentioned in its letter during the organizational meeting held on 27 February 1998. However, pursuant to Article 12.10 of the DSU, "in examining a complaint against a developing country Member, the panel shall accord sufficient time for the developing country Member to prepare and present its argumentation." In light of this provision, and considering the administrative reorganization taking place in India as a result of the recent change in government, the Panel has decided to grant an additional period of time to India to prepare its submission. However, bearing in mind also the need to respect the time frames of the DSU and in light of the difficulties of rescheduling the meeting of 7 and 8 May, the Panel considers that an additional period of ten days would represent "sufficient time" within the meaning of Article 12.10 of the DSU. India is

[269] WT/BOP/R/32, 18 September 1997. See also Section II:A *supra*.

therefore granted until 1 May 1998 (5 p.m.) to submit its first written submission to the Panel. The original date of the first meeting remains unchanged as 7 and 8 May."

2. *Consultation with the International Monetary Fund*

5.11 During the course of its proceedings, the Panel decided to consult with the International Monetary Fund. The parties had divergent opinions on the possible role of the IMF in this instance. The United States was of the opinion that the Panel had before it sufficient evidence, but should consult the IMF if the Panel had any doubts. For the United States, the terms of Article XV:2 of GATT 1994, read as per paragraph 2(b) of the Incorporation Clause of GATT 1994 in Annex 1A of the WTO Agreement, require the WTO to consult with the IMF in specific matters, and the WTO includes panels. For India, on the contrary, to interpret the terms of Article XV to refer to panels ignores the division of functions between the different bodies of the WTO, and only the General Council and BOP Committee are covered by this provision. The parties also had diverging views on the extent of the discretion enjoyed by the Panel with regard to determinations of the IMF. In the view of the United States, the Panel must accept as dispositive the determination of the IMF on the matters of fact specified in Article XV:2, and in particular concerning whether the facts of India's balance-of-payments and reserve situation placed India within the criteria listed in Article XVIII:9(a) and (b). This took nothing away from the efficacy of the Panel's final decision phase. For India, the text of Article XV:2 made it clear that the Committee and the General Council must accept certain determinations of the IMF "in reaching their final decision". In India's view, the argument of the United States, however, allowed the determination of the IMF on the financial aspects of the consultations to determine the legal status of a restriction notified under Article XVIII:B. For India, Articles XV:2 and XVIII:12 left no doubt that the IMF did not take final decisions on the legal status of restrictions under the WTO.

5.12 Article 13.1 of the DSU provides that each panel has "the right to seek information and technical advice from any individual or body which it deems appropriate." Article 13.2 further provides that panels may "seek information from any relevant source and may consult experts to obtain their opinion on certain aspects of the matter". With regard to balance-of-payments issues, the IMF, as a recognized body with extensive expertise in these matters, is obviously a highly relevant source of information. We find that, whatever the interpretation of Article XV:2 of GATT 1994, Article 13.1 of the DSU entitles the Panel to consult with the IMF in order to obtain any relevant information relating to India's monetary reserves and balance-of-payments situation which would assist us in assessing the claims submitted to us. Although the BOP Committee had previously consulted with the IMF, there were two particular reasons for the Panel to consult the IMF on its own account. First, the BOP Committee itself had not made a determination based on Article XVIII:B following its consultation with the IMF. Secondly, the balance-of-payments situation of India might have changed in the meantime. Consequently, the Panel submitted a number of questions to the IMF, by a letter dated 3 July 1998, having regard to Article 13 of the DSU and to Article XV:2 of the GATT 1994.[270] The IMF provided answers to these questions on July 17, 1998. These answers were duly taken into account in our assessment of the claims before us.

5.13 We do not find it necessary for the purposes of this case to decide the extent to which Article XV:2 may require panels to consult with the IMF or consider as dispositive specific determinations of the IMF. As will be seen in Section V.G *infra*, we accept in the circumstances of this case certain assessments of the IMF. In this regard, however, we note that whether or not the provisions of Article XV:2 extend to panels, the Panel has the responsibility of making an objective assessment of the facts of the case and the conformity with GATT 1994, as incorporated into the WTO Agreement, of the Indian measures at issue, in accordance with Article 11 of the DSU.

C. *Scope of the Complaint*

5.14 We note that the product coverage of the complaint is not at issue here. In its first submission, the United States clearly stated that its claims were limited to the measures applicable to the 2,714 HS tariff lines notified by India on 19 May 1997 in Annex I, Part B of document WT/BOP/N/24 under paragraph 9 of the Understanding on the Balance-of-Payments Provisions of the General Agreement on Tariffs and Trade 1994 (hereafter the "1994 Understanding on Balance-of-Payments Provisions" or the "1994 Understanding"). However, in light of the arguments exchanged by the parties, we need to define more precisely our understanding of some of the claims made by the United States. In particular, we must consider (1) whether the claims of violation of Article XIII of GATT 1994 and Article 3 of the Agreement on Import Licensing Procedures are properly before the Panel, (2) the extent to which we should consider the provisions of Article XVIII:B, other than Article XVIII:11, which is the only paragraph of Article XVIII expressly contained in the United States' request for establishment of a panel and (3) the relationship of the United States' claim to India's claim that it is entitled to a phase-out period for its balance-of-payments measures.

1. *Claims of Violation of Article XIII of GATT and of Article 3 of the Agreement on Import Licensing Procedures*

5.15 In its first written submission, the United States claimed that the measures at issue violate Articles XI:1 and XVIII:11 of GATT 1994, as well as Article 4.2 of the Agreement on Agriculture. The United States did not refer at that stage to Article XIII of GATT 1994 or to Article 3 of the Agreement on Import Licensing

[270] The parties were provided with the opportunity to comment on the questions put to the IMF.

Procedures (hereafter the "Import Licensing Agreement"), which were mentioned in its request for the establishment of a panel and hence incorporated in our terms of reference.[271] India claimed that, since the United States did not elaborate on its claims under Article XIII of GATT 1994 and Article 3 of the Licensing Agreement in its first submission, it could not do so later. The United States replied that it is only in the event the Panel does not agree that India lacks justification for the challenged measure that the United States requests a finding that the measures are not applied in accordance with the requirements of Article XIII:2(a) of GATT 1994.

5.16 A claim of violation of Article 3 of the Import Licensing Agreement is contained in the United States' request for establishment of a panel and thus, in our terms of reference. The United States, however, did not develop any legal arguments relating to such claim at any point of the proceedings, nor did it request a finding on the basis of that provision. We therefore do not address that claim.

5.17 With regard to the claim of violation of Article XIII of GATT 1994, since the resolution of the claims under Articles XI and XVIII:B may make it unnecessary to resolve that claim, we will defer consideration of this issue.

2. *Provisions of Article XVIII:B other than Article XVIII:11*

5.18 India has raised the issue of the extent to which the Panel should consider the provisions of Article XVIII:B and the 1994 Understanding on Balance-of-payments Provisions in its analysis of the US claims. In this regard, we note that the United States has not raised any claim regarding violations of Article XVIII:B or the 1994 Understanding, apart from Article XVIII:11. Accordingly, we will not address any claims of the United States based on the 1994 Understanding or on provisions of Article XVIII:B other than Article XVIII:11.

5.19 However, the provisions of Article XVIII:B (other than Article XVIII:11) and the 1994 Understanding are part of the context of those provisions alleged by the United States to have been violated. In addition, India also refers to various provisions of Article XVIII:B in its defence. In our view, the defending party is not restricted in the provisions of the Marrakesh Agreement Establishing the World Trade Organization (hereinafter "WTO Agreement") that it can invoke in its defence. In these circumstances, we find it relevant to consider the provisions of Article XVIII:B and the 1994 Understanding as part of the context in deciding on the claims of the United States and to examine them in relation to the defence raised by India.

[271] WT/DS90/8 and WT/DS90/9.

3. *Phase-Out Period*

5.20 India claims that the central issue in this dispute is the length of the time-schedule that India should be permitted in order to relax progressively and eliminate certain restrictions on imports that India has maintained for balance-of-payments purposes. The United States replies that the case is not about the phase-out schedule for the Indian restrictions. We note that the United States does not seek any findings or recommendations regarding the duration of the phase-out period. The United States seeks findings that the challenged measures are quantitative restrictions subject to Article XI:1 and that they are not justified under the provisions of Article XVIII:11. We therefore consider the issue of the phase-out only to the extent relevant to the defence raised by India and in our suggestions for implementation of the recommendations of the DSB.

D. *Competence of the Panel*

5.21 In their submissions, the parties raise fundamental issues relating to the competence of panels to review balance-of-payments measures and their justification under Article XVIII:B. We therefore examine at the outset these issues of competence.

1. *The Issue: Are Panels Competent to Review the Justification of Balance-of-Payments Measures under Article XVIII:B?*

5.22 In response to the claim of the United States that its balance-of-payments measures violate Articles XI:1 and XVIII:11, India's defence is that, even if its measures violate Article XI:1, they are permitted as balance-of-payments measures under Article XVIII:B and, as such, do not violate Article XVIII:11. Moreover, India considers that this Panel is not competent to make findings with respect to the justification of the measures taken under Article XVIII:B, as this is a matter in respect of which, according to India, exclusive authority has been assigned by GATT 1994 to the BOP Committee and the General Council. India claims that a panel cannot substitute itself for the BOP Committee or the General Council with regard to the justification of measures under Article XVIII:B and that acceptance of the arguments of the United States would result in making whole paragraphs of Article XVIII:B and whole sections of the 1994 Understanding redundant, altering fundamentally the negotiated balance reflected in the text of Article XVIII:B and the 1994 Understanding.

5.23 The United States argues that the texts of neither Article XII nor Article XVIII:B prohibit recourse to dispute settlement under Article XXIII. Nor does the text of Article XXIII or of the DSU contain any such prohibition. Article XVIII of GATT 1994 is among the WTO provisions that have been made subject to the DSU as set forth in Appendix 1 to the DSU and for which no special or additional provisions are found in Appendix 2 of the DSU. In that light, the United States argues that India's suggestion that the committee that holds Article

XVIII:12(c) consultations is the sole body able to decide the question before this Panel is an untenable interpretation of GATT 1994. The United States further argues that footnote 1 of the 1994 Understanding confirms the availability of dispute settlement in relation to measures taken for balance-of-payments purposes.[272]

5.24 Pursuant to Article 3.2 of the DSU, our task is to clarify the existing provisions of the covered agreements in accordance with customary rules of interpretation of public international law. The Appellate Body has stated that these rules are the criteria contained in Articles 31 and 32 of the Vienna Convention on the Law of Treaty (1969) (hereafter the "Vienna Convention").

5.25 In addition, on the basis of Article XVI:1 of the WTO Agreement, we are also guided by the decisions, procedures and customary practices followed by the CONTRACTING PARTIES to GATT 1947. Indeed, the parties refer to the practice of GATT CONTRACTING PARTIES and the role of the procedures under Article XVIII:B of GATT in their arguments regarding the competence issue. Moreover, the first sentence of footnote 1 of the 1994 Understanding, which was negotiated as part of the WTO Agreement, provides that "[n]othing in this Understanding is intended to modify the rights and obligations of Members under Articles XII or XVIII:B of GATT 1994".

5.26 In the light of these elements, we first examine, to the extent relevant to our discussion, the mechanisms which the GATT provided for the surveillance and review of balance-of-payments measures prior to the entry into force of the WTO Agreement. Our focus is first on Article XVIII:B, the provision applicable to balance-of-payments measures taken by developing countries which came into effect in 1957, and its Ad Note, together with relevant texts adopted in 1970, 1972 and 1979 (with a reference, as appropriate, to Article XII, the balance-of-payments provision applicable to developed countries), then on Article XXIII, the provision regarding the settlement of disputes in general under GATT 1947.

5.27 We then proceed with the analysis of the applicable provisions under the WTO Agreement. The text of Article XVIII:B is unchanged. It should now be read together with the 1994 Understanding. The text of Article XXIII of GATT is also unchanged in the WTO. However, it should now be read in conjunction with the DSU.

2. *Surveillance and Review of Balance-of-Payments Measures Prior to the Entry Into Force of the WTO*

(a) Article XVIII:B

5.28 Article XVIII:B was added to the GATT text in 1957 to provide special and differential treatment for developing countries in respect of their balance-of-

[272] For a detailed description of the arguments of the parties, see Section III.D.1 *supra*.

payments measures.[273] Article XVIII:12 established several procedures through which the CONTRACTING PARTIES collectively could exercise surveillance over balance-of-payments measures taken by developing contracting parties and review their consistency with Article XVIII:B. Hereafter, we first identify the nature of these procedures, then examine the practice under Article XVIII:12.

(i) Article XVIII:12 procedures

5.29 Article XVIII:12 provided for two different types of procedures: procedures for consultations (Article XVIII:12(a) and (b)) and dispute-settlement like procedures (Article XVIII:12(c) and (d)). Procedures for consultations on balance-of-payments restrictions were further detailed in decisions approved on 28 April 1970 ("full consultation procedures") and on 19 December 1972 ("simplified consultations"),[274] and in the Declaration on Trade Measures taken for Balance-of-Payments Purposes adopted on 28 November 1979 (hereinafter "the 1979 Declaration"). Article XVIII:12(a) required a contracting party applying new or substantially intensified measures under Article XVIII:B to consult as to the nature of its balance-of-payments difficulties, alternative corrective measures which might be available and the possible effect of the restrictions on the economies of other contracting parties.[275] Article XVIII:12(b) provided for the review of measures applied under Article XVIII:B and for regular consultations on such measures.

5.30 Article XVIII:12(c)(i) provided that if in the course of consultations, the CONTRACTING PARTIES found that the restrictions were not consistent with the provisions of Article XVIII:B or Article XIII, they "*shall*" indicate the nature of the inconsistency and "*may*" advise that the restrictions be suitably modified. Article XVIII:12(c)(ii) further provided that if in the course of consultations, the CONTRACTING PARTIES determined that the restrictions were being applied in a manner involving an inconsistency *"of a serious nature"* with the provision of Article XVIII:B or Article XIII and that damage to the trade of any contracting party was caused or threatened thereby, they "*shall*" make appropriate recommendations for securing conformity with such provisions within a specified period. If the recommendations were not complied with, the CONTRACTING PARTIES could release any contracting party, whose trade was adversely affected by the restrictions, from such obligations under GATT to the contracting party applying the restrictions as they determined to be appropriate.

5.31 Under the terms of Article XVIII:12(d), the CONTRACTING PARTIES were to invite any contracting party applying balance-of-payments restrictions under Article XVIII:B to enter into consultations with them at the request of any

---

[273] For a fuller description of the special and differential treatment provided for in Article XVIII, see *infra* paras. 5.152-5.157.

[274] BISD18S/48-53 and BISD 20S/47-49.

[275] A similar provision is found in Article XII:4(a).

contracting party which could establish a *prima facie* case that the restrictions were inconsistent with the provisions of Article XVIII:B or Article XIII and that its trade was adversely affected thereby. If the consultations were unsuccessful and the CONTRACTING PARTIES determined that the restrictions were being applied inconsistently with such provisions and that damage to the trade of the complaining contracting party was caused or threatened, they were to recommend the withdrawal or modification of the restrictions within a prescribed time period. If the recommendations were not complied with, the CONTRACTING PARTIES could release the complaining contracting party from such GATT obligations to the contracting party applying the restrictions as they determined to be appropriate.

5.32 Determinations under Article XVIII:12 were to be made expeditiously and if possible within 60 days of the initiation of consultations.[276]

5.33 Paragraph 13 of the 1979 Declaration provides that if the BOP Committee finds an inconsistency with, *inter alia*, Article XVIII, it shall in its report to the Council make such findings as will assist the Council in making appropriate recommendations designed to promote the implementation of Article XVIII. The Council is directed to keep under surveillance any matters on which it has made recommendations.

(ii) Practice of the BOP Committee/Council

5.34 Numerous consultations were held in the past under Article XVIII:B concerning balance-of-payments measures taken by developing countries. The consultations led to reports which expressed in most cases the unanimous view of all the contracting parties present and which were subsequently adopted by the Council. We are not aware of instances, at least since 1970,[277] where consultations led to formal recommendations, explicitly based on Article XVIII:12(c)(ii), that measures determined to be unjustified under Article XVIII:B had to be brought into conformity with that provision.

5.35 A Secretariat note concerning the period from 1975 to 1988 indicates that, in a number of cases, the BOP Committee explicitly recognized the existence of a balance-of-payments justification. On the other hand, the Committee never explicitly determined that a particular measure was unjustified under the balance-of-payments provisions of the GATT. Rather, various levels of tone have been used to indicate the strength of the Committee's doubts concerning the justification of measures in particular circumstances. Strong language was, for instance, used in the 1987 report concerning Korea. The report stated that "[t]he prevailing view expressed in the Committee was that the current situation and outlook for

[276] Article XVIII:12(f).

[277] L/4200, 18 July 1975, para. 39 and document MTN.GNG/NG7/W46, 24 June 1988, para. 66, further discussed *infra* at para. 5.35.

the balance-of-payments was such that import restrictions could no longer be justified under Article XVIII:B."[278] With regard to the discussion and adoption of reports, the same Secretariat note indicates that

> "on a number of occasions contracting parties, while not opposing the adoption of reports, have used the occasion of their adoption to express regret at the continued maintenance of import restrictions and to press for faster or more complete liberalization. In some cases, countries have also reserved their GATT rights in relation to measures which they saw as damaging their interests and whose maintenance they believed not to be in conformity with GATT. For example, in 1985 Japan reserved its rights in relation to measures maintained by Portugal, and Hungary did so in relation to a Turkish measure (...). In November 1987 the point was made that contracting parties retain all their GATT rights in respect of measures maintained for balance-of-payments purposes, and that review of such restrictions by the Balance-of-payments Committee, and adoption by the Council of the Committee's report, did not constitute acceptance that they were consistent with GATT."[279]

We also note that it appears that Article XVIII:12(d) has not been resorted to.[280]

(b) Article XXIII

(i) The general procedure for the settlement of disputes

5.36 At the origin of GATT, the general procedure contemplated for the settlement of disputes between contracting parties bore marked similarities with the procedure which was available to contracting parties under Article XVIII:12(d). In the course of time, the procedure based on Article XXIII evolved as a result of the development of the system of panels.

(ii) Practice under Article XXIII with respect to balance-of-payments measures

5.37 Prior to the WTO Agreement, recourse to dispute settlement with regard to balance-of-payments measures occurred from time to time, but it was infrequent. The United States cites in particular the *Belgian Dollar Import Restrictions* case and the *German Import Restrictions* case. The *Belgian Dollar Import Restrictions* case concerned measures maintained by Belgium on imports from the dollar area, which in the view of the United States were not justified by Bel-

[278] BOP/R/171, para. 22.
[279] *Consultations held in the Committee on Balance-of-Payments Restrictions under Articles XII and XVIII:B since 1975*, Note by the Secretariat, MTN.GNG/NG7/W/46, 24 June 1988, para. 66.
[280] Footnote 289 to para.5.47 *infra*.

gium's dollar balance-of-payments position. A Working Party was established in 1952 following a request under Article XXIII, but no ruling was made on the issue, since a settlement was reached between the parties. The measures were progressively reduced and eliminated.[281] The *German Import Restrictions* case did not directly involve a determination of consistency of measures with Article XII through dispute settlement.[282]

5.38 In another case, not cited by the parties and involving the United States and India, the United States initiated consultations regarding the justification of balance-of-payments measures maintained by India. Although a panel was established in November 1987, the parties reached a mutually agreed solution and no report was issued by the panel.[283]

5.39 The only adopted panel report to have addressed explicitly the issue of the availability of dispute settlement procedures under Article XXIII, in relation to the justification of measures taken for balance-of-payments purposes under Article XVIII:B, concerned a dispute relating to measures applied by Korea on the importation of beef.[284]

---

[281] GATT/CP.6/50, GATT/IC/7, GATT/IC/SR.3 and SR.7/11.

[282] In the *German Import Restrictions* case, Germany consulted within the Consultations Committee in June 1957, under Article XII:4(b). At their twelfth session, the CONTRACTING PARTIES decided that the Federal Republic of Germany was no longer entitled to maintain import restrictions under Article XII for balance-of-payments purposes. When the report was presented for approval by the CONTRACTING PARTIES, the Federal Republic of Germany presented a statement announcing further phased liberalization measures and presenting "some facts and points of view" it considered of importance for appreciating the measures. A Working Party was established under Article XII to consider this statement and "to collect and present in an orderly fashion for transmission to the German government the initial reactions and comments of contracting parties [...]". The issue was further examined in 1958 and 1959, and a waiver was eventually adopted, without prejudice to the legal arguments raised by Germany that it was entitled to maintain import restrictions under paragraph 1 (a) (ii) of the Torquay protocol (as existing legislation).

[283] The US request for establishment of a panel was based on Article XXIII:2 of GATT. The United States argued that the import restrictions maintained by India on almonds were "impermissible under Article XI of the General Agreement" and were "not justified under Article XVIII, Section B, as claimed by the Government of India, because India ha[d] not followed the requirements incumbent on a contracting party imposing restrictions under that section." In the discussions of the Council prior to the establishment of the panel, a number of delegations questioned the appropriateness of resort to dispute settlement procedures in relation to balance-of-payments measures taken by developing countries under Article XVIII:B and expressed concern that a precedent might be set by the establishment of a panel in this matter. Other delegations, however, supported the view that there was no reason for dispute settlement procedures under Article XXIII not to be available with regard to balance-of-payments measures as for other measures. Although a panel was established, the parties reached a mutually agreed solution and no report was issued by the panel (See L/6197, C/M/215, p. 5-7, C/154 and C/154/Add.1.).

[284] There were in fact three complaints, leading to almost identical reports. See Panel Report on *Republic of Korea - Restrictions on Imports of Beef, Complaint by the United States,* adopted on 7 November 1989, BISD 36S/268 (hereinafter the "*Korea - Beef* case"). See also Panel Reports adopted on 7 November 1989, *Republic of Korea - Restrictions on Imports of Beef, Complaint by Australia*, BISD36S/202 and *Complaint by New Zealand*, BISD 36S/234.

5.40 In that instance, the BOP Committee had previously reviewed these measures and in its conclusions, noted that

> "The prevailing view expressed in the Committee was that the current situation and outlook for the balance of payments was such that import restrictions could no longer be justified under Article XVIII:B" [...] "[T]he Committee therefore stressed the need to establish a clear timetable for the early, progressive removal of Korea's trade measures maintained for balance-of-payments purposes"[285]

5.41 In the panel proceedings, Korea argued that its import restrictions could not be challenged under Article XXIII and the panel therefore examined the issue of availability of dispute settlement procedures under Article XXIII in relation to import restrictions applied on balance-of-payments grounds:

> "The Panel examined Korea's contention that its import restrictions, referred to under paragraph 111(b) above, were justified under the provisions of Article XVIII:B. The Panel noted Korea's view that the compatibility with the General Agreement of Korea's import restrictions could not be challenged under Article XXIII because of the existence of special review procedures in paragraphs 12(b) and 12(d) of Article XVIII:B, and the adoption by the CONTRACTING PARTIES of the results of the paragraph 12(b) reviews in the Balance-of-Payments Committee. The Panel decided first to consider whether the consistency of restrictive measures with Article XVIII:B could be examined within the framework of Article XXIII.
>
> The Panel considered the various arguments of the parties to the dispute concerning past deliberations by the CONTRACTING PARTIES on the exclusivity of special review procedures under the General Agreement. However, the Panel was not persuaded that any of these earlier deliberations in the GATT were directly applicable to the present dispute. Moreover, the Panel had a clear mandate to examine Korea's beef import restrictions under Article XXIII. The Panel's terms of reference, as agreed by Korea and the United States, and approved by the Council, required the Panel, however, to examine the beef import restrictions "in the light of the relevant GATT provisions", which included Article XVIII:B.
>
> The Panel examined the drafting history of Article XXIII and Article XVIII, and noted that nothing was said about priority or exclusivity of procedures of either Article. The Panel observed that Article XVIII:12(b) provided for regular review of balance-of-payments restrictions by the

[285] BOP/R/171, 10 December 1987, p. 7.

> CONTRACTING PARTIES. Article XVIII:12(d) specifically provided for consultations of balance-of-payments restrictions at the request of a contracting party where that party established a *prima facie* case that the restrictions were inconsistent with the provisions of Article XVIII:B or those of Article XIII, but the Article XVIII:12(d) provision had hitherto not been resorted to. In comparison, the wording of Article XXIII was all-embracing; it provided for dispute settlement procedures applicable to all relevant articles of the General Agreement, including Article XVIII:B in this case. Recourse to Article XXIII procedures could be had by all contracting parties. [...]"

5.42 The panel highlighted the differences between the dispute settlement procedures under Article XXIII and the procedures under Article XVIII:B:

> "[T]he Panel noted that in GATT practice there were differences with respect to the procedures of Article XXIII and Article XVIII:B. The former provided for the detailed examination of individual measures by a panel of independent experts whereas the latter provided for a general review of the country's balance-of-payments situation by a committee of government representatives." (footnote omitted)

5.43 It concluded that it was competent to review balance-of-payments measures in the following terms:

> "[...]excluding the possibility of bringing a complaint under Article XXIII against measures for which there was claimed balance-of-payments cover would unnecessarily restrict the application of the General Agreement. This did not preclude, however, resort to special review procedures under Article XVIII:B. Indeed, either procedure, that of Article XVIII:12(d) or Article XXIII, could have been pursued by the parties in this dispute. But as far as this Panel was concerned, the parties had chosen to proceed under Article XXIII."[286]

5.44 The panel then considered Korea's balance-of-payments justification under Article XVIII:B and examined the balance-of-payments situation of Korea. The panel "considered that it should take into account the conclusions reached by the Committee on balance-of-payments in 1987". The panel also looked at other information available up to February 1989, noted that there was a continued improvement in Korea's balance-of-payments situation and then reached a conclusion similar to that of the CONTRACTING PARTIES when they adopted the Committee report in 1987. The CONTRACTING PARTIES adopted the panel report in November 1989.[287]

[286] Op. Cit., para. 119.
[287] BISD 36S/268.

5.45 India argues that in the *Korea - Beef* case, the panel did not make its own finding on the balance-of-payments situation, since conclusions had been reached in the Committee, which the panel took into account. However, we find no evidence in the report that the panel would have refused to review the claims of the complainants as to the justification of the balance-of-payments measures if the Committee had not issued any report. Indeed, as noted in paragraph 5.41 above, the panel states in its report that it has a clear mandate to examine Korea's beef import restrictions under Article XXIII and that the wording of its mandate was all embracing; it provided for the panel to review the matter in the light of the relevant GATT provisions, which included Article XVIII:B. In particular, the panel discussed expressly the availability of dispute settlement procedures with regard to balance-of-payments measures and concluded that it was competent without reference to the existence of specific Committee conclusions in the case submitted to it. Furthermore, in its assessment of the balance-of-payments situation of Korea, it had not simply taken note of the existence of a violation on the basis of the Committee's conclusions alone. Rather, the panel determined the absence of a balance-of-payments justification, in light of the conclusions of the Committee, and also of updated information relating to the period elapsed since the adoption of the Committee's conclusions. The report thus tends rather to show that even in a situation where conclusions had emerged from the Committee's consultations, the panel, while taking account of such conclusions, felt itself competent to carry out its own updated assessment of the balance-of-payments situation of Korea.

5.46 Thus the *Korea - Beef* case is an example of recourse to the GATT dispute resolution mechanism under Article XXIII with respect to Article XVIII:B. Although it is the only case where the justification of balance-of-payments measures was clearly challenged and fully examined by a panel, its relevance is increased by the fact that it contains a reasoned discussion of the issue and that there was a consensus to adopt it.[288] This would tend to support the view that, as recently as 1989, the time of its adoption, a GATT contracting party could have recourse to Article XXIII with respect to measures for which Article XVIII:B justification was claimed.

(c) Summary

5.47 Numerous consultations were held in the framework of Article XVIII:12(b). However, as indicated in paragraphs 5.34 and 5.35, the specific provisions of Article XVIII:12(c)(ii) and XVIII:12(d) have not been explicitly

288 In that respect, we recall that the Appellate Body, in its report on *Japan - Taxes on Alcoholic Beverages*, adopted on 1 November 1996, WT/DS8/AB/R, WT/DS10/AB/R, WT/DS11/AB/R, DSR 1996:I, 97 at 108, stated that "Adopted panel reports are an important part of the GATT *acquis*. [...] They create legitimate expectations among WTO Members, and, therefore, should be taken into account where they are relevant to any dispute."

referred to by the GATT CONTRACTING PARTIES for the purpose of prescribing the removal of measures unjustified under Article XVIII:B. However, GATT contracting parties, at times, did resort to the general dispute settlement procedures of Article XXIII of GATT in order to obtain a ruling with respect to balance-of-payments measures, including regarding their justification. There are thus instances suggesting acceptance that prior to the entry into force of the WTO Agreement, recourse could be had either to the special procedures of Articles XII or XVIII *or* to Article XXIII in respect of balance-of-payments measures.[289]

3. Applicable Provisions under the WTO Agreement

(a) Article XVIII:B

5.48 As already indicated, the text of Article XVIII:B is unchanged.[290] It should now be read in light of the 1994 Understanding, which clarifies the provisions of Articles XII and XVIII:B and of the 1979 Decision. The 1994 Understanding, which refers to the procedures for balance-of-payments consultations adopted in 1970 ("full consultation procedures") and 1972 ("simplified consultation procedures") as well as the 1979 Decision, contains provisions on the application of balance-of-payments measures, as well as provisions relating to the procedures for balance-of-payments consultations and their conclusion, but it does not explicitly refer to Articles XVIII:12(c) and (d). Footnote 1 to the 1994 Understanding, however, as was previously noted, indicates that "[n]othing in this Understanding is intended to modify the rights and obligations of Members under Articles XII or XVIII:B of GATT 1994". The same footnote further states that "[t]he provisions of Article XXII and XXIII of GATT 1994 as elaborated and applied by the Dispute Settlement Understanding may be invoked with respect to any matters arising from the application of restrictive import measures taken for balance-of-payments purposes". The exact meaning of this reference, which is a subject of debate between the parties, is discussed *infra*.[291]

5.49 Since the entry into force of the WTO Agreement, WTO Members have not to date made express use of or reference to the procedures under Articles

[289] Indeed, a leading treatise on GATT commented in 1969: "All four of these "release remedy" procedures in Article XII and XVIII parallel in many respects the provisions of Article XXIII. But the BOP procedures are both more restrictive than those of Article XXIII, so in all probability a damaged party is likely to use Article XXIII rather than the BOP procedures. This author can find no record of any procedure actually brought under the subparagraph (d) complaint procedures and no record of a release approval under either the (c) or (d) subparagraphs of Article XII, paragraph 4, or Article XVIII, paragraph 12, but some Article XXIII complaints might have been eligible for the BOP procedure". (John H. Jackson, *World Trade and the Law of GATT* (1969), p. 706).

[290] The Ministerial Conference has not formally assigned the functions of the CONTRACTING PARTIES in Article XVIII to any body. However, under the 1979 Declaration and the 1994 Understanding and decisions referred to therein, the oversight of Articles XII and XVIII:B is assigned to the BOP Committee, which reports to the General Council. The General Council acts on recommendations of the BOP Committee.

[291] See *infra* the discussion starting para. 5.55.

XII(c) and (d) and XVIII:12(c) and (d). It should nevertheless be mentioned that the BOP Committee has in one instance found that the measures under review, maintained by Nigeria, "could no longer be justified under Article XVIII:B and the Understanding on Balance-of-Payments Provisions of GATT 1994" and "recalled Nigeria's commitments to make all restrictive trade measures price-based and to eliminate them by disinvoking Article XVIII:B".[292] The Committee did, not, however, expressly refer to a particular provision of Article XVIII:12 in making this determination.

(b) Article XXIII and the DSU

5.50 Article XXIII is now elaborated by the DSU. Pursuant to its Article 1, the Dispute Settlement Understanding applies to all the multilateral agreements, subject to special or additional provisions contained therein. We must therefore first consider whether any such provisions exist which would apply to this dispute and be relevant to the determination of the scope of competence of panels in relation to balance-of-payments measures. We note in this instance that there is no specific provision in the DSU or in Article XVIII that would establish such special or additional rules and procedures applicable to this dispute.

5.51 While parties disagree as to the degree of inter-relation between the DSU and Article XVIII of GATT 1994, neither party claims that the Panel is subject to specific procedures under Article XVIII other than the normal DSU procedures.

5.52 The only provision of Article XVIII:B, the DSU or the WTO Agreement which expressly addresses the relationship between dispute settlement under the DSU and measures taken for balance-of-payments purposes is the second sentence of footnote 1 to the 1994 Understanding, which provides that:

> "The provisions of Article XXII and XXIII of GATT 1994 as elaborated and applied by the Dispute Settlement Understanding may be invoked with respect to any matters arising from the application of restrictive import measures taken for balance-of-payments purposes."

5.53 Hereafter, we discuss the meaning of the second sentence of footnote 1 to the 1994 Understanding, since it bears directly on the relation between Article XVIII:12 and Article XXIII of GATT 1994. As noted in paragraphs 5.24 and 5.25 above, the discussion will be based on the criteria set forth in Articles 31 and 32 of the Vienna Convention. It will also be guided by decisions, procedures and customary practices under GATT 1947.

---

[292] WT/BOP/R/18, 16 October 1996, para. 10. See also the reports of the Committee on the resumed consultations in 1997 and 1998, in WT/BOP/R/25 (27 March 1997) and WT/BOP/R/41 (7 April 1998).

4. *Competence of Panels to Review the Justification of Measures Taken under Article XVIII:B*

5.54 Pursuant to Article 31 of the Vienna Convention, we must interpret the relevant provisions by relying on the ordinary meaning of the terms taken in their context and in the light of the object and purpose of the WTO Agreement. While all these elements are part of one single assessment, for the sake of clarity, we examine the different elements of Article 31 successively, examining first the terms of Footnote 1 of the 1994 Understanding (a), before considering them in their context (b) and in relation to the object and purpose of the WTO Agreement (c)[293]

(a) Terms of the second sentence of footnote 1 to the 1994 Understanding

5.55 The parties disagree on the interpretation of the terms of the second sentence of footnote 1 to the 1994 Understanding, and in particular on the interpretation of the indication that dispute settlement procedures are available regarding "any matters arising from the *application* of measures (...)"(emphasis added). We recall the arguments of the parties relating to the terms of the second sentence of the footnote before analyzing these terms.

(i) Arguments of the parties

5.56 In the view of India, the reference in footnote 1 to the 1994 Understanding to "matters arising from the application of restrictive import measures" requires that a distinction be made between "application" of measures and their "justification" under the balance-of-payments provisions of GATT 1994. According to India, the scope of the footnote is limited to import restrictions that have a valid balance-of-payments justification and it does not modify a Member's right to a determination of the justification of its import restrictions by the BOP Committee in accordance with the provisions of Article XVIII:12. India argues that the consistency of balance-of-payments measures with Articles I, II, X, and XIII of the GATT and the provisions of other WTO agreements, such as the Agreement on Import Licensing Procedures, could be examined by a panel but the question of their balance-of-payments justification should be determined in accordance with the procedures set out in Articles XV:2 and XVIII:B of GATT 1994, the 1979 Declaration on Trade Measures Taken for Balance-of-Payments Purposes and the 1994 Understanding. India is of the opinion that the footnote indirectly confirms that disputes arising from the other matters regulated in the 1994 Understanding, in particular the matters regulated in paragraph 13, are not meant to be resolved

[293] Arguments have been raised relating to the negotiating history. These are addressed as relevant in the course of our discussion in this section, in accordance with Article 32 of the Vienna Convention (see *infra* paras. 5.106-5.111).

by panels. In contrast, the reference to "restrictions... being applied in a manner involving an inconsistency" in Article XVIII:12(c)(ii) must be interpreted to refer both to import restrictions lacking balance-of-payments justification and import restrictions administered in a GATT-inconsistent manner.

5.57 The United States replies that the text of footnote 1 to the 1994 Understanding confirms rather than denies the availability of dispute settlement. In the view of the United States, had the drafters of the GATT 1994 intended to impose restrictions on dispute settlement, they would have used words of prohibition or limitation. For the United States, even if India's interpretation of footnote 1 were to be accepted, this dispute would be properly before the Panel since it has "arisen" precisely because of India's "application" of quantitative restrictions that it originally instituted for balance-of-payments purposes: India is applying the challenged measures in excess of what is necessary to address its balance-of-payments situation. For the United States, lawful application of measures taken for balance-of-payments purposes includes the obligation not to apply measures in excess of what is necessary to address the balance-of-payments situation and the removal of unjustifiable measures is a part of the "application" of such measures. For the United States, footnote 1 served a function by confirming the availability of dispute settlement under Article XXIII in balance-of-payments cases, shortly after the panel reports on *European Communities - Tariff Treatment on Imports of Citrus Products from Certain Countries in the Mediterranean Region* (hereafter *EC - Citrus*),[294] *EEC - Member States' Import Regimes for Bananas* (hereafter *EC- Bananas I*)[295], and *Korea - Beef.*[296] Negotiators were aware of the possibility that panels would examine quantitative restrictions for which balance-of-payments cover had been claimed and intentionally did not exclude them from the scope of panel review in the WTO system. Finally, India's argument would unnecessarily restrict the application of the WTO Agreement. If India's approach were accepted, a mere claim of balance-of-payments cover could be used to frustrate justified access to dispute settlement.[297]

(ii) Ordinary meaning of the terms "application of measures" in footnote 1 to the 1994 Understanding

5.58 We must first consider the ordinary meaning of the terms "application of measures". A dictionary definition of "application" includes "use, employment, a specific use or purpose for which something is put, the bringing of a general or

---

[294] L/5776, 7 February 1985, not adopted. This case, which does not relate to Article XVIII:B of GATT, is discussed in paras. 5.104-5.105 *infra* in section (d) on "Related GATT practice".

[295] DS32/R, 3 June 1993, not adopted. This case, which does not relate to Article XVIII:B of GATT, is discussed in paras. 5.104-5.105 below in section (d) on "Related GATT practice".

[296] See paras. 5.39-5.46 *supra*.

[297] For a detailed description of the arguments of the parties, see Section III.D.1.(b) *supra*.

figurative statement, a theory, principle, etc., to bear upon a matter; applicability in a particular case."[298] The "application" of a measure would thus refer to the fact that a measure is in use. The terms "application of restrictive measures taken for balance-of-payments purposes", in their ordinary meaning, therefore seem to refer simply to the fact that a measure is applied for balance-of-payments purposes. The use of these words, in themselves and taken in their ordinary meaning, therefore does not suggest an opposition between the "application" of the measures and their "justification" under Article XVIII:B. To so interpret them would require additional terms to express a restriction or an opposition between two concepts that does not appear in the sentence at issue.

5.59 Furthermore, taking a word in isolation would be applying Article 31 of the Vienna Convention incorrectly.[299] We therefore look at the other terms of the sentence. The expression "*any matters* arising from the application of restrictive import measures taken for balance-of-payments purposes" (emphasis added), taken in its ordinary meaning, does not contain an explicit limitation to issues relating to the manner in which measures are administered, to the exclusion of their justification, as suggested by India. The sentence is in the form of an affirmative statement, and the expression "any matters arising from" is very broad and all-encompassing. It does not distinguish between one or another possible legal basis for action. The sentence therefore seems to be an affirmation of the availability of dispute settlement rather than an expression of restriction. The use of the term "*any* matters" suggests that the matters that may be considered by a panel include, as in the present case, a question of justification of the measure under Article XVIII:9, i.e. whether the Member actually faces balance-of-payments difficulties within the meaning of Article XVIII:9 and whether it is entitled to maintain balance-of-payments measures. Indeed, if the meaning of the footnote had been intended to be restrictive (i.e. to mean that dispute settlement procedures may *only* be invoked with respect to matters arising from the "application" of measures, as opposed to their justification), the use of the words "*any* matters" would not have been necessary to convey this meaning. In fact it would have confused the meaning of the sentence.

---

[298] See *New Oxford Shorter English Dictionary* (1993), p. 100.

[299] See PCIJ *Advisory Opinion on the Competence of the ILO to Regulate Agricultural Labour*, PCIJ (1922) Series B, No. 2, p. 23:

> "In considering the question before the Court upon the language of the Treaty, it is obvious that the Treaty must be read as a whole, and that its meaning is not to be determine merely upon particular phrases which, if detached from the context, may be interpreted in more than one sense."

See also M. Yassen, *L'Interprétation des Traités d'après la Convention de Vienne sur le Droit des Traités, in* Recueil des Cours de l'Académie de La Haye (1974), p. 9, at p. 26:

> "Il ne s'agit donc pas d'un sens ordinaire abstrait, mais d'un sens ordinaire concret qui ne peut être discerné que par l'examen du terme en question dans le contexte de ce terme et à la lumière du but et de l'objet du traité."

5.60 We also note that reviewing the application of measures is the purpose of dispute settlement. WTO dispute resolution is typically initiated with respect to measures[300] and a measure can only be reviewed by a panel if it is applied (a measure that is not applied can only be reviewed if it is mandatory legislation, i.e., it is certain that it will be applied).[301] Moreover, in a practical sense, the consideration of the application of a measure must necessarily embrace its justification. The notion of application includes both the mode of application and the level of application. Even if one were to confine the review of a measure to its "application" within the meaning that India claims it has, then the review still could find that the level of application consistent with the rule under which it is claimed to be justified is zero. In effect, "justification" within the meaning given to it by India inevitably would have been reviewed. As a result, the wording used by the drafters of the footnote is consistent with dispute settlement principles: by saying that the DSU can be invoked with respect to matters arising from the application of restrictive import measures, the footnote does not in our view qualify the role of dispute settlement in the context of balance-of-payments problems. Rather, as the United States pointed out, it seems to re-affirm the application of the DSU.

5.61 The terms of the second sentence of footnote 1 to the Understanding, in their ordinary meaning, therefore appear to affirm, rather than restrict, the availability of dispute settlement provisions with regard to measures taken for balance-of-payments purposes.

(b) Context

5.62 Our examination of the ordinary meaning of the terms of the second sentence of footnote 1 to the 1994 Understanding so far has not led us to conclude that the indication that dispute settlement procedures are available regarding "any matters arising from the application of restrictive import measures taken for balance-of-payments purposes" would imply that panels are precluded from reviewing the justification of measures taken for balance-of-payments purposes under Article XVIII:B. We must now consider whether, taken in their context, these terms should be understood to imply a distinction between a strict notion of "application" of a measure, as advocated by India, and the "justification" of the measure under the terms of Article XVIII:B.

5.63 We examine successively different elements of the relevant context of the second sentence of footnote 1 to the 1994 Understanding. Firstly, we consider whether the use of the terms "application of measures" or "measures being applied" in the rest of the Understanding and in Article XVIII:B suggests the pro-

---

[300] Panel Report on *Japan - Trade in Semiconductors*, L/6309, adopted on 4 May 1988, paras. 106-107.

[301] Panel Report on *United States - Taxes on Petroleum and Certain Imported Substances ("Superfund")*, adopted on 17 June 1987, BISD 34S/136, paras. 5.2.1-5.2.2.

posed distinction. We then turn to a broader examination of the functions of the consultation procedures for balance-of-payments measures under Article XVIII:B in order to determine whether, as argued by India, exclusive authority has been assigned to the BOP Committee and General Council to make certain determinations, thereby preventing panels established in accordance with Articles XXII and XXIII of GATT 1994 and the DSU from making such determinations. Finally, we consider whether our interpretation of the terms of the provision is consistent with the terms of the first sentence of footnote 1 of the 1994 Understanding, which provides that "[n]othing in this Understanding is intended to modify the rights and obligations of Members under Articles XII or XVIII:B of GATT 1994".

(i) Meaning of the terms "application of measures" or measures "applied" in other provisions of the 1994 Understanding, in Article XVIII:B and in other GATT provisions

5.64 The terms "measures being applied" or "application of measures" appear in other provisions of the 1994 Understanding and of Article XVIII:B. It is therefore relevant to consider whether these uses of the notion of "application" are helpful in interpreting the term as used in the footnote.

5.65 The terms "application of measures", "applied" or "applies" are used in various instances in the Understanding. Paragraphs 1 to 4 of the Understanding are grouped under the heading "Application of Measures". The use of these terms in these paragraphs seems to refer to the fact that a measure is in use. There is no suggestion that the terms are used in a way that assumes the measures referred to are justified, or that their justification cannot be reviewed under the dispute settlement mechanism. Indeed, the first sentence of paragraph 4 implies that the "Application of Measures" encompasses the requirement that measures may not exceed what is necessary to address the balance-of-payments situation.[302] As argued by the United States, if a measure exceeds what is necessary to address the balance-of-payments difficulties within the meaning of Article XVIII:9, then, to the extent that it is excessive, it is not necessary. If there is no justification for balance-of-payments restrictions, no measure applied for that reason can be considered as necessary any longer. Indeed, to the extent that paragraph 4 of the Understanding refers to the way a measure is being implemented, it uses the terms "administration" or "administer", not "application".[303]

5.66 Paragraph 6 of the Understanding also refers to "[a] Member *applying* new restrictions or raising the general level of its existing restrictions [...]" to

[302] This "necessity" test is also found in Article XVIII:9 of GATT 1994.
[303] Paragraph 4 of the 1994 Understanding.

describe situations where consultations may be requested under Article XII:4 (a) or Article XVIII:12 (a). Paragraph 7 further states that "All restrictions *applied* for balance-of-payments purposes shall be subject to periodic review under paragraph 4 (b) of Article XII or under paragraph 12 (b) of Article XVIIII [...]". In both instances, the text refers to situations where review under the consultation procedures of Article XVIII:12 could or would take place and it cannot be assumed that this would refer only to measures having a valid balance-of-payments justification, but rather suggests a situation where measures are being applied and a balance-of-payments justification is claimed for them.

5.67 Thus, it is clear that the word "application" (or "applied" or "applies") is not used in the 1994 Understanding in a way that suggests that a consideration of justification, i.e., whether a balance-of-payments measure is necessary, would be excluded from dispute settlement.

5.68 Since the Understanding aims at clarifying the provisions of, *inter alia*, Article XVIII:B, the terms of the 1994 Understanding should also be read in light of the provisions of Article XVIII:B. In this respect, it is worth noting that Article XVIII:B does not require measures to be authorized before they can be applied. The very mechanism of surveillance and review of import restrictions under Article XVIII:12 rests on the notification of measures which are in application and for which a balance-of-payments justification is claimed. This does not mean that they could not be found to be inconsistent with the provisions of Article XVIII:B in the course of consultations. In this context, the provisions of Article XVIII:B frequently refer to measures being "applied" under Article XVIII:B, but this reference cannot be assumed only to encompass measures which have a valid balance-of-payments justification.

5.69 Likewise, under Article XVIII:12(c) and (d), the Committee and General Council are called upon to determine whether "restrictions are being applied" in a manner involving an inconsistency with Article XVIII:B or Article XIII. Article XVIII:12 (d) refers to the establishment of a *prima facie* case "that the restrictions are inconsistent with the provisions of [Article XVIII:B] or with those of Article XIII" and to a determination that the restrictions are "being applied inconsistently with such provisions". Accordingly, these references to measures being "applied" cannot be assumed to refer exclusively to measures consistent with Article XVIII:B. The fact that consistency with both Article XVIII:B and Article XIII may be reviewed under Articles XVIII:12 (c) and (d) precludes an interpretation of the word "applied" as limiting consideration to the administration of restrictions having a valid balance-of-payments justification.[304]

[304] India itself actually interprets the words "applied in a manner" as used in Article XVIII:12(c)(ii) to cover not only measures which are administered in violation of Article XIII, but also measures which no longer have a justification under Article XVIII:9 (see para. 3.98 in Section III.D.1.(b) *supra*).

5.70 India also draws comparisons between Footnote 1 of the 1994 Understanding and the terms of paragraph 12 of the Understanding on the Interpretation of Article XXIV of the General Agreement on Tariffs and Trade 1994 (hereafter the "Understanding on Article XXIV"), claiming that they are identical in their reference to the application of measures and represent a compromise between the conflicting positions taken by the contracting parties in relation to the application of dispute settlement in those fields. The fact that the same word "application" is found in another provision of GATT 1994 is not in itself sufficient to justify an analogy. In paragraph 12 of the Understanding on Article XXIV, what is referred to is the "application of [...] provisions of Article XXIV", not the "application of measures" as in the 1994 BOP Understanding. The phrase "the application of those provisions of Article XXIV" plainly means "the implementation of the provisions of Article XXIV..." and does not allow for a distinction such as the one proposed by India. India's argument that the terms of paragraph 12 of the Understanding on Article XXIV would represent a compromise limiting the scope of review of panels with respect to Article XXIV agreements is based on the assumption that such a compromise had to be reached because of the debate generated by some panel reports. India did not supply any evidence on this matter that would suggest that we should depart from the plain meaning of the terms of paragraph 12. In any case, such a comparison alone would not have been sufficient to change our conclusion on the meaning of the terms in the footnote to the 1994 Understanding.

5.71 India further refers to Article XX of GATT 1994 to support the proposed distinction between the application and the justification of a measure. Here, the wording of the two provisions is quite distinct, as the preamble of Article XX expressly requires that measures "are not applied *in a manner* which would constitute a means of arbitrary or unjustifiable discrimination"(emphasis added). In that case, the text is explicit in its reference to the *manner* in which the measure is applied. There is no similar wording in the footnote to the 1994 Understanding.

5.72 These elements of context clearly suggest that the terms of the footnote refer to the fact that a measure is being applied, i.e. is in effect, nothing more.

(ii) Respective roles of DSU procedures and Article XVIII:B procedures

5.73 Part of the context of the second sentence of footnote 1 to the 1994 Understanding is Article XVIII:B and the rest of the 1994 Understanding. India argues that this context compels the conclusion that dispute settlement panels are not competent to decide on the justification of balance-of-payments measures. In India's view, a WTO Member has the right to institute balance-of-payments measures without prior approval of any WTO body and it has the right to maintain those measures until the BOP Committee or General Council advises it to modify them under Article XVIII:12 or establishes a time-period for their removal under paragraph 13 of the 1994 Understanding. According to India, its position reflects the carefully negotiated balance struck by WTO Members on this issue, and, in particular, a decision that the justification of balance-of-payments should be determined by WTO Members by consensus in a political setting, not by dispute settlement panels. If the justification of balance-of-payments measures could be decided by dispute settlement panels, India alleges that significant parts of Article XVIII:B and the 1994 Understanding would be rendered redundant and serious conflicts could arise.

5.74 The United States responds that the consultation procedures established in Article XVIII:B are independent of dispute settlement procedures under Article XXIII and the DSU. For the United States, there are two independent tracks for enforcing Article XVIII:B and either may be followed in order to determine the justification of balance-of-payments measures.[305]

5.75 In this section, we examine the position of India on this aspect of the context of the second sentence of footnote 1 and the US response. We start with India's argument that it has a right to maintain balance-of-payments measures until the BOP Committee or the General Council decides otherwise. We then consider whether the procedures of Article XVIII:12(c)-(d) are an exclusive mechanism for assessing compliance with Article XVIII:B. Third, we analyze whether dispute settlement panels are capable of making the necessary determinations on issues related to the justification of balance-of-payments measures. Finally, we assess whether recognizing a role for dispute settlement in determining the justification of balance-of-payments measures would render Article XVIII:B and the 1994 Understanding redundant or result in serious conflicts.

The right to maintain balance-of-payments measures

5.76 India's basic argument is that it has a right to institute balance-of-payments measures without the prior approval of any WTO body and a right to maintain those measures until the BOP Committee or the General Council advises it to modify them under Article XVIII:12 or establishes a time-period for their removal under paragraph 13 of the 1994 Understanding. In the absence of such action by the Committee or General Council, India asserts that the issue of whether its measures are justified under Article XVIII:B cannot be raised in dispute settlement.

5.77 Under Article XVIII:B, it is clear that a Member has the right to institute balance-of-payments measures without the prior approval of any WTO body. India correctly notes that proposals in the past to require such approval were not adopted. As explained above, when a Member institutes or intensifies balance-of-payments measures, it is required to consult with the BOP Committee. Pursuant to Article XVIII:12(c)-(d), the Committee and the General Council[306] have cer-

[305] For a detailed description of the arguments of the parties, see Section III.D.1.(a) *supra*.

[306] As noted earlier, in the absence of a Ministerial Conference allocation, these powers still formally reside in the CONTRACTING PARTIES, but on the basis of the 1979 Declaration (in particular para. 13) and the 1994 Understanding, it is appropriate to refer to the BOP Committee and General Council as the decision-makers. We refer to both bodies, although the BOP Committee only

tain powers to advise or recommend that such measures be modified because of an inconsistency with Article XVIII:B or Article XIII. Paragraph 13 of the 1994 Understanding authorizes the General Council to approve a phase-out period for balance-of-payments measures.

5.78 We note at the outset that there is no explicit statement in Article XVIII:B or the 1994 Understanding that authorizes a Member to maintain its balance-of-payments measures in effect until the General Council or BOP Committee acts under one of the aforementioned provisions. Article XVIII:B, however, addresses the issue of the extent to which balance-of-payments measures may be maintained. Article XVIII:11, which is analyzed in more detail in Part G below, specifies that a Member:

> "shall progressively relax any restrictions applied under this Section [i.e., Article XVIII:B] as conditions improve, maintaining them only to the extent necessary under the terms of paragraph 9 of this Article [XVIII] and shall eliminate them when conditions no longer justify their maintenance."

5.79 The obligation of Article XVIII:11 is not conditioned on any BOP Committee or General Council decision. If we were to interpret Article XVIII:11 to be so conditioned, we would be adding terms to Article XVIII:11 that it does not contain.

5.80 Moreover, the obligation in Article XVIII:11 requires action by the individual Member. It is qualified only by a proviso and Ad Note (which we discuss in Part G and which are not relevant here) and it is not made subject to the accomplishment of other procedures. In light of the unqualified nature of the Article XVIII:11 obligation, it would be inconsistent with the principle *pacta sunt servanda* to conclude that a WTO Member has a right to maintain balance-of-payments measures, even if unjustified under Article XVIII:B, in the absence of a Committee or General Council decision in respect thereof. Thus, we find that India does not have a right to maintain its balance-of-payments measures until the General Council advises it to modify them under Article XVIII:12 or establishes a time-period for their removal under paragraph 13 of the 1994 Understanding.

Are Article XVIII:12 procedures exclusive?

5.81 India also argues that the procedures of Article XVIII:12(c)-(d) are the exclusive route for determining whether balance-of-payments measures taken under Article XVIII:B are justified. This issue is related to the issue of whether India has a right to maintain its balance-of-payments measures in the absence of a Committee or General Council decision. However, the conclusion that India does not have such a substantive right does not necessarily dispose of the procedural

makes recommendations to the General Council, which is the actual decision-making body in these matters.

question of how other Members may challenge India's balance-of-payments measures as unjustified.

5.82 In considering whether the Article XVIII:12 procedures are exclusive, we start with the fact that the text of Article XVIII:12 in itself does not indicate that the BOP Committee procedures thereunder would be exclusive of procedures under Article XXIII or the DSU. Indeed, in the first part of our examination of the context of the second sentence of footnote 1 to the 1994 Understanding, we noted that the authorization in Article XVIII:12 to consider whether balance-of-payments measures were being "applied" in a manner involving an inconsistency with Articles XVIII:B or XIII tended, amongst other contextual elements, to confirm that footnote 1 should be interpreted as permitting dispute settlement panels to consider the justification of balance-of-payments measures (see paragraph 5.69 *supra*). Thus, the text of Article XVIII:12 as a whole does not suggest that Article XVIII:12 procedures are the exclusive means of determining whether balance-of-payments measures are justified under Article XVIII:B.

5.83 Further textual support for the non-exclusivity of Article XVIII:12 procedures is found in the fact that those procedures are specifically authorized to consider violations of Article XIII. In this regard, we note that India concedes that violations of Article XIII may be considered in regular dispute settlement proceedings under the DSU. We understand India's distinction that while certain aspects of the administration (for India, "application") of balance-of-payments measures may be considered under either Article XVIII:B procedures or DSU procedures (such as those involving Article XIII), the issue of the justification of balance-of-payments measures is reserved to Article XVIII:B procedures. We find it significant, however, that India's distinction (i) necessarily concedes that issues subject to Article XVIII:12 procedures are not always exclusively subject thereto, and (ii) has no textual basis in Article XVIII:B.

5.84 The conclusion that Article XVIII:12 procedures do not exclude the application of the general dispute settlement system is also confirmed by the fact that Article XVIII:12(d) is not mentioned as a special or additional procedure within the meaning of Article 1.2 of the DSU.[307] If it had been intended that the DSU should apply subject to Article XVIII:12(d), it could have been expected that this would be specified in the DSU. Moreover, Article 8.5 of the Agreement on Subsidies and Countervailing Measures, which is one of the provisions to which India refers in support of its argument that exclusive procedures exist in the WTO Agreement, is mentioned in Appendix 2 to the DSU. The Panel therefore concludes that the nature of the procedures applied under Article XVIII:B is not a decisive factor in determining whether Article XVIII:B procedures are exclusive.

[307] Since the present complaint is based on Article XXIII and not on Article XVIII:12(d), it is not for this Panel to discuss whether the DSU would apply to a procedure based on Article XVIII:12(d).

5.85 We find accordingly that the Article XVIII:12 procedures are not the exclusive means for determining whether balance-of-payments measures are justified under Article XVIII:B.[308] We reach this conclusion on a provisional basis, however, as India presents several other arguments justifying its position that dispute settlement panels cannot consider the justification of balance-of-payments measures taken pursuant to Article XVIII:B.

The nature of decisions on the justification of balance-of-payments issues

5.86 India argues that the very nature of a decision as to whether balance-of-payments measures are justified or not makes it unsuitable for consideration by a dispute settlement panel. India argues that WTO Members have agreed on a number of provisions that assign the task of determining the legal status of politically delicate issues not to panels but to specialized bodies acting under particular procedures. These include decisions on whether balance-of-payments measures are consistent with Article XVIII:B and whether a phase-out period is appropriate, decisions which are not technical, legal matters in India's view.

5.87 In our view, panels are frequently required to examine issues which may call on consideration of specialized, or more generally "non-legal" matters. With regard to specialized matters, panels have the possibility of consulting with experts and seeking information and technical advice from any individuals and bodies they deem appropriate, under the terms of Article 13 of the DSU. With respect to balance-of-payments issues in particular, the IMF plays an important role and indeed, the panel has consulted with the IMF on the issues pertaining to its areas of expertise (see paragraphs 5.11-5.13 *supra* regarding the consultations with the IMF). In addition, it is quite possible that some disputes submitted to panels may concern politically sensitive matters. The role of panels is defined in Article 3.2 of the DSU which provides that the dispute settlement system "serves to preserve the rights and obligations of Members under the covered agreements, and to clarify the existing provisions of those agreements in accordance with customary rules of interpretation of public international law." Panels are in all instances required to make an objective assessment of the facts of the case and apply the relevant WTO provisions to those facts.[309] We are therefore not con-

[308] To support its argument that panels cannot determine the justification of balance-of-payments measures taken under Article XVIII:B, India also relies on paragraph 13 of the 1994 Understanding, which authorizes the General Council to approve a phase-out period for removal of balance-of-payments measures. In our view, the fact that the General Council has been granted such authority does not affect our conclusion. See *infra* the discussion in paras. 5.229-5.235.

[309] Article 7.1 of the DSU defines standard terms of reference: "To examine, in the light of the relevant provisions in (name of the covered agreement (s) cited by the parties to the dispute, the matter referred to the DSB by (name of the party) in document ... and to make such findings as will assist the DSB in making the recommendations or in giving the rulings provided for in that/those agreement(s)." Finally, Article 11 specifies that "the function of panels is to assist the DSB in discharging its responsibilities under [the DSU] and the covered agreements. Accordingly, a panel should make an objective assessment of the matter before it, including an objective assessment of the facts of the case and the applicability of and conformity with the relevant covered agreements, and

vinced that the specialized or "non-legal" nature of the issues involved in examining the justification of balance-of-payments measures should prevent panels from examining such issues in the light of Article XVIII:B.[310]

Potential redundancies

5.88 According to India, if the Panel were to interpret the right to resort to the DSU confirmed in the footnote to the 1994 Understanding as implying a complete transfer of the competence to determine the justification of balance-of-payments restrictions, including phased removal of such restrictions, from the Committee and the General Council to panels and the Appellate Body, it would

make such other findings as will assist the DSB in making the recommendations or in giving the rulings provided for in the covered agreements".

[310] India further argues that numerous provisions in the WTO Agreement assign the task of determining the legal status of a measure to WTO bodies other than panels. (For a detailed description of the arguments of the parties, see *supra* in Section III.D.1 (a)). However, the examples given by India to illustrate its arguments do not persuade us that our conclusion on this issue is incorrect. These arguments are not directly relevant to Article XVIII:B.

Firstly, in the case of non-actionable subsidies, a specific provision exists to exclude the application of the dispute settlement procedures to notified subsidies and, provided the subsidy being reviewed is found to conform with Article 8.2 of the Agreement on Subsidies and Countervailing Measures (hereafter the "SCM Agreement"), to non-notified subsidies. No similar provision exists in the case of Article XVIII. If anything, the second sentence of footnote 1 to the 1994 Understanding *affirms* the application of the DSU. It is only by interpreting extensively one word of this sentence that India reaches the conclusion that panels are not supposed to review the "justification" of balance-of-payments measures under Article XVIII:B. However, since we found this interpretation unsupported by the ordinary meaning of the terms of footnote 1 in their context and in the light of the object and purpose of the WTO Agreement, we cannot make any analogy with the provisions of Article 8 of the SCM Agreement. In addition, we are not convinced that India's arguments reflect an accurate description of the situation resulting from the cited provisions. Regarding the procedure of Article 8.3 of the SCM Agreement, footnote 35 to that Agreement states that the provisions of Parts III and V of the Agreement shall not be invoked with respect to measures considered non-actionable. However, a subsidy referred to in Article 8.2 conferred pursuant to a non-notified programme can be subject to panel review, even though such subsidy shall be treated as non-actionable if it is found to conform with Article 8.2.

Secondly, the example of Argentina's request for the establishment of a panel to determine its principal supplying interest under Article XXVIII of GATT 1947 in respect of the renegotiation of the concession covering its soyabean exports to the EC is not conclusive. In that case, the discussions of the Council reveal divergent opinions of contracting parties on the appropriateness of recourse to Article XXIII to resolve this issue. The matter was however considered to have been satisfactorily resolved, without establishment of a panel, as the European Communities recognized Argentina's principal supplying interest in the concessions at issue, "without prejudice to any future decision by the CONTRACTING PARTIES with regard to Note 5 to Article XXVIII:1, nor to the future application of the Memorandum relating to Article XXVIII" (C/M/260).

Finally, Article V of GATS contains no express reference to dispute settlement procedures. It is therefore difficult to compare the situation with respect to Article V GATS with one where a provision exists that expressly addresses the relationship between the DSU and Article XVIII:B.

In any case, the argument that the provisions referred to by India provide for exclusive Committee procedures, even if it were to show that such possibility exists in the WTO Agreement, is of no relevance for Article XVIII:B, since no analogy can be deduced from the terms or the structure of the agreement itself.

reduce the whole of Article XVIII:12 and most of the provisions of the 1994 Understanding and the 1979 Declaration to redundancy or inutility.

5.89 In our view, India's argument overstates the effect of a decision that dispute settlement panels may consider the justification of balance-of-payments measures in individual cases. In most cases, it is reasonable to assume that there will be no resort to dispute settlement procedures on such issues. Past practice supports that assumption.

5.90 Even if some balance-of-payments issues are considered in the dispute settlement system, it is our view that the BOP Committee procedures would play a significant role in these cases. To begin with, the issues will first be discussed in the BOP Committee and the results of the Committee process may influence the results of the dispute settlement process (see *infra* paragraphs 5.92-5.97 on potential conflicts). It should also be noted that dispute settlement procedures and the BOP Committee consultation procedures differ in nature, scope, timing and type of outcome. A review of the 1970 and 1979 Declarations, for example, confirms that the BOP Committee is called upon to address a wider range of issues than panels. Moreover, while resort to dispute settlement procedures under Article XXIII was not common in the GATT system, we have seen that recourse to Article XXIII was recognized, without calling into question the utility of the BOP Committee process, which has always provided the permanent framework for considering balance-of-payments issues.

5.91 Thus, we find that allowing dispute settlement panels to consider whether balance-of-payments measures are justified under Article XVIII:B would not render redundant or reduce to inutility either that article or related WTO provisions dealing with balance-of-payments issues. Article XVIII:B and the 1979 Declaration and 1994 Understanding taken together would continue to provide the basic instrument for review of balance-of-payments issues, with the dispute settlement procedures playing a complementary role, if and when necessary.

Potential conflicts

5.92 India argues that if dispute settlement panels are permitted to make findings on whether balance-of-payments measures are justified under Article XVIII:B, there will be a risk of normative conflicts within the WTO system because such decisions may be inconsistent with decisions on the same issue reached by other WTO bodies. In this regard, India additionally notes that different panels acting on different complaints could reach inconsistent conclusions. Moreover, India sees a significant increase in the risk of such conflicts in the WTO system, as opposed to the GATT 1947 system, because of the "automatic" adoption of dispute settlement reports under the DSU. We examine each of these issues in turn.

5.93 **Potential conflicts between a panel report and the BOP Committee**. It is possible that a panel and the BOP Committee could examine successively[311] the issue of whether the same balance-of-payments measures are justified under Article XVIII:B. If there has been no decision in the BOP Committee or General Council at the time of the panel's consideration of the issue, the issue of conflict does not arise at the panel stage, which is the situation in this case. While the BOP Committee and the General Council have considered the justification of India's balance-of-payments measures at issue in this case, they made no determinations and reached no agreed conclusions. Even if this Panel were to decide that India's measures are not justified, nothing would prevent the Committee and the General Council from reaching different conclusions on the basis of new, different facts, in which case the Council could take a decision on a phase-out period under paragraph 13 of the 1994 Understanding on Balance-of-Payments Provisions. Moreover, what Members accepted in the DSB could be modified in the General Council. The discretionary competence of the General Council to waive India's obligations under Article IX of the WTO Agreement would remain unaffected. Similarly, a decision by the Panel that India's measures were justified as of November 1997 would not preclude re-examination by the BOP Committee or the General Council of India's measures in the future.

5.94 If the measures before a panel have been the subject of determinations or recommendations by the BOP Committee or General Council, we see no reason to assume that the panel would not appropriately take those conclusions into account. If the nature of the conclusions were binding (e.g., a decision on a phase-out period pursuant to paragraph 13 of the 1994 Understanding, which provides that the General Council may recommend that "in adhering to such a time-schedule, a Member shall be deemed to be in compliance with its GATT 1994 obligations" or a determination on the basis of Article XVIII:12 (c) or (d)), a panel should respect them. Indeed, paragraph 13 of the Understanding provides that "[w]henever the General Council has made specific recommendations, the rights and obligations of Members shall be assessed in the light of such recommendations". If the conclusions are based on factual matters as of a given point of time, we assume that a panel would take those conclusions into account, as did the panel in the *Korea - Beef* case. In such a case, the fact that a matter before a panel is being considered at a later point in time necessarily means that a different result could be reached because the underlying factual situation may have changed. But in such circumstances, it could not be said that there would be an actual conflict between the Committee and panel determinations.

[311] It is most unlikely that a dispute settlement procedure and a Committee procedure would reach conclusions at the same time. Even if this were to occur, the basis of review by the panel and the Appellate Body is limited to the facts and claims in existence at the time of the establishment of the panel, while the Committee is not under such constraint regarding the materials it can consider in terms of fact, implying that the factual basis of the conclusions of the Committee is likely to be different.

5.95 **Potential conflicts between panels.** India notes that the question of whether or not a Member's balance-of-payments measures are justified must be answered consistently. Yet, if panels may consider the issue of justification, successive panels may reach different results. While such a result cannot be excluded, we do not think it is likely. If the panels are commenced at or about the same time, Article 9.3 of the DSU provides for the same individuals to serve on the panels to the greatest extent possible. In all cases, the reports of such panels would be subject to review by the Appellate Body, which provides a mechanism to ensure consistent decisions. To the extent that the panels were established at significantly different points of time (such that Article 9.3 could not be applied), we note that, if the same factual situation obtained, it is likely that the second panel would take into account the results of the first panel, for the reasons expressed by the panel in *India - Patent Protection for Pharmaceutical and Agricultural Chemical Products*, Complaint by the European Communities and their Member States (hereinafter *India - Patents II*).[312] If the same factual situation did not obtain, a different decision would not necessarily be in conflict.

5.96 **"Automatic" adoption of panel reports.** It is certainly true, as noted by India, that the WTO dispute settlement system functions differently from that of the GATT dispute settlement system, particularly in respect of the procedures for the adoption of panel reports. In the WTO, in the absence of a consensus to the contrary (a "negative" consensus), panel and Appellate Body reports are adopted, while consensus decision-making prevails elsewhere in the WTO. We do not see why this would increase the risk of conflict, however. In fact, the practice of consensus decision-making in the WTO generally reduces the possibility of conflicts since opposition by one Member results in no decision being taken. While the negative consensus rule could result in the adoption of conflicting panel reports, that is true generally for dispute settlement in the WTO and not a problem specific to the balance-of-payments area. But such conflicts are unlikely, as discussed in the preceding paragraph.

5.97 Thus, we cannot accept India's argument that the problem of potential conflicting decisions (panel *vs.* Committee, panel *vs.* panel) in cases considering whether balance-of-payments measures under Article XVIII:B are justified, requires a finding that panels are not competent to consider such issues. In any case, the arguments raised by India concerning any potential conflict do not seem to outweigh the drawbacks which could result from the absence of availability of dispute settlement procedures to deal with balance-of-payments measures taken under Article XVIII:B.

[312] Panel Report on *India - Patent Protection for Pharmaceutical and Agricultural Chemical Products*, Complaint by the European Communities and their Member States, adopted on 2 September 1998, WT/DS79/R, para. 7.30.

(iii) First sentence of footnote 1 of the 1994 Understanding

5.98 Having considered the first two elements of the context of the second sentence of footnote 1 of the 1994 Understanding - the use of the word "applied" in other provisions and the relationship of the BOP Committee procedures to dispute settlement procedures, we now turn to the third element of that context - the first sentence of footnote 1 of the 1994 Understanding. This sentence provides that "[n]othing in this Understanding is intended to modify the rights and obligations of Members under Articles XII or XVIII:B of GATT 1994."

5.99 Our interpretation of the second sentence of footnote 1 so far, which has been based on the ordinary meaning of its terms, taken in their context, and which is consistent with past practice under GATT 1947, does not affect the right of developing country Members to take measures under Article XVIII:B. Nor does it prevent Members from resorting to the procedures of the BOP Committee under Article XVIII:12 and the 1994 Understanding. As such, our interpretation does not modify Members' rights and obligations under Article XVIII:B of GATT 1994.

(c) Object and purpose of the WTO Agreement

5.100 In relation to the object and purpose of the WTO Agreement, we note that the first sentence of Article 3.2 of the DSU provides that "[t]he dispute settlement system of the WTO is a central element in providing security and predictability to the multilateral trading system." It has been one of the major achievements of the Uruguay Round to strengthen the operation of settlement of disputes through the institution of a single integrated framework for the examination of disputes relating to all the multilateral trade Agreements negotiated as part of the "Single Undertaking". This includes GATT 1994 which contains the relevant provisions relating to balance-of-payments measures. It has clearly been intended that this mechanism be very widely available for the preservation of the rights and obligations of Members under the WTO Agreement, subject only to special or additional rules and procedures which are specifically listed.

5.101 With regard to measures taken for balance-of-payments purposes, we have noted that, under GATT 1947, the panel in *Korea - Beef* concluded that it was competent to review balance-of-payments measures. That panel, the only one to have expressly addressed this issue under GATT 1947, found that the availability of dispute settlement procedures with regard to balance-of-payments provisions was consistent with the complete application of the GATT 1947. Under the WTO, the rule of law has been strengthened through increased automaticity of dispute settlement and detailed integrated dispute settlement procedures. All the more so in this context of "thickening of legality", it would be inconsistent with the object and purpose of the WTO Agreement to interpret the relevant provisions as precluding panels from reviewing the justification of measures taken for balance-of-payments purposes in the absence of a clear textual basis to this effect.

5.102 The purpose of Article XVIII:B is to allow developing countries to deviate temporarily from the provisions of the GATT by adopting, under certain specified conditions, import restrictions to safeguard their external position and ensure a level of reserves adequate for the implementation of their programme of economic development. However, to interpret footnote 1 to the 1994 Understanding to confirm the availability of dispute settlement in relation to measures taken for balance-of-payments purposes is not in contradiction with that purpose. The right of developing country Members to take such measures is not affected by the availability of dispute settlement in relation to these measures. This is also consistent with the overall object and purpose of the WTO Agreement described above, as it enables the preservation of Members' rights and obligations in relation to such measures.

5.103 These elements confirm our interpretation that, in the absence of a provision clearly limiting the application of the DSU in balance-of-payments matters, no such limitation should be read in footnote 1 to the 1994 Understanding.

(d) Related GATT practice

5.104 India also referred to practice under Article XXIV of GATT 1947 to support its argument that under the GATT 1947, the established practice was not to allow review by dispute settlement panels of measures justified under provisions for which a specific review procedure exists. India thus refers to the report on *EC-Citrus*, and the panel report on *EC - Bananas I*, both unadopted reports which have addressed the issue of the relationship between Article XXIV and Article XXIII procedures under GATT 1947.[313]

5.105 The reference to panel reports concerning Article XXIV could be relevant, to the extent that they also address issues relating to the availability of dispute settlement procedures to challenge measures taken on the basis of a provision, Article XXIV, under which a specific review procedure exists. However, since both reports cited remained unadopted, they have a very limited weight as a reflection of past practice of the GATT Contracting Parties.[314] Also, they can only be relevant to this dispute by analogy, as they consider the issue of the relationship between Article XXIII and Article XXIV, which is not the issue we are required to examine here. Moreover, these reports do not seem to support India's

[313] See *supra* notes 294 and 295 the references for *EC - Citrus* and *EC - Bananas I* respectively.

[314] We recall that the Appellate Body specified, in its report on *Japan - Taxes on Alcoholic Beverages*, that unadopted panel reports "have no legal status in the GATT or WTO system since they have not been endorsed through decisions by the CONTRACTING PARTIES to GATT or WTO Members. Likewise we agree that 'a panel could nevertheless find useful guidance in the reasoning of an unadopted panel report that it considered to be relevant.'" (WT/DS8/AB/R,WT/DS10/AB/R, WT/DS11/AB/R, DSR 1996:I, 97, adopted on 1 November 1996, p. 108). The Appellate Body confirmed this analysis in *Argentina - Measures Affecting Imports of Footwear, Textiles, Apparels and other Items* (See Report of the Appellate Body, WT/DS56/AB/R, adopted on 22 April 1998, para. 43).

claim that the past practice under GATT 1947 had been not to allow a review under dispute settlement procedures when a specific review procedure exists, such as Article XXIV. At best, this past practice would seem uncertain, and the most recent report on this issue, the second panel report on *EC - Import Regime for Bananas* (hereinafter *EC - Bananas II)*, shows an evolution with respect to Article XXIV towards a result similar to that applied for Article XVIII:B in the *Korea - Beef* case.[315] In addition, the Understanding on the Interpretation of Article XXIV of GATT 1994, concluded after these reports, includes some specific language on the availability of dispute settlement in relation to Article XXIV.

(e) Preparatory work

5.106 India also refers to a US-Canadian proposal for a "Declaration on Trade Measures Taken for Balance-of-Payments Purposes", presented in June 1990 during the Uruguay Round negotiations. The proposal contained detailed provisions relating to surveillance of balance-of-payments measures[316], including, in a final section entitled "Review of Measures Following Balance-of-payments Consultations", the following text:

> "In those cases in which the Committee has been unable to agree on a specific recommendation, the question of the consistency of the measures under review with the Articles and this Declaration has not been resolved. The consulting contracting party or affected contracting parties can, if they wish, attempt to resolve the question in the Council. Alternatively, affected contracting parties can, if they wish, pursue the matter through normal GATT dispute settlement procedures pursuant to Articles XXII and XXIII".[317]

5.107 From the fact that the US-Canadian proposal of June 1990 was not adopted, India derives that the notion of recourse to dispute settlement as an "alternative" mode of determination of the legal status of restrictions taken for balance-of-payments purposes was rejected.[318]

---

[315] In *EC - Bananas II*, the panel "could not accept that tariff preferences inconsistent with Article I:1 would, by notification of the preferential agreement and invocation of Article XXIV against the objections of other contracting parties, escape any examination by a panel established under Article XXIII. If this view were endorsed, a mere communication of a contracting party invoking Article XXIV could deprive all other contracting parties of their procedural rights under Article XXIII:2, and therefore also of the effective protection of their substantive rights, in particular those under Article I:1. The Panel concluded therefore that a panel, faced with an invocation of Article XXIV, first had to examine whether or not this provision applied to the agreement in question." (DS38/R, 11 February 1994, not adopted, para. 158.).

[316] The US-Canada proposal included strongly worded provisions relating to preference to be given to price-based measures over quantitative restrictions, and specific deadlines to announce time-schedules for relaxation and removal of measures and maximum time-periods for such relaxation or removal. This proposal as tabled was not accepted.

[317] "Proposal by Canada and the United States", MTN.GNG/NG7/W/72, 15 June 1990, para. 19.

[318] For a detailed description of the parties' arguments, see Section III.D.(c) *supra*.

5.108 India does not point to any particular source supporting its position. The provision relating to recourse to dispute settlement was only one element of the US-Canadian proposal, which addressed a broad range of issues relating to balance-of-payments measures. At the time this proposal was put forward, there was no agreement to negotiate balance-of-payments matters and discussions in the Negotiating Group seemed to reflect a general lack of support for the proposal by a number of developing countries. A report of the Chairman of the Negotiating Group, dated 23 July 1990,[319] notes that :

> "The Group has discussed at considerable length a number of proposals for negotiations on trade measures taken for balance-of-payments reasons [one from the EC, one from Canada and the United States]. It has not however been able to agree to engage in negotiations on this subject. In these circumstances it is not possible for me to present a text which would have the character of a profile of an agreement. This note therefore describes the main positions taken in the Group's discussions to date." [...]
>
> "The general thrust of these proposals has been supported by a substantial number of developed contracting parties, though some have said that while being prepared to negotiate stronger disciplines in Article XII, it would be difficult for them, at this stage, to commit themselves to avoid recourse to it.
>
> A considerable number of developing countries, on the other hand, have argued that no convincing case has been made out as to why it is necessary to address this issue in the Round, given that as recently as 1979 the CONTRACTING PARTIES approved the Declaration on Trade Measures Taken for Balance-of-Payments Purposes [...]. The payments situation of many developing countries [...] remains critical: if there were to be negotiations regarding trade measures taken under Article XVIII:B, the objective should be to provide greater flexibility in its use rather than to impose more stringent conditions. This applied in particular to countries undertaking major economic reforms. In general, however, these participants have taken the view that the existing provisions and the related procedures in the Balance-of-Payments Committee have worked well and that any perceived problems in their functioning should be addressed in the Committee rather than in the context of the Round."

5.109 However, this document does not specify whether the dispute settlement aspects played any role in the rejection of the US-Canada proposal. Moreover, one should be cautious in drawing from this report any conclusion as to the

[319] MTN.GNG/NG7/W/73, Annex 2, paras. 1 and 4-5.

meaning of the texts finally adopted since negotiations actually continued in spite of the attitude of the parties recorded in that document.

5.110 Article 32 of the Vienna Convention allows a treaty interpreter to have recourse to supplementary means of interpretation, including the preparatory work of the treaty and the circumstances of its conclusion, in order to confirm the meaning resulting from the application of Article 31 or when interpretation according to Article 31 (a) leaves the meaning ambiguous or obscure or (b) leads to a result which is manifestly absurd or unreasonable. In this instance, we find that the meaning resulting from the application of Article 31 is neither ambiguous nor obscure, and does not lead to a manifestly absurd or unreasonable result. We therefore do not need to consider the preparatory work as reflected in the negotiating history to determine the meaning of the terms.[320]

5.111 We also note that the piece of drafting history referred to by India is not unequivocal. The US-Canadian proposal of June 1990 addressed several aspects of the balance-of-payments surveillance. India did not point to any source, such as minutes, which would have expressly stated that the reasons for its rejection was related to the alternative recourse to Article XXIII. The additional negotiating material available to the Panel on the reasons for the rejection of that proposal does not address specifically this aspect.[321] We can only conclude that the piece of negotiating history submitted by India is insufficient evidence that recourse to the general dispute settlement mechanisms was rejected during the

[320] See PCIJ *Lotus* (France *vs.* Turkey), 7 September 1927, PCIJ Reports Series A (1927), No. 10 p. 16.

[321] The results of the negotiations on this issue has been described in the following terms:

"In November 1989 the Americans and Canadians put their earlier views into concrete form in a joint proposal [...] [According to the proposal] action under the balance-of-payments articles should be allowed only in accordance with agreed guidelines. [...] Any deviations from the guidelines, unless explicitly approved by the Committee, would permit other countries to seek redress through the GATT dispute settlement procedures for damage done to their trade, with the onus on the restricting country to show that its measures are justified. [...] The reaction of developing countries was totally negative. [...] By June 1990, the Americans and Canadians had recognized that their earlier proposals were not negotiable, and moved to a position fairly close to that of the Community, although still calling for time limits for the removal of restrictions and not offering anything for infant industries. This was still not enough, however, to persuade developing countries to negotiate on the subject[...]" ... "The fragile compromise that emerged [in 1991] [...] was [...] carried into the Draft Final Act [...]. For the most part, it deals with the procedures for balance-of-payments consultations [...] The Agreement also makes clear that countries resorting to the balance-of-payments provisions may still be subject to complaints under the GATT dispute settlement procedures if they do not follow the rules. As a whole, the Agreement is a far cry from the ambitious controversial and ultimately non-negotiable proposals originally put forward by some countries. But it stands as (in Maciel's words) "a serious effort to clarify the existing provisions and procedures without undermining the right to use balance-of-payments measures". (J. Croome, *Reshaping the World Trading System. A History of the Uruguay Round*, World Trade Organization, 1995, pp. 223-224 and 307. Ambassador Maciel, of Brazil, was Chairman of the Negotiating Group on Rule-Making and Trade-Related Investment Measures during the Uruguay Round negotiations.) This text, apart from being a secondary source of information, is also imprecise on this issue.

Uruguay Round and to lead us to change the conclusions we reached on the basis of the criteria of Article 31.

5. *Conclusion*

5.112 Our examination of the ordinary meaning of the words of footnote 1 to the 1994 Understanding, the only provision expressly addressing the relationship between dispute settlement procedures under the DSU and balance-of-payments measures, has revealed that it could not be assumed, from the use of the terms "application of measures" in the provision, that an implicit distinction is intended between such "application" and the justification of the measure under Article XVIII:B. The ordinary meaning of the words suggests rather that this is a positive requirement that there be a measure currently applied, which will form the basis for the complaint. We find that this wording affirms the application of the WTO dispute settlement system to balance-of-payments matters. It does not limit it. In order to find, as suggested by India, an implicit opposition contained in this text between this notion of "application" and that of "justification", with the effect of very significantly restricting the scope of dispute settlement review by panels regarding balance-of-payments measures, we would have needed to find clear elements supporting such an interpretation. An examination of the context of the provisions and object and purpose of the agreement, as well as past GATT practice, has not led us to a conclusion other than that initially suggested by the terms of the provisions.

5.113 Therefore, we find that the terms of the second sentence of footnote 1 to the 1994 Understanding cannot be construed in such a narrow sense as to preclude the examination by panels of issues relating to the justification of measures taken for balance-of-payments purposes under Article XVIII:B of GATT. Nothing in past panel reports leads us to change our conclusions in this respect. Our finding is also consistent with the terms of the first sentence of footnote 1 of the 1994 Understanding which provides that "[n]othing in this Understanding is intended to modify the rights and obligations of Members under Articles XIII or XVIII:B".

5.114 We are thus competent to review the legal status of balance-of-payments measures and the justification of these measures to the extent necessary to address the claims submitted to us, within the scope of our mandate under the DSU. We are aware of the fact that the BOP Committee and panels have different functions and our finding is without prejudice to the role of the Committee and the General Council in reviewing balance-of-payments measures in the context of consultations under the balance-of-payments provisions of GATT 1994. By finding that panels can review the justification of balance-of-payments measures, we do not conclude that panels can substitute themselves for the BOP Committee, making the Committee procedure redundant and depriving Members of their rights under Article XVIII:B procedures. On the one hand, as shown in paragraphs 5.92 to 5.97, the likelihood of a conflict between conclusions reached under the dispute settlement mechanism and conclusions of the Committee is very low in practice. It is also clear that panels could not ignore determinations by the BOP Committee and the General Council. Moreover, our findings do not affect the right of developing country Members to invoke Article XVIII:B when they face balance-of-payments difficulties. They do not affect their right to maintain those measures in accordance with the requirements of Article XVIII:11 and the Committee procedure remains the only procedure for Members to obtain the authorization to maintain balance-of-payments measures under certain circumstances. On the other hand, our findings also preserve the right of Members aggrieved by balance-of-payments measures to secure the protection of their rights under the WTO Agreement if the measures at issue are no longer justified under Article XVIII:B If India's interpretation were endorsed, a mere notification by a Member under Article XVIII:B could deprive other Members of their procedural rights under the WTO dispute settlement provisions and therefore also of the effective protection of their substantive rights. This would also be contrary to the principle expressed in Article 3.2 of the DSU, which provides that the dispute settlement system of the WTO is a central element in providing security and predictability to the multilateral trading system.[322]

5.115 Having determined our degree of competence in this case, we must address the substantive claims of the United States. Before proceeding with this examination, we clarify the manner in which burden of proof is distributed in the examination of the different claims submitted to us.

E. Burden of Proof with Respect to the Claims

5.116 We consider that the evidence and arguments submitted by the parties regarding Article XI and Article XVIII requires us to state how we review the evidence in this case. In relation to Article XI, the United States has presented detailed evidence regarding four types of measures applied by India to a number of products which it considers violate Article XI:1 of GATT 1994. India does not submit a point-by-point rebuttal of the evidence presented by the United States. Rather, India contests the need for a ruling of the Panel on the question of the legality of the import restrictions at issue since they were notified to the BOP Committee as falling under Article XI:1. With respect to Article XVIII, the issue in this case is the extent to which the United States needs to prove its claim of a violation of Article XVIII:11, when India invokes Article XVIII:B as its justification for the measures at issue.

5.117 We recall that the Appellate Body Report on *United States - Measure Affecting Imports of Woven Wool Shirts and Blouses from India*,[323] stated that:

[322] Panel Report on *European Communities - Import Regime for Bananas*, 11 February 1994, DS38/R, not adopted, para. 158.

[323] WT/DS33/AB/R, adopted on 23 May 1997.

> "the burden of proof rests upon the party, whether complaining or defending, who asserts the affirmative of a particular claim or defence. If that party adduces evidence sufficient to raise a presumption that what is claimed is true, the burden then shifts to the other party, who will fail unless it adduces sufficient evidence to rebut the presumption."

5.118 In addition, we recall that the Appellate Body, in its report on *EC Measures concerning Meat and Meat Products (Hormones)*, stated that:

> "The general rule in a dispute settlement proceeding requiring a complaining party to establish a *prima facie* case of inconsistency of a provision [...] before the burden of showing consistency with that provision is taken by the defending party is *not* avoided by simply describing the same provision as an exception" (emphasis in original)[324]

5.119 We view the above-mentioned principle as requiring the following in terms of burden of proof in this case. In all instances, each party has to provide evidence in support of each of its particular assertions. This implies that the United States has to prove any of its claims in relation to the alleged violation of Article XI:1 and XVIII:11. Similarly, India has to support its assertion that its measures are justified under Article XVIII:B. We also view the rules stated by the Appellate Body as requiring that the United States as the complainant cannot limit itself to stating its claim. It must present a *prima facie* case that the Indian balance-of-payments measures are not justified by reference to Articles XI:1 and XVIII:11 of GATT 1994.[325] Should the United States do so, India would have to respond in order to rebut the claim.

5.120 In this instance, the United States has presented a *prima facie* case for each of its claims. India has responded and presented several defences to which the United States has responded. Subsequently, having regard to Article XV:2 of GATT 1994 and Article 13 of the DSU, we have consulted the IMF on a number of issues related to India's balance-of-payments situation. We have then weighed, on each claim, the evidence favouring India against that favouring the United States to determine on the basis of all evidence before the Panel whether the United States has established its claim. Of course, where the balance of evidence is inconclusive, the party asserting the particular claim or defence will have failed to establish it.

5.121 In the case of the claim of violation of Article XI:1, we shall take into account the fact that the United States intends to prove violations in specific situations, and that India does not deny or reply specifically to some of those allegations. We accordingly determine whether the evidence made available by

---

[324] Op. Cit. para. 104.

[325] Appellate Body Report on *Australia - Measures Affecting Importation of Salmon*, adopted on 6 November 1998, WT/DS18/AB/R, paras. 257-259.

both parties allows the Panel to reach a conclusion for each measure. In the case of Article XVIII, the United States has claimed that India has violated Article XVIII:11 by maintaining balance-of-payments measures that are no longer justified. If the evidence before us supports the US position, the United States will at the same time have negated India's Article XVIII defence.

F. Article XI:1

5.122 India regulates the importation of goods found in a "Negative List of Imports", contained in Chapter 15 of India's Export and Import Policy 1997-2002. The United States identifies four measures which are implemented under India's Export and Import Policy and which it claims constitute quantitative restrictions within the meaning of Article XI:1: (a) discretionary import licensing; (b) canalization of imports through government agencies; (c) the Special Import Licensing (SIL) system; (d) the "Actual User" condition on import licensing. These measures are described in more detail in paragraphs 5.125, 5.132, 5.137 and 5.140. To the extent that India applies these four measures as balance-of-payments restrictions on the products specified in Annex I, Part B of WT/BOP/N/24, we refer to these measures as the "measures at issue" in this dispute.

5.123 While India seeks to rebut some of the United States' arguments, it does not challenge the status of the measures under Article XI:1. India argues that it has already notified all of the import restrictions at issue to the BOP Committee as falling under Article XI:1. In the view of India, there is consequently no dispute regarding the legality of the import restriction under Article XI:1 and it would be sufficient for the Panel to record that India has notified all the measures at issue as import restrictions falling under Article XI:1 and then proceed with the examination of their consistency with Article XVIII:B.

5.124 In our opinion, the notification by India of the measures at issue to the Committee is more than a simple admission of facts, since such notification implies a recognition that the measures at issue are "quantitative restrictions". The fact that India also notified that these measures were justified under Article XVIII, with the legal consequences attached to it (including consultations within the BOP Committee) also gives added value to the statement of India.[326] However, we consider that we need to make a finding on the violation of Article XI:1, for two reasons. First, it is an established practice under GATT and under the

[326] We recall in this context that, as recently stated by the Panel on *United States - Import Prohibition of Certain Shrimp and Shrimp Products,* adopted on 6 November 1998, WT/DS58/R, "it is usual legal practice for domestic and international tribunals, including GATT panels, to consider that, if a party admits a particular fact, the judge may be entitled to consider such fact as accurate" (footnote omitted). See also the panel reports cited in reference in the footnote to the cited text: *EEC - Programmes of Minimum Import Prices, Licences and Surety Deposits for Certain Processed Fruits and Vegetables*, adopted on 18 October 1978, BISD 25S/68, para. 4.9 and *EEC- Quantitative Restrictions against Imports of Certain Products from Hong Kong*, adopted on 12 July 1983, BISD 30S/129, para. 31.

WTO that, even when the legal nature of a particular measure is not challenged, panels have made findings to determine the existence of a violation before addressing any justification invoked by the defending party. Secondly, the United States has asked for a ruling on the legality of each of the import restrictive measures at issue in this case. The United States claims that specific findings on the violation of Article XI:1 would assist in the implementation of the Panel's recommendations. Such a finding would not constitute, as argued by India, a "declaratory judgment" on "potential future inconsistencies". It will be based on an examination of the measures at issue as they are submitted to the Panel, and is required for the effective resolution of this dispute concerning these measures.

1. India's Import Licensing System for Products on the "Negative List of Imports" [327]

5.125 The United States claims that imports of goods falling within the "Restricted Items" list, found in Annex II of the Negative List, require a licence issued by the Director-General of Foreign Trade (DGFT). The "Restricted Items" list covers a number of products, including consumer goods (defined as consumption goods which can directly satisfy human needs without further processing and includes consumer durables and accessories). In WT/BOP/N/24, Annex 1, Part B, the products subject to this condition are identified by the notation "NAL", which stands for "Non-automatic Licensing". According to the United States, imports of these products into India are subject to an arbitrary, non-transparent and discretionary import licensing system, under which licences are granted "on merit" and only to a category of operators called "Actual Users".

5.126 India responds that this system is transparent and rules-based, and notes in particular that under the Foreign Trade (Development and Regulation) Act, 1992, criteria are provided for the granting of licences, refusals to grant a licence must be motivated in writing and decisions on the granting of licences, including refusals, are open to appeal.

5.127 Article XI contains one of the fundamental principles of the GATT/WTO legal system, the general prohibition of quantitative restrictions. Article XI:1 reads as follows:

> "No prohibitions or restrictions other than duties, taxes or other charges, whether made effective through quotas, import or export licences or other measures, shall be instituted or maintained by any [Member] on the importation of any product of the territory of any other [Member] or on the exportation or sale for export of any product of the territory of any other [Member]."

[327] For a detailed description of the measures at issue and of the arguments of the parties, see Sections II.B and III.B *supra*.

5.128 We note that the text of Article XI:1 is very broad in scope, providing for a general ban on import or export restrictions or prohibitions "other than duties, taxes or other charges". As was noted by the panel in *Japan - Trade in Semi-conductors*, the wording of Article XI:1 is comprehensive: it applies "to all measures instituted or maintained by a [Member] prohibiting or restricting the importation, exportation, or sale for export of products other than measures that take the form of duties, taxes or other charges."[328] The scope of the term "restriction" is also broad, as seen in its ordinary meaning, which is "a limitation on action, a limiting condition or regulation".[329]

5.129 Under the GATT 1947, panels have examined whether import and export licensing systems are restrictions under Article XI:1. For example, in a case involving a so-called "SLQ" regime, which concerned products subject in principle to quantitative restrictions, but for which no quota amount had been set either in quantity or value, permit applications being granted upon request, the panel noted "that the SLQ regime was an import licensing procedure which would amount to a quantitative restriction unless it provided for the *automatic* issuance of licences".[330] A similar conclusion was reached in the above-cited *Japan - Trade in Semi-conductors*, where the panel found that "export licensing practices by Japan, leading to delays of up to three months in the issuing of licences for semi-conductors destined for contracting parties other than the United States, had been non-automatic and constituted restrictions on the exportation of such products inconsistent with Article XI".[331] These reports are consistent with the ordinary meaning noted above, as discretionary or non-automatic licensing systems by their very nature operate as limitations on action since certain imports may not be permitted. Thus, in light of the terms of Article XI:1 and these adopted panel reports, we conclude that a discretionary or non-automatic import licensing requirement is a restriction prohibited by Article XI:1.

5.130 In light of the foregoing, we note that it is agreed that India's licensing system for goods in the Negative List of Imports is a discretionary import licensing system, in that licences are not granted in all cases, but rather on unspecified "merits". We note also that India concedes this measure is an import restriction under Article XI:1.[332]

---

[328] Panel Report on *Japan - Trade in Semi-conductors*, adopted on 4 May 1988, BISD 35S/116, para. 104.

[329] *New Shorter Oxford Dictionary* (1993), p. 2569.

[330] Panel Report on *EEC - Quantitative Restrictions Against Imports of Certain Products from Hong Kong*, adopted on 12 July 1983, BISD 30S/129, para. 31 (emphasis added). See also Panel Report on *EEC - Programmes of Minimum Import Prices, Licences and Surety Deposits for Certain Processed Fruits and Vegetables*, adopted on 18 October 1978, BISD 25S/68, para. 4.9.

[331] Op. Cit., para. 118.

[332] We note that a finding that a discretionary licensing system is a restriction for purposes of Article XI does not imply that discretionary licensing systems cannot be used where an exception to Article XI is applicable. Indeed, their use is foreseen by the Import Licensing Agreement, which regulates their use.

5.131 In light of these elements, we find that the import licensing system maintained by India for the products found in Annex II of the Negative List of Imports, to the extent that it applies to the products specified in WT/BOP/N/24, Annex I, Part B, operates as a restriction on imports within the meaning of Article XI:1.

2. *Canalization of Imports through Government Agencies*[333]

5.132 The United States also claims that imports of goods specified as "Canalized Items" in Part III of the Negative List may in principle be imported only by designated canalizing (government) agencies. Among these items are petroleum products, certain fertilizers, various sorts of oil and certain cereals. The DGFT may grant import licences for canalized products to other entities than the designated canalizing agency, but this is subject to a "no objection" certificate from the canalizing agency normally entitled to import. According to the United States, the "canalization" of imports, i.e. the exclusive importation of certain goods through designated government agencies, constitutes restrictions within the meaning of Article XI:1. The United States refers to the Note Ad Articles XI, XII, XIII, XIV and XVIII and to a number of working party and panel reports under GATT 1947 in support of the proposition that import restrictions are no less subject to Article XI:1 when they are imposed through state trading. In this regard, the United States has produced tables indicating the quantities and values of imports of some "canalized" items, taken from India's notification to the State Trading Committee to show that canalization resulted in zero imports in 1992-1995 for wheat and rice.

5.133 As to India, we note that it considers that the restrictions on canalized items are "restrictions" within the purview of Article XI:1, since it has notified them as balance-of-payments restrictions in WT/BOP/N/24.

5.134 In analyzing the US claim, we note that violations of Article XI:1 can result from restrictions made effective through state trading operations. This is made very clear in the Note Ad Articles XI, XII, XIII, XIV and XVIII, which provides that "Throughout Article XI, XII; XIII; XIV; and XVIII, the terms 'import restrictions' or 'export restrictions' include restrictions made effective through state-trading operations." It should be noted however, that the mere fact that imports are effected through state trading enterprises would not in itself constitute a restriction. Rather, for a restriction to be found to exist, it should be shown that the operation of this state trading entity is such as to result in a restriction.[334]

---

[333] For a detailed description of the measures at issue and of the arguments of the parties, see: respectively, Sections II.B and III.B *supra*.

[334] Panel Report on *Korea - Beef*, Op. Cit., para 115: "The mere existence of producer-controlled import monopolies could not be considered as a separate import restriction inconsistent with the

5.135 As noted above, the United States has shown in some instances that there have been zero imports of products reserved to state trading enterprises by India. We note, however, that canalization *per se* will not necessarily result in the imposition of quantitative restrictions within the meaning of Article XI:1, since an absence of importation of a given product may not always be the result of the imposition of a prohibitive quantitative restriction. For instance, the absence of importation of snow ploughs into a tropical island cannot be taken as sufficient evidence of the existence of import restrictions, even if the right to import those products is granted to an entity with exclusive or special privileges.

5.136 In this case, however, the inclusion by India of the canalized items as quantitative restrictions under Article XI:1 in its notification to the BOP Committee, combined with the evidence submitted by the United States, leads us to conclude that the "canalization" measures specified in Part III of the Negative List of Imports, to the extent that they apply to products specified in WT/BOP/N/24, Annex I, Part B, operate as a restriction on imports within the meaning of Article XI:1.

3. The Special Import Licence (SIL) System[335]

5.137 The United States claims that imports of certain designated goods require a Special Import Licence (SIL) issued by the DGFT or an authorized licensing authority. SILs are granted in proportion to the applicant's exports or net foreign exchange earnings (Chapter 12 of India's Export and Import Policy 1997-2002). According to the United States, the SIL system is a non-automatic licensing regime under which approval of licence applications is not granted in all cases. The United States considers that the restrictive effect of the SIL system on imports is shown by the quota premium for purchase of special import licences (which may be transferred in certain cases). As such, the United States argues that the SIL system is equally in violation of Article XI:1.

5.138 As for India, we note that it considers that the SIL system is a "restriction" within the purview of Article XI:1, since it has notified it as a balance-of-payments restriction in WT/BOP/N/24.

5.139 It appears that the SIL system, like the general import licensing regime examined above, is a discretionary or non-automatic licensing regime. Licences under this regime can be granted only to certain categories of exporters and licences are not always granted. Accordingly, we find that the SIL system, to the extent that it applies to the products specified in WT/BOP/N/24, Annex 1, Part B, operates as a restriction on imports within the meaning of Article XI:1.

General Agreement. The Panel noted, however, that the activities of such enterprises had to conform to a number of rules contained in the General Agreement, including those of Article XVII and Article XI:1".

[335] For a detailed description of the measures at issue and of the arguments of the parties, see: respectively, Sections II.B and III.B *supra*.

4. *The Actual User Requirement*

5.140 The United States also claims that under India's Export and Import Policy 1997-2002, import licences are generally available only to "Actual Users", which are defined in Chapter 3 thereof as follows: an "Actual User" means an actual user who may be either industrial or non-industrial. "Actual User (industrial)" means a person who utilizes the imported goods for manufacturing in his own industrial unit or manufacturing for his own use in another unit including a jobbing unit. "Actual User (non-industrial)" means a person who utilizes the imported goods for his own use in (i) any commercial establishment carrying on any business, trade or profession; or (ii) any laboratory, scientific or research and development institution, university or other educational institution or hospital; or (iii) any service industry.

5.141 The United States argues that the granting of licences only to "Actual Users" also constitutes a restriction on imports, as it effectively prevents imports by intermediaries. Although India states that licences might be granted to any person "including an industrial user who was engaged in production solely for the domestic market", the definition of "actual user" quoted above appears to include only persons who will employ the imported goods "for their own use".

5.142 As noted above, Article XI:1 is "comprehensive" in that it prohibits import restrictions "made effective through quotas, import or export licences *or other measures*"[336], excluding from its coverage only "duties, taxes or other charges". In considering the scope of the prohibition, it is instructive to consider how it has been dealt with in prior panel reports. For example, a minimum import price system has been considered to be a restriction within the meaning of Article XI:1.[337] In a case involving limitations on the points of sale available to imported beer, a panel found that such limitations were restrictions within the meaning of Article XI:1.[338] These reports are in accord with the ordinary meaning of the term "restriction", which, as noted above, is "a limitation on action, a limiting condition or regulation".[339] Applied to the "Actual User" condition, they lead to the conclusion that it is a restriction on imports because it precludes imports of prod-

336 (emphasis added).

337 Panel Report on *EEC - Programmes of Minimum Import Prices, Licences and Surety Deposits for Certain Processed Fruits and Vegetables*, adopted on 18 October 1978, BISD 25S/68, para. 4.9. Similarly, a panel found that a measure limiting exports below a certain price was within the scope of Article XI:1. Panel Report on *Japan - Trade in Semiconductors*, Op. Cit., para. 105.

338 Panel Report on *Canada - Import, Distribution and Sale of Alcoholic Drinks by Canadian Provincial Marketing Agencies*, adopted on 22 March 1988, BISD 35S/37, para. 4.24. This case involved state trading operations and the panel emphasized that the Note Ad Articles XI, XII, XIII, XIV and XVIII referred to "restrictions" generally and not to "import restrictions". It accordingly considered restrictions on distribution as within the meaning of "other measures" under Article XI:1, even though such measures might be examined also under Article III:4. Here the restrictions at issue, although related to distribution, are on importation.

339 *New Shorter Oxford Dictionary* (1993), p. 2569.

ucts for resale by intermediaries, i.e. distribution to consumers who are unable to import directly for their own immediate use is restricted.

5.143 Accordingly, we find that the Actual User condition, to the extent that it applies to the products specified in WT/BOP/N/24, Annex I, Part B, operates as a restriction on imports within the meaning of Article XI:1.

5. *Summary*

5.144 In conclusion, we find that the import licensing system applied by India to the importation of goods falling within the "Restricted Items" list found in Annex II of the Negative List of Imports, the canalization through government agencies of imports specified in Part III of the Negative List of Imports, the SIL system and the Actual User requirement, to the extent that they apply to the products specified in WT/BOP/N/24, Annex I, Part B, impose restrictions or prohibitions on imports within the meaning of Article XI:1 of GATT 1994 and therefore violate Article XI:1.

G. *Article XVIII:B of GATT 1994*

5.145 Having determined that the measures at issue are quantitative restrictions within the meaning of Article XI:1 and therefore prohibited, we must examine the United States' second claim, i.e. violation of Article XVIII:11, and India's defence under the balance-of-payments provisions of GATT 1994 in order to determine whether India, by maintaining the measures at issue, violates Article XVIII:11.

5.146 The claims of the parties can be summarized as follows: the United States claims that India's measures are in violation of Article XVIII:11 because they are not necessary under the terms of Article XVIII:9. In the view of the United States, Article XVIII:11 allows for progressive relaxation of balance-of-payments measures as the balance-of-payments situation improves, but this progressive relaxation is required to take place only during the period when the conditions of Article XVIII:9 are met, not afterwards. For the United States, the concept of a phase-out after that period is entirely absent from Article XVIII:B, and once there is no longer any balance-of-payments justification, the measures must be eliminated. India considers that it is allowed to maintain balance-of-payments measures until the General Council decides, upon recommendation by the BOP Committee, that they are no longer justified. India further claims that under the Note Ad Article XVIII:11, even if it is not currently experiencing balance-of-payments difficulties within the meaning of Article XVIII:9, it should not be required to relax or remove restrictions if such relaxation or removal would thereupon produce conditions justifying the intensification or institution, respectively, of restrictions under paragraph 9 of Article XVIII. Moreover, India claims that, in any event, it is entitled, under the 1994 Understanding and other GATT 1994 provisions, to a gradual phase-out of its quantitative restrictions.[340]

5.147 Under the terms of Article XVIII:9,

> "the import restrictions instituted, maintained or intensified shall not exceed those necessary:
>
> (a) to forestall the threat of, or to stop, a serious decline in monetary reserves, or
>
> (b) in the case of a Member with inadequate monetary reserves, to achieve a reasonable rate of increase in its reserves"

due regard being paid to any special factors that may be affecting the reserves of the Member or its need for reserves.

5.148 The second sentence of Article XVIII:11 provides:

> "[The Member concerned] shall progressively relax any restrictions applied under this section as conditions improve, maintaining them only to the extent necessary under the terms of paragraph 9 of this Article and shall eliminate them when conditions no longer justify such maintenance; Provided that no Member shall be required to withdraw or modify restrictions on the ground that a change in its development policy would render unnecessary the restrictions which it is applying under this section.*"

5.149 The Note Ad Article XVIII:11 provides:

> "The second sentence in paragraph 11 shall not be interpreted to mean that a Member is required to relax or remove restrictions if such relaxation would thereupon produce conditions justifying the intensification or institution, respectively, of restrictions under paragraph 9 of Article XVIII."

5.150 In light of these provisions and the arguments of the parties, it is therefore necessary to examine in the first instance whether India's balance-of-payments situation is such that the conditions foreseen in Article XVIII:9 are fulfilled. If this were the case, India would be in the situation in which the United States admits that it would be entitled to maintain and progressively relax any measures maintained for balance-of-payments purposes as the balance-of-payments situation improves, without being required to eliminate them. If we determine that this is not the case, however, we will need to consider India's position that restrictions can be maintained on the basis of Article XVIII:11 even when the balance-of-payments situation does not meet the conditions of Article XVIII:9. Finally, we must consider whether India could claim a right to maintain the measures as long as the General Council has not determined them to be inconsistent with Ar-

[340] For a detailed description of the arguments of the parties, see Section III.D.3-4 *supra*.

ticle XVIII:B[341] or otherwise has a right to phase out its balance-of-payments measures.

5.151 Before we address these claims and having regard to Article 12.11 of the DSU, we first consider the concept of special and differential treatment in relation to Article XVIII:B of GATT 1994, which is relevant to our examination under Article XVIII:B of GATT 1994 as a whole.

1. *Special and Differential Treatment*

5.152 India argues that Article XVIII:B is the most important expression of the principle of special and differential treatment in the GATT. India further argues that the provisions of Article XVIII:B embody a presumption that developing country Members would face balance-of-payments difficulties on account of economic development and that the sequence of the terms of Article XVIII:11 suggested a dynamic linkage between domestic policy reform and improvements in the balance-of-payments and that such improvements would enable Members to progressively relax and eliminate import restrictions as the balance-of-payments situation improved. Therefore, Article XVIII:11 was premised on the notion that trade liberalization must follow upon improvements of the balance-of-payments situation and not vice-versa. In the view of India, there was no requirement in Article XVIII:B that a Member must provide evidence that maintaining import restrictions would result in improvements in its balance-of payments or conversely, that the removal of import restrictions would cause deterioration in its balance-of-payments. For India, in view of the presumption underlying Article XVIII:B, the burden was on the United States to establish that maintaining import restrictions would not result in improvement, or would cause a deterioration, in India's balance of payments.[342]

5.153 In Article XVIII:8, Members recognize that developing countries "tend, when they are in rapid process of development, to experience balance-of-payments difficulties arising mainly from efforts to expand their internal markets as well as from the instability in their terms of trade." In Article XVIII:2, it is recognized that

> "it may be necessary for those Members, in order to implement programmes and policies of economic development designed to raise the general standard of living of their people, to take protective or other measures affecting imports, and that such measures are justified in so far as they facilitate the attainment of the objectives of this Agreement. [Members] agree, therefore, that those members should enjoy additional facilities to enable them [...] (b)

[341] This issue was already considered in paras. 5.76-5.80 *supra*, but as it is relevant to the analysis of India's defence under Article XVIII:B, we also address it in this context, with reference to our previous conclusions.

[342] For a detailed description of the arguments of the parties, see Section III.D.5 *supra*.

> to apply quantitative restrictions for balance-of-payments purposes in a manner which takes full account of the continued high level of demand for imports likely to be generated by their programmes of economic development."

5.154 Article XVIII:4(a) further provides that:

> "Consequently, a Member, the economy of which can only support low standards of living and is in the early stages of development, shall be free to deviate temporarily from the provisions of the other Articles of this Agreement, *as provided* in Sections A, B and C of this Article." (emphasis added)

5.155 It is clear from these provisions that Article XVIII, which allows developing countries to maintain, under certain conditions, temporary import restrictions for balance-of-payments purposes, is premised on the assumption that it "may be necessary" for them to adopt such measures in order to implement economic development programmes. It allows them to "deviate temporarily from the provisions of the other Articles" of GATT 1994, as provided for in, *inter alia*, Section B. These provisions reflect an acknowledgement of the specific needs of developing countries in relation to measures taken for balance-of-payments purposes. Article XVIII:B of GATT 1994 thus embodies the special and differential treatment foreseen for developing countries with regard to such measures. In our analysis, we take due account of these provisions. In particular, the conditions for taking balance-of-payments measures under Article XVIII are clearly distinct from the conditions applicable to developed countries under Article XII of GATT 1994.[343]

5.156 We also find that while Article XVIII:2 foresees the possibility that it "may" be "necessary" for developing countries to take restrictions for balance-of-payments purposes, such measures might not always be required. These restrictions must be adopted within specific conditions "as provided in" Section B of Article XVIII. The specific conditions to be respected for the institution and maintenance of such measures include Article XVIII:9, which specifies the circumstances under which such measures may be instituted and maintained, and Article XVIII:11 which sets out the requirements for progressive relaxation and elimination of balance-of-payments measures.

5.157 Article 12.11 of the DSU requires us to indicate explicitly the form in which account was taken of relevant provisions on special and differential treatment for developing country Members that form part of the covered agreements which have been raised by the developing country Member in the course of the dispute settlement procedures. In this instance, we have noted that Article

[343] In particular, the conditions to be met for the institution of balance-of-payments measures are different in Article XVIII:9 and Article XII, and an Ad Note which applies to the conditions for progressive relaxation and elimination of restrictions under Article XVIII:11 has no analogue in Article XII.

XVIII:B as a whole, on which our analysis throughout this section is based, embodies the principle of special and differential treatment in relation to measures taken for balance-of-payments purposes. This entire part G therefore reflects our consideration of relevant provisions on special and differential treatment, as does Section VII of our report (suggestions for implementation).

2. *Is India Experiencing Balance-of-Payments Difficulties within the Meaning of Article XVIII:9?*

(a) Conditions under Article XVIII:9

5.158 As noted above, Article XVIII:11 requires Members to "progressively relax any restrictions applied under this section as conditions improve, maintaining them only to the extent necessary under the terms of paragraph 9 of this Article and shall eliminate them when conditions no longer justify such maintenance [...]". We recall that, under the terms of Article XVIII:9, "the import restrictions instituted, maintained or intensified shall not exceed those necessary:

> (a) to forestall the threat of, or to stop, a serious decline in monetary reserves, or
>
> (b) in the case of a contracting party with inadequate monetary reserves, to achieve a reasonable rate of increase in its reserves"

due regard being paid to any special factors that may be affecting the reserves of the Member or its need for reserves.

(b) Date at which the situation of India's monetary reserves must be reviewed

5.159 The United States argues that the dispute began with the United States' request for consultations on 15 July 1997 and that the DSU treats consultations as the initiation of a dispute. Therefore, in its view, 15 July 1997 is the date as of which this Panel should determine whether India's measures were justified under Article XVIII:B. If the Panel disagrees, the United States considers that the latest date should be the date of establishment of the Panel. India generally considers that the Panel must determine the legality of the import restrictions under India's obligations "as of the date the United States submitted this request". However, India also considers that taking into account external or internal developments affecting India's economy since the establishment of the Panel would be appropriate because much of the evidence introduced by the United States in the dispute relates to the period after the establishment of the Panel.[344]

5.160 With respect to the date at which India's balance-of-payments and reserve situation is to be assessed, we note that practice, both prior to the WTO and since

[344] For a detailed description of the arguments of the parties, see Section III.D.9(c)(i) *supra*.

its entry into force, limits the claims which panels address to those raised in the request for establishment of the panel, which is typically the basis of the panel's terms of reference (as is the case here).[345] In our opinion, this has consequences for the determination of the facts that can be taken into account by the Panel, since the complainant obviously bases the claims contained in its request for establishment of the panel on a given set of facts existing when it presents its request to the DSB.

5.161 In the present situation, the United States primarily seeks a finding that, at the latest on the date of establishment of the Panel (18 November 1997), the measures at issue were not compatible with the WTO Agreement and were not justified under Article XVIII:11 of GATT 1994. Therefore, it would seem consistent with such a request and logical in the light of the constraints imposed by the Panel's terms of reference to limit our examination of the facts to those existing on the date the Panel was established.

5.162 This result is also dictated by practical considerations. The determination of whether balance-of-payments measures are justified is tied to a Member's reserve situation as of a certain date. In fixing that date, it is important to consider that the relevant economic and reserve data will be available only with some time-lag, which may vary by type of data. This is unlikely to be a problem if the date of assessment is the date the panel is established, since the first written submission is typically filed at least two (and often more) months after establishment of a panel. However, using the first or second panel meetings as the assessment date is more problematic since data might not be available and, if the date of the second panel meeting were chosen, it could significantly reduce the utility of the first meeting.

5.163 We note that, in the case on *Korea - Beef*, the panel relied on the conclusions of the BOP Committee reached before its establishment, but also considered "all available information", including information related to periods after the establishment of the panel.[346] In this case, the parties and the IMF have supplied information concerning the evolution of India's balance-of-payments and reserve situation until June 1998. To the extent that such information is relevant to our determination of the consistency of India's balance-of-payments measures with GATT rules as of the date of establishment of the Panel, we take it into account.[347]

---

[345] Appellate Body Report on *European Communities - Regime for the Importation, Sale and Distribution of Bananas*, adopted on 25 September 1997, WT/DS27/AB/R, para. 143 and Appellate Body Report on *India - Patent Protection for Pharmaceutical and Agricultural Chemical Products*, adopted on 16 January 1998, WT/DS50/AB/R, paras. 87-89.

[346] Adopted on 7 November 1989, BISD 36S/268, paras. 122-123.

[347] We note for instance that such information might be relevant to an examination of the existence of a threat of serious decline in monetary reserves under Article XVIII:9 or to an examination of the conditions contemplated in the Note Ad Article XVIII:11.

(c) Information provided by the IMF

5.164 The Panel put the following questions to the IMF which are relevant to our examination of India's balance-of-payments situation:

> "1. (a) (i) As of 18 November 1997, the date of establishment of the Panel, was India experiencing a serious decline in its monetary reserves, or facing a threat thereof? (ii) Was India experiencing an inadequate, or a very low level of monetary reserves? (iii) Was India experiencing a reasonable rate of increase in its monetary reserves?
>
> (b) In connection with responding to these questions, could the IMF indicate what would have constituted a serious decline in India's monetary reserves, what would have constituted an inadequate, or a very low level of monetary reserves for India, and what would have constituted a reasonable rate of increase in India's monetary reserves?"

5.165 The IMF's replies to the questions show that foreign currency reserves of India's monetary authorities stood at US$25.1 billion (excluding gold) on 21 November 1997, which represented an increase of US$5.6 billion from a year earlier, and of US$2.8 billion from end-March 1997. The IMF indicates that "[a]t about six months of imports of goods and non-factor services, India's reserves appeared to provide sufficient external liquidity and a reasonable degree of protection against unforeseen external shocks. In particular, reserves were sufficient to deal with debt service payments and potential outflows of portfolio investment, covering 2½ times the amount of maturing debt obligations in the next twelve months and 1½ times the stock of short-term debt and cumulative inflows of portfolio investment. Therefore, it was the Fund's view that India's level of foreign currency reserves on November 18, 1997 was adequate". The IMF notes that the establishment of the panel coincided with a period of turbulence in the foreign exchange market in India, but concludes that "with an appropriate macroeconomic response and the containment of contagion, India's foreign currency reserves on 18 November 1997 did not appear to be under a threat of a serious decline; since there was no threat, the question of whether an imminent threat existed is moot". Having noted that gross foreign currency reserves fell by US$1.9 billion in November 1997, the Fund nevertheless determines that "there has been a reasonable rate of accumulation of reserves since India's balance-of-payments crisis in 1991".

5.166 In response to question 1 (b), the Fund, noting the considerable degree of subjective judgment involved in an assessment of the adequacy of the level and rate of change of reserves, based its view on "the size of the existing and potential claims on reserves, examined in the context of the country's economic circumstances. In the case of India, policy had prudently aimed at ensuring that reserve coverage is ahead of the outstanding short-term liabilities (by remaining maturity) and potential outflows of portfolio investment. As of November 1997, short-term liabilities (by remaining maturity) and the stock of portfolio investment (after marking to market) were estimated at US$16 billion. A decline in reserves to significantly below this level would be considered serious, and such levels could be deemed inadequate or very low".

Table 1: Evolution of India's level of reserves (1995-1998)

Year	31 March 1995	31 March 1996	31 March 1997	31 March 1998	30 June 1998
Level of reserves (US$ billions)	20.8	17	22.4	26	24.1

(Source: IMF)

5.167 India comments that the events described by the IMF in its answer to question 1(a)(i) constitute recognition by the IMF of the threat of a serious decline in India's reserves. India notes that the Reserve Bank of India (RBI) had to change its monetary policy goals in order to defend the rupee, and would not have done so had it not felt that it faced a threat of a serious decline in foreign currency reserves which it had been unable to control using other policy instruments. With regard to questions 1(a)(ii) and 1(b), India notes that experts have suggested alternative indicators to evaluate the adequacy of India's foreign currency reserves, which, in India's view, would be more appropriate than the standard measure used by the IMF.[348] Using these measures, India calculated that its reserves should be at higher levels to ensure adequacy.

5.168 The United States comments that the IMF's replies are fully consistent with the evidence furnished by the United States to the Panel and make it clear that India's balance-of-payments situation does not meet the criteria of the proviso of Article XVIII:9. The United States also points out that the IMF's analysis of India's balance-of-payments situation is more complete than that presented by India, in that it considers the whole balance-of-payments situation, whereas India's analysis focuses mostly on its trade account, which is only one element of the analysis.[349]

(d) Assessment of India's balance-of-payments situation in relation to the conditions of Article XVIII:9

(i) Article XVIII:9(a)

5.169 The issue to be decided under Article XVIII:9 (a) is whether India's balance-of-payments measures exceeded those "necessary ... to forestall the threat of, or to stop, a serious decline in monetary reserves". In deciding this issue, we

---

[348] For a description of these methods, see para. 5.171 *infra*.

[349] For a detailed description of the arguments of the parties, see Section III.D.9.(c)(iii) *supra*.

must weigh the evidence favouring India against that favouring the United States and determine whether on the basis of all evidence before the Panel, the United States has established its claim under Article XVIII:11 that India does not meet the conditions specified in Article XVIII:9(a).

5.170 The United States relies principally upon the following evidence and argument: it notes in the first instance that in the view of the IMF, as of 18 November 1997[350] India was not facing a threat of a serious decline in monetary reserves and that the IMF had expressed an identical view to the BOP Committee in January 1997 and June 1997. In addition, the United States notes the statement in the Annual Report of the Reserve Bank of India for the year July 1, 1996 to June 30, 1997 (para. 7.23), where it is stated:

> "The level of foreign exchange reserves (including gold and SDRs) rose to US$ 29.9 billion by August 14, 1997[351] equivalent to seven months of imports and well above the thumb rule of reserve adequacy (three months of imports). In the context of the changing interface with the external sector and the importance of the capital account, reserve adequacy needs to be evaluated in terms of indicators other than conventional norms. By any criteria, the level of foreign exchange level reserves appears comfortable. They are equivalent of about 25 months of debt service payments and 6 months of payments for imports and debt service taken together. Thus, even if exchange market developments accentuate the leads and lags in external receipts and payments, the reserves would be adequate to withstand both cyclical and unanticipated shocks."

5.171 India responds that its monetary authorities had to change their monetary policy goals in the latter part of 1997 in order to defend the rupee during this period and argues that they would not have taken such actions if there had not been a threat of a serious decline in monetary reserves. Moreover, it contends that there are different ways to measure reserve adequacy. In this regard, it points to the answers of the IMF, where the IMF states that "A considerable degree of subjective judgment is involved in an assessment of the adequacy of the level and rate of changes of reserves". According to India, there are four other methods of assessing reserve adequacy:

(a) import coverage of at least 6 months: US$22 billion;

(b) import coverage of three months plus 50% of debt service payments plus one months' imports and exports to account for leads and lags: more than US$22 billion;

[350] The IMF relied on Indian balance-of-payments data as of 21 November 1997, which was closest date to the date of the establishment of the Panel for which the relevant Indian balance-of-payments data were available.

[351] The IMF statistics exclude gold.

(c) short-term debt and portfolio stock should not exceed 60% of reserves and incremental short-term debt and portfolio liabilities should be accompanied by equivalent increases in reserves: more than US$27 billion; and

(d) foreign assets to currency ratio should not be less than 40% and a desirable level would be 70%: US$16 billion (minimum); US$28 billion (desirable).

5.172 In evaluating the evidence and arguments presented by the parties, we note India's argument that its monetary authorities changed their monetary policy goals in the latter part of 1997 to defend the rupee. However, the Indian authorities' action does not in itself demonstrate that there was a serious decline in India's monetary reserves or a threat thereof during that period, in terms of Article XVIII:9(a).

5.173 The question before us is whether India was facing a serious decline or threat thereof in its reserves (Article XVIII:9(a)) or had inadequate reserves (Article XVIII:9(b)). In analyzing India's situation in terms of Article XVIII:9(a), it is important to bear in mind that the issue is whether India was facing or threatened with a *serious* decline in its monetary reserves. Whether or not a decline of a given size is serious or not must be related to the initial state and adequacy of the reserves. A large decline need not necessarily be a serious one if the reserves are more than adequate. Accordingly, it is appropriate to consider the adequacy of India's reserves for purposes of Article XVIII:9(a), as well as for Article XVIII:9(b).

5.174 In this connection, we recall that the IMF reported that India's reserves as of 21 November 1997 were US$ 25.1 billion and that an adequate level of reserves at that date would have been US$ 16 billion. While the Reserve Bank of India did not specify a precise level of what would constitute adequacy, it concluded only three months earlier in August 1997 that India's reserves were "well above the thumb rule of reserve adequacy" and although the Bank did not accept that thumb rule as the only measure of adequacy, it also found that "[b]y any criteria, the level of foreign exchange reserves appears comfortable". It also stated that "the reserves would be adequate to withstand both cyclical and unanticipated shocks".

5.175 We have also considered the four alternative methods of assessing reserve adequacy cited by India. We note that India concedes that its reserves of US$25.1 billion would have been adequate under two of the alternatives (a and b). Under a third alternative (d), the reserves of US$25.1 billion were at the higher end of the range between the minimum (US$16 billion) and desirable (US$28 billion) reserve levels. Under the fourth method (c), reserves of US$27 billion would be considered adequate. While it might be following a prudential approach in suggesting method (c), India does not explain why it would be superior to the IMF method or to the other three Indian alternatives under which reserves could be considered adequate. Moreover, India's alternatives do not seem to be consistent with the approach of the Reserve Bank of India quoted above.

5.176 Having weighed the evidence before us, we note that only one of the four methods suggested by India for measuring reserve adequacy supports a finding that India's reserves are inadequate, and even under that method, the issue is a close one (US$25.1 billion vs. US$27 billion, or less than 10 per cent difference). Overall, we are of the view that the quality and weight of evidence is strongly in favour of the proposition that India's reserves are not inadequate. In particular, this position is supported by the IMF, the Reserve Bank of India and three of the four methods suggested by India. Accordingly, we find that India's reserves were not inadequate as of 18 November 1997.

5.177 Turning now to the question of whether India was facing a serious decline or threat thereof in its reserves, it is appropriate to consider the evolution of its reserves in the period prior to November 1997. As noted above, as of 31 March 1996, India's reserves were US$17 billion; as of 31 March 1997, India's reserves were US$22.4 billion. We note that at the time of the BOP Committee's consultations with India in January and June 1997, the IMF reported that India did not face a serious decline in its reserves or a threat thereof. As of 21 November 1997, India's reserves had risen to US$25.1 billion and the IMF continued to be of the view that India did not face a serious decline in its reserves or a threat thereof. In our view, in light of the foregoing evidence, and taking into account the provisions of Article XV:2, as of the date of establishment of the Panel, India was not facing a serious decline or a threat of a serious decline in monetary reserves as those terms are used in Article XVIII:9(a). In the event that it might be deemed relevant to add support to our findings concerning India's reserves as of November 1997, we have also examined the evolution of India's reserves after November 1997. We note that India's reserves fluctuated around the November level in subsequent months, falling to a low of US$23.9 billion in December 1997 and rising to a high of US$26.2 billion in April 1998. They were US$24.1 billion as of the end of June 1998.

5.178 The anticipated evolution of India's reserves after June 1998 shows that no serious decline was foreseen. Indeed, in response to a question as to whether there had been developments since November 1997 that could lead to a modification of the IMF's answers to the Panel's questions, the IMF responded:

> "There has been a deterioration in the economic outlook and market sentiment over the past few months, and short-term risks have increased. [...] [O]n the basis of developments thus far, the balance-of-payments situation is expected to worsen and a decline in reserves ($2½-4 billion) is anticipated for 1998/99. Nevertheless, it remains the Fund view that the external situation can be managed using macroeconomic policy instruments and that quantitative restrictions are not needed for balance-of-payments adjustment."

Thus, not only the evolution until June 1998, but also assessments in relation to 1998 as a whole and 1999 support the view that no threat of serious decline existed as of November 1997.

5.179 As a result, the evolution of India's reserve situation in the seven months after November 1997 does not, in our view, call into question our conclusion that as of the date of the establishment of the Panel, India was not facing a serious decline or a threat of a serious decline in its monetary reserves as those terms are used in Article XVIII:9(a).

5.180 Accordingly, we find that as of the date of establishment of this Panel, there was not a serious decline or a threat of a serious decline in India's monetary reserves, as those terms are used in Article XVIII:9(a).

(ii) Article XVIII:9(b)

5.181 The issue to be decided under Article XVIII:9(b) is whether India's balance-of-payments measures fall into the category of those "necessary ... in the case of a Member with inadequate monetary reserves, to achieve a reasonable rate of increase in its reserves". In deciding this issue, we must weigh the evidence favouring India against that favouring the United States and determine whether on the basis of all evidence before the Panel, the United States has established its claim under Article XVIII:11 that India does not meet the conditions specified in Article XVIII:9(b).

5.182 The United States relies upon the views of the IMF and the statement of the Reserve Bank of India, as cited in paragraph 5.170 above. As noted therein, in the view of the IMF, as of 18 November 1997 an adequate level of monetary reserves for India was US$16 billion. As noted above in paragraph 5.171, India suggests use of four other ways of measuring the adequacy of its reserves, which lead to a calculation of adequate reserves being between US$16 and US$28 billion.

5.183 For the reasons outlined in paragraphs 5.174-5.176 above, we find that as of the date of establishment of this Panel, India's monetary reserves of US$25.1 billion were not inadequate as that term is used in Article XVIII:9(b) and that India was therefore not entitled to implement balance-of-payments measures to achieve a reasonable rate of growth in its reserves.

(e) Summary

5.184 We find that, as of the date of establishment of this Panel, India's balance-of-payments measures were not necessary to forestall the threat of, or to stop, a serious decline in its monetary reserves and that its reserves were not inadequate. As a result, its measures were not necessary and therefore "exceed those necessary" under the terms of Article XVIII:9 (a) or (b). Therefore, India would appear to be in violation of the requirements of Article XVIII:11 by maintaining its measures. However, a Note Ad Article XVIII:11 specifies that a Member need not remove its balance-of-payments measures, if such removal would thereupon produce conditions justifying their reinstitution. Moreover, a proviso to Article XVIII:11 states that a Member shall not be required to withdraw balance-of-payments measures on the grounds that a change in its development policy would render them unnecessary. Accordingly, we now turn to an examination of the Ad Note and the proviso of Article XVIII:11.

3. Is India Entitled under the Ad Note to Article XVIII:11 to Maintain Measures for Balance-of-Payments Purposes when the Conditions Contemplated in Article XVIII:9 are no Longer Met?

5.185 India argues that it should not be required to remove its quantitative restrictions immediately, even if it were found that it currently does not experience balance-of-payments difficulties within the meaning of Article XVIII:9, because immediate removal would create the conditions for their reinstitution. India's argument is based on the Note Ad Article XVIII:11. The United States argues that those conditions are not met and that, since India does not experience any current balance-of-payments difficulties, it should disinvoke Article XVIII:B, with the possibility of invoking it again if such difficulties were to occur in the future. The United States recalls that the terms of Article XVIII:4 show that balance-of-payments measures must be temporary.

5.186 The arguments of the parties raise three questions: (a) Does the Ad Note cover situations where the conditions of Article XVIII:9 are no longer met? (b) What conditions must be met in order to allow for the maintenance of measures under the Ad Note? (c) Are these conditions met in the present case? We examine these three questions successively.

(a) Does the *Ad* Note cover situations where the conditions of Article XVIII:9 are no longer met?

5.187 We recall that the Note Ad Article XVIII:11 reads as follows:

> "The second sentence in paragraph 11 shall not be interpreted to mean that a Member is required to relax or remove restrictions if such relaxation or removal would thereupon produce conditions justifying the intensification or institution, respectively, of restrictions under paragraph 9 of Article XVIII."

5.188 It seems clear to us that the use of the word "respectively" in this provision allows the sentence to be read to refer to two situations, so that the second sentence of paragraph 11 should not be interpreted to mean (i) that a Member is required to relax restrictions if such relaxation would thereupon produce conditions justifying the intensification of restrictions under paragraph 9 of Article XVIII or (ii) that a Member is required to remove restrictions if such removal would thereupon produce conditions justifying the institution of restrictions under paragraph 9 of Article XVIII.

5.189 The ordinary meaning of the words therefore suggests that the Ad Note could cover situations where the conditions of Article XVIII:9 are no longer met but are threatened. This would make it possible for a developing country having validly instituted measures for balance-of-payments purposes and whose situation has sufficiently improved so that the conditions of Article XVIII:9 are no longer fulfilled, not to eliminate the remaining measures if this would result in the reoccurrence of the conditions which had justified their institution in the first place.

5.190 This appears consistent with the context of the provision, in particular with the general requirement of gradual relaxation of measures as balance-of-payments conditions improve, under Article XVIII:11. The notion of "gradual relaxation" contained in Article XVIII:11 should itself be read in context, together with Article XVIII:9. Article XVIII:9 requires that the measures taken shall not "exceed those necessary" to address the balance-of-payments situation justifying them. The institution and maintenance of balance-of-payments measures is only justified at the level necessary to address the concern, and cannot be more encompassing. Paragraph 11, in this context, confirms this requirement that the measures be limited to what is necessary and addresses more specifically the conditions of evolution of the measures as balance-of-payments conditions improve: at any given time, the restrictions should not exceed those necessary. This implies that as conditions improve, measures must be relaxed in proportion to the improvements. The logical conclusion of the process is that the measures will be eliminated when conditions no longer justify them.

5.191 The Ad Note clarifies that the relaxation or removal should not result in a worsening of the balance-of-payments situation such as to justify strengthened or new measures. It thus seeks to avoid a situation where a developing country would be required to remove the measures, foreseeing that in doing so, it will create the conditions for their reinstitution. In light also of the need to restore equilibrium of the balance-of-payments on a sound and lasting basis, acknowledged in the first sentence of Article XVIII:11, it appears that removal should be made when the conditions actually allow for it. In this sense, we can agree with India that the developing country Member applying the measures is not required to follow a "stop-and-go" policy. It is worth noting, however, that in circumstances where the balance-of-payments situation has gradually improved, if measures have been gradually relaxed as conditions improved under the terms of Article XVIII:11 and maintained only to the extent necessary under the terms of Article XVIII:9, it could be anticipated that only a minor portion of the measures initially instituted would remain to be removed by the time the balance-of-payments conditions have improved to the extent that the country faces neither a serious decline in monetary reserves or a threat thereof, or inadequate reserves. The elimination of these measures would thus constitute the final stage of a gradual relaxation and elimination.

5.192 We therefore conclude that the Note Ad Article XVIII:11 could apply to both situations where balance-of-payments difficulties still exist and when they have ceased to exist but are threatened to return. It is therefore possible for India to invoke the existence of such risk in order to justify the maintenance of the measures. However, this possibility is available only to the extent that the conditions foreseen in the Ad Note are fulfilled. We must therefore determine what these conditions are before examining whether they are fulfilled in this instance.

(b) Conditions to be met to allow for the maintenance of measures under the Ad Note

5.193 We recall that the Ad Note provides that the second sentence of Article XVIII:11 shall not be interpreted to require relaxation or removal of measures "*if such relaxation or removal would thereupon produce conditions justifying the intensification or institution, respectively, of restrictions under paragraph 9 of Article XVIII.*"

5.194 Three elements thus appear to be contemplated in this text:

(i) that conditions justifying the intensification or institution, respectively, of restrictions under paragraph 9 of Article XVIII would occur

(ii) that the relaxation or removal of the measures *would produce* occurrence of these conditions

(iii) the relaxation or removal would *thereupon* produce these conditions.

5.195 The first two conditions appear to be quite clear. The expression "conditions justifying the intensification or institution, respectively, of restrictions under paragraph 9 of Article XVIII" would seem to refer necessarily to the two situations envisaged in paragraph 9, i.e. (a) a threat of or a serious decline in monetary reserves or (b) inadequate monetary reserves. We have determined in the previous section that the Ad Note covers situations where these circumstances would not currently exist but would reoccur. The second element ("would produce") states the requirement of a causal link between the occurrence of these conditions and the removal. The assessment of the existence of the conditions foreseen in the Ad Note thus requires a prospective assessment of whether, if the measures were relaxed or removed, this relaxation or removal would *result* in the conditions of paragraph 9 reoccurring (in cases where they do not currently exist).

5.196 The text further foresees that the relaxation or removal would "thereupon" produce the conditions. This term requires further interpretation. Dictionary definitions of the term "thereupon" are "upon that or it", "on that being done or said", "(directly) after that", "in consequence of that"[352], "immediately" or "at once".[353] While several variations of meaning can be identified in those definitions, we are of the view that the most appropriate meaning should be "immediately". In particular, we note that this interpretation is consistent with, and arguably compelled by the Spanish and French versions of the Agreement ("inmediatamente" and "immédiatement", respectively). The context of the term tends to confirm this choice. If "thereupon" had been intended to mean only "in consequence of that",

[352] *New Shorter Oxford English Dictionary* (1993), p. 3275.

[353] *Webster's New Encyclopedic Dictionary* (1993), p. 1075.

the word would not have been necessary. The causality between the removal of the measures and the occurrence of the "conditions" is clear without that word.[354]

5.197 We conclude that, in order to give an effect to the word "thereupon", we have to interpret it as meaning "immediately". We do not consider that our interpretation would introduce an additional condition to Article XVIII:9, nor would it be contrary to the purpose of Article XVIII:B. In particular, bearing in mind that the conditions foreseen for the institution of balance-of-payments measures by developed countries under Article XII are not the same as those applicable to developing countries under Article XVIII:B, we note that saying that removal would thereupon produce the conditions of Article XVIII:9 does not imply that we would introduce in that paragraph the condition of "imminent" threat found in Article XII, but not in Article XVIII.[355] "Produce *immediately* conditions such that action is necessary to forestall a threat" is not the same as "produce conditions such that action is necessary to forestall an *imminent* threat". We mean that those conditions would have to appear immediately, and that they would have to be of the type and degree contemplated in Article XVIII:9. Our interpretation implies that not every balance-of-payments difficulty that might occur as the Liberalisation process continues could be considered as falling within the scope of the Note Ad Article XVIII:11. The location of the term in the sentence shows in our opinion that "thereupon" refers to the situation where re-occurrence of the conditions justifying balance-of-payments measures would immediately follow removal of the measures.

5.198 This is in our view the only useful meaning possible for the word "thereupon". Other interpretations, in addition to being contrary to the principles of interpretation followed in this paragraph and the paragraphs above, could in practice turn the provision into providing a means to maintain balance-of-payments indefinitely, which would be contrary to the objective of Articles XVIII:4, XVIII:9 and the Ad Note, as well as contrary to the object and purpose of the WTO Agreement. Our interpretation of the term "thereupon" as a notion of time is also consistent with the structure of the sentence which deals with the moment when measures may have to be removed. We do not mean that the term "thereupon" should necessarily mean within the days or weeks following the relaxation or removal of the measures; this would be unrealistic, even though in-

---

[354] In this regard, we note that in its report on *Japan-Taxes on Alcoholic Beverages*, Op. Cit., at p. 106, the Appellate Body recalled that:

> "A fundamental tenet of treaty interpretation flowing from the general rules of interpretation set out in Article 31 is the principle of effectiveness (*ut res magis valeat quam pereat*). [...] [O]ne of the corollaries of the general rules of interpretation in the Vienna Convention is that interpretation must give meaning and effect to all the terms of the treaty. An interpreter is not free to adopt a reading that would result in reducing whole clauses of paragraphs of a treaty to redundancy or inutility".

[355] See India's argument highlighting the absence of requirement of an "imminent" threat under Article XVIII:11, Section III.D.3 *supra*, para. 3.180).

stances of very rapid deterioration of balance-of-payments conditions could occur. We consider that the purpose of this word is to ensure that measures are not maintained because of some distant possibility that a balance-of-payments difficulty may occur, which would be possible if India's interpretation was accepted.

5.199 We therefore conclude that, in order to be allowed to maintain the measures at issue, it must be determined that one of the conditions contemplated in sub-paragraphs (a) and (b) of Article XVIII:9 would appear immediately after the removal of the measures, and a causal link must be established between the anticipated reoccurrence of the conditions of Article XVIII:9 and the removal. It should be noted that the text requires more than a mere possibility of reoccurrence of the conditions ("*would* produce"). The Ad Note therefore allows for the maintenance of measures on the basis only of clearly identified circumstances, and not on the basis of a general possibility of worsening of balance-of-payments conditions after the measures have been removed. Such an interpretation could lead to the maintenance of balance-of-payments measures for indefinite periods, as it could almost always be argued that there exists a risk of worsening of balance-of-payments conditions at some time in the future. This would be in contradiction with the terms of the second sentence of Article XVIII:11 and the principle expressed in Article XVIII:4 that balance-of-payments measures should be temporary. Our interpretation is of course without prejudice to the possibility of institution of measures for balance-of-payments purposes if the circumstances should justify such measures again.

5.200 Having determined the conditions under which measures can be maintained in accordance with the Ad Note to Article XVIII:11, we now examine whether these conditions are fulfilled in this instance.

(c) Are the conditions contemplated in the Ad Note met in this case?

5.201 We have determined that under the Note Ad Article XVIII, three aspects have to be taken into account: (i) that a situation contemplated in Article XVIII:9 (a) or (b) would occur; (ii) that such situation would occur immediately after the removal or the relaxation of the measures at issue and (iii) that such a situation be causally linked to the removal. We recall that we have already determined that India did not face the situation foreseen in Article XVIII:9 as of the date of establishment of the panel. The question here is to determine whether the removal of the measures would immediately produce such conditions so as to justify India's maintenance of the measures at issue under this provision.

5.202 The United States' argument that India does not meet the conditions contained in the Ad Note and is not entitled to a phase-out period may be summarized as follows. First, it notes that India told the BOP Committee in 1994 that if its balance-of-payments showed sustained improvement, India's aim was to move by 1996/97 to a regime in which import licensing restrictions would only be maintained for environmental reasons. The United States notes that India's reserves increased from US$20.3 billion in 1994 to US$25.0 billion in 1997. Second, the United States recalls the statements by the IMF in the January 1997 BOP Committee consultations to the effect that India's "external situation can be well managed using macroeconomic policy instruments without recourse to QRs", that "India should be able to meet all external payments requirements without difficulties, and to weather the consequences of potential external shocks without undue disruption", and that "the removal of quantitative restrictions, in conjunction with other measures, could be expected [*inter alia*] to strengthen the external position over the medium term". Third, the United States notes the IMF statement at the June 1997 BOP Committee consultations that "[i]t remains the Fund's view that the external situation can be well managed using macroeconomic policy instruments alone, [quantitative restrictions] are not needed for balance-of-payments adjustment".

5.203 In addition, the United States notes that the IMF's answers to questions 3 and 5 of the Panel support its position that India does not meet the conditions in the Ad Note. In this regard, we note that in response to Panel Question 3 on whether relaxation or removal of India's restrictions as of 18 November 1997 would have been likely to produce thereupon the conditions specified in the Ad Note, the IMF repeated the view it had already expressed before the Committee and further stated:

> "A time-bound program for eliminating the remaining QRs over a relatively short period would reduce distortions to investment and promote an efficient, export-oriented consumer goods sector."

5.204 In reply to Panel Question 5 concerning the impact of immediately removing quantitative restrictions on India's development policy, the IMF stated:

> "Some problems in import substituting sectors and a temporary decline in reserves cannot be ruled out in the event India immediately removed the remaining QRs. ... However, there would also be considerable benefits to such a move, if it were implemented in a phased manner over a relatively short period. First, increased customs revenue from the tariffs applied to previously restricted consumer goods imports would contribute toward deficit reduction and could provide the necessary resources for essential spending in infrastructure and the social sectors. Second, a more competitive, efficient, and quality-conscious consumer goods sector could contribute strongly to export growth. Finally, the structural measures advocated in response to question 3 would improve the allocation of investment, promote efficiency, and enhance the growth prospects of the economy."

5.205 In analyzing whether the United States has provided sufficient evidence to establish that the conditions foreseen in the Ad Note are not met in this case, we consider the US position in light of the responses thereto by India.

5.206 In commenting on the IMF answer to Question 3, India first notes that the IMF admits in answering Question 5 that there may be a temporary decline in reserves on removal of its balance-of-payments restrictions and that the IMF endorses removal of the restrictions in a "relatively short period of time", not immediately. As we noted earlier (paragraph 5.173), a decline in reserves does not necessarily mean that balance-of-payments restrictions may be imposed consistently with Article XVIII:9; one must examine the size of the decline in relation to the stock of reserves. We do not believe that the possibility of some decline in reserves calls into question the IMF's conclusion that the removal of the measures would not thereupon produce the conditions foreseen in the Ad Note. Nor does the IMF condition its conclusion on the use of a phase-out as opposed to an immediate lifting of the restrictions. However, we note that the IMF suggests that it would be advisable from the standpoint of adjustment in the Indian economy as a whole - as opposed to the standpoint of managing India's monetary reserves -, for the restrictions to be removed within a relatively short period of time, rather than immediately. We view this as a matter of how India should implement an adverse DSB ruling or recommendation, as opposed to a justification for maintaining its balance-of-payments restrictions. We discuss this issue below in Section VII.

5.207 Second, according to India, the removal of import restrictions would certainly lead to an increase in imports, although the magnitude of the increase would depend upon a number of factors. India notes, however, that if the percentage share of products that are currently subject to import restrictions rises to the level reached by products that are no longer subject to such restrictions, the additional import bill from the removal of import restrictions would have been approximately US$30.6 billion in 1996-1997, as compared to the total merchandise import bill for that year of US$ 43.5 billion. Moreover, India argues that private transfers and investment flows which in the recent past have helped to finance the increase in imports may not be adequate to do so in the future. While we agree that the removal of restrictions will lead to an increase in imports over time, we do not consider that the information presented by India about possible future problems establishes that conditions justifying reimposition of balance-of-payments measures would occur immediately on lifting the current balance-of-payments measures. We note in this respect that India does not appear always to take into account the distinction between a projected change in imports and a projected change in its reserves. Expecting a surge in imports is not sufficient to establish that the conditions of Article XVIII:9 will immediately reoccur. India does not give much attention to the potentially favourable effects on India's balance-of-payments following the removal of import restrictions, such as the attraction of foreign capital into the distribution of consumer goods and other service industries, stating instead that private transfers and investments flows may be inadequate in the future.

5.208 Third, India argues that the robust growth in non-oil imports in the past couple of years is partially attributable to the surge in consumer goods imports as a result of the removal of import restrictions on some consumer goods. In its comments to the IMF answers to Question 5, India expands on this point to note the problems of transitional adjustment that removal of balance-of-payments restrictions may cause in its consumer goods industry. We note, however, that problems of structural adjustment to import competition are not *per se* justifications for balance-of-payments measures. The WTO Agreement on Safeguards has established rules for dealing with such problems. Moreover, we note that Article XVIII:C of GATT 1994 also allows developing countries to adopt, under certain conditions, measures to promote the establishment of a particular industry.

5.209 Fourth, India notes that in response to Questions 3 and 5, the IMF suggests various other policy reforms that India should implement. We agree with India that pursuant to the proviso to the second sentence of Article XVIII:11, India cannot be required to change its development policy so as to render balance-of-payments measures unnecessary. Initially, we note that our finding that India's balance-of-payments measures are unnecessary in terms of Article XVIII:9 does not assume that there will be any change in India's development policy. Rather, that conclusion is based on our consideration of the factors specified in Article XVIII:9 (e.g., the level of India's reserves). In considering India's comments on the IMF's reply to our questions, we address in the next section (paragraphs 5.216-5.223) India's objections to the IMF 's statement that it could use macroeconomic policy instruments to avoid balance-of-payments problems. We address in this section India's arguments related to the IMF's reference in its reply to Question 3 to "structural measures". In that regard, we note that the IMF stated: "The macroeconomic policy instruments would need to be complemented by structural measures such as scaling back reservations on certain products for small-scale units and pushing ahead with agricultural reforms." It is not clear that the IMF has linked the structural measures to the balance-of-payments situation.

5.210 We note that India made general claims that implementation of the IMF's views would require a change in its development policy at several points in this proceeding.[356] Although invocation of the proviso is in the nature of an affirmative defence to be established by India, India's arguments on development policy have been expressed in very general terms. However, India addresses the issue in some more detail in its comments on the IMF's reply to Question 3.[357] In those comments, India states that it "has been autonomously engaged in a programme of economic reform". Thus, it appears that India's development policy now envisages some changes and reforms. However, India does not explain how the IMF's suggestions are not consistent with its development policy, except to say that the "pace of change cannot be forced" and that "a period of transition is necessary for structural reforms of this nature".

5.211 The IMF's suggestions on "structural measures" should not be taken in isolation from the context in which they are made. We recall that the IMF began its reply to Question 3 by stating that India's "external situation can be managed by using macroeconomic policy instruments alone". Its comments on structural measures appear only at the end of its answer after it has suggested other liberalization measures, such as tariff reductions. The adoption by India of "structural

[356] Section III.D.7 at paras. 3.232-3.235.

[357] Section III.D.9(c)(iii) at paras. 3.398-3.401.

measures" is not suggested as a condition for preserving India's reserve position. Thus, we cannot conclude that the removal of India's balance-of-payment measures would thereupon lead to conditions justifying their reinstitution that could be avoided only by a change in India's development policy.

5.212 Finally, India points to several other factors that may lead to a worsening of its reserve position in the future. For example, it cites the South-East Asia currency crisis which it argues almost certainly will affect India's export competitiveness, as well as the legislatively mandated imposition of economic sanctions on India and the postponement of fresh approvals of bilateral and multilateral assistance as a result of its recent nuclear test which it argues will affect inflows of foreign capital. We note that the sanctions and assistance postponements had not occurred and were not foreseen as of the date of establishment of the Panel, which is the date at which we have assessed the consistency of India's measures with its GATT obligations. In addition, the magnitude and implications of the South-East Asia currency crisis were not fully developed or foreseen at that time. In this regard, we recall that we considered the evolution of India's reserve situation from November 1997 through June 1998 and concluded that it did not call into question our findings on Article XVIII:9 (see paragraphs 5.177-5.179).

5.213 We have weighed the foregoing evidence and considered the arguments of the parties. In determining whether the requirements of the Ad Note are met, we must bear in mind that it refers to prospective events, i.e., if a certain action is taken, will one of certain specified conditions occur. When dealing with the future, there can be no certainty. Instead, we must satisfy ourselves with probabilities. In order to meet the requirements of the Ad Note ("would produce"), the probability of occurrence of the conditions would have to be clear. We must also bear in mind our conclusion that the Ad Note requires the specified conditions (i.e., those specified in Article XVIII:9(a) and (b)) to manifest themselves immediately as a result of the removal.

5.214 In our view, on the basis of the evidence before the Panel, the immediate removal by India of the measures at issue may generate some potential decline of reserves and adjustment difficulties. In relation to such adjustment difficulties, we note that the IMF suggests a phase-out over a short period of time. However, with regard to the potential decline in reserves, there is no evidence that such a decline would be of the magnitude required by Article XVIII:9 to allow the imposition of balance-of-payments measures.

5.215 Consequently, we find that, while India could in principle invoke the Note Ad Article XVIII:11 even when the conditions contemplated in Article XVIII:9 are no longer met, the information available to the Panel leads to the conclusion that a removal of the measures at issue would not immediately produce conditions justifying the re-imposition of import restrictions for balance-of-payments reasons. We therefore find that the measures at issue maintained by India are not justified by reference to the Note Ad Article XVIII:11. However, we must now consider whether India is entitled under the proviso to Article XVIII:11 to maintain these measures.

4. *Is India Entitled to Maintain its Balance-of-Payments Measures on the Basis of the Proviso to Article XVIII:11?*

5.216 Article XVIII:11 contains a proviso as follows: "[n]o Member shall be required to withdraw or modify restrictions on the ground that a change it its development policy would render unnecessary the restrictions which it is applying under [Article XVIII:B]". India argues that some of the statements made by the IMF, in particular its response to Questions 3 and 5, suggest that the IMF position that there is no current justification for India's balance-of-payments measures is based on the assumption that India should change its development policy. We respond to certain aspects of this argument in paragraphs 5.209-5.211 *supra*. In this section, we address in particular India's arguments that the IMF's statement that its reserve levels can be managed through monetary policy instruments reflects the same assumption. India notes that while it is true that the Reserve Bank of India raised interest rates in 1997 in a successful defence of the value of the rupee, the increase had a negative impact on the Indian economy.

5.217 In analyzing India's argument, we note that we must consider the proviso to Article XVIII:11 in light of the first sentence of Article XVIII:11, which provides that "[i]n carrying out its domestic policies, the Member concerned shall pay due regard to the need for restoring equilibrium in its balance of payments on a sound and lasting basis and to the desirability of assuring an economic employment of productive resources."

5.218 We recall that our finding that India's balance-of-payments measures are unnecessary in terms of Article XVIII:9 does not assume that there will be any change in India's development policy. Rather, that conclusion is based on our consideration of the factors specified in Article XVIII:9 (e.g., the level of India's reserves). Here, we consider whether our conclusion in the preceding section that those measures are not justified either by reference to the Note Ad Article XVIII:11 is based on the assumption that conditions justifying reinstitution of those measures can be avoided by policies that would require changes in India's development policy, contrary to the proviso to Article XVIII:11.

5.219 Since India's reference to the proviso to Article XVIII:11 is in the nature of an affirmative defence, we would have expected India to provide sufficient arguments and evidence to prove it. However, India did not supply convincing evidence that the removal of its balance-of-payments measures would generate balance-of-payments problems, within the meaning of Article XVIII:9, the avoidance or prevention of which would imply changes in its economic policy which, themselves, would require changes in its development policy in the sense of the proviso. India addresses the IMF replies and the impact of the removal of the measures only in general terms.

5.220 In our consideration of India's argument, we note that India has in the past used macroeconomic policy instruments to defend the rupee (see paragraph 5.172), suggesting that the use of macroeconomic policy instruments as mentioned by the IMF would not necessarily constitute a change in India's development policy. Moreover, India has not been precise in specifying what it considers to be its development policy in the terms of the proviso.

5.221 India argues in its reply of 6 July 1998 to Question 5 posed by the Panel that the removal of quantitative restrictions would cause decreased use of industrial capacity and increased unemployment. It argues that this result would be inconsistent with the "economic employment of productive resources" (Article XVIII:11, first sentence). This phrase in Article XVIII:11 refers to domestic policies: import restrictions cannot be regarded as domestic policies. Thus, Article XVIII:B does not allow the retention of balance-of-payments measures to support the use of industrial capacity or reduce unemployment. Furthermore, the Panel is not persuaded that the removal of import restrictions would, in fact, cause reduced use of industrial capacity in the economy as a whole, or cause increased unemployment. Reducing barriers to imports may lead to decreased activity in some domestic industries but to increased activity in others.

5.222 We therefore conclude that India is not entitled to maintain its balance-of-payments measures on the basis of the proviso to Article XVIII:11. We note, however, that our findings do not preclude the possibility that adjustments to domestic policies (other than development policies) embraced by the first sentence of Article XVIII:11 may be necessary or prudent from time to time.

5.223 Having determined that India's measures are not necessary under the terms of Article XVIII:9 and are not justified under the terms of the Note Ad Article XVIII:11, we must now examine the other potential justifications advanced by India for the maintenance of its measures.

5. *Right to Maintain Balance-of-Payments Measures until they are Found to be Inconsistent by the General Council and the Right to a Phase-Out of Balance-of-Payments Measures*

(a) Article XVIII:12(c)(i) and (ii)

5.224 India claims that a Member invoking a balance-of-payments justification is entitled to maintain the measures until the General Council, following a recommendation from the BOP Committee, requires it to modify or remove them under Article XVIII:12(c)(i) or (ii). India further claims that this provision confirms the existence of a "right to a phase-out" for measures which no longer meet the criteria set out in Article XVIII:9, by providing for a "specified period of time" to be granted to secure compliance with the relevant provisions when an inconsistency has been identified.

5.225 The United States claims that Article XVIII:12(c)(ii) does not provide a basis for a gradual reduction of measures that do not have a balance of payments justification and that this interpretation is consistent with the wording of the first sentence of Article XVIII:12(c)(ii) which uses the phrase "restrictions are being applied in a manner involving an inconsistency".

5.226 We have already considered India's argument that under Article XVIII:12 it is entitled to maintain its balance-of-payments measures until requested to remove them by the General Council, and for the reasons explained in Section D of these findings, we have not accepted it.[358]

5.227 India also argues that Article XVIII:12(c)(ii) confirms the existence of a right to a phase-out for measures no longer justified by current balance-of-payments difficulties. We note that Article XVIII.12(c)(ii), provides a specific mechanism in order for the BOP Committee to address possible violations of the provisions of, *inter alia*, Article XVIII:B and provides for a period of time to be granted to the Member in order to implement the requirement to remove or modify the inconsistent measures. In the situation envisaged by Article XVIII:12(c)(ii), a period of time is granted when an inconsistency with the provisions of either Article XVIII:B or Article XIII has been identified. The period of time which is allocated to the Member in order to bring its measures into conformity is thus comparable, but not identical, to an implementation period of the sort provided for in Article 21.3 of the DSU. However, this specific mode of determination of the "implementation" period applies to procedures initiated under Article XVIII:12(c), which is not the procedure under which this Panel is acting. We consider the issue of whether a phase-out would be appropriate in this case in our suggestions in respect of implementation, where we note this provision of Article XVIII:12(c)(ii).

5.228 We therefore conclude that Article XVIII:12(c) does not entitle India to maintain measures which no longer meet the criteria of Article XVIII:9 and are not covered by the Note Ad Article XVIII:11.

(b) Paragraphs 1 and 13 of the 1994 Understanding

5.229 Paragraph 1 of the 1994 Understanding provides:

> "Members confirm their commitment to announce publicly, as soon as possible, time-schedules for the removal of restrictive import measures taken for balance-of-payments purposes. It is understood that such time-schedules may be modified as appropriate to take into account changes in the balance-of-payments situation. Whenever a time-schedule is not publicly announced by a Member, that Member shall provide justification as to the reasons therefor."

5.230 Paragraph 13 of the 1994 Understanding further provides:

> "The Committee shall report on its consultations to the General Council. When full consultation procedures have been used, the report should indicate the Committee's conclusions on the different elements of the plan for consultations, as well as the facts and rea-

[358] See *supra* in section V.D.4.(b)(ii) the discussion on the right to maintain balance-of-payments measures (paras. 5.76-5.80).

> sons on which they are based. The Committee shall endeavour to include in its conclusions proposals for recommendations aimed at promoting the implementation of Articles XII and XVIII:B, the 1979 Declaration and this Understanding. In those cases in which a time-schedule has been presented for the removal of restrictive measures taken for balance-of-payments purposes, the General Council may recommend that, in adhering to such a time-schedule, a Member shall be deemed to be in compliance with its GATT 1994 obligations. Whenever the General Council has made specific recommendations, the rights and obligations of Members shall be assessed in the light of such recommendations. In the absence of specific proposals for recommendations by the General Council, the Committee's conclusions should record the different views expressed in the Committee. When simplified consultation procedures have been used, the report shall include a summary of the main elements discussed in the Committee and a decision on whether full consultation procedures are required."

5.231 During its 1997 consultations, India presented a time-schedule for the Committee to consider. This time-schedule was not approved, as consensus was not reached.[359] The commitment to present a time-schedule to the Committee and, the possibility, if it is approved, of obtaining from the General Council a specific recommendation that the member applying the schedule should be deemed to be in conformity with its obligations under GATT 1994 in carrying out the schedule, are an integral element of BOP Committee procedures. In this sense, it is a specific feature of balance-of-payments consultations, expressly provided for by the Understanding. Had India's time-schedule been approved by the Committee, together with a recommendation that India be deemed in conformity with its obligations in carrying it out, we would then have assessed India's rights and obligations in light of this important factor, in accordance with paragraph 13 of the 1994 Understanding. In this instance, however, although a time-schedule was presented, it was not approved.

5.232 India argues that all members of the Committee, including the United States, accepted the principle of a progressive relaxation, and that all members, except the United States, consider the schedule of progressive relaxation followed by India to be satisfactory. In the view of India, this creates a presumption that India is in conformity with its obligations. We can agree with India that the absence of approval of its time schedule should not in itself adversely affect the status of its measures. However, in the absence of recommendations approving India's proposed time schedule, the Panel is not in a position to substitute its own assessment of the Committee's position for the Committee's absence of consen-

[359] In accordance with the established practice, no vote was requested in the General Council pursuant to Article IX of the Agreement Establishing the World Trade Organization.

sus. The rights and obligations of India must be assessed in the light of the relevant provisions of Article XVIII:B.[360] We are therefore not in a position to give a specific weight to the fact that India presented a time-schedule to the Committee, when this schedule was not approved by the Committee or Council.

5.233 India further argues that paragraphs 1 and 13 of the Understanding provide an incentive for Members to present a time-schedule for removal even when there are no current balance-of-payments difficulties within the meaning of Article XVIII:9, thereby confirming the existence of a "right" to a phase out even in the absence of current balance-of-payments difficulties within the meaning of Article XVIIII:9. The text of paragraph 13 of the Understanding itself does not specify whether the balance-of-payments difficulties which justified the imposition of the measures should still be in existence when a time schedule is presented for their elimination. However, the notion of presentation of a time-schedule, starting when the balance-of-payments difficulties still exist, is consistent with the temporary nature of balance-of-payments measures and with the requirement for their gradual elimination. Also, the time-schedules referred to in paragraphs 1 and 13 of the 1994 Understanding are the same and paragraph 1 specifies that "such time-schedules may be modified as appropriate to take into account changes in the balance-of-payments situation." This suggests that a time-schedule would have to be presented before the balance-of-payments difficulties disappear, otherwise, the reference to "take into account changes in the balance-of-payments situation" would become redundant.

5.234 This does not mean that the General Council has no margin of discretion in deciding whether or not to accept or not a time-schedule that would provide protection to the Member concerned. We have seen that the Ad Note suggests also that measures could, under certain circumstances, be maintained for a time when balance-of-payments difficulties which initially justified their institution are no longer in existence. In addition, paragraph 13 of the 1994 Understanding provides that "the General Council may recommend that, in adhering to such a time-schedule, a Member *may be deemed* to be in compliance with its GATT 1994 obligations" (emphasis added). There is no clear evidence that this phrase has to be interpreted as covering only situations under which a phase-out period would exactly coincide with the gradual disappearance of balance-of-payments difficulties.

5.235 In light of the above, we conclude that the procedure for submission and approval of a time-schedule incorporated in the 1994 Understanding, which is specific to the Committee consultations, does not give WTO Members a "right" to a phase-out period which a panel would have to protect in the absence of balance-of-payments difficulties in the sense of Article XVIII:B.[361] Even assuming

[360] See *supra* in section V.D.4. (b) (ii) the discussion on potential conflicts (paras. 5.92-5.97).

[361] As we note in our suggestions for implementation, a phase-out period typically has been negotiated (see text accompanying footnotes 366-368).

that such a "right" could be recognized under paragraph 13 of the 1994 Understanding, such a recognition would in any case require a prior decision of the General Council.

6. *Conclusion*

5.236 In conclusion, with regard to our examination of the United States' claim of violation by India of Article XVIII:11 and India's defence that its measures are justified under Article XVIII:B, we have found that India's balance-of-payments situation was not such as to allow the maintenance of measures for balance-of-payments purposes under the terms of Article XVIII:9, that India was not justified in maintaining its existing measures under the terms of Article XVIII:11, and that it does not have a right to maintain or phase-out these measures on the basis of other provisions of Article XVIII:B which it invoked in its defence. We therefore conclude that India's measures are not justified under the terms of Article XVIII:B.

5.237 It should be noted that our finding is without prejudice to any future developments in India's balance-of-payments situation which might justify India invoking the provisions Article XVIII:B and the Understanding, should one of the conditions contemplated in Article XVIII:9 be met. It is also without prejudice to the possible determination of a reasonable period of time under Article 21 of the DSU for India to bring its measures into conformity with its obligations under the WTO Agreement.[362]

H. Article 4.2 of the Agreement on Agriculture

5.238 The United States claims that, of the 2,714 HS lines listed as subject to quantitative restrictions in Annex II, Part B of India's 1997 notification of quantitative restrictions, 710 (26%) are products covered by the Agreement on Agriculture. Since processed food, fresh fruits and vegetables, coffee, poultry, and many other agricultural products are consumption goods which could directly satisfy human needs without further processing, India's ban on imports of consumer goods also serves as a form of agricultural protectionism. For the United States, since the IMF has conclusively found that there is no balance-of-payments necessity for India's import restrictions, with respect to these items, India is in violation of its obligations under Article 4.2 of the Agreement on Agriculture.

5.239 India considers that footnote 1 to Article 4.2 of the Agreement on Agriculture makes it clear that Article 4.2 does not extend to measures imposed under the balance-of-payments provisions of GATT 1994. The question of the consistency of India's measures with Article 4.2 depends on their consistency with Article XVIII:B of the GATT 1994. The legal status of India's import restrictions

[362] See *infra* Section VII on "suggestions for implementation."

under the Agreement on Agriculture is consequently identical to that under GATT 1994.

5.240 Article 4.2 of the Agreement on Agriculture provides that "Members shall not maintain, resort to, or revert to any measures of the kind which have been required to be converted into ordinary customs duties [...] ". Footnote 1 to Article 4.2 clarifies that "These measures include quantitative import restrictions [...] discretionary import licensing, non-tariff measures maintained through state-trading enterprises [...] and similar border measures other than ordinary customs duties, whether or not the measures are maintained under country-specific derogations from the provisions of GATT 1947, but not measures maintained under balance-of-payments provisions or under other general, non-agriculture-specific provisions of GATT 1994 or of the other Multilateral Trade Agreements in Annex 1A to the WTO Agreement."

5.241 In paragraph 5.139 above, we found that the measures at issue violate Article XI:1 of the GATT 1994, which is equally applicable to industrialized and agricultural products. In paragraph 5.223 above, we also found that the measures at issue were not justified under Article XVIII:B and violated Article XVIII:11. India did not contest that Article 4.2 was applicable to the agricultural products subject to the measures at issue. We agree with India's claims that the question of the consistency of India's import restrictions with Article 4.2 depends on their consistency with Article XVIII:B. We therefore conclude that the Indian restrictions are not "measures maintained under balance-of-payments provisions" within the meaning of footnote 1 to Article 4.2 of the Agreement on Agriculture.

5.242 Since India does not invoke any of the other exceptions contained in the footnote to Article 4.2, we find that the measures at issue violate Article 4.2 of the Agreement on Agriculture.

I. Article XIII of GATT 1994

5.243 In view of our findings that the measures at issue violate Article XI:1 of GATT 1994 and are not justified under Article XVIII:B, the United States does not request findings under Article XIII of GATT 1994.

J. Nullification or Impairment

5.244 The United States claims that, since India is in violation of its WTO obligations and is not excused by the exception for balance-of-payments import restrictions in Article XVIII:B, nullification or impairment of benefits is presumed, as provided in Article 3.8 of the DSU. In the view of the United States, past GATT panels have regarded violation of Article XI:1 in a special light with regard to nullification or impairment, because of the fundamentally trade-distorting nature of quantitative restrictions.[363]

5.245 India considers that its measures are justified under Article XVIII:B and applied pursuant to its development policy as it conceives it.

5.246 We have found that India's measures at issue violate Articles XI:1 and XVIII:11 of GATT 1994 and Article 4.2 of the Agreement on Agriculture, and that they are not justified under Article XVIII:B of GATT 1994. Since Article 3.8 of the DSU provides that "[i]n cases where there is an infringement of the obligations assumed under a covered agreement, the action is considered *prima facie* to constitute a case of nullification or impairment", we conclude that India's measures have nullified or impaired benefits accruing to the United States under GATT 1994 and the Agreement on Agriculture.

VI. CONCLUSIONS AND RECOMMENDATIONS

6.1 We conclude that

(i) the measures at issue[364] applied by India violate Articles XI:1 and XVIII:11 of GATT 1994 and are not justified by Article XVIII:B;

(ii) the measures at issue, to the extent they apply to products subject to the Agreement on Agriculture, violate Article 4.2 of the Agreement on Agriculture; and

(iii) the measures at issue nullify or impair the benefits of the United States under GATT 1994 and the Agreement on Agriculture.

6.2 We therefore *recommend* that the DSB request India to bring the measures at issue into conformity with its obligations under the WTO Agreement.

VII. SUGGESTIONS FOR IMPLEMENTATION

7.1 Article 19.1 of the DSU provides that in addition to its findings and recommendations, the Panel may suggest ways in which the Member concerned could implement the recommendations. In the light of this provision, we wish to highlight some factors which , in our considered opinion, are relevant to the manner in which India should bring its measures into conformity with its obligations under the WTO Agreement.

7.2 At the outset, we recall that the Preamble to the WTO Agreement recognizes both (i) the desirability of expanding international trade in goods and services and (ii) the need for positive efforts designed to ensure that developing

[363] The United States refer to the Panel Reports *on Japan - Restrictions on Imports of Certain Agricultural Products*, adopted on 2 February 1988, BISD 35S/163, para. 5.4.3, and on *Japanese Measures on Imports of Leather*, adopted on 15/16 May 1984, BISD 31S/94, para. 55.

[364] The "measures at issue" are defined in paragraph 5.122 *supra*.

countries secure a share in international trade commensurate with the needs of their economic development. In implementing these goals, WTO rules promote trade liberalization, but recognize the need for specific exceptions from the general rules to address special concerns, including those of developing countries.

7.3 The process of trade Liberalisation is often fragile and can be interrupted by balance-of-payments problems, even when these problems are not attributable to trade Liberalisation. Liberalisation is also fragile with respect to internal adjustment problems. This fragility suggests an implementation period which is attuned to sustaining support for Liberalisation in the presence of external shocks, and to the internal adjustment process.

7.4 As reflected in our report, we have found that the balance-of-payments measures in question were inconsistent with India's obligations under Articles XI:1 and XVIII:11 of GATT 1994 and Article 4.2 of the Agreement on Agriculture, and therefore recommended that India bring those measures into conformity with its obligations under the WTO Agreement. India has claimed that it is entitled to a phase-out period in connection with the removal of those measures and that it should not be required to eliminate them immediately. We concluded that, under Article XVIII:B and in the circumstances of the case, India had no right to a phase-out of its balance-of-payments restrictions, which the dispute settlement system would have to "preserve" as provided by Article 3.2 of the DSU. However, we wish to stress that our findings and recommendations do not imply that the measures at issue must be removed instantly.

7.5 The DSU provides for "prompt compliance" with recommendations of the DSB, but it contemplates the possibility that it might be impractical for a Member to comply immediately, in which case "the Member shall have a reasonable period of time in which to do so" (Article 21.3). This panel suggests that a reasonable period of time be granted to India in order to remove the import restrictions which are not justified under Article XVIII:B. Normally, the reasonable period of time to implement a panel recommendation, when determined through arbitration, should not exceed fifteen months from the date of adoption of a panel or Appellate Body report. However, this 15-month period is "a "guideline for the arbitrator", not a rule",[365] and as indicated in Article 21.3(c) of the DSU, "that time may be shorter or longer, depending upon the particular circumstances". In light of the factors mentioned above, the panel suggests that the "reasonable period" in this case could be longer than fifteen months. In this regard, the panel would also bring the following points to the attention of the DSB:

> First, while no agreement was reached in the BOP Committee as to the period in which India should remove its measures, we note that India has concluded bilateral agreements with a number of Mem-

[365] Award of the Arbitrator, Arbitration under Article 21.3 (c) of the DSU, *EC Measures concerning Meat and Meat Products (Hormones)*, WT/DS26/15, WT/DS48/13, 28 May 1998, para. 25.

bers providing for a gradual elimination of the measures on an MFN basis.[366]

Second, in a proceeding under Article XVIII:12(c)(ii) or (d), it is provided that in the event that an inconsistency, even of a serious nature, is found, recommendations shall be made requiring the measure to be brought into conformity within a specified period. While not directly applicable in a panel proceeding, it is significant that immediate removal of even seriously inconsistent measures is not required.

Third, the IMF has not recommended immediate removal, but rather a phase-out over a relatively short period of time. As an indication, in 1995, when the balance-of-payments situation of India was more uncertain, the IMF had suggested a transition period of two years.

Fourth, in practice - both prior to and since the entry into force of the WTO Agreement: (a) in the *Korea - Beef* case, in 1989, the panel, following the BOP Committee, recommended that a time schedule be established, this in fact being done at the same time as Korea disinvoked Article XVIII[367]; (b) in a number of later cases where Members have disinvoked Article XVIII, the balance-of-payments measures at issue were phased-out.[368]

7.6 The foregoing factors take an added importance in light of the principle of special and differential treatment. This principle should be highlighted, given that Article 21.2 of the DSU requires that "Particular attention should be paid to matters affecting the interests of developing country Members with respect to measures which have been subject to dispute settlement"[369]

---

[366] See *India - Quantitative Restrictions on Imports of Agricultural, Textiles and Industrial Products*, notifications of mutually agreed solutions, circulated pursuant to Article 3.6 of the DSU, WT/DS92/8 and WT/DS92/8/Corr.1, WT/DS93/8, WT/DS94/9 and WT/DS94/9/Corr.1; WT/DS96/8 and WT/DS96/8/Corr.1 and WT/DS90/2/Add.1, WT/DS91/2/Add.1, WT/DS92/2/Add.1, WT/DS93/2/Add.1, WT/DS94/2/Add.1, WT/DS96/2/Add.1.

[367] Op. Cit., BISD 36S/268, para. 131. See also BOP/R/171 paras. 22-23. A seven-year phase-out period was applied (see BOP/R/183/Add.1, paras. 12-13).

[368] Under the GATT: Brazil (1991) - one year phase-out (See BOP/R/194, 24 July 1991). Under the WTO: Egypt (1995) - three to five year phase-out (See WT/BOP/R/2, 30 June 1995); The Philippines (1995) - two year phase-out (WT/BOP/R/9, 24 November 1994). Two of these cases were dealt with under both Committees: GATT and WTO. See also the case of Tunisia (1997), where the Committee recommended to the General Council that, in adhering to its three year phase-out plan, Tunisia be deemed to be in compliance with its GATT 1994 obligations (see WT/BOP/R/31).

[369] See Award of the Arbitrator in the case on *Indonesia - Certain Measures Affecting the Automobile Industry*, WT/DS54/15, WT/DS55/14, WT/DS59/13, WT/DS64/12, 7 December 1998, para. 24.

7.7 Accordingly, we suggest that the parties negotiate an implementation/phase-out period. Should it be impossible for them to do so, we suggest that the reasonable period of time, whether determined by arbitration (Article 21.3(c) of the DSU) or other means, be set in light of the above-listed factors.

CANADA - MEASURES AFFECTING THE IMPORTATION OF MILK AND THE EXPORTATION OF DAIRY PRODUCTS

Report of the Appellate Body

WT/DS103/AB/R
WT/DS113/AB/R*

Adopted by the Dispute Settlement Body on 27 October 1999

Canada, *Appellant*	Present:
New Zealand, *Appellee*	Matsushita, Presiding Member
United States, *Appellee*	Feliciano, Member
	Lacarte-Muró, Member

TABLE OF CONTENTS

* WT/DS103/AB/R/Corr.1, WT/DS113/AB/R/Corr.1.

I. INTRODUCTION

1. **Canada** appeals from certain issues of law and legal interpretations developed by the Panel in *Canada - Measures Affecting the Importation of Milk and the Exportation of Dairy Products* (the "Panel Report")[1] Following their requests for consultations, the United States[2] and New Zealand[3] requested that the Dispute Settlement Body (the "DSB") establish panels to examine certain alleged export subsidies that they contended Canada or its provinces had granted, through the Special Milk Classes Scheme, to support the export of dairy products and to examine a claim by the United States regarding imports into Canada of fluid milk and cream within the 64,500 tonnes tariff-rate quota committed in Canada's Schedule of Commitments under the *Marrakesh Agreement Establishing the World Trade Organization* (the "*WTO Agreement*"). On 25 March 1998, the DSB agreed to establish two panels in accordance with these requests and further agreed that the two panels would be consolidated into a single panel pur-

[1] WT/DS103/R, WT/DS113/R, 17 May 1999.
[2] WT/DS103/4, 2 February 1998.
[3] WT/DS113/4, 12 March 1998.

suant to Article 9.1 of the *Understanding on Rules and Procedures Governing the Settlement of Disputes* (the "DSU") with standard terms of reference.

2. The Panel considered claims made by the United States and New Zealand that Canada's measures are inconsistent with Articles II, X, XI and XIII of the *General Agreement on Tariffs and Trade 1994* (the "GATT 1994"); Articles 3, 4, 8, 9, and 10 of the *Agreement on Agriculture*; Article 3 of the *Agreement on Subsidies and Countervailing Measures* (the "*SCM Agreement*"); and Articles 1, 2 and 3 of the *Agreement on Import Licensing Procedures*. The Panel Report was circulated to Members of the World Trade Organization (the "WTO") on 17 May 1999. In paragraph 8.1 of its Report, the Panel concluded that Canada:

> (a) through Special Milk Classes 5(d) and (e) - and this for all of the dairy products in dispute (butter, cheese and "other milk products") and for both marketing years at issue (1995/1996 and 1996/1997) - has acted inconsistently with its obligations under Article 3.3 and Article 8 of the Agreement on Agriculture by providing export subsidies as listed in Article 9.1(a) and Article 9.1(c) of that Agreement in excess of the quantity commitment levels specified in Canada's Schedule; and
>
> (b) by restricting the access to the tariff-rate quota for fluid milk to (i) consumer packaged milk for personal use and (ii) entries valued at less than C$20, acts inconsistently with its obligations under Article II:1(b) of GATT 1994.

3. In paragraph 8.3 of its Report, the Panel made the following recommendation:

> We *recommend* that the Dispute Settlement Body requests Canada: (i) to bring its dairy products marketing regime into conformity with its obligations in respect of export subsidies under the Agreement on Agriculture; and (ii) to bring its tariff-rate quota for fluid milk into conformity with GATT 1994.

4. On 15 July 1999, Canada notified the DSB of its intention to appeal certain issues of law covered in the Panel Report and legal interpretations developed by the Panel, pursuant to paragraph 4 of Article 16 of the DSU, and filed a Notice of Appeal with the Appellate Body, pursuant to Rule 20 of the *Working Procedures for Appellate Review* (the "*Working Procedures*"). On 19 July 1999,

Canada filed its appellant's submission.[4] On 6 August 1999, the United States and New Zealand filed their respective appellees' submissions.[5]

5. The oral hearing in the appeal was held on 6 September 1999.[6] The participants presented oral arguments and responded to questions put to them by the Members of the Appellate Body Division hearing the appeal.

II. BACKGROUND

A. *The Canadian Dairy Regime*

6. The relevant factual and regulatory aspects concerning the Canadian dairy regime, including the Special Milk Classes Scheme, are fully described in paragraphs 2.1 to 2.66 of the Panel Report. For the purposes of this appeal, we summarize certain of the principal aspects of the Panel's factual findings.

1. *Institutions*

7. Regulatory jurisdiction over trade in dairy products in Canada is divided between the federal and the provincial governments.[7] The Canadian federal government has the power to regulate inter-provincial and international trade generally, including trade in milk, while the provincial governments have jurisdiction over aspects of the production and sale of milk within the provinces.[8] Three entities have decision-making roles with respect to the production and sale of milk in Canada: the Canadian Dairy Commission (the "CDC"), the provincial milk marketing boards and the Canadian Milk Supply Management Committee (the "CMSMC").

(a) CDC

8. The CDC is a Crown corporation established under the Canadian Dairy Commission Act (the "CDC Act"), a federal statute.[9] The CDC is funded by the Canadian federal government as well as by its market activities and by producers.[10] The chairman, the vice-chairman and the commissioner of the CDC are appointed by the federal government of Canada, and the CDC is accountable to the federal Parliament, reporting to the Minister of Agriculture and Agri-Food.[11]

---

4 Pursuant to Rule 21(1) of the *Working Procedures*.
5 Pursuant to Rule 22(1) of the *Working Procedures*.
6 Pursuant to Rule 27 of the *Working Procedures*.
7 Panel Report, para. 2.7.
8 *Ibid*.
9 *Ibid*., para. 2.12.
10 *Ibid*., para. 2.14.
11 Panel Report, para. 2.14.

9. The CDC Act empowers the CDC, *inter alia*, to establish national target prices for industrial milk[12]; to buy and sell dairy products, including through importation and exportation; and to operate pools for the marketing of milk and cream.[13] As the chair of the CMSMC[14], the CDC participates both in the implementation of the Comprehensive Agreement on Special Class Pooling[15] and in the establishment of the annual national production quota.[16] The CDC also chairs the Advisory Group on Preemptive Surplus Removal (the "Surplus Removal Committee"), which determines when and whether there is surplus milk available for exports.[17]

(b) Provincial Milk Marketing Boards

10. In each province, a milk marketing board has been established to "[regulate] the production for marketing, or the marketing, in intraprovincial trade of any dairy product."[18] Membership of the provincial milk marketing boards is comprised mostly or exclusively of dairy producers.[19]

11. The provincial milk marketing boards operate within a legal framework established under federal and provincial legislation, and they exercise powers, given by the federal and provincial governments, in respect of the issuance and administration of quotas, the pooling of returns at the provincial level, pricing, record-keeping and reporting, inspection and agreements to cooperate with other provinces and the CDC.[20] Milk producers cannot sell milk without using the provincial milk marketing boards as an intermediary.[21] Orders or regulations issued by the provincial milk marketing boards can be enforced in the Canadian courts.[22]

(c) CMSMC

12. The CMSMC is a body established under the NMMP, a federal-provincial agreement whose purpose is to regulate the marketing of milk and cream prod-

---

[12] Industrial milk includes all milk utilized in the preparation of processed dairy products, such as butter, cheese, milk powder, ice cream and yoghurt (see Section F of the National Milk Marketing Plan (the "NMMP")).

[13] Panel Report, para. 2.13. The CDC's powers are set out in full in this paragraph of the Panel Report.

[14] *Ibid.*, para. 2.28.

[15] *Ibid.*, para. 2.27.

[16] *Ibid.*, para. 2.29.

[17] Section C.1(ii) of Annex B of the Comprehensive Agreement on Special Class Pooling. "Surplus milk" is milk that is surplus to Canadian domestic requirements.

[18] Panel Report, para. 2.16. The Panel quotes from Section 2 of the CDC Act.

[19] *Ibid.*, para. 2.18.

[20] *Ibid.*, para. 2.17.

[21] *Ibid.*, para. 2.19.

[22] *Ibid.*, para. 7.76.

ucts in Canada.[23] The NMMP is signed by nine of the provincial milk marketing boards, some provincial governments, and the CDC.[24] The CMSMC is composed of the representatives of the signatory provincial milk marketing boards and the respective provincial governments and is chaired by the CDC.[25] The Dairy Farmers of Canada, the National Dairy Council and the Consumers Association of Canada also participate in the CMSMC but have no voting rights.[26]

13. The CMSMC oversees the implementation of the Comprehensive Agreement on Special Class Pooling, pursuant to which the Special Milk Classes Scheme is established.[27] The CMSMC sets the annual national production target for industrial milk (known as the national market sharing quota, the national "MSQ").[28] The CMSMC then allocates the national MSQ among the provinces based on historical production levels.[29]

2. *The Special Milk Classes Scheme*

14. Industrial milk in Canada is subject to a national common classification system, under which the pricing of milk is based on the end use to which the milk is put.[30] The classification system establishes five different "Classes" of milk, the first four of which cover milk used exclusively in the domestic market.[31] The "Special Milk Classes" are the five sub-classes of Class 5 milk. Special Classes 5(a) to 5(c) cover milk used for the preparation of certain dairy products that are either sold in the domestic market or exported.[32] Special Class 5(d) is for milk used in products exported to "traditional" export markets.[33] Special Class 5(e) is for the removal of surplus milk from the domestic market.[34] Surplus milk may be either milk that is produced within production quota limits ("in-quota milk") or milk that is produced in excess of production quota limits ("over-quota milk").[35]

---

[23] Panel Report, para. 2.22. The Panel quotes from Section 2 of the CDC Act.
[24] *Ibid.*, para. 2.21.
[25] Panel Report, para. 2.28.
[26] *Ibid.*
[27] *Ibid.*, para. 2.27.
[28] *Ibid.*, para. 2.29.
[29] *Ibid.*, paras. 2.29 and 2.31.
[30] *Ibid.*, para. 2.38.
[31] The Panel describes Classes 1 to 4 of the classification system in paragraph 2.38 of the Panel Report.
[32] Panel Report, para. 2.39.
[33] *Ibid.* Further details as to the operation of Special Class 5(d) are given at paragraphs 2.49, 2.51, 2.53 to 2.56, 7.68 and 7.69 of the Panel Report.
[34] *Ibid.* Further details as to the operation of Special Class 5(e) are given at paragraphs 2.49, 2.51, 2.53 to 2.58 and 7.70 to 7.72 of the Panel Report.
[35] Further details regarding in-quota and over-quota milk are given at paragraphs 2.40, 2.42 to 2.46 and 2.53 to 2.58 of the Panel Report.

3. *Price of Milk to the Processor*

15. The price of Special Classes 5(d) and 5(e) milk is negotiated by the CDC and the processors/ exporters on a transaction-by-transaction basis.[36] The price at which industrial milk is made available under Special Classes 5(d) and 5(e) is "significantly lower" than the price of industrial milk destined for domestic use.[37] In the case of export sales of milk under Special Classes 5(d) and 5(e), processors are guaranteed a "margin" which "covers the cost of transforming milk ... and a return on investment ...".[38]

4. *Returns to the Producer - Pooling*

16. Returns to producers from the sale of milk are calculated on the basis of a system of pooling. Two separate pooling mechanisms are used to pool returns from sales of in-quota and over-quota milk. Revenues from all in-quota sales are pooled on a regional basis, whether the milk sold was destined for domestic use or for export.[39] Over-quota sales are subject to a much more limited pooling of returns that covers only over-quota sales. This pooling is conducted on a national basis.[40]

B. *Canada's Tariff-Rate Quota for Fluid Milk*

17. The factual aspects relating to Canada's tariff-rate quota for fluid milk are fully provided at paragraphs 7.142 and 7.143 of the Panel Report.

III. ARGUMENTS OF THE PARTICIPANTS

A. *Claims of Error by Canada - Appellant*

1. *Article 9.1(a) of the Agreement on Agriculture*

(a) "direct subsidies, including payments-in-kind"

18. Canada contends that the interpretation of the term "export subsidies" in the *Agreement on Agriculture* must take into account the related provisions of the *SCM Agreement*. The *Agreement on Agriculture* and the *SCM Agreement* are both Multilateral Agreements on Trade in Goods and, in the language of Article II:2 of the *WTO Agreement*, are "integral parts" of the *WTO Agreement*. The two Agreements reflect the latest statement of WTO Members as to their rights

---

36 Panel Report, para. 2.51.

37 *Ibid.*, para. 7.50. See also para. 2.51, Table 3, and para. 7.40 of the Panel Report.

38 *Ibid.*, para. 7.59.

39 Further details regarding the pooling mechanism for in-quota milk are given at paragraphs 2.59 to 2.63 and 7.107 to 7.111 of the Panel Report.

40 Further details regarding the pooling mechanism for over-quota milk are given at paragraph 7.112 of the Panel Report.

and obligations concerning agricultural subsidies. The clear inference is that, if possible, there should be consistency of interpretation between the two Agreements, particularly with respect to the notions of "subsidies" and "export subsidies". In Canada's view, the Panel did not give proper consideration to this need for consistent interpretation.

19. Canada submits that the interpretation of the expression "direct subsidies, including payments-in-kind", in Article 9.1(a) of the *Agreement on Agriculture*, should begin with the word "subsidies". That word, although not defined in the *Agreement on Agriculture*, is defined in Article 1.1 of the *SCM Agreement*. If the elements identified in Article 1.1 are present, Article 9.1(a) of the *Agreement on Agriculture* requires examination of whether the "subsidies" are "direct". The Panel erred by failing to do this. In Canada's view, a subsidy is "direct" if: it is funded directly from government funds; it is paid directly to the beneficiary by the government itself; *and* it does not involve the activities of non-governmental actors acting through a government-mandated scheme. In this case, since the alleged subsidy is not funded by government, it is not "direct".

20. The Panel also erred by "equating 'payments-in-kind' with 'direct subsidies'".[41] A subsidy may take the form of a "payment-in-kind", but a "payment-in-kind" is not necessarily a "subsidy". By collapsing these separate legal concepts, the Panel failed to address the two fundamental elements of Article 9.1(a): namely, the terms "direct" and "subsidies".

21. Canada contends that the Panel also substituted for the ordinary meaning of "payments", in the term "payments-in-kind", a special meaning of "gratuitous act, a bounty or benefit".[42] The end result is that the Panel equates "payments-in-kind" with "direct subsidies", and "payments", in "payments-in-kind", with "benefit". In so doing, the Panel has confused the *form* of a transaction ("payments-in-kind") with its *economic consequences* ("benefit").

22. Moreover, by holding that the "provision of a good at a price lower than the normal price"[43] was a "payment-in-kind", the Panel departed from the ordinary meaning of that term, which Canada sees as reflecting a requirement to show a "financial contribution". When goods are sold at less than the "normal" price, purchasers are not receiving payments-in-kind but are simply paying less for the goods they receive.

23. Although the Panel correctly set out to establish the existence of a "benefit", it misconstrued and misapplied that concept. The Panel established two "benchmarks" to test whether a benefit was conferred.[44] Canada submits that the Panel erred in relying on the domestic price of milk as the first benchmark since that price is influenced by lawful, bound tariffs. On the basis of the Panel's ap-

---

41 Canada's appellant's submission, para. 46.

42 Panel Report, para. 7.44.

43 Panel Report, para. 7.45.

44 *Ibid.*, para. 7.47.

proach, the exportation of any product, subject to an import tariff, at the prevailing world market price is, effectively, an export subsidy. It is, however, normal commercial practice for domestic and export prices to be different. Indeed, several provisions of WTO law suggest that price differentiation on the basis of market realities is acceptable.

24. Canada notes that the Panel's "benefit" test is based on whether processors obtain milk under Special Classes 5(d) and 5(e) at a price more advantageous than the prevailing world market price for competing products, *whether or not processors choose to source the product from those markets.* The Panel's approach overlooks the commercial reasons why certain access opportunities are not pursued. The Panel was also wrong to presume that there is a "world market" price for raw milk, since raw milk is rarely traded internationally.

25. Canada states that the legal error committed in connection with the second benchmark was compounded: by a failure to take into account relevant factual considerations and by making unwarranted presumptions concerning the import of milk under the Import for Re-export Program; by engaging in unwarranted speculation about the commercial viability of importing fluid milk into Canada from the United States; and, by relying on evidence that was deemed to contain "certain inaccuracies"[45], without providing a basic rationale under Article 12.7 of the DSU to justify placing reliance on such evidence.

(b) "governments or their agencies"

26. Canada argues that the Panel erred by finding that the provincial milk marketing boards are government agencies "solely on the basis of one characteristic: the delegation of some governmental authority."[46] The mere fact of delegation of authority from government is not sufficient to conclude that an entity is an agency of government.

27. Canada notes that, in Article 9.1(a), marketing boards are identified as potential recipients of "direct subsidies". The implication is that a marketing board is distinct from "governments or their agencies". Moreover, if marketing boards are deemed to be "government agencies", the result would be that subsidies are being provided by a government to itself.

28. According to Canada, the Panel was misguided in relying on Article XVII of the GATT 1994 to support its conclusion that marketing boards may be government agencies. That provision has no bearing on the status of the marketing boards at issue under Article 9.1(a). Similarly, the Panel's reference to Article XXIV:12 does not advance its reasoning. That provision states that "regional" or "local" authorities are subject to GATT obligations but does not define such authorities.

---

[45] Panel Report, para. 7.56, footnote 404.

[46] Canada's appellant's submission, para. 116.

29. Canada notes that Item (d) of the Illustrative List of Export Subsidies in Annex I of the *SCM Agreement* (the "Illustrative List"), distinguishes between the provision of subsidies by "government-mandated schemes" and by "governments or their agencies". "Government-mandated schemes" will usually entail the delegation of authority by government to a private entity. Yet, under Item (d), such an entity does not become a government agency as a result of that delegation of authority.

30. Canada emphasizes that under Canadian domestic law, the provincial milk marketing boards are neither part of the executive branch of any Canadian government nor are they government "agencies". The Panel failed to address the high degree of independence, private accountability and discretion enjoyed by the boards. An entity, such as the provincial milk marketing boards, which act in the private interest of a specific group, cannot be said to be performing government functions, even if it enjoys powers delegated to it by government.

31. Canada adds, finally, that the judgment in the *Bari III* case, referred to by the Panel, provides no support for the proposition that the provincial milk marketing boards should be deemed to be government agencies because they enjoy some delegated powers.

2. *Article 9.1(c) of the Agreement on Agriculture*

(a) "payments"

32. Canada contends that the Panel erred by collapsing the distinction between the term "payments" in Article 9.1(c) and the term "payments-in-kind" in Article 9.1(a). These words have different meanings: where the drafters intended the word "payments" to include "payments-in-kind", this was indicated in the text, as in the case of Article 9.1(a) and of paragraph 5 of Annex 2. The absence of an express reference to "payments-in-kind" in other provisions of the *Agreement on Agriculture* indicates a different intention. Canada argues that its interpretation is supported by the French and Spanish texts of that Agreement.

33. The Panel also erred by equating a "payment-in-kind" with the provision of a good at a discounted price or "revenue foregone". As regards "revenue foregone", the Panel erred in concluding that, because such revenue counts against a Member's budgetary outlay commitments, *every* type of subsidy listed in Article 9.1 covers "revenue foregone". In Canada's view, it is only if the *specific* subparagraph of Article 9.1 can be interpreted to include "revenue foregone" that such revenue is relevant to the subsidy concerned. The Panel also fails to differentiate between "payments-in-kind" and "revenue foregone". In effect, therefore, the Panel errs by collapsing the separate terms, "payments", "payments-in-kind" and "revenue foregone", into a single concept.

(b) "financed by virtue of governmental action"

34. Canada argues that the Panel's finding under Article 9.1(c), that "payments" were "financed by virtue of governmental action", is based expressly on the Panel's findings under Article 9.1(a) regarding "governments and their agencies". The finding under Article 9.1(c) is, therefore, wrong for the same reasons Canada submitted under Article 9.1(a).

35. Canada also points to what it considers to be significant differences between in-quota and over-quota milk as regards the degree of government involvement and contends that the Panel erred by dismissing these differences.[47] Neither the boards nor the CDC determine how much over-quota milk will actually be produced. Canada also underlines the differences in the pooling of returns to producers as between in-quota and over-quota milk.

3. Article 10.1 of the Agreement on Agriculture

36. Canada observes that Article 10.1 applies to "subsidies contingent upon export performance", other than those subsidies listed in Article 9.1. The Panel erred by suggesting that the scope of the measures covered by Article 10.1 is drawn from the items listed in Article 9.1. The Panel indicated that a measure, which is partially, but not completely, covered by Article 9.1, should, for that reason, be included under Article 10.1. Canada emphasizes that a practice not included in Article 9.1 can only be an "export subsidy" if it satisfies the definition of that term in Article 1(e) of the *Agreement on Agriculture*. Approximations will not suffice.

37. In interpreting Article 10.1, the Panel sought guidance from the *SCM Agreement*. Although it mentioned both Article 1 and the Illustrative List, the Panel overlooks consideration of Article 1, moving directly to Item (d) of the Illustrative List. The Illustrative List cannot be applied in isolation, but must be considered together with Article 1 of the *SCM Agreement*. Moreover, the Panel also erred by finding that Special Classes 5(d) and 5(e) fulfil the substantive requirements of Item (d) of the Illustrative List.

4. Article II:1(b) of the GATT 1994

38. Canada argues that the Panel overlooked the scope and meaning of Canada's entry in its Schedule of Commitments. In effect, the Panel reduced the language contained in the entry to a nullity by failing to ascribe any limiting effect to it. Instead, the Panel found that the entry contained "terms" relating solely to the way in which the size of the quota was determined. The Panel thereby failed to interpret the word "term" according to its ordinary meaning, which is "limiting

[47] The factors regarding in-quota and over-quota milk that Canada identified are mentioned by the Panel in paragraphs 7.83 and 7.99 of the Panel Report.

conditions". The Panel also erred by failing to set out the basic rationale behind its finding, as required by Article 12.7 of the DSU.

39. The Panel did not take sufficient account of the language in Article II:1(b) of the GATT 1994 which means, in effect, that Canada's access commitments are subordinated to the "terms and conditions" set out in its Schedule of Commitments. By giving the notation no limiting effect on Canada's access obligations, the Panel ignored the words "subject to" in Article II:1(b).

40. Canada acknowledges that the two specific requirements at issue are not expressly provided for in its notation. But the Panel should have recognized a strong presumption that the notation was intended to restrict access to the tariff-rate quota to "cross-border purchases imported by Canadian consumers".

41. Canada submits that because the Panel failed to ascribe any substantive meaning to Canada's terms and conditions, the Panel also failed properly to interpret the meaning of the word "consumer" in the notation. As a result of its approach, the Panel failed to rule on the central issue, namely, whether Canada must permit commercial import shipments of fluid milk within the two tariff lines in question.

42. In view of the doubts regarding the interpretation of the notation, the Panel should have clarified the meaning by considering the negotiating history pursuant to Article 32 of the *Vienna Convention on the Law of Treaties* (the "*Vienna Convention*").[48] Canada asserts that it was clear from the record before the Panel that Canada proposed to maintain its existing access opportunities, unless the United States removed barriers to Canadian access to the United States' market. Those existing access opportunities did not extend to commercial imports.

B. Arguments of New Zealand - Appellee

1. Article 9.1(a) of the Agreement on Agriculture

(a) "direct subsidies, including payments-in-kind"

43. New Zealand disagrees with Canada's view that the export subsidy provisions of the *Agreement on Agriculture* and the *SCM Agreement* form a single, comprehensive statement and must, therefore, be interpreted consistently. Even though the *WTO Agreement* may constitute a single undertaking, that does not mean that the provisions of one part are to be governed by the provisions of another part. The various WTO agreements contain provisions that establish a hierarchy between them and this hierarchy must be respected. Furthermore, on Canada's argument, neither Agreement could be applied in isolation, since only by applying the Agreements together could consistency be ensured.

48 Done at Vienna, 23 May 1969, 1155 U.N.T.S. 331; (1969) 8 International Legal Materials 679.

44. Canada seems to argue that the Panel erred because it found that any "payment-in-kind" constitutes a "direct subsidy". New Zealand does not concur in this reading of the Panel Report. The Panel makes it clear that a "payment-in-kind" is *capable* of being a "direct subsidy", *provided* that it can be shown to confer a "benefit".

45. New Zealand agrees with the Panel that provision of goods at a reduced price can constitute a "payment-in-kind". If processors were to purchase milk at a higher price and receive a rebate, the rebate would undoubtedly be a "payment". In the case of Special Classes 5(d) and 5(e), the rebate is in the form of the provision of milk instead of money.

46. In New Zealand's view, a "benefit" is conferred if access to milk under Special Classes 5(d) and 5(e) results in processors obtaining milk for export at a price which is lower than the price of milk from alternative sources. As the Panel concluded, Special Classes 5(d) and 5(e) do provide a "benefit" because processors would have to pay significantly higher prices for alternative supplies of milk.

47. New Zealand observes that the Panel employed the two benchmarks to assess whether the terms offered under Special Classes 5(d) and 5(e) were available elsewhere in the marketplace. Such an approach was endorsed by the Appellate Body in its Report in *Canada - Measures Affecting the Export of Civilian Aircraft* ("*Canada - Aircraft*").[49]

48. Finally, New Zealand argues that Canada's interpretation of the word "direct" in Article 9.1(a) of the *Agreement on Agriculture* rewrites that provision. If "direct" means funded through government funds, the words "the provision by governments or their agencies" are redundant. Canada's interpretation would also mean that the word "provision" should be understood as being preceded by the word "direct". In New Zealand's opinion, a "direct subsidy" is one that affects trade directly rather than indirectly.

(b) "governments or their agencies"

49. New Zealand notes that Canada challenges only the Panel's conclusion that the provincial milk marketing boards are governmental in character. New Zealand maintains that the provincial milk marketing boards fall within the definition of "governments or their agencies" under Article 9.1(a). It defends this position on the basis of the delegation of power by the government to the boards and on the nature of those powers, which would normally inure to the federal or provincial governments.

50. New Zealand does not share Canada's view that the reference to "marketing boards" as potential recipients of subsidies under Article 9.1(a) means that they cannot be government agencies. There is no single definition of the term "marketing board" and the Panel properly evaluated the particular characteristics

[49] Appellate Body Report, WT/DS70/AB/R, adopted 20 August 1999.

of the provincial milk marketing boards at issue here. New Zealand also contends that both the *Ad* note to Article XVII:1, and Article XXIV:12 of GATT 1994 indicate that marketing boards are capable of being agencies of government, although neither purports to provide a universal definition of government agency.

51. New Zealand disagrees with Canada's argument on Item (d) of the Illustrative List. Item (d) says nothing about the "government" status of "government-mandated schemes" since Item (d) does not depend upon whether those schemes are governmental or non-governmental.

52. Finally, New Zealand contends that Canada's argument that the status of the provincial milk marketing boards should be determined by Canadian domestic law is contrary to Article 3.2 of the DSU, which provides that the WTO Agreements are to be interpreted "in accordance with customary rules of interpretation of public international law."

2. *Article 9.1(c) of the Agreement on Agriculture*

(a) "payments"

53. New Zealand maintains that the Panel properly applied the appropriate principles of treaty interpretation in its examination of the word "payments". A "payment-in-kind" is a *form* of payment. Canada has offered no substantive argument to show that this is wrong.

54. According to New Zealand, Canada's argument regarding revenue foregone suggests that such revenue would be excluded from the assessment of budgetary outlay commitments made for "export subsidies" under Article 9.1, unless there is explicit reference to revenue foregone in a particular sub-paragraph of Article 9.1. Since none of the sub-paragraphs in Article 9.1 refers specifically to revenue foregone, the implication of the Canadian argument is that revenue foregone need not be included at all in the calculation of "budgetary outlay" commitments. This is a rewriting of Articles 1(c), 9.1 and 9.2(a) of the *Agreement on Agriculture*.

(b) "financed by virtue of governmental action"

55. New Zealand submits that, for the reasons given in its arguments on the meaning of "governments or their agencies", the Panel's analysis under Article 9.1(c), insofar as it is based on its analysis under Article 9.1(a), is correct. Canada is attempting to reargue the facts of the case by focusing on differences between in-quota and over-quota milk that the Panel did not regard as significant. The important point is that "governmental action" is involved regardless of whether the milk is in-quota or over-quota.

3. Article 10.1 of the Agreement on Agriculture

56. New Zealand submits that Canada fails to take proper account of the purpose of Article 10.1, which is to prevent Members of the WTO circumventing reduction commitments made in respect of export subsidies listed in Article 9.1. When the Panel indicated that Article 10.1 covered subsidies that did not meet all of the definitional elements of Article 9.1, it was precisely this type of circumvention that the Panel was aiming at. The Panel did not find that it suffices that a measure approximates an "export subsidy" under Article 9.1. The Panel emphasized that the alleged subsidy must meet the requirements of Article 1(e) of the *Agreement on Agriculture*.

57. As with Article 9.1(a) of the *Agreement on Agriculture*, New Zealand considers that the *SCM Agreement* is not the appropriate starting-point for interpretation of the *Agreement on Agriculture*. That Agreement must be interpreted according to its own terms. In any event, New Zealand agrees with the Panel that Special Classes 5(d) and 5(e) are "export subsidies" within the meaning of Item (d) of the Illustrative List.

C. Arguments of the United States - Appellee

1. Article 9.1(a) of the Agreement on Agriculture

(a) "direct subsidies, including payments-in-kind"

58. The United States submits that the Panel correctly concluded, first, that Special Classes 5(d) and 5(e) provide a "payment-in-kind" to dairy processors and, second, that the "payment-in-kind" is a "direct subsidy" provided by the Canadian federal and provincial governments, working through the provincial milk marketing boards.

59. Canada argues that the provision of goods at a price lower than their value is not a "payment-in-kind", although the provision of goods free of charge is. However, this position would allow circumvention of Article 9.1(a) by the imposition of a minimal fee, regardless of how small, for the goods.

60. The United States agrees with Canada that the *SCM Agreement* is relevant to the interpretation of the *Agreement on Agriculture*, but its provisions are not to be given more weight than those of the *Agreement on Agriculture*. A practice which falls within Article 9.1 of the *Agreement on Agriculture* is an "export subsidy" for the purposes of that Agreement, irrespective of whether the practice is also an "export subsidy" under the *SCM Agreement*.

61. The United States does not consider that the Panel "equated" "payments-in-kind" with "subsidies". First, the Panel focused on the circumstances of this case by referring to the "instant matter".[50] Furthermore, the Panel's finding under

---

[50] Panel Report, para. 7.43.

Article 9.1(a) is not dependent solely on the term "payments-in-kind", but was an application of the provision in its entirety. The Panel's analysis of whether the "payment-in-kind" conferred a "benefit" is part of the Panel's consideration of the subsidy issue under Article 9.1(a) as a whole.

62. Canada's argument as to the meaning of "direct" is also flawed. The term "direct" reveals nothing about either the grantor of a subsidy or the source of the funds. Indeed, Canada's own Special Import Measures Act (SIMA) Handbook relies on a very different understanding of the word "direct". It states that "a direct ... benefit is one which accrues directly to the person, firm, or industry which is the intended recipient". This is in contrast to "an indirect benefit ...which does not accrue directly, but which alters the economic environment within which firms operate."

63. The United States contends that Canada's argument on the first benchmark is superfluous to the appeal because the Panel relied on the second benchmark, and not the first, in making its finding. Under the second benchmark, the Panel established that there were no alternative supplies of milk, or competing products, that were available to processors on terms as favorable as those offered under Special Classes 5(d) and 5(e).

(b) "governments or their agencies"

64. The United States notes that Canada does not challenge either the governmental status or the role of the CDC in the regulatory framework. Canada's appeal against the Panel's findings on this issue turns exclusively on the status of the provincial milk marketing boards.

65. The Panel did *not* focus simply on the delegation of powers to the marketing boards. Instead, the Panel also considered the functions of the boards, as well as the extent to which the provincial and federal governments retain supervisory oversight over the boards.

66. The ordinary meaning of the word "agency" is not restricted to a department or other section of the government itself but also embraces entities acting on an agency basis. This meaning clearly does not exclude private entities acting for the government.

67. The United States disagrees with Canada that the reference in Article 9.1(a) to "marketing boards" as potential recipients of "direct subsidies" precludes "marketing boards" from being government agencies in appropriate circumstances. This interpretation is not justified by the text of Article 9.1.

68. Finally, Canada's argument on Item (d) of the Illustrative List is based entirely on the assumption that "government-mandated schemes" always involve the delegation of governmental authority. The United States does not agree with this assumption.

2. *Article 9.1(c) of the Agreement on Agriculture*

(a) "payments"

69. Contrary to Canada's arguments, the Panel did not equate "payment" with "payment-in-kind". The Panel correctly found that "payments-in-kind" represent a subset of the broader term "payment". Canada, however, treats the two terms as mutually exclusive. This position is untenable given the ordinary definition of "payment" as the "remuneration of a person with money or its equivalent".[51]

70. Canada is also incorrect to suppose that "payments-in-kind" are only included in the scope of the *Agreement on Agriculture* where express provision is made to that effect. To the contrary, the express reference to "payments-in-kind" is necessary to prevent the terms "direct subsidy" (in Article 9.1(a) of the *Agreement on Agriculture*) and "direct payment" (in Paragraph 5 of Annex 2 of that Agreement) from being interpreted narrowly to exclude "payments-in-kind".

71. According to the United States, the Panel was correct to find that the word "payment" in Article 9.1(c) includes "revenue foregone". The drafters did not qualify the word "payment" in Article 9.1(c) in any way. Consistently with its ordinary meaning, the word covers transfers of value to another person or entity. Such a transfer occurs when one party foregoes revenue for the advantage or benefit of another. The fact that the Panel found that the word "payment" encompassed both "payments-in-kind" and "revenue foregone" does not mean, as Canada argues, that these terms are synonymous.

(b) "financed by virtue of governmental action"

72. The United States argues that "financed by virtue of governmental action" under Article 9.1(c) is a less demanding requirement than "the provision by governments or their agencies of direct subsidies" under Article 9.1(a). Activities of "governments or their agencies" that do not fall within Article 9.1(a) may satisfy the requirement of Article 9.1(c).

73. The United States disputes Canada's suggestion that the Panel's findings under Article 9.1(c) do not stand independently from the Panel's conclusions under Article 9.1(a). Under Article 9.1(c), the Panel examined in exhaustive detail the involvement of government in the functioning and control of Special Classes 5(d) and 5(e) and Canada has not refuted the Panel's specific factual findings concerning the breadth of that involvement.

74. The United States considers that, for all relevant purposes, the role of the Canadian governments and of the provincial milk marketing boards under Special Classes 5(d) and 5(e) is the same. It makes no difference from the perspective of the *processors* whether the milk they receive is in-quota or over-quota because the price to them is the same. The United States rejects Canada's argument that it

[51] See Panel Report, 7.92.

is significant that producers decide themselves whether to produce over-quota milk. If mandating the production of milk were a prerequisite for a finding of a subsidy, the subsidies disciplines would be altogether eviscerated.

3. Article 10.1 of the Agreement on Agriculture

75. Canada's arguments on Article 10.1 reflect a mistaken reading of the Panel Report. Contrary to Canada's argument, the Panel did not state that any measure which does not satisfy some of the elements of Article 9.1 would, without more, be an export subsidy under Article 10.1. The Panel found that even a measure which meets most of the criteria in Article 9.1 must still satisfy the requirements of Article 1(e) of the *Agreement on Agriculture*.

76. By arguing that the Panel should have assessed Special Classes 5(d) and 5(e) in terms of Article 1.1 of the *SCM Agreement*, rather than just in light of Item (d) of the Illustrative List, Canada is implicitly suggesting that the export subsidies identified in the Illustrative List might not satisfy the criteria set forth in Article 1.1. This is not possible. As a matter of definition, Article 3.1 of the *SCM Agreement* mandates that *all* subsidies described in the Illustrative List are subsidies for purposes of Article 1 of the *SCM Agreement*.

77. The United States argues, in any event, that Special Classes 5(d) and 5(e) involve "subsidies" within the meaning of Article 1.1 of the *SCM Agreement* and, moreover, that the Panel was correct to conclude that these Special Classes fall within Item (d) of the Illustrative List.

4. Article II:1(b) of the GATT 1994

78. Consistently with the rules of treaty interpretation, the Panel was aware of the context of the language in the notation in Canada's Schedule. Nevertheless, the Panel could not find, in that language, the specific access restrictions contended for by Canada.

79. The United States disagrees with Canada that the most relevant meaning of the word "term" is "limiting conditions", as this meaning would render the word "conditions", in the phrase "terms and conditions", entirely superfluous. It is reasonable to assume that the words "other terms and conditions" contained in Canada's Schedule are intended to mirror the language used in Article II:1(b). The similar language in this provision has been interpreted as indicating not simply additional conditions.[52] Accordingly, there is no reason for giving the entry a narrower interpretation than is justified by the ordinary meaning of its wording.

80. According to the United States, the only operative word in Canada's notation is the word "represents". However, that word gives the notation no legally

[52] The United States cites the panel report in *United States - Restrictions on Imports of Sugar*, adopted 22 June 1989, BISD 36S/331, para. 5.6.

operative effect. It is not the same as saying "access is limited to", or "this quantity is available only for", language which Canada could have added, as it did with respect to yoghurt and ice cream.

81. The United States agrees with the Panel's interpretation of the word "consumer".[53] The Panel was not required to spell out that "consumer" also embraces entities such as processors that "consume" milk in manufacturing. The Panel did not ignore the core issue, but found that the notation did not support the two restrictions imposed by Canada.

82. The requisite conditions for resorting to Article 32 of the *Vienna Convention* were not met and, thus, the Panel was not compelled to take into account the negotiating history. Moreover, even if Article 32 were applicable, a panel is not *required* to look to the negotiating history. That is simply "permitted". In any event, the negotiating history does not establish the existence of a common understanding between Canada and the United States that confirms Canada's interpretation of the notation.

IV. ISSUES RAISED IN THIS APPEAL

83. This appeal raises the following issues:

(a) whether the Panel erred in its interpretation and application of Article 9.1(a) of the *Agreement on Agriculture*, in particular, with respect to:

i) the expression "direct subsidies, including payments-in-kind", and

ii) the expression "governments or their agencies";

(b) whether the Panel erred in its interpretation and application of Article 9.1(c) of the *Agreement on Agriculture*, in particular, with respect to:

i) the term "payments", and

ii) the expression "financed by virtue of governmental action";

(c) whether the Panel erred in its interpretation and application of the term "export subsidies" in Article 10.1 of the *Agreement on Agriculture*; and

(d) whether the Panel erred in finding that Canada has acted inconsistently with its obligations under Article II:1(b) of the GATT 1994 by restricting access to the tariff-rate quota for fluid milk to consumer packaged milk for personal use, valued at less than C$20, imported under the authority of General Import Permit No. 1.

---

[53] See Panel Report, para. 7.152.

V. ARTICLE 9.1(a) OF THE AGREEMENT ON AGRICULTURE

A. *"Direct Subsidies, Including Payments-In-Kind"*

84. The Panel stated that "'payments-in-kind' are a form of direct subsidy."[54] For the Panel, it followed that "a determination in the instant matter that *'payments-in-kind'* exist *would also be* a determination of the existence of a *direct subsidy*."[55] (emphasis added) The Panel next proceeded to consider the meaning of the term "payments-in-kind". It concluded that the ordinary meaning of the word "payments", in the term "payments-in-kind", "connotes a gratuitous act, a bounty or benefit provided, for example, in pursuit of a policy objective".[56] According to the Panel, this meaning is "mandated by the general context of this provision which includes Article 1 of the SCM Agreement."[57] On the basis of this interpretive framework, the Panel examined whether Special Classes 5(d) and 5(e) provide a "benefit". It reached the conclusion that a "benefit" was conferred and that there was, therefore, a "payment-in-kind".[58] On the grounds that this "payment-in-kind" was provided by Canada's "governments or their agencies", the Panel found that "the making available of milk under Classes 5(d) and (e) constitutes an export subsidy within the meaning of Article 9.1(a)."[59]

85. Canada submits that the Panel's interpretive approach is flawed. It believes that the Panel has equated "payments-in-kind" with "direct subsidies", and "payments", as used in "payments-in-kind", with "benefit". Thus, in Canada's view, the Panel, in essence, equated "direct subsidies" with "benefit".

86. On our reading of the Panel Report, the Panel took the view that if "payments-in-kind" were provided by "governments or their agencies", "direct subsidies" were also provided. In other words, the Panel found that a "payment-in-kind" is *necessarily* a "direct subsidy". This is clear from the Panel's statement that "a determination ... that 'payments-in-kind' exist would also be a determination of the existence of a direct subsidy."[60] Moreover, this understanding of the Panel's reasoning is borne out by the Panel's subsequent analysis. At no point did the Panel examine whether the "payments-in-kind" that it found to exist were "subsidies", let alone "direct subsidies". To the contrary, the Panel's finding under Article 9.1(a) resulted from its conclusion that the provision of reduced priced milk to processors for export under Special Classes 5(d) and (e) constitutes "payments-in-kind" provided by Canada's "governments or their agencies".[61] In making this finding, the Panel did not make any reference to the meas-

---

[54] Panel Report, para. 7.43.
[55] *Ibid.*
[56] *Ibid.*, para. 7.44.
[57] Panel Report, para. 7.44.
[58] Panel Report, paras. 7.58 and 7.62.
[59] *Ibid.*, para. 7.87.
[60] *Ibid.*, para. 7.43.
[61] *Ibid.*, para. 7.87.

ures being "direct subsidies". It assumed that because the measures were "payments-in-kind" they were, therefore, also "direct subsidies".

87. In our view, the term "payments-in-kind" describes one of the *forms* in which "direct subsidies" may be granted. Thus, Article 9.1(a) applies to "direct subsidies", *including* "direct subsidies" granted in the form of "payments-in-kind". We believe that, in its ordinary meaning, the word "payments", in the term "payments-in-kind", denotes a transfer of economic resources, in a form other than money, from the grantor of the payment to the recipient. However, the fact that a "payment-in-kind" has been made provides no indication as to the economic *value* of the transfer effected, either from the perspective of the grantor of the payment or from that of the recipient. A "payment-in-kind" may be made in exchange for full or partial consideration or it may be made gratuitously. Correspondingly, a "subsidy" involves a transfer of economic resources from the grantor to the recipient for less than full consideration. As we said in our Report in *Canada - Aircraft*, a "subsidy", within the meaning of Article 1.1 of the *SCM Agreement*, arises where the grantor makes a "financial contribution" which confers a "benefit" on the recipient, as compared with what would have been otherwise available to the recipient in the marketplace.[62] Where the recipient gives full consideration in return for a "payment-in-kind" there can be no "subsidy", for the recipient is paying market-rates for what it receives. It follows, in our view, that the mere fact that a "payment-in-kind" has been made does not, *by itself*, imply that a "subsidy", "direct" or otherwise, has been granted.

88. We, therefore, conclude that the Panel erred in finding that "a determination in the instant matter that 'payments-in-kind' exist would also be a determination of the existence of a direct subsidy."[63] The Panel should have considered whether the particular "payment-in-kind" that it found existed was a "direct subsidy". Instead, because the Panel assumed that a "payment-in-kind" is necessarily a "direct subsidy", it did not address specifically either the meaning of the term "direct subsidies" or the question whether the provision of milk to processors for export under Special Classes 5(d) and 5(e) constitutes "direct subsidies".

89. We have just found that the term "payments-in-kind" describes a transfer of economic resources, in a form other than money, but that the term gives no indication as to the economic value of that transfer or as to whether there is a subsidy.[64] The Panel, however, interpreted the word "payments", in the term "payments-in-kind", as connoting "a *gratuitous* act, a *bounty* or *benefit*".[65] (emphasis added) To us, each of these meanings describes the economic value of a transfer, both from the perspective of the grantor and of the recipient. These meanings all infer that the economic resources transferred by way of the payment were given in exchange for less than full value and, in the case of a "gratuitous"

[62] *Supra*, footnote 49, paras. 156 and 157.

[63] Panel Report, para. 7.43.

[64] *Supra*, para. 87.

[65] Panel Report, para. 7.44.

payment, without any exchange of value at all. While we acknowledge that a "payment" *may* be made "gratuitously", the ordinary meaning of the word also encompasses a transfer of economic resources made for full or partial consideration. We, therefore, find that the Panel erred in holding that the word "payments", in the term "payments-in-kind", *necessarily* "connotes a gratuitous act, a bounty or benefit".[66]

90. We also note that the Panel's reliance on the *SCM Agreement* in interpreting Article 9.1(a) of the *Agreement on Agriculture* was not consistent. The concept of "benefit" is an integral part of the definition of "*subsidy*" in Article 1.1 of the *SCM Agreement*. Yet, on the one hand, the Panel used this term, not to assist in defining the term "direct *subsidies*" in Article 9.1(a) of the *Agreement on Agriculture*, but to define the word "*payment*". However, on the other hand, the Panel failed entirely to make any mention of the other integral aspect of a "subsidy" under Article 1.1 of the *SCM Agreement*, namely the need for a "financial contribution". The Panel did not explain why one aspect of the definition of a "subsidy" in the *SCM Agreement* is relevant in interpreting Article 9.1(a) of the *Agreement on Agriculture*, while the other is not.

91. Thus, on our reading of the Panel Report, the Panel equated a "payment-in-kind" with a "direct subsidy", and then equated a "payment-in-kind" with a "benefit". For the Panel, it followed logically from the existence of a "benefit" that a "direct subsidy" also existed. If the "benefit" was provided by "governments or their agencies", it followed, furthermore, that there was an export subsidy as listed in Article 9.1(a) of the *Agreement on Agriculture*. It was on the basis of this flawed interpretive approach that the Panel found, in paragraph 7.87 of its Report, that export subsidies as listed in Article 9.1(a) are granted through Special Classes 5(d) and 5(e). Since we have held that the interpretive approach which underlies the finding in paragraph 7.87 of the Panel Report is wrong, it follows that that finding is itself tainted by the same errors of law. The conferral of a "benefit" does not necessarily constitute a "payment-in-kind", and a "payment-in-kind" is not necessarily a "direct subsidy".[67] Thus, the Panel's assessment that a "benefit", and hence a "payment-in-kind", are provided by "governments or their agencies" does not, in our view, warrant the conclusion that export subsidies are conferred.

92. We, therefore, reverse the Panel's interpretive approach, in paragraphs 7.43 and 7.44 of its Report, regarding the terms "direct subsidies" and "payments-in-kind". Since the Panel's finding in paragraph 7.87 of its Report that Special Classes 5(d) and 5(e) involve export subsidies under Article 9.1(a) of the *SCM Agreement* is based, in part, on the Panel's flawed interpretive approach, which we hereby reverse, we also reverse the finding of the Panel in paragraph 7.87. However, in view of our findings below on Article 9.1(c) of the

---

[66] Panel Report, para. 7.44.

[67] Panel Report, paras. 7.43 and 7.58.

Agreement on Agriculture, we do not find it necessary to examine in this Report whether export subsidies, as listed in Article 9.1(a), are conferred through Special Classes 5(d) and 5(e) and we, therefore, reserve our judgment on this question.

B. "Governments or their Agencies"

93. The Panel identified the CDC, the provincial milk marketing boards and the CMSMC as playing "a direct decision-making role" in administering Special Classes 5(d) and 5(e).[68] Canada does not appeal the Panel's conclusion that the CDC, a federal Crown corporation, is an "agency" of government within the meaning of Article 9.1(a), nor does Canada specifically appeal the Panel's finding regarding the CMSMC. As regards the provincial milk marketing boards, the Panel found that they were:

> ... established and operate *within a legal framework set up by federal and provincial legislation*. These boards exercise powers in respect of inter-provincial and external trade delegated to them by the federal government through the CDC, as well as powers delegated to them by provincial authorities. Three of these boards (Alberta, Nova Scotia and Saskatchewan) are, according to Canada, agencies of the provincial government. Orders or regulations issued by the provincial marketing boards can be *enforced before the Canadian courts*. In most provinces, individual decisions by the boards are subject to appeal to a provincial supervisory board or commission (of which Canada recognizes the governmental nature).[69] (emphasis added)

94. It was against this factual background that the Panel concluded that:

> It is precisely *because* the boards receive the authority from the governments to regulate certain areas themselves that their actions become governmental. What is important though is that Canadian governments maintain the ultimate control and supervision of most, if not all, of the boards' activities. These governments define, and approve changes to, the boards' mandates and functions.[70] (underlining added)

95. Since the Panel found that all of the bodies that play a decision-making role in the CMSMC are "government agencies", the Panel found that the actions of the CMSMC were the actions of a "government agency".[71]

---

[68] Panel Report, para. 7.74.

[69] Panel Report, para. 7.76.

[70] *Ibid*., para. 7.78.

[71] *Ibid*., para. 7.80. The bodies involved in the CMSMC are set forth in paragraph 7.79 of the Panel Report.

96. Canada's appeal focuses on the Panel's findings that the provincial milk marketing boards are "government agencies". Canada takes the view that the Panel erred in law in deciding that these boards are "government agencies" "*solely on the basis of one characteristic*: the delegation of some governmental authority."[72] (emphasis added)

97. We start our interpretive task with the text of Article 9.1(a) and the ordinary meaning of the word "government" itself. According to *Black's Law Dictionary*, "government" means, *inter alia*, "[t]he *regulation*, *restraint*, *supervision*, or *control* which is exercised upon the individual members of an organized jural society *by those invested with authority*".[73] (emphasis added) This is similar to meanings given in other dictionaries.[74] The essence of "government" is, therefore, that it enjoys the effective power to "regulate", "control" or "supervise" individuals, or otherwise "restrain" their conduct, through the exercise of lawful authority. This meaning is derived, in part, from the *functions* performed by a government and, in part, from the government having the *powers* and *authority* to perform those functions. A "government agency" is, in our view, an entity which exercises powers vested in it by a "government" for the purpose of performing functions of a "governmental" character, that is, to "regulate", "restrain", "supervise" or "control" the conduct of private citizens. As with any agency relationship, a "government agency" may enjoy a degree of discretion in the exercise of its functions.[75]

98. In the present case, the Panel seems to us to have applied precisely these concepts in concluding that the provincial milk marketing boards are "government agencies". Contrary to Canada's assertions, the Panel's conclusion is not based on the *sole* fact that the provincial milk marketing boards enjoy authority delegated to them by governments. To the contrary, the Panel examined both the *source* of the provincial boards' powers and the *functions* performed by those boards in the exercise of their powers. We note, furthermore, that as regards three of the provincial boards, Canada acknowledged that they were "agencies" of certain provincial governments of Canada.[76]

99. As regards the *source* of the provincial milk marketing boards' powers, it is clear that, in the words of the Panel, they "operate within a legal framework set up by federal and provincial legislation."[77] Furthermore, the provincial boards'

---

72 Canada's appellant's submission, para. 116.

73 *Black's Law Dictionary* (West Publishing Co., 1990), p. 695. The same dictionary states that "[t]he term 'jural society' is used as the synonym of 'state' or 'organized political community'" (p. 851).

74 *The New Shorter Oxford English Dictionary*, Lesley Brown (ed.) (Clarendon Press, 1993), Vol. I, p. 1123; *Merriam Webster's Collegiate Dictionary*, Frederick Mish (ed.) (Merriam Webster Inc., 1993), p. 504.

75 *Black's Law Dictionary*, *supra*, footnote 73, pp. 62 and 63.

76 The boards in question are those of Alberta, Nova Scotia and Saskatchewan.

77 Panel Report, para. 7.76.

powers and functions may only be modified by "governments".[78] In these circumstances, it is clear, as the Panel said, that "these boards act under the *explicit authority delegated to them by either the federal or a provincial government.*"[79] (emphasis added) Indeed, we are of the view that Canada accepts that the provincial milk marketing boards act on the basis of delegated powers vested in them by federal and provincial "governments". On appeal, Canada does not argue that there is *no* delegation of powers by its "governments" to these boards, but, rather, that the delegation of powers is not a sufficient basis, *on its own*, for a finding that such entities are "government agencies".[80]

100. The Panel did not, however, rely solely on the fact of the delegation of powers. The Panel also examined the *functions* of the provincial milk marketing boards and concluded that their powers enable them, again in the words of the Panel, to "*regulate*" a particular sector of the economy, namely the dairy sector.[81] The "governmental" character of the boards' functions, as well as the extent of their regulatory control, is underlined by the fact that their orders and regulations are enforceable in courts of law.[82] Thus, the powers of the provincial boards are augmented by the machinery of the State itself, and the boards have at their disposal the public force to ensure that their regulatory functions and decisions are carried out. Although the provincial boards enjoy a high degree of discretion in the exercise of their powers, governments retain "ultimate control" over them.[83] The Panel was, therefore, correct to conclude that the provincial milk marketing boards are "government agencies".

101. Moreover, the presence of dairy producers as officers of the provincial boards does not compel a change in our view. Irrespective of the composition of the boards, the source of their powers is still "governments" and the nature of the functions that they exercise is still "governmental". Nor is our opinion altered by the fact that the provincial boards exercise their powers with a view to promoting the interests of particular traders, namely, the producers. In our view, it is part of the normal functioning of "governments" to promote the perceived interests of the State, and this may involve securing the interests of one or more sectors of the community.

102. In light of the foregoing, we uphold the Panel's finding in paragraph 7.80 of the Panel Report, that the provincial milk marketing boards are "agencies" of Canada's governments.

---

78 Panel Report, para. 7.78.
79 *Ibid.*, para. 7.77.
80 *Supra*, para. 96.
81 Panel Report, para. 7.77.
82 *Ibid.*, para. 7.76.
83 *Ibid.*, para. 7.78.

VI. ARTICLE 9.1(c) OF THE AGREEMENT ON AGRICULTURE

A. *"Payments"*

103. In determining whether Special Classes 5(d) and 5(e) involve "payments" under Article 9.1(c), the Panel recalled that it had already found that "the provision of milk at a discounted price under Classes 5(d) and (e) involves 'payments-in-kind' in the sense of Article 9.1(a)".[84] It followed that, if the word "payments" in Article 9.1(c) embraced "payments-in-kind", Special Classes 5(d) and 5(e) would involve "payments".[85]

104. Based on the *Oxford English Dictionary* definition of the word "payment", the Panel took the view that:

> ... the ordinary meaning of the word "payment" includes both the act of remunerating a person with money and the act of remunerating a person with its equivalent in kind, a so-called "payment in kind".[86]

105. The Panel found that this meaning was confirmed by the context of the word, which in the Panel's view, included: the words "a charge" and "financed" in Article 9.1(c) itself; the concept of "revenue foregone", that is included in the term "budgetary outlays", mentioned in Article 9.2(a) and defined in Article 1(c); as well as the other "export subsidies" listed in Article 9.1 of the *Agreement on Agriculture*. On this basis, the Panel found that Special Classes 5(d) and 5(e) involved "payments" within the meaning of Article 9.1(c).[87]

106. Canada argues that the Panel erred by collapsing the distinction between "payments" in Article 9.1(c) and "payments-in-kind" in Article 9.1(a). Canada maintains that the concept of "payments-in-kind" is only included in those provisions of the *Agreement on Agriculture* that make express mention of the concept, which Article 9.1(c) does not. Moreover, Canada asserts that the Panel erred by relying on "revenue foregone" under Article 9.1(c). "Revenue foregone" is not relevant to all the sub-paragraphs of Article 9.1, but only to those which can be interpreted as including "revenue foregone". Article 9.1(c) is not such a sub-paragraph. Finally, even if Article 9.1(c) were to apply to "payments-in-kind", Canada disagrees with the Panel that Special Classes 5(d) and 5(e) involve "payments-in-kind".

107. We have found that the word "payments", in the term "payments-in-kind" in Article 9.1(a), denotes a transfer of economic resources.[88] We believe that the same holds true for the word "payments" in Article 9.1(c). The question which we now address is whether, under Article 9.1(c), the economic resources that are

[84] Panel Report, para. 7.90.
[85] Panel Report, para. 7.90.
[86] *Ibid.*, para. 7.92.
[87] *Ibid.*, para. 7.101.
[88] *Supra*, para. 87.

transferred by way of a "payment" must be in the form of money, or whether the resources transferred may take other forms. As the Panel observed, the dictionary meaning of the word "payment" is not limited to payments made in monetary form. In support of this, the Panel cited the *Oxford English Dictionary*, which defines "payment" as "the remuneration of a person with money *or its equivalent*".[89] (emphasis added) Similarly, the *Shorter Oxford English Dictionary* describes a "payment" as a "sum of money (*or other thing*) paid".[90] (emphasis added) Thus, according to these meanings, a "payment" could be made in a form, other than money, that confers value, such as by way of goods or services. A "payment" which does not take the form of money is commonly referred to as a "payment in kind".

108. We agree with the Panel that the ordinary meaning of the word "payments" in Article 9.1(c) is consistent with the dictionary meaning of the word. Under Article 9.1(c), "payments" are "financed by virtue of governmental action" and they may or may not involve "a charge on the public account". Neither the word "financed" nor the term "a charge" suggests that the word "payments" should be interpreted to apply solely to money payments. A payment made in the form of goods or services is also "financed" in the same way as a money payment, and, likewise, "a charge on the public account" may arise as a result of a payment, or a legally binding commitment to make payment by way of goods or services, or as a result of revenue foregone.

109. The context of Article 9.1(c) also supports a reading of the word "payments" that embraces "payments-in-kind". That context includes the other subparagraphs of Article 9.1. As the Panel explained, *none* of the export subsidies listed in Article 9.1 is restricted to grants made solely in money form and several expressly involve subsidies granted in a form other than money.[91] Under Article 9.1(a), "payments-in-kind" are specifically included as a form of "direct subsidies". Similarly, under Articles 9.1(b), the export subsidy identified may involve the disposal of agricultural goods *at less than domestic price*. Under Article 9.1(e), the provision of transport services for export shipments at *prices lower than the price charged for domestic shipments* is also an export subsidy. Thus, each of these three sub-paragraphs of Article 9.1 specifically contemplates that the export subsidy may be granted in a form other than a money payment.

110. The context, in our view, also includes Article 1(c) of the *Agreement on Agriculture*. In terms of that provision, "revenue foregone" is to be taken into account in determining whether "budgetary outlay" commitments, made with respect to export subsidies as listed in Article 9.1, have been exceeded. In our view, the foregoing of revenue usually does not involve a monetary payment. Thus, if a restrictive reading of the words "payments" were adopted, such that

---

[89] Panel Report, para. 7.92.

[90] *The Shorter Oxford English Dictionary*, C.T. Onions (ed.) (Guild Publishing, 1983), Vol. II, p. 1532.

[91] See Panel Report, para. 7.95.

"payments" under Article 9.1(c) had to be monetary, no account could be taken, under Article 9.1(c), of "revenue foregone". This would, we believe, prevent a proper assessment of the commitments made by WTO Members under Article 9.2, as envisaged by Article 1(c) of the *Agreement on Agriculture*. We, therefore, prefer a reading of Article 9.1(c) that allows full account to be taken of "revenue foregone". The contrary view would, in our opinion, elevate form over substance and permit Members to circumvent the subsidy disciplines set forth in Article 9 of the *Agreement on Agriculture*.

111. It is true, as Canada argues, that Article 9.1(c) does not expressly include "payments-in-kind" within its scope, whereas Article 9.1(a) and paragraph 5 of Annex 2 to the *Agreement on Agriculture* do. However, we do not regard the express inclusion of "payments-in-kind" in these two provisions as necessarily implying the exclusion of "payments-in-kind" under Article 9.1(c). In Article 9.1(a) and in paragraph 5 of Annex 2, the term "payments-in-kind" is used in conjunction with the words "*direct* subsidies" and "*direct* payments", respectively. We believe that reference is made to "payments-in-kind" in these two provisions to counter any suggestion that the ordinary meaning of the terms "*direct* subsidies" and "*direct* payments" does *not* include "payments-in-kind". By contrast, since the ordinary meaning of the word "payments" in Article 9.1(c) includes "payments-in-kind", there was no need for "payments-in-kind" to be expressly provided for. Moreover, if "payments-in-kind" are *included* in the qualified concept of "direct payments" under Annex 2, paragraph 5, it would be incongruous to *exclude* them from the broader concept of "payments" in Article 9.1(c).

112. We, therefore, agree with the Panel that the ordinary meaning of the word "payments" in Article 9.1(c) encompasses "payments" made in forms other than money, including revenue foregone.

113. In our view, the provision of milk at discounted prices to processors for export under Special Classes 5(d) and 5(e) constitutes "payments", in a form other than money, within the meaning of Article 9.1(c). If goods or services are supplied to an enterprise, or a group of enterprises, at reduced rates (that is, at below market-rates), "payments" are, in effect, made to the recipient of the portion of the price that is not charged. Instead of receiving a monetary payment equal to the revenue foregone, the recipient is paid in the form of goods or services. But, as far as the recipient is concerned, the economic value of the transfer is precisely the same.

114. We, therefore, uphold the Panel's finding, in paragraph 7.101 of the Panel Report, that the provision of discounted milk to processors or exporters under Special Classes 5(d) and 5(e) involves "payments" within the meaning of Article 9.1(c) of the *Agreement on Agriculture*.

B. "Financed by Virtue of Governmental Action"

115. The Panel noted at the outset of its analysis on this issue that the parties did not contest that:

> ... payments-in-kind made under Classes 5(d) and (e) do *not* directly involve a charge on the public account. The cost of selling milk at a reduced price for export is not borne by the government. It is borne by the milk producers ...[92] (underlining added)

116. The Panel observed that such "producer-financed payments" can nonetheless be covered by Article 9.1(c), provided they are "financed by virtue of governmental action".[93] The Panel found that the "payments" made under Special Classes 5(d) and 5(e) were financed in this way.[94] In reaching this conclusion, the Panel relied on a number of factors. These included the facts that: the supply of milk under Special Classes 5(d) and 5(e) is managed by "agencies" of the Canadian federal or provincial governments, within the meaning of Article 9.1(a); these "agencies" determine when and what quantity of milk may be processed for export under those Special Classes; they negotiate the sale price of the milk with the processor or exporter; they enable the processor or exporter to take delivery of the milk; they collect the price paid for the milk by the processors or exporters; they determine the rules for the pooling of returns to producers for in-quota milk, as well as the rules for the more limited pooling of returns for over-quota milk; in the implementation of these rules, they determine the effective selling price of milk for the producers; they pay out those returns to producers; and, they monitor and supervise the operation of Special Classes 5(d) and 5(e).[95]

117. In arguing that the Panel erred in finding that "payments" made under Special Classes 5(d) and 5(e) are "financed by virtue of governmental action", Canada maintains, first, that this finding is based on the Panel's earlier finding that the provincial milk marketing boards are "government agencies" under Article 9.1(a). Since Canada believes that the Panel's finding under Article 9.1(a) is erroneous, Canada also believes that the finding under Article 9.1(c) is flawed. Canada contends, moreover, that the "payments" are not "financed by virtue of governmental action" because the provincial milk marketing boards are composed, at least in part, of milk producers and act in the interest of those producers. Finally, Canada considers that the Panel failed to take sufficient account of important differences between the treatment of in-quota and over-quota milk, in particular, as regards the pooling of returns to producers.

118. We have rejected Canada's appeal against the Panel's finding that the provincial milk marketing boards are "government agencies".[96] Canada's first argument that the Panel's finding under Article 9.1(c) is flawed to the extent that it is based on the Panel's finding under Article 9.1(a) must, therefore, be dismissed. In our view, since all of the bodies involved in the supply of milk under Special

---

[92] Panel Report, para. 7.102.

[93] *Ibid.*, para. 7.102.

[94] *Ibid.*, paras. 7.106, 7.111 and 7.112.

[95] The considerations relied on by the Panel are set out in detail in paragraphs 7.103, 7.104, 7.105, 7.108, 7.109, 7.110, 7.111 and 7.112 of the Panel Report.

[96] *Supra*, para. 102.

Classes 5(d) and 5(e) are "government agencies" under Article 9.1(a), a strong presumption arises that their conduct in managing those Special Classes may appropriately be regarded as "governmental action".

119. In assessing whether the Panel erred in finding that the "payments" made under Special Classes 5(d) and 5(e) are "financed *by virtue of* governmental action", it is appropriate to look to the "governmental" involvement as whole and not just to the role of the provincial milk marketing boards. The functioning of the system depends on a complex regulatory web involving the CDC and the CMSMC, acting together with the provincial milk marketing boards. It is, therefore, the "action" of all these bodies together which must be examined.

120. While the "cost of selling milk at a reduced price for export is not borne by the government"[97], "governmental action" is, in our view, indispensable to the transfer of resources that takes place as a result of the operation of Special Classes 5(d) and 5(e). The factors relied upon by the Panel, which we have summarized above[98], demonstrate that at *every* stage in the supply of milk under Special Classes 5(d) and 5(e), from the determination of the volume and the authorization of the purchase of milk for processing for export, to the calculation of the price of the milk to the processors and the return to the producers, "governmental action" is not simply involved; it is, in fact, indispensable to enable the supply of milk to processors for export, and hence the transfer of resources, to take place. In the regulatory framework, "government agencies" stand so completely between the producers of the milk and the processors or the exporters that we have no doubt that the transfer of resources takes place "by virtue of governmental action".

121. We have already found, in our reasoning under Article 9.1(a), that the fact that the provincial milk marketing boards are composed, in part, of producers and act in their interests, does not alter the "governmental" character of the provincial boards' "actions".[99] Nor does the fact that, under Special Class 5(e), in-quota returns to *producers* are pooled very differently from over-quota returns alter our conclusion. The price paid for the milk by the *processors* is not, in any way, dependent on whether milk is part of in-quota or over-quota production. Moreover, even though the two pooling mechanisms differ in significant respects, they both nevertheless involve "governmental action" that remains an essential aspect of the financing of the "payments" to processors or exporters.

122. For these reasons, we, therefore, agree with the Panel's findings[100] that the "payments" made under Special Classes 5(d) and 5(e) are "financed by virtue of governmental action" within the meaning of Article 9.1(c) of the *Agreement on Agriculture*.

---

97 Panel Report, para. 7.102.
98 *Supra*, para. 116.
99 *Supra*, para. 101.
100 Panel Report, paras. 7.106, 7.111 and 7.112.

123. In light of all of the foregoing, we believe and so hold that the Panel was correct in finding, in paragraph 7.113 of the Panel Report, "that the making available of milk under Classes 5(d) and (e) constitutes an export subsidy within the meaning of Article 9.1(c)."

VII. ARTICLE 10.1 OF THE *AGREEMENT ON AGRICULTURE*

124. Canada has also appealed the Panel's alternative finding that, if Special Classes 5(d) and 5(e) do *not* constitute export subsidies under either Article 9.1(a) or Article 9.1(c) of the *Agreement on Agriculture*, they nevertheless constitute export subsidies under Article 10.1 of that Agreement.[101] This finding was expressly declared by the Panel to be made on the condition that the Canadian measures do *not* fall within Article 9.1 of the *Agreement on Agriculture*. Moreover, the Panel's final conclusions in Section VIII of the Panel Report, contain no reference to this alternative finding. Since we believe that the provision of lower priced milk to processors for export under Special Classes 5(d) and 5(e) constitutes export subsidies, as listed in Article 9.1(c), those subsidies *cannot*, by definition, be "export subsidies *not* listed in paragraph 1 of Article 9", as required by Article 10.1. Therefore, the condition on which the Panel's alternative line of reasoning is predicated does not arise. In these circumstances, both the Panel's reasoning and its finding under Article 10.1 are completely moot and, thus, of no legal effect. There is, therefore, no reason for us to examine Canada's appeal of the Panel's finding under Article 10.1.

VIII. ARTICLE II:1(b) OF THE GATT 1994

125. We approach this last issue by recalling the factual background to this aspect of the dispute. The Panel stated that:

> In Part I of Canada's Schedule to GATT 1994, Canada established a tariff-rate quota for fluid milk (HS 0401.10.10 and 0401.20.10) of 64,500 tonnes. In-quota imports are subject, initially, to a maximum duty of 17.5 per cent (a rate to be decreased to 7.5 per cent in 2001). Fluid milk imports outside of the 64,500 tonnes tariff-rate quota bear an initial rate of duty equal to 283.8 per cent, declining to 241.3 per cent in 2001. In its Schedule, Canada specified under 'Other terms and conditions' that '[t]his quantity [64,500 tonnes] represents the estimated annual cross-border purchases imported by Canadian consumers'.[102]

[101] See Panel Report, para. 7.133. See also Panel Report, para. 7.117.
[102] Panel Report, para. 7.142.

126. Canada asserts the right, on the basis of these "Other Terms and Conditions", to restrict access to the tariff-rate quota to imports authorized and actually allowed under the relevant practice followed by Canada at the time of the conclusion of the Uruguay Round. In 1970, Canada issued General Import Permit No. 1. The amended version of this Permit provides that "any person may, under the authority of this General Import Permit, import into Canada ... any dairy products for the personal use of the importer and his household not exceeding $20 in value for each importation."[103] Nevertheless, for such imports, no individual permits and no customs entries are required and no customs duties are imposed and collected, even in the case of imports within the in-quota quantity.[104] Indeed, Canada does not monitor imports made under the authority of General Import Permit No. 1.[105] Commercial shipments of milk are not, however, allowed by Canada within the tariff-rate quota.[106] The United States claims that the restrictions that Canada places on access to its market for fluid milk are inconsistent with its obligations under Article II:1(b) of the GATT 1994.

127. The Panel found, *inter alia*, that:

> The words "[t]his *quantity represents* the *estimated* annual ..." are, in our view, introducing "terms" related to the *quantity* of the quota - i.e., describing the way the size of the quota was determined - rather than setting out "conditions" as to the *kind* of imports qualified to enter Canada under this quota. In particular, the ordinary meaning of the word "represent" in this context does not, in our view, call to mind the setting out of specific restrictions or conditions.[107] (emphasis in original)

128. The Panel went on to state:

> Even if the phrase could be said to include restrictions on access to the tariff-rate quota, we do not see how the two conditions *at issue in this dispute* could be read into this phrase. First, the restriction that only entries valued at less than C$20 qualify for the tariff-rate quota can nowhere be found in Canada's Schedule. Nowhere is any reference made to a maximum value per entry. ... [I]n our view, the ordinary meaning of the words "cross-border purchases" by "consumers" in this context does not warrant the conclusion that only *consumer packaged* milk *for personal use* can enter under the tariff-rate quota. An imported good, by definition, crosses a border. Also, the dictionary meaning of "consumer" is not restricted to a person buying *for personal use in small retail packages*. All dic-

[103] General Import Permit No. 1 was amended in 1978 to allow imports of a value of C$20, instead of C$10.

[104] Panel Report, para. 7.143.

[105] Panel Report, para. 7.143.

[106] *Ibid*.

[107] *Ibid*., para. 7.151.

> tionary definitions of "consumer" referred to by the parties include wider definitions without these restrictions.[108] (emphasis in original)

129. The Panel held that the meaning of the terms in Canada's Schedule could be gleaned from an examination of the "ordinary meaning [of those terms] in their context and in the light of the object and purpose of GATT 1994."[109] The Panel saw "no need to also examine the historical background against which these terms were negotiated."[110] It noted, furthermore, that the "drafting history ... is inconclusive, possibly supporting both the view of Canada and that of the United States."[111] Finally, the Panel concluded that:

> ... Canada, by restricting the access to the tariff-rate quota for fluid milk to (i) consumer packaged milk for personal use and (ii) entries valued at less than C$20, acts inconsistently with its obligations under Article II:1(b) of GATT 1994.[112]

130. On appeal, Canada argues, in essence, that the Panel erred by failing to ascribe any meaning, in the sense of "limiting effect", to the language in the notation in its Schedule.[113] In Canada's view, the Panel ought to have established the meaning and content of the language in the Schedule, before considering whether the specific restrictions imposed under General Import Permit No. 1 were justified by that language.

131. We explained in *European Communities - Customs Classification of Certain Computer Equipment* ("*European Communities - Computer Equipment*") that:

> A Schedule is ... an integral part of the GATT 1994 ... . Therefore, the concessions provided for in that schedule are part of the terms of the treaty. As such, the only rules which may be applied in interpreting the meaning of a concession are the general rules of treaty interpretation set out in the *Vienna Convention*.[114]

132. These rules call, in the first place, for the treaty interpreter to attempt to ascertain the ordinary meaning of the terms of the treaty in their context and in the light of the object and purpose of the treaty, in accordance with Article 31(1) of the *Vienna Convention*. However, as we also said in *European Communities - Computer Equipment*:

---

[108] Panel Report, para. 7.152.
[109] Panel Report, para. 7.155.
[110] *Ibid*.
[111] *Ibid*.
[112] *Ibid*., para. 7.156.
[113] Canada's appellant's submission, para. 152.
[114] Appellate Body Report, WT/DS62/AB/R, WT/DS67/AB/R, WT/DS68/AB/R, adopted 22 June 1998, para. 84.

> ... if after applying Article 31 the meaning of the term remains ambiguous or obscure, or leads to a result which is manifestly absurd or unreasonable, Article 32 allows a treaty interpreter to have recourse to:
>
> > ... supplementary means of interpretation, including the preparatory work of the treaty and the circumstances of its conclusion.
>
> With regard to "the circumstances of [the] conclusion" of a treaty, this permits, in appropriate cases, the examination of the historical background against which the treaty was negotiated.[115]

133. It is also well to recall that the task of the treaty interpreter is to ascertain and give effect to a legally operative meaning for the terms of the treaty. The applicable fundamental principle of *effet utile* is that a treaty interpreter is not free to adopt a meaning that would reduce parts of a treaty to redundancy or inutility.[116]

134. We start our interpretive task by noting that the language at issue in Canada's Schedule is included under the heading "Other Terms and Conditions". Under Article II:1(b) of the GATT 1994, the market access concessions granted by a Member are "*subject to*" the "terms, conditions or qualifications set forth in [its] Schedule". (emphasis added) In our view, the ordinary meaning of the phrase "subject to" is that such concessions are without prejudice to and are *subordinated to*, and are, therefore, *qualified by*, any "terms, conditions or qualifications" inscribed in a Member's Schedule. We believe that the relationship between the 64,500 tonnes tariff-rate quota and the "Other Terms and Conditions" set forth in Canada's Schedule is of this nature. The phrase "terms and conditions" is a composite one which, in its ordinary meaning, denotes the imposition of qualifying restrictions or conditions. A strong presumption arises that the language which is inscribed in a Member's Schedule under the heading, "Other Terms and Conditions", has some *qualifying* or *limiting* effect on the substantive content or scope of the concession or commitment.[117]

135. In interpreting the language in Canada's Schedule, the Panel focused on the verb "represents" and opined that, because of the use of this verb, the notation

---

[115] *Supra*, footnote 114, para. 86.

[116] Appellate Body Report, *United States - Standards for Reformulated and Conventional Gasoline*, WT/DS2/AB/R, DSR 1996:I, 3, adopted 20 May 1996, p. 17; Appellate Body Report, *Japan - Taxes on Alcoholic Beverages*, WT/DS8/AB/R, WT/DS10/AB/R, WT/DS11/AB/R, DSR 1996:I, 97, adopted 1 November 1996, p. 106.

[117] The United States contends, on the basis of the panel report in *United States - Restrictions on Imports of Sugar* (*supra*, footnote 52), that "terms and conditions" may encompass "additional concessions". We take no position as to whether "terms and conditions" may encompass "additional concessions"; but we do, however, note that, even assuming that the United States is correct on this point, an "additional concession" may well embody a qualification to a concession by expanding its scope or adding to it.

was no more than a "*description*" of the "way the size of the quota was determined".[118] The net consequence of the Panel's interpretation is a failure to give the notation in Canada's Schedule *any* legal effect as a "term and condition". If the language is *merely* a "description" or a "narration" of how the quantity was arrived at, we do not see what purpose it serves in being inscribed in the Schedule. The Panel, in other words, acted upon the assumption that Canada projected no identifiably necessary or useful qualifying or limiting purpose in inscribing the notation in its Schedule. The Panel thus disregarded the principle of effectiveness in its interpretive effort.

136. We note that the Panel also adopted an overly literal and narrow view of the words "cross-border purchases imported by Canadian consumers" in the notation at issue. Moreover, the Panel erred in failing to give meaning to *all* of the words in that notation. On the basis of its ordinary meaning, the Panel stated that the language in the notation could *not* refer only to "*consumer packaged* milk *for personal use*."[119] (emphasis in original) We do not agree that the ordinary meaning of that phrase in the notation is so unequivocal. We do not see anything in the text of the notation which necessarily *precludes* such an interpretation. The notation refers to "cross-border purchases imported by Canadian consumers". It seems, to us, that this language may well be taken to refer to imports of fluid milk made by Canadian consumers for personal use in the course of cross-border shopping.

137. Moreover, we do not share the Panel's view as to the significance of the object and purpose of Article II of the GATT 1994 for the interpretive question at issue. It is true, as the Panel said, that the object and purpose of Article II is "to preserve the value of tariff concessions...".[120] However, the issue facing the Panel was what was the *scope and content* of the concession? The Panel's reference to the object and purpose of Article II appears to us to beg the very question that the Panel should have addressed: namely, what *is* the meaning of that notation? That is, what *is* the shape and tenor of the concession that Canada had set forth in its Schedule of Commitments?

138. In our view, the language in the notation in Canada's Schedule is *not* clear on its face. Indeed, the language is general and ambiguous, and, therefore, requires special care on the part of the treaty interpreter. For this reason, it is appropriate, indeed necessary, in this case, to turn to "supplementary means of interpretation" pursuant to Article 32 of the *Vienna Convention*. In so doing, we are unable to share the apparent view of the Panel that the meaning of the notation at issue is so clear and self-evident that there was "*no need* to also examine

[118] Panel Report, para. 7.151.

[119] *Ibid.*, para. 7.152.

[120] See Panel Report, para. 7.154. The Panel is citing from our Report in *Argentina - Measures Affecting Imports of Footwear, Textiles, Apparel, and Other Items*, adopted on 27 March 1998, WT/DS56/AB/R, para. 47.

the historical background against which these terms were negotiated."[121] (emphasis added)

139. In considering "supplementary means of interpretation", we observe that the "terms and conditions" at issue were incorporated into Canada's Schedule after lengthy negotiations between Canada and the United States, regarding reciprocal market access opportunities for dairy products.[122] Both Canada and the United States agree that those negotiations failed to produce any agreement between them.[123] Our reading of the circumstances surrounding the conclusion of the *WTO Agreement* leads us to observe that, although Canada's commitment on fluid milk was made unilaterally[124], both Canada and the United States understood that this commitment represented a continuation by Canada of "current access" opportunities, not a commitment to provide "minimum access" opportunities under the *Agreement on Agriculture*.[125]

140. The next issue we must address is whether the measure promulgated by Canada in the form of General Import Permit No. 1 is consistent with the commitment for fluid milk in Canada's Schedule, as we read it. General Import Permit No. 1 authorizes:

> Any person ... [to] *import into Canada* from any country ... *any dairy products* for *the personal use* of the importer and his household *not exceeding $20 in value for each importation*. (emphasis added)

141. The first condition of General Import Permit No. 1 is that the dairy products, including fluid milk, imported into Canada must be for "the personal use of the importer and his household". This condition appears to us to be reflected in the following phrase in the notation in Canada's Schedule: "cross-border purchases imported by Canadian consumers". General Import Permit No. 1 allows, in the words of the notation, "Canadian consumers" to "import into Canada" fluid milk and other dairy products that they purchase in the United States. These are, therefore, "cross-border purchases" for the "personal use" of Canadian importers.

---

[121] Panel Report, para. 7.155.

[122] Canada's appellant's submission, para. 173; United States' appellee's submission, para. 148.

[123] Canada's appellant's submission, para. 176; United States' appellee's submission, paras. 146 and 148.

[124] This is borne out by the positions taken by both Canada and the United States in this appeal. See Canada's appellant's submission, paras. 173 to 176, and the United States' appellee's submission, paras. 146 and 148.

[125] The Panel stated that "[t]he United States, on the other hand, submits that the *phrase at issue was added to clarify that the tariff-rate quota was a continuation of 'current access' opportunities already available before the Uruguay Round negotiations*; not a phrase limiting access to the quota as such. In so doing, the United States argues, Canada avoided granting the 'minimum access opportunities' for products for which there are no significant imports (ranging from 3 to 5 per cent of domestic consumption) referred to in the Agreement on Modalities for the Establishment of Specific Binding Commitments under the Reform Program ...." (emphasis added) (Panel Report, para. 7.155, footnote 530) See also the summary of the United States' submissions to the Panel at paragraph 4.499 of the Panel Report.

Thus, we see the first condition of General Import Permit No. 1 as consistent with the notation at issue in Canada's Schedule.

142. The second condition of General Import Permit No. 1 is that the value of "each importation" of any "dairy products" not exceed "$20 in value". In this connection, we note that General Import Permit No. 1 applies to "dairy products" generally, not just to fluid milk. The tariff-rate quota commitment and the accompanying notation in Canada's Schedule, however, apply only to "fluid milk". Moreover, the notation at issue in Canada's Schedule does not place any limit on the value of each importation. To the extent that the second condition of General Import Permit No. 1 is not reflected in the notation at issue, the Canadian measure is not consistent with Canada's commitment on fluid milk set forth in its Schedule.

143. In light of the foregoing, we do not agree with the Panel's interpretation of the notation at issue relating to the tariff-rate quota commitment on fluid milk in Canada's Schedule. Nor do we agree with the Panel's finding that by restricting access to the tariff-rate for fluid milk to "consumer packaged milk for personal use", Canada acts inconsistently with its obligations under Article II:1(b) of the GATT 1994. However, we do agree with the Panel's finding that by restricting access to the tariff-rate quota for fluid milk to "entries valued at less than C$20", Canada acts inconsistently with its obligations under Article II:1(b) of the GATT 1994.

IX. FINDINGS AND CONCLUSIONS

144. For the reasons set out in this Report, the Appellate Body:

(a) reverses the Panel's interpretation of the terms "direct subsidies" and "payments-in-kind", as used in Article 9.1(a) of the *Agreement on Agriculture,* and, in consequence, reverses the Panel's finding that Canada, through Special Milk Classes 5(d) and 5(e), has acted inconsistently with its obligations under Article 3.3 and Article 8 of the *Agreement on Agriculture* by providing export subsidies as listed in Article 9.1(a) of that Agreement in excess of the quantity commitment levels specified in Canada's Schedule; but, in light of the finding in paragraph (b) below, sees no reason to examine whether export subsidies as listed in Article 9.1(a) are conferred through Special Milk Classes 5(d) and 5(e);

(b) upholds the Panel's finding that Canada, through Special Milk Classes 5(d) and 5(e), has acted inconsistently with its obligations under Article 3.3 and Article 8 of the *Agreement on Agriculture* by providing export subsidies as listed in Article 9.1(c) of that Agreement in excess of the quantity commitment levels specified in Canada's Schedule;

(c) declines to examine the Panel's alternative finding under Article 10.1 of the *Agreement on Agriculture* since, in light of our finding in paragraph (b) above, that alternative finding has no legal effect; and

(d) reverses the Panel's finding that Canada, by restricting access to the tariff-rate quota for fluid milk in its Schedule to consumer packaged milk, imported by Canadian consumers for personal use, acts inconsistently with its obligations under Article II:1(b) of the GATT 1994; but upholds the Panel's finding that Canada, by restricting access to the tariff-rate quota for fluid milk in its Schedule to entries valued at less than C$20, acts inconsistently with its obligations under Article II:1(b) of the GATT 1994.

145. The Appellate Body recommends that the DSB request that Canada bring its measures found in this Report, and in the Panel Report as modified by this Report, to be inconsistent with its obligations under the *Agreement on Agriculture* and the GATT 1994 into conformity with those agreements.